Placing Movies

Placing Movies

The Practice of Film Criticism

Jonathan Rosenbaum

UNIVERSITY OF CALIFORNIA PRESS

BERKELEY / LOS ANGELES / LONDON

University of California Press
Berkeley and Los Angeles, California

University of California Press
London, England

Copyright © 1995 by The Regents of the University of California

Library of Congress Cataloging-in-Publication Data

Rosenbaum, Jonathan.

 Placing movies : the practice of film criticism / Jonathan
Rosenbaum.
  p. cm.
 Includes bibliographical references and index.
 ISBN 0–520–08632–5 (alk. paper).
 ISBN 0–520–08633–3 (pbk. : alk. paper)
 1. Motion pictures—Reviews. 2. Film criticism. I. Title.
PN1995.R65 1995
791.43'75—dc20   93–42954
                           CIP

Printed in the United States of America

1 2 3 4 5 6 7 8 9

The paper used in this publication meets the minimum requirements of
American National Standard for Information Sciences—Permanence of
Paper for Printed Library Materials, ANSI Z39.48–1984 ∞

Contents

Dedication and Acknowledgments

To my editors, official and unofficial. The list is too long and goes too far back in time to be exhaustive here, but I'd like to cite, in particular, Gilbert Adair, Peter Cole, Richard Combs, Richard Corliss, Edward Dimendberg, Nataša Durovičová, Bernard Eisenschitz, Pamela Falkenberg, Sandy Flitterman-Lewis, Noah Forde, Marilyn Goldin, Holly Greenhagen, Penelope Houston, Richard T. Jameson, Kitry Krause, Bill Krohn, Michael Lenehan, Lorenzo Mans, Tom Milne, Laura Molzhan, John Pym, Bérénice Reynaud, Lauren Sedofsky, Jeffrey Skoller, Garrett Stewart, Christine Tamblyn, Alison True, Jeramy Turner, Melinda Ward, and Tracy Young.

Grateful acknowledgment is also made to the publications in which these pieces first appeared: *Chicago Reader, Cinematograph, Film Comment, Modern Times, Monthly Film Bulletin, Sight and Sound, Soho News,* and *Tikkun.*

Starting Out in Film Criticism

This book is intended as a companion and sequel to an autobiographical experiment I carried out in the late 1970s, published in 1980 by Harper & Row as *Moving Places: A Life at the Movies.* The present volume doesn't require a reading of that earlier book—long out of print, though recently reprinted by the University of California Press so as to reappear alongside this collection; however, since many of this volume's premises are predicated on either extensions or inversions of the premises of its predecessor, a few words about that book and the material it covers are in order.

Most of *Moving Places* is concerned with my childhood in northwestern Alabama, specifically in relation to my family and what was known as the family business from around 1914 to 1960. This business began when my grandfather, Louis Rosenbaum, started operating his first movie theater in Douglas, Wyoming, and it existed until Rosenbaum Theaters, owned by my grandfather and managed by my father, was sold to a larger chain. I was born in 1943, and the family business afforded me a steady diet of free movies through the age of sixteen, when I went away to school in Vermont. As a consequence of this perk, I saw practically every feature that had national distribution between the late 1940s and the autumn of 1959.

The focus of *Moving Places*—written after I had been working professionally as a film critic for several years—included all the circumstantial, personal, historical, and ideological aspects of experiencing movies that criticism generally factors out. The project had personal urgency for me because I wanted to forge links between two mainly disconnected portions of my life— my childhood in Alabama, and my career as a critic in New York, Paris, London, and San Diego. My initial points of entry were movies with no critical standing of any kind—principally BIRD OF PARADISE and ON MOONLIGHT

1

BAY—that I had not seen since the early 1950s. Seeing them again on television in 1977 and 1978, I was interested in discovering first what they told me about myself as a child (through Proustian recollections of my initial responses), and then what these findings told me about movies in general. Later, this material was supplemented by detailed and obsessive research—much of it conducted in Florence, my hometown—about the history of what I had seen (and when, and under what circumstances), and, beyond that, the history of the family theater chain.

I had written a great deal as a child, but until the late 1960s my writing had basically consisted of fiction and poetry, not criticism. (In fact, I was working on the first of my three unpublished novels when the theaters were sold during my senior year in boarding school, and the other two novels were written over the next decade.) Part of the synthesis I was pursuing in *Moving Places* had to do with this discontinuity as well: as a writing project it was literary and personal/historical rather than critical in any conventional sense, and I naively hoped at the time that such a book could pave my way out of film criticism and into a literary career. Unfortunately, apart from a few reviews (mainly in newspapers west of the Hudson and film magazines), it was regarded exclusively as a film book—it had no impact at all on the literary world—and not as a kind of film book with any status in relation to sociology, social history, film history, or film exhibition. (To the best of my knowledge, it has never appeared in bibliographies related to any of these subjects—or to "cultural studies," for that matter.) It *did* achieve some genuine success and longevity as a cult item, but basically among film buffs, and not of the sort that could be parlayed into any sort of career opportunities, journalistic or academic. To make a living—both during and after the writing of the book—I had to return to whatever freelance work I could find, which proved to be journalism, criticism, and teaching.

At the same time, I should stress that writing *Moving Places* permanently altered some of my positions as a film critic, which is another reason why it seems necessary to define that book as a watershed in my evolution. It taught me that subjectivity in critical writing is never something to be avoided—to try to do so is merely to make one's self the passive victim of its complex operations—but always something to be defined and accounted for. It also taught me, as a corollary to this, that where and when one is viewing a movie has an inextricable relation to what that movie means, and that consequently no meanings should ever be regarded as universal or eternal. To put it more simply, it forced me to recognize that moviegoing—and therefore film criticism—is a social act.

■

I offer this account to set the stage for this volume, which presents an autobiographical placement of my film criticism, designed for both serious moviegoers and for those people among that group who are considering serious film criticism as a profession. The critical pieces I've selected are thus intended to serve double duty, functioning both as essays and reviews in their own right and as particular cases (or case histories) that point to some of their sources, circumstances, and functions.

One part of my aim coincides with the project of *Moving Places* almost identically—to objectify my own positions in the autobiographical segments that follow rather than set myself up as some sort of hero or role model. Although I have obvious biases as a critic which will become increasingly clear as the book develops—and do my utmost to argue on their behalf, though I also try to contextualize and *place* these positions so that readers will know as much as possible where they're coming from—it is not my intention to advise or instruct potential critics in how to duplicate my own tastes and procedures. As in *Moving Places,* I can best be regarded as a test case, and with this in mind, I have done my best to draw attention to some of my own critical shortcomings—insofar as I'm aware of them—and encourage readers to draw their own conclusions about them. Although a central part of my concern is to provide a guided tour through film criticism as a profession—one intersecting and interacting with editors, readers, publicists, fans, and filmmakers alike—I think it would be more useful for readers to regard me as a vehicle in this enterprise than for them to regard me as a definitive tour guide, much less as an ultimate destination. (As Godard usefully put it in an interview I once had with him, "I'd like to regard myself as an airplane, not an airport.")

■

One of the consequences that writing *Moving Places* had on some of my earliest film memories was to paralyze and then evacuate them—which means that if I want to trace certain facts or strands relating to my prehistory as a film critic, I'm often better off referring to the book than to my own recollections. This book tells me, among other things, that two of my first pieces of sustained film criticism were written during my teens—at the ages of fourteen and nineteen, respectively. Together, they form a dialectic of sorts which defines what film criticism has personally meant for me ever since.

The first piece was a guest column written for the *Florence Times,* "reviewing" the major releases that Rosenbaum Theaters were showing that week. Every other week, this column was written by my father, and my frequent criticisms of his efforts led to him inviting me to take over the job on a one-shot basis. Like him in most cases, I hadn't seen most of the movies, but the fact that I'd already seen the Disney cartoon accompanying FANTASIA out of town a few months earlier—an Oscar-winning CinemaScope effort called TOOT, WHISTLE, PLUNK AND BOOM—gave my plug the status of a genuine testimonial. ("Frankly, it's the best cartoon I've ever seen.") I'm sure that if anyone had asked me at the time, I would have considered such a statement of in-house promotion film criticism, and a sincere form of it at that.

My second opus, never published, was a brief essay arguing on behalf of the moral and aesthetic superiority of FOLLOW THAT DREAM, a flaky and somewhat pro-anarchist Elvis Presley comedy, over SWEET BIRD OF YOUTH, a Richard Brooks desecration of a Tennessee Williams play I had previously seen on stage and loved in that form. The piece was written about a year and a half after Rosenbaum Theaters had been sold, shortly after I had gone to see the movie with my grandfather at the largest of the theaters he had built. The fact that he had howled with pleasure at some of the movie's crudest jokes goaded me into some sort of rebellious self-definition, which was undoubtedly a major source of the piece.

Two years after that came one of my first serious published efforts—an extended, troubled review of Kubrick's DR. STRANGELOVE for the *Bard Observer,* my college newspaper, that attempted to square the film's virulent misanthropy with its comedy. The piece concluded: "Basically, I believe that the movie is hateful as far as it is successful, and unsuccessful insofar as it is likeable; for its success depends on the strength of its vision and its ability to convince us, and I doubt seriously whether any of us [is] un-man enough to take it. As an experience, however, none of us is likely to forget it." The review prompted an unsolicited favorable comment from the best teacher I ever had—Heinrich Bluecher, the husband of Hannah Arendt and Bard's presiding philosophical guru—and, come to think of it, its dialectical play undoubtedly bore the mark of his Hegelian influence. But another reason why I'm recalling this early review is to point to a concrete example of how the cast of a particular period can inflect and even determine a movie's meaning. A week or so before, when I'd gone to see the movie near Times Square with some of my best friends, one of them—Kathy Stein, who sixteen years later became my editor at *Omni*—emerged from the shock of that experience devastated and in tears. For her, seeing the end of the world as comic was not only frightening but morally hateful, and her passionate response made a permanent impression on me. The unlikelihood of anyone of college age having that sort of reaction to DR. STRANGELOVE today tells us something important, I suspect, about what's happened to our sensibilities since then—not only in relation to the idea of nuclear holocaust, but also in relation to comedy. I think it's possible that we've lost something.

■

Although I had achieved a modicum of literary success during my early teens—one poem won first prize in a national contest, and I sold a vignette to Anthony Boucher's *The Magazine of Fantasy & Science Fiction* in 1956 that was eventually published in English, Spanish, and Japanese—none of my subsequent fiction was published outside of school and college literary magazines, and even the fact that I was writing occasional film and literary reviews for student newspapers and running a film series at Bard didn't suggest to me that I would eventually be doing this sort of work for a living.

After spending five years as an undergraduate English major at Washington Square College (1961–1962) and Bard College (1962–1966), most of them enjoyable—it was at Bard that I had close friends, and likewise felt I was a respected member of an intellectual community, for the first time in my life—I wound up wasting two and a half years as a graduate student in English at the State University of New York at Stony Brook (1966–1968). Although the hefty number of military enlistments in Alabama kept me safe from the draft after 1968, the possibility of getting drafted prior to that kept me enrolled in a program I had little respect for, vaguely motivated by the assumption that I would wind up teaching English and American literature for a living. Even then, I was enough of a film buff to propose doing a dissertation involving film and literature, but when I quit Stony Brook about a year later, I still hadn't succeeded in getting any sort of support from the faculty.

In retrospect, I consider myself highly fortunate that the option of becoming a graduate student in film study was not open to me at the time, because I might well have taken it. The reason why I "broke into" film criticism professionally was equally circumstantial: an acquaintance who was starting a series of monographs and books on film directors, with the aim of selling the whole package to a publisher, hired me to edit a collection of pieces on major directors—an anthology that he or we dubbed *Film Masters*—at the same time that I was looking for a good excuse to quit graduate school. (Another excuse was my third novel, which I had already started writing. But *Film Masters* provided the additional inducement of a modest income to supplement my inheritance from my grandfather, which was my main means of support—an alternative, in other words, to my salary for teaching freshman English at Stony Brook.) A further incentive was that I was provided with a budget to commission translations from the French, and I was finding the research involved in the project—the screenings as well as the readings—a lot more exciting than the enforced and pedantic labors of graduate school.

By the time *Film Masters* was sold to Grosset and Dunlap, I believe I had already decided to move from Greenwich Village to Paris, which I wound up doing in the fall of 1969. By that time, I had written my first "serious" extended piece of film criticism—an essay about my favorite film at the time, SUNRISE. For this piece, I had made special research trips to the George Eastman House in Rochester and the Cinémathèque Royale de Belgique in Brussels to look at other films by F. W. Murnau and had paid for a special screening of TABU at the Museum of Modern Art. (Stephen Koch, a friend from Stony Brook, had brought along Annette Michelson to the screening, and it was the first time we met. She went on to become a good friend and strong influence and for a brief period was interested in getting *Film Masters* published at Praeger—until my employer opted for bigger bucks by going with Grosset and Dunlap. Things started to unwind between us around 1977, the time that "Regrouping" [see bibliography] was published, which Annette scornfully told me might have been written by Penelope Gilliatt.) I had also spent a highly enjoyable summer in Paris and London pursuing my research and meeting various contributors to the book while working on my third novel.

Professionally speaking, however, all these activities ended in grief. If painful memory serves, *Film Masters* twice made it into galleys at Grosset and Dunlap before being yanked from production by editors who had second thoughts on the project. (It's possible that they were wrong. I would estimate now that the book was a few years ahead of its time in some of its selections and emphases, though hardly as earthshaking as I then believed; within a few years, many of the pieces I had selected for translation or commissioned wound up in print elsewhere.) The man who had hired me to edit the book—a Scientologist in that period who had disappeared with the book's illustrations when he flew to the west coast with Grosset and Dunlap's advance in order to finance further "auditing"—was not to be heard from again for years, so the book no longer had an agent to defend or promote it. Even after I flew back to New York, hired a lawyer, recovered the stills, and acquired some legal protection, I still couldn't convince anyone to publish the book in any form, and having by this time moved all my belongings to Paris, I was ill-prepared to shop it around. Nor did my novel, when I finally finished it, fare any better. I still had the dregs of my inheritance to keep me going in Paris, as well as a passionate interest in movies that my ambitious work on *Film Masters* and my subsequent move to Paris had only intensified.

So it seemed only natural, during one of my trips back to New York, to ask the staff—specifically Richard Corliss, the editor, and his assistant, Melinda Ward—of a recently refurbished film magazine there called *Film Comment* if they could use a Paris correspondent. The reply was an invitation to send them a sample piece, which I did, and which ran in their Fall 1971 issue, two years after my move to Paris. From then on, I resolved to write something for every issue, even after they went from quarterly to bimonthly, and was delighted to discover that they printed everything I wrote for them. It wasn't a living, to be sure, but it was a beginning; and after my name appeared on the cover of the November–December 1972 issue—occasioned by a piece on Orson Welles's first Hollywood project, HEART OF DARKNESS, which had entailed an interview with Welles in Paris—even my grandmother, who had denounced me for wasting my life a year or so before, was duly impressed.

Earlier in 1971, with the encouragement of Andrew Sarris—whom I had met in connection with the ill-fated *Film Masters*—I began writing occasional pieces for the *Village Voice,* starting with a pedestrian account of having been an extra on Robert Bresson's FOUR NIGHTS OF A DREAMER

(29 April) and moving on from there to Cannes Film Festival coverage (1971 and 1972), occasional reviews during visits back to New York (GLEN AND RANDA in 1971, REMINISCENCES OF A JOURNEY TO LITHUANIA and MOON-WALK ONE in 1972), and then book reviews—Thomas Pynchon's *Gravity's Rainbow,* Noël Burch's *Theory of Film Practice,* Dwight Macdonald's *Discriminations,* Gore Vidal's *Myron,* and, many years later, *Jerry Lewis in Person* and Martin Gardner's *Science: Good, Bad and Bogus.*

I have gone to the trouble of recounting this minihistory in spite of my decision to omit all my (mainly less than durable) *Voice* pieces from this collection because I have to confess that the personal-confessional and vernacular mode associated with the *Voice* had an enormous effect on my writing for other magazines—especially my "Journals" for *Film Comment,* but also a few of my *Sight and Sound* articles as well (see, especially, the Edinburgh piece). The gonzo journalistic mode associated nowadays with Tom Wolfe and Hunter S. Thompson—neither of whom, I should add, ever impressed me as much as their reputations seemed to warrant—surely had some of its roots in the nonfiction of Norman Mailer, who wrote a column for the *Voice* in the 1950s and who influenced my prose a lot more.

I don't mean to imply by this association, however, that the macho branch of autobiographical writing in the *Voice*—a tradition sustained today by J. Hoberman—was the only kind that affected me. Undoubtedly even more influential was the passionately sincere and hypersensitive critical writing of James Stoller, a *Voice* proofreader in the 1960s and 1970s who launched a wonderful (albeit short-lived) magazine called *Moviegoer* with Roger Greenspun when I was still an undergraduate, and who wrote a *Voice* column for a time called "16mm." (Eventually, I'm sorry to say, Stoller gave up writing and transferred his love of film to opera; he still works as a proofreader, but not for the *Voice.* And Roger has remained a friend for almost thirty years.) Still another important influence at this time was Susan Sontag, whom I'd been instrumental in inviting up to Bard for a talk during the same period—soon after her notorious "Notes on Camp" was published in *Partisan Review* (and her essay on Godard's VIVRE SA VIE appeared in the second issue of *Moviegoer*), but prior to the publication of "On Style," which is what she read that evening. I was running the Friday night film series at the time and had been getting some flak from fellow students for showing such movies as THE LADY FROM SHANGHAI, UNDERWORLD, TRIUMPH OF THE WILL, and SUN-RISE. The fact that Susan cited the first three films with some approval in her essay, and later told me that she had burst into tears when she'd first seen SUNRISE, won me over to her heart and soul that evening.

■

A few words on some of the principles of selection I've followed in this collection. Automatically eliminated are capsule reviews, book reviews,

annual ten-best list columns, production stories, inverviews, film festival reports, and all of my pieces that have been reprinted in other books. (These
latter omissions, as well as all the other major film pieces of mine that have
been excluded for one reason or another, are listed in the bibliography, in
order of their original publication.) Including my capsule reviews, I estimate
I've published over twenty-six hundred pieces in sixty magazines and newspapers; this selection comprises thirty-one, drawn from seven publications.

I've tried to strike a balance between pieces included for their critical
value and those that are included because of the importance of the films and
filmmakers I'm writing about—often being guided, in the latter case, by
works and figures that I believe have been unjustly neglected elsewhere. This
means that a certain number of pieces deal with films that are either difficult
to come by in the United States or completely unavailable. Although the customary approach in collections of this kind is to avoid at all costs writing about
films that can't be seen, I strongly object to this practice as a means of passively promoting—by continuing—a vicious circle. Most uncommercial (or
"uncommercial") films of value only get shown if critics clamor loud and
long enough to stir up some interest in them; this is what I've been trying to
do for virtually my entire career as a critic, and it would betray the thrust and
meaning of that work if I avoided that policy here.

—September 1993

Part One

The Critical Apparatus

Introduction

Although this entire book is devoted to film criticism as a practice, this section emphasizes this fact by dealing with film criticism directly as a subject. This includes both specific examinations of the work of other critics and polemical forays into questions about how critics and reviewers operate on a day-to-day basis. A broader look at the same topic might question whether film criticism as it's presently constituted is a worthy activity in the first place—if in fact the public would be better off without it.

I should add that it's the institutional glibness of film criticism in both its academic and mainstream branches—above all in the United States, where it seems most widespread *and* least justifiable—that has led me on occasion to raise this latter question. Speaking as someone who set out to become a professional writer but not a professional film critic, I've never felt that movie reviewing was an especially exalted activity, but I didn't start out with any contempt or disdain for the profession either. It was only after the institutionalizing of academic film studies got started in the early 1970s and the glamorizing of mainstream film reviewing got started a little after that that I began to wonder about whether the public was often being sold a bill of goods about the so-called "credentials" of film critics.

Admittedly, film academics had to begin by weathering both the scorn and the envy of other humanities professors, who were formerly free to handle film however or whenever they saw fit without the nuisance of specialists glancing over their shoulders. The rapidity with which academic film study developed and promulgated its own jargon undoubtedly had a lot to do with the impatience of pioneers in the field to establish their own sphere of expertise; like the difficult unison lines composed by the best of the early beboppers in

1940s jazz, this jargon was designed not only to scare off amateurs, but also to allow the "experts" to strut their stuff. Unfortunately, a grasp of this jargon didn't necessarily have much bearing on any historical or technical or aesthetic understanding of film; it served mainly as a badge of entry for "film studies," which often proved to be a different thing entirely.

Some of the reasons for this were initially quite positive. The absence of any firmly established canon for film studies left the field potentially wide open. But the only way this canon could grow would be if academics decided to work collectively to expand both what they knew and what was already available, and this has rarely happened. (The sheer scarcity of curiosity in the field is often breathtaking.) What's happened instead is that film study has mainly tended to establish a canon passively and reactively—refining the discoveries of theoretical or nonacademic auteurist critics while often defining its own canon mainly on the basis of what distributors have already made available.

Similarly, as it's usually practiced, journalistic film reviewing is a profession that has often remained dangerously close to simple news reporting (at best) and unabashed advertising (at worst), and whenever it dares to stray beyond those functions, an inordinate amount of hubris usually comes along with the presumption. Sometimes, as in the criticism of Jean-Luc Godard, this hubris turns out to be more than justified, although it's worth adding that it's mainly Godard's critical intelligence as a filmmaker that created a receptive audience for his written criticism.

"Theory and Practice: The Criticism of Jean-Luc Godard" was the first piece I ever published in *Sight and Sound,* my favorite film magazine in English at the time, and I can recall putting an unusual amount of time into writing and rewriting it because I was aspiring to become a regular writer for the magazine. The strategy paid off, and two years later, thanks to the support of the magazine's editor, Penelope Houston, I even found myself moving from Paris to London to become assistant editor of *Monthly Film Bulletin* and staff writer for *Sight and Sound,* which were sister publications edited from adjoining offices at 81 Dean Street for the British Film Institute. (Getting a work permit was no easy matter and took about six months of effort and patience on Penelope's part, as well as legal help from the late Richard Roud— votes of confidence that I still feel enormously grateful for.) I remained for two and a half years; "Edinburgh Encounters" and the pieces on Ozu and Rivette in the next two sections were written during this period—the first in my life when I had steady employment as a film critic. (The second period came in 1980—when I became a regular film and literary critic for *Soho News* in New York for a year and a half—and the third in 1987, when I moved to Chicago to become the film critic for the *Chicago Reader,* where I have been ensconced ever since.)

Almost exactly two decades after my first article appeared in *Sight and Sound,* when Penelope commissioned her last article from me before she departed as editor (it wound up in the Winter 1990/1991 issue), I deliberately made it a companion piece to my first, entitled "Criticism on Film," which again dealt with "criticism composed in the language of the medium," and concluded symmetrically with a discussion of Godard's HISTOIRE(S) DU CINÉMA. By that time, however, the tone of my approach to both criticism and cinema was distinctly more elegiac, and, under the circumstances, less celebratory.

■

One of the more practical of Jean-Luc Godard's gnomic utterances might be, "Trusting to chance is listening to voices." Film critics, who usually put their faith in chance more than they care to admit—hoping to predict audience responses and trends, "banking" on certain favorite directors and actors—tend to read and listen to one another compulsively. To a certain extent, Pauline Kael first came into prominence through attacking other critics, and although editor William Shawn got her to curb this impulse when she arrived at *The New Yorker,* she never lost the habit of using the responses of other viewers—friends or foes, often alluded to anonymously—as the springboards for her own polemics.

Most other critics follow suit even when the original sources of their bile (or agreement) go unmentioned. "I'm a reactive critic," Manny Farber told Richard Thompson in a fascinating interview in the May–June 1977 *Film Comment*; "I like to listen to someone else and cut in." Although my sense of Farber's singularity as a critic—explored in an autobiographical piece that concludes this section—originally made this remark seem curious (he rarely mentioned other critics by name in his writing, and he never assigned reading in his classes), I gradually discovered that it was essential to his method, in teaching and writing alike. Whether acknowledged or not, virtually all critical discourse is part of a conversation that begins before the review starts and continues well after it's over; and all the best critics allude in some fashion to this dialogue, however obliquely. The worst usually try to convince you that they're the only experts in sight.

One rather grotesque illustration of this is a feeble assigned review I did of Satyajit Ray's DISTANT THUNDER for *Sight and Sound* in 1975 that confused certain characters with one another, as one irritated reader wrote the magazine to point out. When I started investigating how I could have committed this gaffe, it emerged that part of my preparation for the review was reading another critic's account of the movie at the 1973 Berlin Festival, published in the same magazine, which made the identical error. To make matters worse, two daily newspaper critics repeated the same blunder after *my* review appeared, which suggested that they, like me, were prone to believe more in the printed word—anybody's printed word—than in the fleeting evidence on the screen. In just such a fashion, an enormous amount of misinformation routinely gets passed along from one critic to the next, sometimes over the span of several decades. (One would like to think that the availability of many movies on video began to put some damage control on this situation by the early 1980s.)

The same thing happens with critics copying or paraphrasing sentences cribbed from pressbooks—a practice much harder to spot and, consequently, even more prevalent, because ordinary viewers never see these publicity handouts. The one time in my career when I put together a pressbook myself—a service performed gratis for London's Contemporary Films in 1976 to help them launch CELINE AND JULIE GO BOATING—I was amazed to find my own unsigned prose being parroted by most of the critics in town when the movie opened, even by those who detested the film.

An even more general problem rules critics' social etiquette in *admitting* that they pay attention to one another. A striking difference between the behavior of critics in London and New York is that the former find many more occasions to socialize with one another, largely because the atmosphere is noticeably less competitive. After many evening press shows in London—those most commonly held for magazine reviewers, who require longer lead times—drinks and hors d'oeuvres are served, in effect inviting the critics to swap opinions and theories about what they've just seen. It's always struck me as an agreeable and helpful custom—the equivalent of what one finds at most film festivals, where one's overall sense of a critical community is also very pronounced. When I once asked a prominent American critic why this was never done in New York, his response was swift and emphatic: "You can't talk about a film right after you've seen it—other critics will steal your ideas!"

It was hard to explain to him that in London, where ideas are less likely to be seen as private property, critics are often delighted if their ideas are stolen, because this means that their ideas have power. In New York, only the critics are supposed to have power, and the ideas have to fend for themselves. This creates a different notion of criticism, a different notion of community, and a different notion of ideas. It also helps to explain why film critics are regarded as stars in America—a situation that has only existed since the 1970s—but nowhere else. (At the moment a critic becomes a star, the critical discourse becomes a nightclub act.) To be a star means to have an aura, and in a media ruled by the marketplace, auras are strictly personal possessions, not to be shared.

What seems most ironic about this is such auras always depend more on institutional bases than they do on ideas, expertise, or even personalities. As writer-director Samuel Fuller once put it to me with characteristic bluntness and lucidity, "If Vincent Canby got fired from the *Times* today, and he went to a bar and started talking about a movie he'd just seen, nobody there would give a fuck what he thought. They'd probably just tell him to shut up."

This helps to dramatize the fact that authority in matters of film judgment is often an illusory construct—a point emphasized in my piece on Bèla Tarr. (Seeing a particular movie because "the *Times* says it's good" means in effect trusting not Canby but the people who hired him—and what do *they* know about movies?—as well as all the traditions and particular interests that *The New York Times* embodies, for better and for worse.) Public opinion of a given movie generally grows out of a general "buzz" that circulates around it, and publicists, reviewers, and audiences—usually in that order—all contribute to that drone and influence each other in the process. The buzz usually starts well before the picture's release and grows (or dies) over many weeks afterward, and the cacophonous overlaps that compose it often make it hard to determine which voices are the most dominant or influential.

■

Although I've omitted my earliest pieces for *Film Comment,* I've included extracts from my "Journals" (from Paris, London, and elsewhere) for that magazine from the mid-1970s which represent for me today some of the best as well as some of the worst tendencies of that column. (For purposes of illustration, I ask for the reader's indulgence; the commentary on film criticism is more fleeting here than elsewhere in this section.) Although the freedom granted me by Richard Corliss and the personal-confessional mode I adopted enabled me to spread my nets fairly widely—eventually leading to a kind of research and writing in *Moving Places* that took me outside reviewing entirely—it also fostered a certain intolerance and belligerence that probably reached its shrillest level in my "London and New York Journal." Some of this undoubtedly grew out of a sense of impotence and ineffectuality in relation to American film culture which was only exacerbated by my years of living abroad. When I was living in New York during the 1960s, one could count to some degree on such writers as Andrew Sarris and Pauline Kael for a defense of a certain intellectual approach toward cinema; but as their audiences grew, their intellectual partisanship tended to wane, and the philistinism and xenophobia that seemed to me on the rise in New York film criticism often sent me into intemperate rages.

Here's a characteristic sentence from my May–June 1977 column—entitled, like the ones immediately following it, "Moving," and written while I was in the process of moving from London to San Diego, shortly after a brief trip to Paris: "The first indication I had that Alain Resnais' PROVIDENCE might be something special—apart from the enthusiasm of the French press— was the report that most Manhattan critics hated it." It was undoubtedly remarks of this kind that eventually led Andrew Sarris to write (in the January– February 1978 *Film Comment*): "I have been disturbed for some time by a note of unending apologia in [Robin] Wood's writing for *Film Comment,* particularly in apposition to the boringly relentless pugnacity of Jonathan Rosenbaum."

This was undoubtedly one of the periods in my career when my writing habits were proving to be most irksome to some of my colleagues. In the 22 October 1976 issue of the [London] *Times Educational Supplement,* Wood himself had already gone further than Sarris would later and virtually linked me to the downfall of Western civilization—specifically for some flip comments comparing moviegoing and sex apropos of CELINE AND JULIE GO BOATING in London's *Time Out,* and for the nature of my praise of FAMILY PLOT in my "London and New York Journal," which Wood saw as being darkly related: "The implicit trivialization of art and life is the ultimate stage in our alienation," he concluded.

This scarcely begins to describe some of the repercussions that my anger in print was having, and not only among active critics. To cite another example, the 27 March entry in my "London and New York Journal" provoked a distressed letter half a year later from François Truffaut, whom I had been working with at the time—I was translating André Bazin's *Orson Welles* for Harper & Row, and had been serving as both editor and translator on a lengthy preface that Truffaut was writing for that book. (For those who want to read that letter and follow our ensuing exchange, see pages 461–464 in Truffaut's *Letters* [Faber and Faber, 1989].) And it's possible that the closing two sentences of the same two paragraphs permanently prevented any *rapprochement* or future friendship between myself and Pauline Kael, whom I had already undoubtedly alienated by writing an attack on her essay "Raising KANE" for *Film Comment* four years earlier.

I can't say I look back on my former venom with pride—some of it is stridently over-the-top and unpleasantly self-righteous, although I still agree with most of the positions I took. What surprised me at the time, however, and continued to surprise me for years afterward, was that established critics with vastly more power and influence like Kael and Sarris would be as unforgiving as they were about the criticism of a relatively unknown upstart like myself.

In the case of Kael, the first time we met face to face, and then only briefly, was at the New York Film Festival in 1978; both before and after that, mutual friends advised me that I could never hope to become friends with her because of what I'd written about her. I had wrongly assumed that because she'd been so merciless herself about attacking others at the start of her career that she'd be a good sport about being at the receiving end. In fairness to Pauline, however, I should report that after I became a member of the National Society of Film Critics in 1989, she came up to me at the end of the next annual meeting and told me that she had voted for me because (I quote from memory) "no one else has attacked me so consistently over the years." I laughed and replied, "That's because no one else has *read* you so consistently over the years." The following year—the last meeting she attended before retiring—she was kind enough to tell me that she had only been kidding the previous year and that there were other good reasons to have voted for me.

As for Andy, who was never very fond of polemics to begin with, I've been told that he refused to speak to me for a couple of years in the early 1980s because of some critical remarks I had written about him in my entry on Erich von Stroheim in Richard Roud's *Cinema: A Critical Dictionary*—an entry I had written six or seven years earlier. In recent years, I should add, he's been friendly. This paragraph, of course, may conceivably lead him to cut me again, but I should stress that I'm less interested here in settling old scores—or opening old sores—than in revealing to disinterested students the prices that have to be paid sometimes for speaking one's mind in print, especially when it concerns critics in the New York area.

■

A final note on "A Bluffer's Guide to Bèla Tarr," the first of a dozen of my *Chicago Reader* columns included in this book. As with my other *Reader* reviews reprinted here, I have retained their original formats, including the star ratings, because I consider these to be inextricably tied to their meanings. (I've adopted the same principle for my *Monthly Film Bulletin* review in the next section.) The explanation of these ratings, printed in the *Reader* with each review, is "★★★★ = Masterpiece, ★★★ = A must-see, ★★ = Worth seeing, ★ = Has redeeming facet, and ● = Worthless." Star ratings tend to be common currency in Chicago film reviewing, and it's a system I inherited when I started working at the *Reader* in 1987.

Theory and Practice
The Criticism of Jean-Luc Godard

Godard's collected criticism[1] is many things at once: informal history (1950–1967) of the arts in general and film in particular, spiritual and intellectual autobiography, a theory of aesthetics, a grab bag of puns. For those who read the pieces when they first appeared—chiefly in the yellow-covered *Cahiers du Cinéma* and the newspaper format of *Arts*—it was frequently ill-mannered gibberish that began to be vindicated (or amplified) when the films followed, retrospectively becoming a form of prophecy:

> [E]ach shot of MAN OF THE WEST gives one the impression that Anthony Mann is reinventing the Western, exactly as Matisse's portraits reinvent the features of Piero della Francesca . . . in other words, he both shows and demonstrates, innovates and copies, criticises and creates.

For those who encounter the films first, it is likely to seem like an anthology of footnotes serving to decipher and augment what may have once seemed like ill-mannered gibberish on the screen. But for those more interested in continuity than cause and effect, it rounds out a seventeen-year body of work—from an article on Joseph Mankiewicz in *Gazette du Cinéma* to the "Fin du Cinéma" title concluding WEEKEND—that has already transformed much of the vocabulary and syntax of modern narrative film, further illustrating a style that has passed from avant-garde to neoclassical in less than a decade. And as a fringe benefit, for those interested in Getting Ahead in the Commercial Avant-Garde, it is probably the best casual guidebook since Francis Steegmuller's recent biography of Cocteau.

Like Cocteau, Godard commands a vigorous rhetoric that crosses nimbly from one medium to another, registers most effectively in aphorisms, playfully orbits the work of other artists into a toylike cosmology of its own, and instantly changes whatever it touches by assimilating it into a personal aesthetic. Look long enough at his criticism and virtually every departure in Godard's films will be theoretically justified; study the films with enough scrutiny, and even the most outrageous reviews will start to make sense.

Generally less pugnacious than Truffaut, less logical than Rivette, and less Catholic than either Chabrol or Rohmer, Godard tops all four as a critic on the few occasions when he works at full steam. In "Defence and Illustration of Classical Construction" (a brilliant riposte to Bazin's antimontage theories), "Take Your Own Tours" (a mosaic of travelogue, festival reporting, and aesthetics), and reviews of THE WRONG MAN, A TIME TO LOVE AND A TIME TO DIE, and MAN OF THE WEST, he displays a rigor, imagination, and feeling for nuance that few other critics of the period have equaled. In the least interesting pieces—mainly volleys of dull spite against films that usually don't warrant the effort—he becomes a semi-anonymous journalist typing out his obligatory notice. Some articles, such as the one on Mizoguchi, seem to be paste-ups of remembered conversations with colleagues; others are unabashed advertisements for the films of friends; while a few (notably reviews of BITTER VICTORY and MONTPARNASSE 19) forsake critical decorum altogether, take off into the clouds, and deliver impassioned dithyrambs to the gods who inspired the ascent—moving and daring declarations even when one is less than clear about the precise meanings:

> MONTPARNASSE 19 is a film of fear. In this sense, it might be subtitled "the mystery of the film-maker." For in unwittingly investing Modigliani's unbalanced mind with his own perturbation, Jacques Becker—clumsily, admittedly, but infinitely movingly—allows us to penetrate the secret of artistic creation more effectively than Clouzot did by filming Picasso at work. After all, if a modern novel is fear of the blank page, a modern painting fear of the empty canvas, and modern sculpture fear of the stone, a modern film has the right to be fear of the camera, fear of the actors, fear of the dialogue, fear of the montage. I would give the whole of post-war French cinema for that one shot, badly acted, badly composed, but sublime, in which Modigliani asks five francs for his drawings on the terrace of the Coupole.
>
> Then, but only then, everything pleases in this displeasing film. Everything rings true in this totally false film. Everything is illuminated in this obscure film. For he who leaps into the void owes no explanations to those who watch.

The spirited, nonstop babble of this voice, heard the same year (1958) dubbing Jean-Paul Belmondo in CHARLOTTE ET SON JULES, is a guttural, rasping monotone that somehow manages to traverse enormous distances quickly; using epigrams as stepping stones, it proceeds by leaps and bounds across vast reaches of contemporary culture. Perhaps the most distinguishing feature of this style is impatience. Consider Truffaut's memories of Godard around 1950:

> What struck me most . . . at the time was the way he absorbed books. If he were at a friend's house, during one evening he would open easily forty books, and he always read the first and last pages. . . .
> He liked cinema as well as any of us, but he was capable of going to see fifteen minutes each of five different films in the same afternoon.

This frenzied rush—a race with destiny, like Belmondo's attempted flight at the end of BREATHLESS—appears to be the impetus behind most of the achievements, from the jump cuts of the early films to the extended, autonomous takes of the later ones. At the point of self-parody, it is "Bouvard and Pecuchet" in a cafe in 2 OR 3 THINGS I KNOW ABOUT HER, speedily reciting and copying down random passages from a mountain of books. In Godard's prose as much as in his films, this sense of urgency creates a form of criticism in the present tense, an endeavor that no other recent critic—with the possible exception of Manny Farber—has even approximated. It is essential to this method that everything remains *in process*: ideas are introduced in order to spawn other ideas rather than flesh out careful exegeses, and movement invariably takes precedence over explanation: "There was theatre (Griffith), poetry (Murnau), painting (Rossellini), dance (Eisenstein), music (Renoir). Henceforth there is cinema. And the cinema is Nicholas Ray." In a footnote to the first sentence, Godard spends three paragraphs trying to explain away all his paradoxes; but each argument becomes still another leap into the void.

The continuities between Godard's reviews and other films he has seen, and still others which he will eventually make, create a dense network. DERRIÈRE LE MIROIR, the French title of Ray's BIGGER THAN LIFE, crops up frequently as an image in reviews that presumably have nothing to do with Ray.

A line delivered by Mai-Britt Nilsson in Bergman's SOMMARLEK—about not being able to close her eyes as tightly as she wants to—fails to appear in Godard's tribute to the film in "Bergmanorama," but surfaces nine months later in his review of A TIME TO LOVE AND A TIME TO DIE, where he uses it to define the theme of Sirk's film ("blackness") without mentioning either Bergman or the film's title; shortly thereafter, Jean Seberg delivers the line in BREATHLESS. Four years later, Sirk's film in its turn becomes an important source for LES CARABINIERS—particularly the shooting of a partisan woman who denounces her assassins (a Russian peasant in Sirk's film, a French girl quoting Mayakovsky in Godard's). Another variation of the scene appears at the indoor swimming pool in ALPHAVILLE . . . but why go on? Undoubtedly hundreds of such threads could be traced through Godard's labyrinth.

■

By his own admission, Godard's films are also criticism, and it is worth considering how—and how effectively—they fulfill this function. Blake's

"Imitation is criticism" is not quite enough; indeed, Eliot's "Between the emotion / And the response / Falls the Shadow" probably comes closer to explaining Godard's distance from his models. BREATHLESS works intermittently as a thriller, but self-consciousness about the genre tends to veer it in another direction; BANDE À PART—like Monicelli's BIG DEAL ON MADONNA STREET—mainly comments on other "big heist" films by failing to match them. Just as Faulkner, by his own account, developed his prose style out of an inability to write lyric poetry, Godard's modernism—at least until PIERROT LE FOU—largely stems from his inability to make pure "classic" or genre films. (After that, one would probably have to substitute "refusal" for "inability.") And it is in the shadow between emotion and response, model and imitation, that his criticism must be located.

In ALPHAVILLE, this shadow is blackness—specifically, the blackness of the German expressionist cinema (CALIGARI and LULU, MABUSE and METROPOLIS, THE GOLEM and FAUST) and the cinema that derives from it (SCARFACE and KISS ME DEADLY, ORPHÉE and THE TRIAL). Perhaps the two latter films, in addition to furnishing the Orpheus myth and Akim Tamiroff, also suggested the use of real locations instead of sets. But by relating this use to science fiction (which itself has important links with German expressionism), Godard criticizes the conventions of the genre—and subsequently alters its possibilities, to judge from offspring like THX 1138. More profoundly, he comments on the implicit thematic values of light and darkness in German expressionism by making them explicit, even self-conscious, in the film's symbology. "Light that goes . . . light that returns," chants Natasha in the film's central love scene, as the light modulates back and forth from blinding intensity to darkness—as it does throughout much of the film, usually at a faster, blinking tempo. "From needing to know, I watched the night create the day . . . " "What transforms the night into day?" Alpha-60 asks Lemmy, who replies: "Poetry." Even the abrupt shifts to negative express the same dialectic.[2] Quite aside from the specific homages (figures clinging to the wall like Cesare sleepwalking in CALIGARI, a track through the hotel's revolving door from THE LAST LAUGH, Professor Nosferatu, etc.), ALPHAVILLE has more to say about the silent German cinema than any of the passing references in Godard's essays. Criticism composed in the language of the medium, it brings social and aesthetic insight equally into focus, and certainly deserves a place next to Kracauer and Eisner.

The relative cohesiveness of ALPHAVILLE's imagery gives it a steadier critical reference than most of Godard's other films: perhaps only LES CARABINIERS, his critique of the war film, sticks as closely to its subject. More frequently, he comments on genres by mixing them, or playing one off against the other. PIERROT LE FOU is largely a colorful fruit salad of Hollywood forms—crime thriller, comedy, chase film, musical, adventure. In UNE FEMME EST UNE FEMME, neorealism can't do justice to the dreams of Angela, and musical comedy would gloss over the drabness of her days, so Godard attempts a "neorealist musical" to paint her life. Unfortunately, the drabness is itself pretty banal, the comedy laborious, and Michel Legrand's musical score—neither synchronized nor asynchronized with the action in a convincing manner—consistently unmemorable. The net result is fairly constant clumsiness, in nearly every department, and in order to justify this film—as criticism or art—one would ultimately have to evoke Godard's review of MONTPARNASSE 19 as a support (as Jean-André Fieschi once did in *Cahiers*).

In MADE IN U.S.A., however—one of the most maligned films in Godard's pre-1968 canon, and undeservedly so—the crossbreeding of the violent action thriller with the animated cartoon yields much more interesting results. Confronting a web of impenetrable, anxiety-producing mysteries (the Kennedy assassination, the Ben Barka affair, etc.), Godard chooses—much like Rivette in PARIS NOUS APPARTIENT—to evoke their terrors by making his intrigue as ambiguous and complex as possible. Turning to seemingly incompatible Hollywood genres for illustration, he begins to suggest what the two have in common: tendencies toward sadism and hysteria, idealization of types with occasional right-wing implications; the wish-fulfillment and fantasy of the crime thriller, the primal violence and terror of the cartoon. (To exemplify these strains in two recent releases, consider Disney's SONG OF THE SOUTH and Siegel's DIRTY HARRY.) The aggressive antilogic of various elements in the dialogue and plot helps to abstract these genres, for Godard's purposes, into simplified, almost schematic formal diagrams: lots of red paint and brutal noises, rapid transitions, and dreamlike ellipses. This pungent blend of sensual and compositional "essences" recaptures some of the spirit of both genres while revealing their formal and political meeting points. Numerous annotations are offered on the subject: "a film by Walt Disney, but played by Humphrey Bogart," "Walt Disney plus blood"; a dedication of the film to Nick (Ray) and Samuel (Fuller) in bold primary colors; characters named David Goodis, Inspector Aldrich, Mark Dixon, Dr. Korvo,[3] and Widmark, the last of whom (Laszlo Szabo) imitates Tweety Pie; a black car parked in front of a Disney display. Unlike ALPHAVILLE, this cannot be called criticism in depth; but it is provocative commentary nonetheless.

■

Although WEEKEND, the last of Godard's features to be completed before May 1968, probably contains more filmic allusion per square foot than any that preceded it, the direction of his criticism from MASCULINE–FEMININE (1966) increasingly turns from cinematic to social and political subjects. Not that an interest wasn't already there: his second published essay, dated 1950, is entitled "Toward a Political Cinema." But judging from his subsequent prose, it probably isn't until "Take Your Own Tours" nine years later that the world outside the cinema begins to become more important than the movies inside. And even in LE PETIT SOLDAT, an attempt to confront the Algerian war, Godard's sources are politics in literature and cinema rather than in the street. The tempo, duration, and dry, objective treatment of Bruno's extended torture and suicide attempt seem partially derived from Dashiell Hammett's *The Glass Key* (which already supplied BREATHLESS with a wisecrack about wearing silk and tweeds together). Moreover, the existential decision of Hammett's hero to submit to brutality rather than betray his friend, a corrupt politician—essentially resolving to stick by one crook instead of another— closely parallels the moral arbitrariness of Bruno's choice of Right over Left, which leads to his own torture at the hands of the FLN. Within each scale of values, taking a position and remaining steadfast seems more of an issue than the actual position taken.

According to Jean Collet, in his book *Jean-Luc Godard,* Godard's "point of departure" for LE PETIT SOLDAT was the character of O'Hara in THE LADY FROM SHANGHAI. Bruno's final words in the film do have a somewhat familiar ring: "Only one thing was left to me: learn not to be bitter. But I was happy, because I had a lot of time in front of me." And the following comparison of dialogue from JOHNNY GUITAR and LE PETIT SOLDAT speaks for itself, further suggesting that the doomed romanticism of Hammett, Welles, and Ray appealed more to Godard at the time than the social and political questions they dealt with:

> *Johnny* (Sterling Hayden): Lie to me, tell me that all these years you've waited
> for me, tell me.
> *Vienna* (Joan Crawford): All these years I've waited for you.
> *Johnny*: If I hadn't returned, you would have died.
> *Vienna*: If you hadn't returned, I would have died.
>
> *Bruno* (Michel Subor): Lie to me . . . Say you aren't sad that I'm leaving.
> *Véronica* (Anna Karina): I'm not sad that you're leaving. I'm not in love with
> you. I won't join you in Brazil. I don't kiss you tenderly.

When Godard cast Jean Seberg as a journalist in BREATHLESS, this may have been prompted by his own immediate past, which had at least as much to do with journalism as with criticism. When he recast her as a television reporter in LE GRAND ESCROC, changing her name from Franchini to Leacock, he was resuming a line of inquiry that continues, unabated, into the present: the heroine of TOUT VA BIEN, Susan DeWitt (Jane Fonda), is also an American journalist, holding a somewhat implausible job as a radio correspondent. But the climax of his concern with reporting and documentary comes in 2 OR 3 THINGS I KNOW ABOUT HER, surely the most ambitious of all his attempts to create a new language of truth-telling. Just as, in all of the previous films, the spirit of documentary brushes against his fictions—criticizing, testing, and impinging on them—so his criticism of documentary in 2 OR 3 THINGS makes liberal use of the techniques of fiction. Similar in this respect to both Agee's *Let Us Now Praise Famous Men* and Mailer's *Armies of the Night,* it is a meditation composed of reflections on a shifting subject (Paris, Juliette, prostitution, suburban housing) and continual questions about how to reflect on this subject—a seesawing operation that undermines the nature of "content" as well as "style." Are the enormous close-ups of coffee filling the screen an exposition of the real, or—coupled with Godard's poetic narration—an expression of the infinite? Is the remarkable montage sequence at the garage an analysis of an event, or the construction of one? The probing voice and camera question everything, refusing to stay within a single viewpoint or method, thereby challenging *cinéma-vérité* (and cinema itself) at its very sources, reaching out for something else.[4]

Notes

1. *Godard on Godard.* Translation and commentary by Tom Milne (Secker and Warburg, £3.50, 1972). Milne's translation is a careful—and for the most part, successful—attempt to render Godard legibly, and his commentaries, spread out over nearly forty pages, are rich with information and opinions about minor French directors, multiple cross-references between articles and films, and wide-ranging gossip (e.g., the snack bars Godard frequented in 1959). One regrets, however, the omission of nearly all of the reviews' original titles, a somewhat cumbersome and incomplete index, and the loss of several of Godard's best puns, which perhaps only G. Cabrera Infante of *Three Trapped Tigers* could do adequate justice to. A final quibble, which relates equally to the French edition: since this collection is so close to being complete, why were a few stray pieces (like "Trois mille heures de cinéma" in *Cahiers du Cinéma*, no. 184) left out?

2. By a stroke of unusual good fortune, the American dubbed version of ALPHAVILLE improves on the original in one scene: as fluorescent lights flicker on in a dark corridor, the remark of the guide leading Lemmy, in place of "Le jour se lève," is "Sunrise."

3. As Tom Milne informs us in *Godard on Godard,* Dixon and Korvo are characters in two thrillers directed by Otto Preminger—WHERE THE SIDEWALK ENDS and WHIRLPOOL, respectively. Still other references are made in the dialogue to "rue Preminger" and "rue Ben Hecht." The surname of Donald (Jean-Pierre Léaud) is never given, but one is tempted to assume it to be either "Duck" or "Siegel."

4. The gradual clarification and articulation of this "something else"—Godard's increased political mobilization after May 1968, and his collaboration with Jean-Pierre Gorin—fall beyond the scope of this study. It is worth noting, however, that in VENT D'EST one finds a Marxist critique of the Western, while TOUT VA BIEN offers explicit auto-critiques of LE MÉPRIS and other earlier works.

—*Sight and Sound*, Summer 1972

Film Comment Journals, 1974–1977

Excerpts

February 16. As a friend has pointed out, Chaplin doesn't really belong to the history of cinema; he belongs to history. What for another artist might only come across as misjudgment, naivete, or bad taste often registers in a Chaplin film as personal-historical testimony of the most candid and searing sort. Thus the total inadequacy of his impassioned speech at the end of THE GREAT DICTATOR—as art, as thought, as action, as anything—becomes the key experience that the film has to offer, revealing the limitations of human utterance in the face of the unspeakable. For roughly two hours, Chaplin has been trying to defeat Hitler by using every trick that he knows; finally exhausting his capacities for comedy and ridicule, and realizing that neither is enough, he turns to us in his own person and tries even harder, making a direct plea for hope. But although he effectively annihilates the Tramp before our eyes, he simultaneously re-creates him in a much more profound way, exposing the brutal fact of his own helplessness. Seen with historical hindsight, there are few moments in film as raw and convulsive as this desperate coda. Being foolish enough to believe that he can save the world, Chaplin winds up breaking our hearts in a way that no mere artist ever could.

February 20. Carmelo Bene's SALOME. Unlike several of my colleagues, I've never been able to take Bene quite as seriously as he seems to take himself, but this is the first time he's consistently entertained me from first frame to last. Delivering the text of Wilde's play in delirious tirades, locating it in some Exploding Plastic Inevitable of the mind, and then fracturing his Day-Glo visions into a mosaic of jerky and jumbled glimpses, he triumphantly succeeds in turning his ideas about decadence into a cubistic three-ring circus, an explosive shower of shots that are scattered about like opulent jewels.

February 27.   Bertrand Tavernier's L'HORLOGER DE SAINT-PAUL. One of the less endearing plagues of contemporary film criticism is the formula of trying to exalt the conventional by calling it classical. In this fashion, the silly plagiarisms of John Milius's DILLINGER are applauded as commentaries on Our National Heritage, Chabrol's playful (and enormously entertaining) James Cain exercises are treated as though they were etched in acid by a Balzac or carved into marble by a Racine, and a film as uninspired and soporific as this Georges Simenon adaptation gains mystical association in the French press with some imagined "classical" tradition. Certainly the relatively brief and accelerated history of film has led to many radical foreshortenings of the history of art when comparisons are evoked; my semifrivolous reference to cubism one paragraph back is but one example out of thousands. But when decades begin to be treated as though they were centuries or even millennia, what kind of justice are we doing to a Hawks or a Ford, much less a dull craftsman like Tavernier? A former critic—and one who specialized with considerable competence in what is usually called "classic" American cinema—Tavernier already seems well on his way up the Bogdanovich ladder, and we're all beginning to discover where *that* leads. If this is *le cinéma classique,* give me *le cinéma sauvage* any time.

March 8.   My prayer is answered. Seeing a work print of the new Jacques Rivette film—to be called either CÉLINE ET JULIE VONT EN ZIZANIE or CÉLINE ET JULIE VONT EN BATEAU in French, probably PHANTOM LADIES OVER PARIS in English, and running a bit over three hours—I come upon *le cinéma sauvage* in all its exhilarating and barbaric splendors. It's a comedy (a comedy by Rivette? yes), it's wild and funny and unsettling and rigorous (often—if not invariably—at the same time), and when I see the work print again the following week, it still scares me out of my wits. . . .

—from "Paris Journal," *Film Comment,* July–August 1974

March 27.   [New York.] THE STORY OF ADELE H., or GIDGET GOES HEGELIAN. Truffaut's pretty, nonobsessive postcards about obsession are a gift to the eye in Nestor Almendros's photography, but a dull bromide to the mind. Apart from offering a veritable film festival to the spectator who wants to wallow in self-pity and call it literary, the camera's habit of cutting away to another quaintly posed setup every time the heroine's perversity starts to become interesting only underlines how steadily Truffaut has been veering away from any serious risks. A crowd pleaser in the tradition of Chaplin, he has yet to make his MONSIEUR VERDOUX or A KING IN NEW YORK because he always looks for the easy way out.

Much as his collected movie pieces . . . exclude all his polemical writing, and his editing of Bazin has tended to follow suit—with comparable implications of historical whitewash—this movie takes the tang out of its heroine's madness by giving us a healthy, talented ingenue in place of an actress. Of course, one can understand Pauline Kael believing this to be a great work of art, just as one can understand many American intellectuals believing that Kael is a great aesthetician. Given the right sort of climate and training, anything's possible, even the Nixon administration and'snuff movies.

March 29.   Which brings me to TAXI DRIVER, another Kael favorite. Great Bernard Herrmann score, great performances, the best Scorsese direction to date—turning New York into an expressionist moonscape and another Capital of Pain—all pressed into the service of . . . what? Check out Paul Schrader's marathon interview in the March–April [1976] *Film Comment,* which tells you the exciting answer: a transcendental movie about his gun collection influenced by Bresson. But better than Bresson (whom Kael finds "perversely academic"), because it also gives you a simulated snuff movie (Scorsese's endearing monologue) and an exceptionally arty My Lai massacre sequence—obligatory to all Serious American Films, because all Serious American Films are about America, right? Just as Bresson's films, according to Schrader's transcendental mystifications, are about what you *don't* see or hear in them, rather than anything so mundane as their own ingredients. . . .

April 9.   FAMILY PLOT. Hitchcock, on the other hand, has made a movie about his own sexy forms of duplicity and deception, which include sound and image, sumptuous musical scores, and cuddly Hollywood types . . . what better subject for him? But to judge from a lot of local remarks, this gem is apparently one of the Master's lightweights because it doesn't contain any guilt (unless one counts the wealthy dowager's regrets about the past that set the double plot in motion) or murders or contemporary gloss. Apparently death, sex, and money aren't as significant as New York or Watergate unless they're seen through a stained glass, darkly.

Three separate friends have complained that the sequence with Barbara Harris and Bruce Dern in the brakeless car is "embarrassing": I'm not sure whether this means corny or old-fashioned or something else, although this clearly wasn't the experience of the three audiences I saw it with during the first eight days of its run. If by "embarrassing" they mean that it makes its own strategies evident and obvious, I can only concur. In a rare burst of candor, Hitchcock finally places the transcendental where it belongs—in a crystal ball—and devotes his energy to showing us how a thriller works. That the film's visual structure is witty enough to rhyme its crystal ball with a religious amulet and symbol of wealth (the giant diamond) and to suggest elsewhere that both are like TV screens—so that Hitchcock's own appearance consists of his video silhouette, behind glass—only helps to show that FAMILY PLOT's true lucidity (like Lang's in SPIES and THE 1000 EYES OF DR. MABUSE) is its manner of equating its own narrative devices with its character's actions, creating a mirror surface that lets an audience watch its own responses rather than get lost in them. All mirrors, to be sure, are potentially "embarrassing." . . .

April 15.   [Reseeing PLAYTIME in an NYU film class.] . . . With the possible exception of Snow's nonnarrative LA REGION CENTRALE, I know of nothing in cinema which physically exhausts me as much. Fifteen minutes after it's over, I find myself inadvertently crashing into a wall like one of Tativille's inhabitants, still overwhelmed by the notion that *any* slab of sound and image—reality included—can be so richly orchestrated. The crucial catalyst, I've come to feel, is the music played in the restaurant by two successive orchestras, then sung by a chanteuse who is later joined by all the people present—an element that ultimately helps one to deal creatively with Tati's overload of invention by supplying one with a rhythmic base to work from. Thanks to this music, each set of visual options offers a different choice of *rhythmic* trajectories in relation to the underlying pulse, a number of evolving figurations through which spectators can join Tati in charting out their own choreographies, improvising their own organizations of emphasis in relation to the director's massive "head arrangement."

What other film converts work into play so pleasurably by turning the very acts of seeing and hearing into a form of dancing? . . .

—from "London & New York Journal,"
Film Comment, July–August 1976

Paris in Early February.   Seeing PROVIDENCE on two successive nights in a large, crowded Left Bank cinema, I'm part of a rapt audience, and both times there's applause at the end. Can this be accounted for by the hypothesis of a New York colleague—that the audience doesn't understand the subtitled English? I don't think so. Even if one can't accept David Mercer's self-conscious, middlebrow, English-theater script as a fair rendering of the mind of John Gielgud's self-conscious, middlebrow English novelist, it's still a damn sight better written than most reviews I've read of PROVIDENCE. And there's a lot more to the movie than the script: directed by anyone else, it might not have been worth the bother.

The irony is that PROVIDENCE is a warm, old-fashioned realist film, made with a kind of clout that has long since vanished from Hollywood. To see reality as a form of Lovecraftian enchantment filtered through a writer's rambling emotions and imagination isn't a very radical thing to be doing in the mid-1970s, and I'd be the last to claim that Resnais is onto anything innovative. I'm simply grateful for his demonstration of movie magic at a time when the standard upholstery of most film fiction has become astonishingly meager. . . .

To enjoy the film, of course, you have to believe that reality is constructed rather than given, and intuited rather than grasped—in the luminous final sequence no less than in the others. All Resnais' films are about the inexpressible, but the moving sweetness of PROVIDENCE is that although *all* the successive incarnations and versions of Dirk Bogarde, Ellen Burstyn, Elaine Stritch, and David Warner are equally idealized and "unreal," their collective resonances comprise, along with Gielgud, the five most solid characters in any film I've seen this year—phantoms perceived, like all "real" people, through the intimate biases of the mind. In this respect, they resemble the haunted Tyrones in *Long Day's Journey into Night*. Finely tuned in a way that exposes such creations as Stallone's Rocky or Bergman's SCENES FROM A MARRIAGE couple as stereotypes cut from the crudest cardboard, they project a mysterious *density* through Resnais' poetic mélange of props and places that his musically measured editing contrives to convey, not unravel. Thus the 360-degree crane around a gorgeous landscape in the last scene, taking in the breadth of a supposedly material and ordered world, is as pregnant with wonder and latent meaning as the beautiful earlier image of a werewolf in a wheelchair being lifted into an ambulance.

"The cinema is necessarily fascination and rape, that is how it acts on people," Rivette remarked in 1968 . . . ; "it is something pretty unclear, something one sees shrouded in darkness, where you project the same things as in dreams." I doubt that any more than half of me believes this today; the other half is more prone to root out the mysteries and curse the darkness. But for the dark side of me, I can't think of any recent movie quite as ravishing as PROVIDENCE.

—from "Moving," *Film Comment*, May–June 1977

Edinburgh Encounters

A Consumers/Producers Guide-in-Progress to
Four Recent Avant-Garde Films

The role of a work of art is to plunge people into horror. If the artist has a role, it is to confront people—and himself first of all—with this horror, this feeling that one has when one learns about the death of someone one has loved.

—Jacques Rivette
interview, circa 1967

For interpersonal communication, [the modernist text] substitutes the idea of collective production; writer and reader are indifferently critics of the text and it is through their collaboration that meanings are collectively produced . . .

The text then becomes the location of thought, rather than the mind. The mind is the factory where thought is at work, rather than the transport system which conveys the finished product. Hence the danger of the myths of clarity and transparency and of the receptive mind; they present thought as prepackaged, available, given, from the point of view of the consumer . . . Within a modernist text, however, all work is work in progress, the circle is never closed. Incompatible elements in a text should not be ironed out but confronted.

—Peter Wollen
Signs and Meaning in the Cinema, rev. ed., 1972

Are these two statements contradictory or complementary? The former describes art in visceral terms, as mutual emotional devastation; the latter in intellectual terms, as mutually "indifferent" criticism and production of meaning. But both, in a way, are temperamentally different descriptions of a process that might be regarded as the same. If the first prerequisite of an avant-garde work is that it makes one nervous—disrupting a familiar pattern of consumption, creating a sense of loss or absence which must be filled by the consumer's initiative—the second could be that it somehow rewards productive efforts to come to terms with it.

Since the responsibility for both conditions rests with work and consumer alike, it stands to reason that acceptance without conflict and rejection without compunction are the least productive responses to avant-garde films that can be imagined. Yet broadly speaking, the polarization today between defenders and detractors is such that no other public stances are readily acknowledged. To oversimplify somewhat, one faction is play-acting while the other is fleeing in terror.

These stances take the form of two kinds of rhetoric, each of which ignores and alienates the other. "Inside" critics with the benefit of theoretical contexts and larger funds of background information—some of it gossipy and anecdotal, some of it contextual and crucial—usually devote their energies to describing and discussing the text of a work, the concrete elements composing it. "Outside" critics, often limited by less information and more journalistic constraints, are more concerned with their subjective experiences. Thus the insider fails to address or even acknowledge private experience, leaving the uninitiated out in the cold; the outsider, conversely, makes his own experience public while remaining relatively cavalier about the text, effectively banishing the film itself.

The presumption I have adopted for the present context is that "avant-garde" can only be defined in relation to the beholder: whether or not it causes enough discomfort to push one forward. If a spectator finds WAVE-LENGTH as easy or as automatic to read as a Western, then he isn't watching an avant-garde film; if he is a film novice encountering a SUNRISE or a CITIZEN KANE for the first time, he conceivably might be. Any "reading" (definition, discussion, *or* experience) of a modernist work entails a perpetual dialogue between spectator and text, and I have attempted to bear witness to this process in the formula devised for dealing with the films treated below. All four were screened during the Edinburgh Festival late last August, and I have referred to this context whenever it has seemed relevant.

Feeling myself to occupy a certain middle ground between the vantage points of insider and outsider, producer and consumer, I have made my remarks deliberately confessional and provisional to the point of embarrassment, in an effort to demystify, if I can, some of the more rigid attitudes outlined above. I have been particularly interested in charting some of the means by which my own biases, engagements, disengagements, and evaluations have been formed. Limited by single screenings and/or restrictions of space and time, I cannot give these films' texts the kind of close scrutiny that is due to them (which is why I have suggested supplementary texts whenever possible); the same applies to my experiences, all of which are still in progress.

MOSES UND ARON (Straub/Huillet)

Expectations.   There are probably no filmmakers alive who intimidate me more than the team of Straub and Huillet. I can't believe anyone who describes their works as "easy to take": easy to consume, perhaps, on a strictly material level—I'm always excited by their use of direct sound and intrigued by the camera movements which appear to counter this openness, as didactic and final in their effects as Lang's reverse angles. But it's no summer picnic when it comes to reading and coproducing their texts. My usual experience combines an unrigorous respect for what they are doing with a frustrated sense of straggling behind them, which leads me to regard them as utopians aiming their films at "ideal" spectators who don't yet exist.

It's not merely a matter of following, say, the plots of NICHT VERSÖHNT and OTHON without prior knowledge of the Böll and Corneille texts which they utilize; I also have the more immediate problem of assimilating the spoken texts of CHRONICLE OF ANNA MAGDALENA BACH and HISTORY LESSONS in the time spans allotted me, particularly after the musical performances in the former and the car rides in the latter have slowed my motor impulses down to a more contemplative gait. And turning to Straub/Huillet's interviews, I'm again confronted with nearly equal amounts of admiration and confusion. Clearly they're alive to much of the best in cinema, and their theoretical articulations usually make me feel guilty for not reading more Marx and Engels. But when they proceed to enumerate precise reasons for all that they do, I often find myself split between fascination with these details—as ingenious, autonomous critiques in their own right—and dismay that they seldom correspond to my own readings of the films.

Case in point: at a delightfully good-natured and informative public discussion in Edinburgh, Danièle Huillet parenthetically notes that the sections of black leader punctuating the recitation of Schoenberg's second letter to Kandinsky in INTRODUCTION TO THE ACCOMPANIMENT TO A CINEMATO-GRAPHIC SCENE BY ARNOLD SCHOENBERG are introduced to mark elisions in the text. I've seen the short twice, and spent some time pondering the function of those black strips of film: rhythmic, ideological, formal, a kind of distanciation, or merely arbitrary? Some would argue that it doesn't matter; but the strongest impact of any Straub/Huillet film, it seems to me, is that everything matters.

I'm glad to have Huillet's explanation, but I also question the ultimate usefulness of my former blind alleys. Being thrown back on one's habits and resources is valuable if something grows out of the confrontation, but in this case—and comparable ones could be cited in their work—I feel as if I'd been sent out on a singularly unenlightening ride around the block. If, as they frequently state, Huillet/Straub dream of showing their films to factory workers, do they intend to bring along notes explaining such procedures?

Responses to text. Their film of MOSES UND ARON is my initial encounter with the Schoenberg opera, and from the moment the music begins I am grateful for having had this innocence. For the first time in *any* film, I have the sensation of listening to a piece of music without any kind of interference. This isn't true in the Bach film, which obliges one to watch musicians performing in an overall context of "work." Here we see the singers performing live and, along with them, hear the offscreen prerecorded orchestra (facts I heard about before the screening), and in no way do the pans or cuts or actors' movements contrive to interpret the music (although they *do* interpret the libretto). Furthermore, natural sounds of footsteps, breathing, and other movements are so beautifully captured along with the music that I know in advance that Gielen's separate recording of the opera will always sound somewhat incomplete, at least as a soundtrack score. This is the anti-FANTASIA par excellence; and long before the film arrives at the Golden Calf in act 2, it becomes clear that this is an anti-DeMille approach to spectacle as well.

But a question presents itself about the revels staged around this calf. If Moses represents Idea and Aron stands for Image, one might suppose that their conflict would become most intense when Desire rears its orgiastic head. Elsewhere, the voices of the burning bush have been kept offscreen so that (as Straub later explains), after the camera is panning up from Moses and across the landscape, these voices will subsequently seem to be those of "The People," who appear two scenes later as the chorus—a subversive turnaround of the material indeed. The miracle of the staff becoming a snake has been similarly transformed by cutting from one to the other rather than resorting to any trickery, while the Pillar of Fire becomes the sudden increase in light over a landscape brought about by a passing cloud. But when we get to the orgy, images of desire, passion, and bloodshed are so radically stripped of potential resonance that it seems the Calf's temptations aren't even getting a decent look-in. On the other hand, this is where I find the music most exciting and expressive, which makes me reconsider these tactics. Accompanying the musical fury with nude bodies, dancing, and violence that in no way compete with *or* duplicate any of its power may be the best possible way of serving it; who else in cinema would have really left Schoenberg's music alone?

Act 3—spoken by Moses and Aron, without music—is striking but enigmatic. Filmed in one take, it begins with Aron at the feet of Moses and two soldiers in long shot, a towering vista of mountain and lake behind them, and ends with Moses in close-up.

Afterthoughts. Immediately after the screening, I'm told that according to Schoenberg's instructions, Aron is supposed to drop dead after Moses sets him free. Straub "explains" this later in the public discussion by noting that at the end of the film Moses and Aron have destroyed one another ("They are simply two aspects of the same thing") and only The People are left—a fact I can accept and understand ideologically but not materially, because the film doesn't end that way.

In many respects, my work on the film has scarcely begun. Buying the recording and listening to it with the libretto in German and English, seeing the film again in Paris and taking notes, matching these notes with both the libretto and a copy of the script in German, have all been enlightening projects. One cannot appreciate a great deal of the film properly unless one has read Schoenberg's stage directions and then seen how they have or haven't been followed. When, for example, it is indicated that "From the audience Moses and Aron . . . appear to change their respective positions—with Moses shifting from foreground to background to foreground, and Aron vice versa—this transition is effected by one elaborate camera movement. Like many other details, it makes me think that Straub/Huillet aren't so much "minimalists" (as they're often called) as "essentialists" . . . Whatever my qualms about their stimulating statements regarding what *should* be evident in the film (and isn't), the deeper that I delve into its textures, the richer it becomes.

Suggested.   Interview with Straub and Huillet (*Cahiers du Cinéma,* no. 258–259), script of MOSES UND ARON (*Filmkritik,* May–June 1975), Michael Gielen's recording of the opera (with libretto) on Phillips.

RAMEAU'S NEPHEW BY DIDEROT (THANX TO DENNIS YOUNG) BY WILMA SCHOEN (Michael Snow)

Expectations.   Even though a New York friend warned me some months ago that this nearly five-hour film doesn't have the seductive qualities of Snow's earlier work, there's nothing at Edinburgh that I'm more curious or anxious to see. Speaking of "seduction" in relation to WAVELENGTH, BACK AND FORTH, and THE CENTRAL REGION may raise some smiles among those readers who shun them like the bubonic plague—a group that may well constitute the majority. But seductive, provocative, challenging, eye-opening, and mind-bending they certainly are, if only one can profitably get past the point of realizing that Snow has brought possibilities and points of reference to cinema that it never had before.

Large claims, to be sure; yet the beauty and terror of Snow's films are both essential functions of this uniqueness. The route of a cinéphile into the work of Godard, Rivette, and Straub is largely predicated on the experience and knowledge these men have of film history—informed by a history of taste, one might add, which is basically common to all three. For me, Straub's claim to interest is immediately enhanced by his enthusiasm for Renoir's LA NUIT DU CARREFOUR and Mizoguchi, his appreciations of Griffith and Ford. By contrast—and speaking still from a limited cinéphile viewpoint—Snow's

films effectively come out of nowhere and "refer back" to nothing. And because his formation largely *can* be traced back through his work in painting
and sculpture (along with his career as a free-jazz musician and his work in
animation for TV commercials with George Dunning, Richard Williams, and
others), certain art journals have shown more interest in him than most film
magazines.

Snow's three earlier features are based on the consequences of inexorable
camera movements: a gradual zoom across an 80-foot loft; horizontal (and
eventually vertical) pans swiveling "back and forth" across parts of a class-
room; 360-degree rotations of a camera scanning a spectacular vista of sky,
rocks, and mountains. The challenge in each case is to determine just what
one is to *do* in relation to these relentless trajectories. Adventures and lessons
in the potentialities of perception, their liberating power is to reveal that there
is much more to do—to see, grasp, and come to terms with—than one initially supposes.

The progress of the zoom in WAVELENGTH, punctuated by fragments of an
implied storyline (including a mysterious death and its later discovery) and
informed by a sense of finite destination (the opposite wall), entails a mixture
of narrative suspense and a more "painterly" response to shifting aspects of
light, color, texture, and visual field. BACK AND FORTH turns most of its potential narrative elements (the intermittent presence and activity of people)
into painterly subjects while sending its inanimate objects into paroxysms of
movement (as in one rapid section, where the accelerated scannings of a row
of windows appear successive rather than adjacent, like flickering movie
frames). Continuous movement and a total lack of human presence in THE
CENTRAL REGION establishes tensions between a gradually unfolding "landscape painting" and the kinetic sensation of losing one's center of gravity in
an experience roughly akin to riding a demonic ferris wheel. In each film, one
can either "follow" the camera movement or work out one's own looking/
seeing/staring/gazing patterns in opposition to it: either procedure leads to
a different set of problems, and throughout one is participating in a dialectic
which illuminates at every stage.

Although sound usually plays only a subsidiary role in these films—duplicating in some mechanical rhythmic fashion the operations of the camera
and/or supplementing the presence of people "realistically"—Snow's new
work is said to be *devoted* to relationships between sound and image.

Responses to text.   And so it is. Over 285 minutes and twenty-four sections of varying lengths separated by flashes of colors. RAMEAU'S NEPHEW focuses its attention on little else. And that, indeed, is what I find most disconcerting—a sense of reductiveness in relation to the preceding films. In one
respect, Snow's estrangement from the "dominant" film tradition makes itself
felt negatively here. In the Edinburgh festival booklet, he refers to "image-

sound relationships in the cinema" as a "fabulous practically uncharted artistic area." Practically uncharted indeed, if one excludes Bresson, Dovzhenko, Dreyer, Eisenstein, Godard, Hanoun, Mizoguchi, Ozu, Pollet, Portabella, Pudovkin, Renoir, Resnais, Rivette, Sternberg, Straub, Tati, and Welles, among others.

To be fair, he isn't pursuing this concern in a narrative context, which does make for substantial differences. But the seemingly arbitrary order of most sections leads me to regard them more as an interrelated collection of shorts than as a sustained experience, which raises the question of why one has to take it all in one serving . . . Space limitations make it impossible to describe every section, so I'll restrict myself to the rudiments of a few which seem most amusing or interesting:

No. 4, the credit sequence: superimposed over a passing train, a long succession of names drifts upward while a stammering voice reads them off, occasionally corrected by Snow's voice when the pronunciation is wrong. We get title, dedication (to Alexander Graham Bell), and a "cast" of over one hundred fifty names, some quite nonsensical (Lemon Coca Wish, Nice Slow Ham, Malice Shown, Show Me a Ling); meanwhile, one's attention playfully stammers between following the spoken words and those on the screen as they go in and out of synch with one another.

7, a long sequence inside an airplane, comes closest to resembling earlier Snow by following disconnected phrases spoken by various people with fast pans away from them, separated by jump cuts; this one, too, keeps you on your toes. The verbiage is a mixture of clichés, puns, jokes, statements about language, nonsense ("Vivaldi was a big influence on Johann Sebastian Fuck"); finally, moving back in time, one hears Snow offscreen instructing each person on what to say.

8 shows two hands beating the sides of a sink like bongos, continuing as it is filled with water and then emptied. The sound is so close to that of bongos that I wonder if dubbing is involved; if so, it's a skillful job indeed, and the bongo playing isn't bad either.

12 has the camera zooming away from another camera to reveal a group of people sitting around it, babbling incomprehensibly (tape manipulations?); eventually the image is reversed and the shot is run backward, the dialogue now becoming only semi-incomprehensible (something about a bad smell).

16, a delightful bit, juxtaposes the rearrangement by hand of numerous objects on a desk (including a copy of *Rameau's Nephew* in Penguin) with a voice describing these actions: again, like 4, a dance of variations as the one gradually strays behind or ahead of the other.

19, wordless, shows Joyce Wieland (Snow's wife) at the window of a cabin. A loud noise sounding (to me) rather like a wheelbarrow pushed over gravel starts up, and one becomes aware of a sheet of glass *in front of the window* that is now becoming streaked and obscured by raindrops. Is it in fact rain that one hears? An interesting demonstration of relative surfaces, and sight helping to identify sound.

Among the games played in other sections are multiple superimpositions of sound *and* image, recited texts from various sources (including Mao), a disembodied voice in an office, certain words of dialogue replaced by guitar strums followed by images of guitar strums shown silent, syllables synchronized with strokes of a violin, and a wonderful MURIEL-like mosaic of shots accompanying the successive syllables of a story being recited (too bad I can't follow the story as well). A jokey leitmotif recurring throughout the film—critic P. Adams Sitney holds forth on it in section 22—is that each time the words *4, four, for,* or *fore* occur visually or aurally, a separate shot acknowledges the total of these appearances to date.

As the reference in the title to Diderot suggests, Snow's aspiration appears to be encyclopedic. In parts, I find it intriguing; *in toto,* indigestible. Encyclopedias are useful things to have around, but who wants to plough through from A to Z in a single sitting?

Afterthoughts. I speak with Snow after the screening, and he clarifies a number of points: 8 and 19 are indeed sequences in synch sound, and a central point of the former is the synch/sink pun, which eluded me. The first half of 12 has the dialogue played backwards, while the second takes the dialogue spoken *phonetically* backwards and reverses that . . . Peter Wollen observes that the nonsensical "cast" names—forty by my count—are all anagrams of "Michael Snow," as is Wilma Schoen in the title. (Dennis Young, on the contrary, is alive and living in Canada, and Snow speaks of adding another shot to the film to prove that he exists; nobody I ask seems to know who he is.) Simon Field recalls his experience in helping to shoot part of sequence 10; Laura Mulvey points out that one of the texts in 21 comes from *Pride and Prejudice*; James Pettifer objects to the depoliticized use of a Mao text in the same sequence; Ben Brewster comments favorably on the film's looseness, which he compares to concerts of the music of Cornelius Cardew; Tony Rayns argues that section 21 largely explains and justifies the rest of the film. Such swapping sessions are partially what makes a festival like Edinburgh so useful; certainly they can help one map out the coherence of certain films after the fact.

What still rattles me about RAMEAU'S NEPHEW is not having enough information about certain technical procedures either before or after the screening to appreciate (or identify) what Snow is doing in certain cases. And the perceptual investigation it offers is finally less stimulating than what his earlier work explores. Snow calls it a "musical comedy," and perhaps I approached it with the wrong attitude. The shifting strategies turn much of it into a series of teasing puzzles, but beyond a certain point one can lose interest in solving them; and the implied play between sound and color never adds up to *anything* substantial that I can discern. While the earlier features demand to be consumed and produced whole, wasting nothing, it seems that certain sequences here, once one isolates their basic concepts, leave a lot of dead matter behind—like eggshells and orange peel in the wake of a picnic.

Suggested.   Program notes by Marjorie Keller for the screening at Film Center, School of the Art Institute of Chicago, 30 May 1975 (including a detailed *précis*).

SPEAKING DIRECTLY: SOME AMERICAN NOTES (Jon Jost)

Expectations.   Virtually none.

Responses to text.   From the moment Jost traces an animated fish in the air with his finger, I suspect I may be in for some surprises, and prove to be right as well as wrong. As a very personal self-presentation, the film frequently runs me through exercises that I recall from fictional and nonfictional counterparts: Godard in the late 1960s, Jim McBride's DAVID HOLZMAN'S DIARY and MY GIRLFRIEND'S WEDDING, Jonas Mekas's REMINISCENCES OF A JOURNEY TO LITHUANIA. But Jost is so distinct a presence that I gradually start to accept his exercises—didactic section titles like "I-They" and "I-You," "A Geography (Here)" and "A Geography (There)"; voice-over identifications of people and places; detailed inventories of the film's financing and equipment—as means rather than ends, and my focus turns increasingly toward the subjects at hand: Jost himself, the film he is making. And before long it becomes apparent that he is going about his business with a rare sort of honesty, a directness of address that makes even Godard himself seem like an illusionist.

At the same time, I'm wary about the lure that can be exerted by this brand of all-American confessional—the note of cranky individualism which dictates that all the most well-worn discoveries have to be reasserted anew, like homemade appliances, as if no one had ever thought of them before. It's the precise reverse of that assumed tradition of several centuries, languages, and ideologies lurking behind every gesture which I find in Straub/Huillet. An American and a contemporary of Jost, I'm constantly tempted to indulge in this rhetoric—what else am I doing now?—which may give me a high tolerance for it, extended further by a familiarity with the lifestyles and idioms. It's quite different in this way from the urban, apolitical stance of Yvonne Rainer's films—although there, too, my enjoyment is partially dictated by a prolonged exposure to self-analytical New York voices and idioms, which often make her films sound like cooler, more intellectual versions of Woody Allen and Elaine May.

So Jost's painstaking expositions of his life, his cabin in rural Oregon, friends, acquaintances, daily habits, feelings, auto-critiques, and political convictions remind me of other lives I know, and a sensibility that stretches all the way back to Thoreau by way of Mailer and Agee that seeks to justify and bear witness to all the concrete matters at hand, the speaker first of all. But no sooner have I flashed on Thoreau after Jost has begun describing his rustic home—and gotten ready to dismiss his naive pretensions—than Jost takes up this very issue himself and proceeds to explore its ramifications in some detail.

This sort of thing happens more than once and can lead to irritation as well as respect. The combination of thoughtful earnestness and analytical rectitude imposes itself as a personality as much as a sensibility, making it quite difficult to judge film and filmmaker separately. An especially thorny instance occurs in a section devoted to Elayne, the woman he lives with, when one hears her attempts at self-expression doomed from the start by the fact that *he* is dictating the context. Instructed that she has to speak about herself in relation to him for the purposes of the film, she finally reverts to the text he has already prepared for her, and the effect could hardly be more devastating. Should I admire Jost for letting the distastefulness of this episode stand intact or recoil from the fact that he perpetrates it in the first place? I wind up doing a bit of both, which effectively means liking the film more and Jost less.

By the same token, I'm delighted when in another section someone named Dennis lodges a vitriolic protest against the film as a form of self-indulgence, urging the audience (me) to burn the print I'm watching or at least to leave the cinema, finally declaring that he intends to do just that on *his* side of the camera, by leaving the frame—which he promptly does. The paradox is that I'm delighted but *don't* leave the cinema. Is Dennis being self-indulgent as well? Am I?

To Jost's credit, he seems to have much more political sophistication than most of his peers—largely, I think, because as with everything else he tackles in this film, he takes very little for granted. Unlike a lot of Marxist rhetoric I encounter in and about cinema on both sides of the Atlantic, Jost's political stances appear to have nothing to do with social, professional, or academic conformity, self-flattery, or coquetry, and most of his analyses teach me something.

Afterthoughts.   Why then don't I recount these lessons in some detail? The extent of Jost's anti-illusionism prompts me to attempt a little of my own, helping me to appreciate how hard it is to get rid of artifice. In fact, I don't recall most of his political sequences with any precision; what I mainly remember is that I was impressed at the time. My notes allude to one about Vietnam composed of an endlessly repeated film loop of American bombing accompanied by a woman's personal testimony about tortures, heard simultaneously with a man reciting facts and figures about the U.S. involvement—none of which, I should add, taught me anything essential that I hadn't already known. (I recognize the intention of revealing the war's televised monotony and remoteness, but that's nothing new either.) I also recorded some statistics that are cited elsewhere, that the United States comprises 7 percent of the world's land, 5 percent of its population, and consumes 60 percent of its material resources. Perhaps I'd heard *this* before, too, but Jost nevertheless places it in a context where its meaning is renewed for me.

I've neglected to mention several crucial episodes, including a long sequence showing only a stopwatch on the top of a blank white frame, before a hand enters to remove it (rather like a call to silent prayer in a religious service, but I like it anyway); and various striking visual tropes, such as a very slow dissolve that shows the sun appearing in an egg yolk. As some of my selective inventory may suggest, Jost has included a little of everything to flesh out his statement; what I haven't tried to convey, however, is the rather precise way he has structured it all. What I like most about the film is the way it lives up to its title and addresses me in the act of watching it, and not in some imaginary netherworld outside this experience.

Suggested.   Articles by Julia Lesage and Jon Jost in *Jump Cut,* no. 5 (January–February 1975).

JEANNE DIELMAN, 23 QUAI DE COMMERCE — 1080 BRUXELLES (Chantal Akerman)

Expectations.   Acquaintances who've seen this unsubtitled Belgian film at Cannes or Berlin describe it with some bemusement as a film over three hours long showing Delphine Seyrig, as the title heroine, doing a lot of mundane things like polishing shoes and washing dishes. The festival booklet notes that she kills a man "unpremeditatedly" toward the end and that the film covers a time span of two days. Akerman has made other films, but at this point I know nothing about them, apart from the fact that she has some reputation as a feminist.

Responses to text.   Seyrig/Dielman dries dishes, adds salt to potatoes on the stove. After she greets an old man at the door of her flat, takes his coat and scarf, and goes off into another room with him, there's an ellipsis—here, as elsewhere, covered by a straight cut. They emerge, he hands her some money ("Alors, la semaine prochaine"), and leaves. She puts the money in a ceramic pot on the dining room table, returns to the kitchen, pours out the boiling water, transfers the potatoes to another pot, takes a towel off her bed and drops it in a hamper, closes a bedroom window, turns out the light. Another ellipsis: she finishes taking a bath, dries and dresses herself, cleans the tub, sets the dining room table. A boy of sixteen or so arrives; she kisses him on the cheek, serves him soup; he reads while eating until she asks him not to. (A neon sign flashes from outside in the small adjoining living room.) She returns to the kitchen to fetch meat and potatoes, turns off the kitchen light, serves the food. "C'est bon?" "Oui, oui," he mutters, dawdling over the food. She chides him for not eating more, removes his half-eaten plate, then takes out a letter from a friend or relative and reads it aloud, very mechanically. She gives him chewing gum . . . corrects his pronunciation while he reads Baudelaire's "L'Ennemi" twice (significant? I doubt it) . . . turns on the radio . . . knits.

She and her son go out, take the lift down to street level, leave the building. Ellipsis; they return, take the lift back up again. She makes up his sofa-bed in the living room and they talk about her dead husband (his father); in response to questions, she remarks drily that making love with him had no importance for her apart from having a child. She goes to bed—ellipsis—gets out of bed, brings him fresh underwear, polishes his shoes, grinds coffee beans, etc., serves him breakfast, ties his scarf, gives him money from the pot in the dining room, sees him off. Folds up the sofa-bed, washes cutlery and dishes.

By now, I've used up less than a quarter of my abbreviated notes, but there's no need to extend the rundown indefinitely. It all proceeds at the same naturalistic crawl in sharp, uninflected color (shot by Babette Mangolte), with characters always shown frontally, from behind or in profile but never in intermediate angles, and no camera movements that I can recall.

I'm neither bored (exactly) nor interested (exactly), just curious. I tend to like movies that allow me breathing space in which to think, but this one gives me so much freedom that I don't know what to do with it—one reason, perhaps, why I take so many notes . . . The film continues to chronicle the remainder of the second day: a trip to a post office and shoe repair; she runs into a friend who invites her for coffee but she says she doesn't have time, maybe next week. Comes home with groceries, writes a letter, takes charge of a neighbor's baby while preparing wiener schnitzel, puts on makeup, goes out and buys yarn, drinks coffee alone in a cafe, returns home. Is drying her hands in the kitchen when the doorbell rings; greets another male customer—this one Jacques Doniol-Valcroze!—and continues through much the same patterns as the previous day.

At one point I leave the cinema for a few minutes—partially for a cigarette and partially to see what it feels like *not* watching the movie—and when I return, I don't feel as if I've missed anything important. Yet something keeps me watching, although I'm not sure precisely what. I know that some of it is Seyrig's performance—probably her best since MURIEL—which is remarkable for conveying almost no psychological nuances whatever; apart from her very precise movements and rituals, all perfectly executed, it is virtually impossible to guess what she's thinking at any given moment. As with Bresson, this makes her movements more interesting rather than less, but no sort of spiritual project is implied. Indeed, what baffles me about the movie is its absolute *lack* of resonance. What could Akerman possibly have in mind but a *reductio ad absurdum* of neorealism? It doesn't even qualify as polemic because the facts are too uninflected and ordinary.

Or are they? Is it "ordinary" that this archetypal bourgeois workhorse squeezes a prostitute's career so discreetly and unobtrusively into her daily routine? And can I believe, even in advance, that this woman could commit an unpremeditated murder?

Anticipating the latter event, I notice that by the third day, little cracks in her timetable and behavior have already started to appear. In the kitchen, she pauses uncharacteristically over a plate, and even drops a spoon—quite a dramatic moment. Outside, she seems disconcerted about the post office and certain shops being closed for lunch; back in her bedroom, she looks at a clock: is her schedule breaking down? Last night, she fell behind in cooking the vegetables and made two restless stabs at writing a letter before giving up and reading the paper instead. What's bugging her?

After preparing meat in the kitchen, she pours herself a cup of coffee and seems to find something wrong with it. She actually sits in a chair and *thinks* at one point; and after going downstairs to check her mailbox (nothing there), she sits again and thinks for about two minutes more. She has trouble when the neighbor leaves her baby—can't stop it from crying, can't decide whether to play with it or not. She goes out twice looking for a kind of button that she's told is no longer available and finds a package containing a nightgown when she returns the second time.

The third male customer arrives, and this time we cut to her bedroom. She unbuttons her blouse beside a mirror; we hear a cough offscreen. Then we see him make love to her on the towel laid out on the bed while her face remains expressionless, gradually showing some semblance of emotion as she reaches orgasm. She gets dressed; in the mirror behind her the man, smiling contentedly, is still visible on the bed. She picks up a pair of scissors, walks to the other side of the bed, and stabs him in the neck. Ellipsis; we find her seated at the dining room table, blood on her hands. She sits thinking for about five minutes while the neon sign flashes from outside: it is the last shot of the film, and probably the longest. At last, I think, she—and I—have something to think about.

Afterthoughts.   Of all the major films I saw in Edinburgh, JEANNE DIELMAN had the least to offer me immediately, while watching it, and perhaps the most to offer me eventually, recalling it afterward. In a slow, cumulative way, everything about it becomes interesting, and the apparent simplicity of "content" and manner is deceptive. I've spent hours discussing the film with friends, and countless details that initially seemed mechanical or inconsequential have assumed interest and meaning retrospectively. The fact that Akerman seems to have kept resolutely silent about the film is undoubtedly for the best, because any precise definitions of intention could inhibit the viewer and reduce the film's possibilities. Strictly illusionistic from first frame to last, it nonetheless demonstrates, like Dreyer's GERTRUD, just how subversive such a mode can still be.

Does Dielman commit murder in the penultimate shot because she has just had an orgasm (possibly for the first time), or because the customer doesn't get dressed right away (thus further jeopardizing her household schedule), or because she hasn't been able to find the kind of button she wants, or because of some radical feminist awakening? That the film doesn't allow us to say is wholly to its credit; if any reasons were supplied, I think the act would be still harder to accept, simply because it is not an act performed by the woman we have been watching for the preceding three hours. (I spoke briefly with a friend of Akerman's at Edinburgh who suggested that the murder was not introduced for any psychological reasons, but simply as a means for ending the film.) By breaking decisively with a naturalistic mode, Akerman throws considerable doubt on the apparent naturalism leading up to it. How "realistic" is the film, after all? From moment to moment it creates the illusion of showing us "everything," but it obviously doesn't; the film's running time is roughly one-sixteenth of the time span it covers, and even if we omit two nights of sleep we still have thirty-odd hours unaccounted for.

The film's paradoxical fascination is that it's both naturalistic and nonnaturalistic; everything is a clue and nothing offers a solution. Retracing the narrative's itinerary, one finds a startling demonstration of just how much mundane work is required merely to keep the bourgeois world of Jeanne Dielman intact and static, and how slight and imperceptible the ingredients are that might throw this system out of order. An easy conclusion would treat her as a simple social victim à la Fassbinder, her act of violence as spontaneous rebellion. But rebellion against whom or what? What we *see* in the film appears to be self-imposed, a way of life that seems partially designed to rule out the possibility of extended thinking. And if practically all her activity is directly or indirectly in the service of men—her customers and son—the only sort of affection she offers to either looks as mechanical and unspontaneous as her other duties.

With the ceramic pot in the dining room serving as economic index to her existence on Quai de Commerce, the rituals sustaining this cash flow could hardly be more universal; why, then, should the film be "difficult" to watch? Clearly it needs its running time, for its subject is an epic one, and the overall sweep of two days allows one to observe the patterns and their variations, trains one to recognize and respond to fluctuations and nuances. If a radical cinema is something that goes to the roots of experience, this is at the very least a film that shows where and how some of these roots are buried.

By focusing so exclusively on a part and aspect of life that art generally omits, abbreviates, idealizes, takes for granted, or refines out of existence, Akerman enables one to contemplate and analyze its repetitions, interrelations, and consequences—above all, its centrality—allowing one a great deal of leeway in what one finds while obliging one to come to terms with the implications. Politically, it functions like a bomb with a nearly interminable fuse, but the explosion it eventually effects is not so much a murder on the screen as a fission in the mind. Within the limits of the world we see, the heroine's work is not merely what makes everything else "possible"; one could just as concretely define it as what makes everything else *im*possible— a prison as much as a refuge, a safety catch as well as a trigger. To what extent is Jeanne Dielman a consumer, and to what extent a producer? And if, shifting the argument, we should conclude that she is *being* consumed and *being* produced, who is performing these tasks but the filmmakers, in collaboration with ourselves?

—*Sight and Sound*, Winter 1975/1976

1 Barthes & Film?

One reason for looking at the late Roland Barthes's writings about film is that we all tend to be much too specialized in the ways that we think about culture in general and movies in particular. Far from being a film specialist, Barthes could even be considered somewhat *cinephobic* (to coin a term), at least for a Frenchman. Speaking to Jacques Rivette and Michel Delahaye in 1963, he confessed, "I don't go very often to the cinema, hardly once a week"—inadvertently revealing the French passion for movies that can infect even a relative nonbeliever.

Cinephobic? Perhaps. He certainly mistrusted the hypnotic spell exerted by cinema and the attendant problem, for an analyst, of having to reconcile this continuity of appeal with a discontinuity of what he called signs. Yet what he had to say about literature, theater, photography, and music (his first loves) may wind up telling us more about film than the entire output of many movie critics. And what Barthes had to say about cinema—both in general and in many specific cases—is often interesting enough in its own right.

2 Movie Problems

"Resistance to the cinema . . ." he wrote in the self-regarding *Roland Barthes* (1975), trying to get a fix on what he didn't like about the medium. "Without remission, a continuum of images; the film . . . *follows,* like a garrulous ribbon: statutory impossibility of the fragment, of the haiku." A lover of the fragment and the haiku, he possibly came closest to analyzing a film when he devoted an essay ("The Third Meaning") to a few stills taken from Eisenstein's IVAN THE TERRIBLE. He virtually began his last book, *Camera Lucida: Reflections on Photography,* with the admission that "I decided I liked photography *in opposition* to the cinema, from which I nontheless failed to separate it."

Nor was this his only problem with movies. As he went on to say in *Roland Barthes,* "Constraints of representation (analogous to the obligatory rubrics of language) make it necessary to receive everything: of a man walking in the snow, even before he signifies, everything is given to me; in writing, on the contrary, I am not obliged to see how the hero wears his nails—but if it wants to, the Text describes, and with what force, Hölderlin's filthy talons." The trouble, in short, was that film—that "festival of affects," as Barthes called it—offered the spectator too much, yet not enough.

3 A Late Starter

Born in 1915, Barthes didn't publish his first book, *Writing Degree Zero,* until he was thirty-seven. He suffered from pulmonary tuberculosis for much of his youth and published his first articles (1942–1944) in a magazine put out by the Sanitorium des Étudiants, where he was staying much of the time. I haven't been able to track down the third of these pieces—a review of the first feature directed by Robert Bresson, LES ANGES DU PÉCHÉ.

Barthes apparently didn't deal with film again until about 1954, when he started to write a series of magazine articles that eventually became grouped together under the heading "Mythologies." This involved writing about all kinds of cultural activity, ranging from wrestling to striptease to tourist guides, in which films were allowed to play a significant part. In the course of developing this approach—initially with the aid of semiology, and later with the help of psychoanalysis—he constructed a critique of cinema that took shape in such essays as "The Third Meaning" (1970) and "Upon Leaving the Movie Theater" (1975).

In the late 1970s, not long before his death, Barthes agreed to play the novelist William Thackeray in his friend André Téchiné's film THE BRONTË SISTERS. (He had earlier refused to play himself in Godard's ALPHAVILLE in 1965.) And after that, he even contemplated writing a film script which Téchiné would direct, based on the life of Marcel Proust.

4 Hair, Sweat, & Semiology

Contemporary resistance to semiology as a dry academic pursuit can't be dealing with the spirited polemical and political use of it made by Barthes as a journalist over a quarter of a century ago, when he was defining and attacking current mythologies in the pages of *Les Lettres Nouvelles*. Semiology—a term and concept first formulated by linguist Ferdinand de Saussure in the early years of this century, when he called for a "science that studies the life of signs within society"—was in fact brought to the attention of a wide public largely through Barthes's efforts.

Inaugurating the chair of Literary Semiology at the Collège de France in the late 1970s, Barthes reminded his audience that:

> Semiology, so far as I am concerned, started from a strictly emotional impulse. It seemed to me (around 1954) that a science of signs might stimulate social criticism, and that Sartre, Brecht, and Saussure could concur in the project. It was a question, in short, of understanding (or of describing) how a society produces stereotypes, i.e., triumphs of artifice, which it then consumes as innate meanings, i.e., triumphs of nature. Semiology (my semiology, at least) is generated by an intolerance of this mixture of bad faith and good conscience which characterizes the general morality, and which Brecht, in his attack upon it, called the Great Habit.

In "The Roman in Films" (1954), some of these stereotypes, as evidenced in Joseph L. Mankiewicz's film of *Julius Caesar*, turn out to be fairly amusing. For instance, Barthes notices that all the male characters in the film sport fringes in order to demonstrate that they are Romans:

> We therefore see here the mainstream of the Spectacle—the *sign*—operating in the open. The frontal lock overwhelms one with evidence, no one can doubt that he is in Ancient Rome. And this certainty is permanent: the actors speak, act, torment themselves, debate "questions of universal import," without losing, thanks to this little flag displayed on their foreheads, any of their historical plausibility. Their general representativeness can even expand in complete safety, cross the ocean and the centuries, and merge into the Yankee mugs of Hollywood extras: no matter, everyone is reassured, installed in the quiet certainty of a universe without duplicity, where Romans are Romans thanks to the most legible of signs: hair on the forehead.

From this observation, Barthes goes on to trace two intriguing "subsigns" in the film: (1) "Portia and Calpurnia, woken at dead of night, have conspicuously uncombed hair," and (2) "all the faces" in the film "sweat constantly," a sign of "moral feeling." ("To sweat is to think—which evidently rests on the postulate, appropriate to a nation of businessmen, that thought is a violent, cataclysmic operation, of which sweat is only the most benign symptom." Hence, Caesar himself, "the *object* of the crime," is the only man in the film who remains dry.)

5 A Galaxy of Stars, A Plurality of Texts

On the subject of stars, Barthes had many intriguing things to say. Four months after his bout with JULIUS CAESAR, he was decrying the excessive use of movie stars in Sacha Guitry's SI VERSAILLES M'ÉTAIT CONTÉ:

> In the final analysis, the star system is not without a kind of chicanery: it consists of popularising History by Cinema, and of glorifying Cinema by History. It's a form of barter judged useful by both powers: for instance, Georges Marchal passes a little of his erotic glory over to Louis XIV, and in return, Louis XIV surrenders a little of his monarchical glory to Georges Marchal.

Barthes went on to reproach Guitry for not taking a lesson from the costume styling of the Folies Bergère, where the forms of period dress are false but "superbly so, with a fine contempt for accuracy and a desire to give fancy dress an epic dimension."

The same year, he praised Charlie Chaplin as a Brechtian artist, showing "the public its blindness by presenting at the same time a man who is blind and what is in front of him," that is, "a kind of primitive proletarian, still outside Revolution" in MODERN TIMES. Twenty-five years later, in a regular column he was writing for *Le Nouvel Observateur,* he expressed his fascination with an image from LIMELIGHT—Chaplin applying makeup in front of a mirror—as "literally a metamorphosis, such as only mythology and entomology could speak about it." And a few years before that, writing about himself in the third person in *Roland Barthes,* R. B. had this to say:

> As a child, he was not so fond of Chaplin's films; it was later that, without losing sight of the muddled and solacing ideology of the character, he found a kind of delight in this art at once so popular (in both senses) and so intricate; it was a *composite* art, looping together several tastes, several languages. Such artists provoke a complete kind of joy, for they afford the image of a culture that is at once differential and collective: plural. This image then functions as the third term, the subversive term of the opposition in which we are imprisoned: mass culture *or* high culture.

Writing poetically about the face of Greta Garbo—that mythic object *par excellence*—the same year, Barthes found that it represented a "fragile moment when the cinema is about to draw an existential from an essential beauty, when the archetype leans towards the fascination of moral faces, when the clarity of the flesh as essence yields its place to a lyricism of Woman." Comparing her face to the more individualized face of Audrey Hepburn, he concluded that, "As a language, Garbo's singularity was of the order of the concept, that of Audrey Hepburn is of the order of the substance. The face of Garbo is an Idea, that of Hepburn, an Event." The preceding translation is by Annette Lavers. When another Barthes translator, Richard Howard, published his own version of this essay in the 1960s, this formulation was updated by substituting Brigitte Bardot for Audrey Hepburn, leading to a more topical closing line: "Garbo's face is an Idea, Bardot's a Happening."

6 I Didn't Know the Gun Was Coded

There's another way of looking at Barthes and film, less poetic, that has been favored by certain academics. This involves seeing him as a great system builder, whose famous phrase by phrase textual analysis of a novella by Balzac called *Sarrazine,* a study known as *S/Z,* breaks down "the realist text" into "five levels of connotation" or "codes." From the methodology of analyzing prose narrative—which Barthes derived collectively from one of his seminars—certain film academics have tried to establish a more systematic approach in studying movies.

Without wishing to dismiss this sort of work, I can't say I've found it as useful as Barthes's more poetic and suggestive (if less systematic) writings. Maybe this is because I value his work more for its questions than its answers, and more for its art (and play) than its science (and work). In this respect, stylistically and iconoclastically, Barthes is closer to an American film critic like Manny Farber—above all, in the peculiarly *cinematic* flux, speed, and movement of his thought—than he is to fellow French semiologists like Raymond Bellour and Christian Metz.

One could also argue that the more "teachable" an analytic approach is, the easier it becomes to apply it mechanically—as, indeed, a generation of graduate students and professors has often tended to apply *S/Z,* without much thoughtfulness or insight.

7 Art as Immobility

> Ideology is, in effect, the imaginary of an epoch, the Cinema of a society.
>
> —*"Upon Leaving the Movie Theater"*

In 1959, when the French New Wave was just beginning to make itself felt, Barthes published a critique of Claude Chabrol's first film, LE BEAU SERGE, which called it right-wing for imposing a static image of man. The same year, in *Cahiers du Cinéma,* Chabrol wrote, "There's no such thing as a big theme and a little theme, because the smaller the theme is, the more one can give it a big treatment. The truth is, truth is all that matters." The problem about this position for Barthes was that it led to political complacency. The offhand way one looked at someone or something, he wrote, could become "the basis for an act of sarcasm or one of tenderness, in short, a truth," but the offhand way one arrived at a theme could be a falsehood. "What is terrible about the cinema," he added, "is that it makes the monstrous viable; one could even say that currently our entire avant-garde lives on this contradiction: true signs, a false meaning."

Summing up what he liked in Chabrol's provincial melodrama as "micro-realism," Barthes compared its "descriptive surface"—as in the gestures of children playing football in the street—with that of Flaubert. "The difference—which is considerable—is that Flaubert never wrote a *story*." Flaubert had the insight to realize that the ultimate value of his realism was its insignificance, "that the world signified only that it signified nothing."

> Chabrol, on the contrary, his realism firmly in place, invests a pathos and a moral—that is to say, whether he wills it or not, an ideology. There are no inno-cent stories: for the past hundred years, Literature has been struggling with this calamity.

For Barthes, Chabrol's "art of the right" always assigned meanings to human misfortunes without examining the reasons:

> The peasants drink. Why? Because they're very poor and have nothing to do. Why this misery, this abandon? Here the investigation stops or becomes subli-mated: they are undoubtedly stupid in essence, it's their nature. One certainly isn't asking for a course in political economy on the causes of rural poverty. But an artist should acknowledge his responsibility for the terms he assigns to his explanations: there is always a moment when art immobilises the world, and the later it comes, the better. I call art of the right this fascination with immobil-ity, which makes one describe outcomes without ever asking about, I won't say causes (art isn't deterministic), but functions.

8 Buñuel Versus Chabrol

Four years later, interviewed by *Cahiers du Cinéma,* Barthes pursued this notion further by evoking an art which challenged ideology by suspending meaning—a development in some ways of Brecht's ideas about alienation and New Novelist Alain Robbe-Grillet's ideas about nonhumanistic art:

> What I ask myself now is if there aren't arts which are more or less reactionary by their very natures and techniques. I believe that of literature; I don't believe a literature of the left would be possible. A problematic literature, yes—that is, a literature of suspended meaning: an art which provokes responses but doesn't supply them. I think literature is that in the best of cases. As for cinema, I have the impression that, in this respect, it's very close to literature, and because of its structure and material, it's a lot better prepared than theatre is for a certain responsibility for forms that I've called the technique of suspended meaning. I think cinema has trouble supplying clear meanings and that, in its present state, this *shouldn't* be done. The best films (for me) are those that suspend meaning

the most . . . an extremely difficult operation, requiring at once great technique
and total intellectual honesty. For that means disentangling oneself from all the
parasite meanings . . .

As a prime example of what he meant, Barthes cited Luis Buñuel's recent
THE EXTERMINATING ANGEL—a brilliant comic horror film about wealthy
guests who inexplicably find themselves incapable of leaving a dinner party.
Here, Barthes said, meaning was deliberately suspended without becoming
nonsensical or absurd, in a film that jolted one "profoundly, beyond dogma-
tism, beyond doctrines." In the vulgar but accurate sense, it was a film that
"made one think."

A few years later, Barthes's notion of suspended meaning would develop
still further into two major utopian, cultural models. In his beautiful *Empire
of Signs* (1970), Barthes posited Japan and its culture as a system consisting
of the "play" of "empty" signs—a concept that was crucially to influence
Noël Burch when the latter wrote his history of Japanese cinema, *To the
Distant Observer*. And in *The Pleasure of the Text* (1973), this became the
notion of a reader's "bliss" as opposed to his or her "pleasure" in reading a
text—the former a discontinuity of signs akin to the experience of sexual orgasm, when meaning again becomes suspended.

9   This Way, Myth

Passing references to films in Barthes's writings form a significant part of
their overall color and texture. Describing the mythical properties of the new
Citroën in 1955, he saw it "originating from the heaven of METROPOLIS." The
same year, stirred in part by Jacques Becker's TOUCHEZ PAS AU GRISBI, he analyzed the "coolness" of gangsters in gangster films, marveling at the visual
and nonverbal emphasis of their behavior, which insured that "each man re-
gains the ideality of a world surrendered to a purely gestural vocabulary, a
world which will no longer slow down under the fetters of language: gangsters and gods do not speak, they nod, and everything is fulfilled." The next
year, writing about the myth of exoticism revealed by a documentary about
the Mysterious Orient, THE LOST CONTINENT, he noted the various means by
which Buddhism was treated as "a higher form of Catholicism," and dryly
observed that, "Faced with anything foreign, the Established Order knows
only two types of behavior, which are both mutilating: either to acknowledge
it as a Punch and Judy show, or to defuse it as a pure reflection of the West."

10   Barthes and Films

Sometimes a particular film could goad Barthes into a major formulation.
For many readers, the key passage in *The Pleasure of the Text* is a paragraph

that links storytelling to the myth of Oedipus. This was written, Barthes notes at the end, after having seen F. W. Murnau's CITY GIRL—a silent Hollywood film of 1929 that had just been shown on French television. In *Roland Barthes,* he delighted in the "textual treasury" of a Marx Brothers movie, A NIGHT AT THE OPERA—including "the liner cabin, the torn contract, the final chaos of the opera décors"—as emblems of "the logical subversions performed by the Text." In the same book, he compared the process of his own writing to a theater rehearsal in a film by Jacques Rivette (who, in turn, has spoken often of Barthes's influence on his own work), a rehearsal that is "verbose, infinite . . . shot through with other matters."

Later, in *A Lover's Discourse: Fragments* (1978), he would cite a scene from Buñuel's THE DISCREET CHARM OF THE BOURGEOISIE—a curtain rising "the wrong way round—not on an intimate stage, but on the crowded theater"—as an emblematic image for the painful revelation of commonplace information by a lover's informer about his or her beloved. And in a magazine column in 1979, he recorded his distress at an audience laughing at the very things in Eric Rohmer's PERCEVAL (like the hero's simplicity) that he loved the most, and his amusement at seeing "a very French film," VINCENT, FRANÇOIS, PAUL . . . AND THE OTHERS, on French television ("The stereotype here is nationalised; it forms part of the décor, not part of the story").

11 Ugly Excess

In "The Third Meaning," Barthes distinguishes three levels of meaning in the stills from IVAN THE TERRIBLE that he examines. The first is informational, on the level of communication, to be analyzed by semiology. The second is symbolic, on the level of signification, to be analyzed by "the sciences of the symbol (psychoanalysis, economy, dramaturgy)." The third, which Barthes calls the "obtuse meaning," constitutes that surplus of meaning which can't be exhausted by the other two.

This level of "excess" (as it has been called by film scholar Kristin Thompson) is the hardest to describe with any clarity, for most criticism, by equating a film with its story and interpretation, fails to acknowledge that this third meaning can exist on any level at all. Barthes finds it in his own subjective observations of such details as the ugliness of the character Euphrosinia, which "exceeds the anecdote, becomes a blunting of the meaning, its deflection":

> Imagine "following" not Euphrosinia's machinations, nor even the character . . . nor even, further, the countenance of the Wicked Mother, but only, in this countenance, that grimace, that black veil, the heavy, ugly dullness of that skin. You will have another temporality . . . another film. A theme with neither variations nor development . . . the obtuse meaning can proceed only by appearing and disappearing.

12 On the Way Out

"Upon Leaving the Movie Theater" begins with Barthes's description of how much he loves that curious activity, which he compares to coming out of hypnosis. Reflecting on the theater's darkness and what it suggests to him—the "lack of ceremony" and "relaxation of postures"—he settles on the poetic image of the cocoon: "The film spectator might adopt the silk worm's motto: *inclusum labor illustrat*: because I am shut in I work, and shine with all the intensity of my desire."

> Submerged in the darkness of the theatre (an anonymous, crowded darkness: how boring and frustrating all those so-called "private" screenings), we find the very source of the fascination exercised by film (any film). Consider, on the other hand, the opposite experience, the experience of television, which also shows films: nothing, no fascination; the darkness is dissolved, the anonymity repressed, the space is familiar, organised (by furniture and familiar objects), tamed. Eroticism—or, better yet, in order to stress its frivolity, its incompleteness, the eroticisation of space—is foreclosed. Television condemns us to the Family, whose household utensil it has become just as the hearth once was, flanked by its predictable communal stewing pot in times past.

Linking the ideological stereotype with the still image, Barthes wonders if we all don't have "a dual relationship with platitudes: both narcissistic and maternal," in psychoanalytic terms. And the only way to pry oneself from the mirror (i.e., the screen) is to break "the circle of duality/ . . . filmic fascination" and "loosen the glue's grip, the hypnosis of verisimilitude" that is commonly referred to as suspension of disbelief. This can be done "by resorting to some (aural or visual) critical faculty of the spectator—isn't that what is involved in the Brechtian distancing effect?"

Yet instead of going to movies "armed with the discourse of counterideology," Barthes suggests another way. This involves letting himself become involved as if he had two bodies at once, one of them narcissistic, and the other one "perverse," making a fetish not of the image but of what "exceeds" it: "The sound's grain, the theatre, the obscure mass of other bodies, the rays of light, the entrance, the exit . . ." The distance with respect to the image, he concludes, is finally what fascinates us—a distance which is not so much intellectual as "amorous" . . . And despite all the numerous quarrels with cinema that Barthes maintained over a quarter of a century of writing, one suspects that many of them, in the final analysis, were a lover's quarrels, a lover's discourse.

*The author's thanks to Stephen Heath,
Michael Silverman, and Bérénice Reynaud*

—*Sight and Sound*, Winter 1982/1983

A Bluffer's Guide to Bèla Tarr

★★★

ALMANAC OF FALL
Directed and written by Bèla Tarr
With Hedi Temessy, Erika Bodnar, Miklós B. Szekely,
Pal Hetenyi, and János Derzsi

Problems

One reason that Eastern European films often don't get the attention they deserve in the West is that we lack the cultural and historical contexts for them. If Eastern Europe's recent social and political upheavals took most of the world by surprise, this was because most of us have been denied the opportunity to see the continuity behind them: they seemed to spring out of nowhere. The best Eastern European films tend to catch us off guard in the same way, and for similar reasons.

My own knowledge of Hungarian cinema is spotty at best, despite the fact that, according to David Cook in *A History of Narrative Film,* the Hungarians "seem to have identified film as an art form before any other nationality in the world, including the French." (One of the first major film theorists, Béla Balazs, was Hungarian, and a contemporary film studio in Budapest is named after him.) Among the pioneers were Mihaly Kertesz and Endre Toth, who emigrated to the United States and became known as Michael Curtiz and André de Toth. Paul Fejos (1897–1963) was one of the great filmmakers of the late silent and early sound periods, a shamefully neglected figure who made films all over the world—as a Hollywood director (LONESOME, THE LAST PERFORMANCE, BROADWAY), as a restless European independent (FANTOMAS, SONNENSTRAHL), and finally as an anthropologist in Madagascar, the East Indies, Siam (A HANDFUL OF RICE), and Peru. Yet only one of his Hungarian films, TAVASZI ZAPOR (1932), appears to have survived, and it can be seen only in Europe, although it is one of the supreme masterpieces of world cinema.

Otherwise, I have seen several pictures by Miklós Jancsó (a major figure in the 1960s and 1970s for such films as THE RED AND THE WHITE and RED PSALM, but someone whose films are no longer distributed in the United States), and the odd film or two by István Szábo (CONFIDENCE), Márta Mészáros (NINE MONTHS), Gyula Gazdag (A HUNGARIAN FAIRY TALE), the team of István Dárday and Gyorgyu Szalai (THE DOCUMENTATOR), and others.

Last year, I was bowled over by my first encounter with Bèla Tarr when I saw DAMNATION (1987), his fifth feature. And now that I've seen ALMANAC OF FALL (1984), his fourth (showing this week at Facets Multimedia Center), I want to see his earlier features—FAMILY NEST (1977), THE OUTSIDER (1980), and THE PREFAB PEOPLE (1982). The fact that I lack a comprehensive Hungarian context in which to situate these films doesn't create any serious obstacles to the great deal of pleasure Tarr's movies provide. But this lack of expertise *does* usher in a whole set of potential problems when it comes to writing about Tarr's work, and if I'm breaking with conventional critical etiquette in admitting to this anxiety here, it's only because I think a related form of anxiety dissuades a good many viewers from seeing films as exciting as DAMNATION and ALMANAC OF FALL. I believe that these problems are less serious than we tend to make them out to be; rather than pretend that they don't exist, it seems more honest and useful to acknowledge them—in the process of showing how and why they don't matter much.

Three problems should be broached right away: (1) I have no idea what the title ALMANAC OF FALL means, or how it relates to the film; (2) I no longer remember the film's opening quote from Alexander Pushkin, the relevance of which was also unclear; and (3) I'm not sure I understood all the dialogue, because some of the subtitles here (and in DAMNATION) are grammatically and/or typographically slipshod. All three problems have to do with linguistic uncertainty. The fact that I've searched the indexes of *Cahiers du Cinéma* and *Sight and Sound* in vain for any references to Tarr's work creates an additional layer of uncertainty, although one that is surely connected to the linguistic and cultural uncertainties of French and English film critics confronting the same work, many of whom would rather not see or write about films over which they feel no mastery.

The one piece of data I have at my disposal about Bèla Tarr is an entry in a Hungarian film directory—an entry worth quoting for the information it imparts, though it raises some of the same linguistic and cultural uncertainties cited above. After telling us that Tarr was born in 1955, the entry goes on to say:

He started making amateur films at the age of 16. In the meantime he was a labourer, the caretaker at a House for Culture and Recreation, and a free-lance intellectual. It was through his activities as an amateur film maker that he came into contact with the Béla Balazs Studio of which he became a member and that is where he made FAMILY NEST for which he won the Grand Prix (shared) at the

Mannheim Festival. Afterwards, in 1977, he became a student at the Academy for Theatre and Film Art. It was while he was still a student that he was given an opportunity to make his next film THE OUTSIDER which was also made with the methods of the "Budapest School" as was his first film. He graduated in 1981 and made his film THE PREFAB PEOPLE where the lead roles were played by film actors and actresses but the method was a repetition of his previous films.

Apart from its awkward and vague English, this entry raises such questions as: What is a House for Culture and Recreation? What is a freelance intellectual? What is the Budapest School, and what are its methods? And if the lead roles of his third feature were played by "film actors and actresses," who played the lead roles in the first two? (We may deduce that Tarr went from using nonprofessional actors to professionals, but can we be absolutely sure?)

Solutions

The plot and characters of ALMANAC OF FALL are crystal clear. All of the action takes place in the roomy apartment of Hedi (Hedi Temessy), an elderly woman who lives with her son János (János Derzsi) and her nurse Anna (Erika Bodnar). A recent addition to the household is Miklós (Miklós B. Szekely), Anna's lover; another recent addition is Pal (Pal Hetenyi), János's former and now unemployed schoolmaster, who moves in at János's insistence.

The main issue for all five characters is money, which Hedi has and the other four characters want. The relations between them are often edgy and quarrelsome and at times even violent, although at the outset, Anna gets along quite well with Hedi, serving as a friend as well as a nurse. The action proceeds mainly through a series of dialogues between two characters at a time, in or between various rooms, during which they either form temporary alliances or engage in conflicts: Anna speaks to Miklós in their bedroom, Hedi and János quarrel about money in the living room, Anna in the kitchen addresses Hedi in the bathroom, and so on.

Over the course of the film, Anna sleeps with all three men, and Pal, desperate to pay back a loan, steals and pawns Hedi's gold bracelet, an act that eventually unites the other four characters against him. Most of the time, each character seems to be acting on his or her own behalf, conspiring against the others; the emotional climate is Strindbergian, reflecting a continual series of power struggles, and it suggests at times the films of John Cassavetes in its intensity. The amount of time that passes over the course of the film is somewhat ambiguous; scenes usually follow one another abruptly, without much sense of how much time has passed between them.

The writing and acting are sufficiently controlled and effective to give this story a strong dramatic appeal, but what gives the film its greatest interest is

Tarr's elaborately choreographed mise en scène: he treats every scene as an individually shaped and sculpted set piece. This is also the case in DAMNA-TION, where the plot is much more minimal (a recluse in love with a singer gets her husband involved in a smuggling scheme so that he can spend time with her), and the mise en scène is more systematically blocked out and structured in lengthy takes. The two films are quite different in other respects. DAMNATION is in black and white and steeped in gloomy atmospherics (in exterior shots rain, fog, mud, and stray dogs, and in interiors lots of murk and decay). ALMANAC OF FALL is in color and has the dramatic economy of a tightly scripted play. But the two films have one striking thing in common: the story and the mise en scène are constructed in counterpoint to one another, like the separate melodic lines in a fugue.

In DAMNATION, this sometimes has the effect of making the story seem an afterthought, or at least a secondary element. A very slow camera movement proceeds through a given setting for no apparent reason apart from conjuring up a mood and creating a powerful sensation of formal suspense, similar to the look and effect of such camera movements in Tarkovsky films like SOLARIS and STALKER; then, toward the end of the sequence, something will appear in the shot or on the sound track that will retroactively connect this scene with the preceding story. The mise en scène in ALMANAC OF FALL, by contrast, is rarely used to suspend our perception of the plot; but it frequently has the effect of following a distinct agenda of its own. Another way of describing this process would be to say that in conventional movies, the action usually represents a precise congruence between what the characters do and what the camera does; in DAMNATION and ALMANAC OF FALL, where the congruence is not precise, the "action" consists of what the characters and the camera do in relation to one another—creating a set of shifting power relationships every bit as intricate as the shifting power relationships between the characters.

One of the most beautiful aspects of Tarr's mise en scène is a recurring lighting scheme: most areas in a given shot are divided between blue gray and orange red, isolating the characters from one another in the process. There doesn't appear to be anything systematic or programmatic about the color coding of various characters and spaces; it differs from scene to scene (Bèla Tarr is much more of an artist than Peter Greenaway), and its use is much too varied and expressive to register as a simple manneristic device. (Although the lighting is usually plotted in relation to the actors, the division of colors isn't absolute; a character bathed in blue light might be outlined in orange, for instance.)

Some of the unorthodox camera angles, like those of Raúl Ruiz, provide disturbingly uncanny and nonhuman vantage points on the action: in some scenes in the bathroom, the camera peers down at the characters from a point somewhere near the ceiling, and in one startling and violent scene in the kitchen, the wide-angle camera peers *up* at them through a transparent floor.

(Because the camera is some distance below the floor, the characters seem to be floating eerily in midair, like astronauts frozen in free-fall.) More often, the camera frames the actors at eye level from a certain distance while moving slowly past or around them—glimpsing them from outside the apartment through a succession of windows, or gliding between them so that their relationships to each other and to the frame are in continual flux. Reflections in mirrors and in other kinds of glass are often ingeniously incorporated; a dialogue between János and Miklós is framed in such a way that, thanks to double reflections, they appear to be simultaneously facing and looking away from each other, so that we get the equivalent of both an angle and its reverse angle within the same shot.

Some of the elaborate staging helps alert us to the characters' hidden agendas and duplicitous motives, almost as if the camera were whispering to us about the scene, adding to the overall paranoid and conspiratorial atmosphere. But at other times this mise en scène seems to express a certain detachment toward the characters that borders on contempt or indifference—it pursues a distracted path of its own that has little to do with them. This is especially true in the final sequence, when the camera, moving around a festive banquet to the strains of a Hungarian version of "Que sera, sera," is only intermittently attentive to what the characters are doing.

Here, as in DAMNATION, Tarr's approach ultimately becomes a set of strategies for creating or locating various kinds of movement within stasis, and freedom within confinement. Should his approach be read in political and allegorical terms, as a direct or indirect statement about the rigidity of life under Hungarian communism? Certainly it *can* be read that way—a veritable cottage industry has grown up out of interpreting the elaborate camera movements in Jancsó's films in an analogous fashion. But applying this interpretation to DAMNATION and ALMANAC OF FALL as a literal skeleton key to their meanings seems both facile and needlessly simplistic. It's part of these films' beauty and fascination that they don't have to be read this way in order for them to breathe, function, and speak to us. (All American films are about America—and a strict ideological reading might say that they're all about capitalism, too—but it's surely reductive to limit the range of their meanings to this notion.) With or without the Hungarian context, ALMANAC OF FALL is a riveting experience.

—*Chicago Reader*, 25 May 1990

They Drive by Night

The Criticism of Manny Farber

"What is the role of evaluation in your critical work?" Manny Farber was once asked in an interview. "It's practically worthless for a critic," Farber replied. "The last thing I want to know is whether you like it or not; the problems of writing are *after* that. I don't think it has any importance; it's one of those derelict appendages of criticism. Criticism has nothing to do with hierarchies." A few years later, in another interview—published only in French, so I can't quote from it verbatim—he expressed his irritation with Pauline Kael writing about RAGING BULL as if she knew what was good or bad in every shot, in every scene. He wondered what would happen if the same critical method were applied to Cézanne, or to Mozart.

In fact, some of the most authentic moments in Farber's criticism—following his lead, I won't say the best—are those in which you can't be sure whether he's praising or ridiculing the subject before him. Maybe he's doing both:

> The fact that Academy Award Lee Marvin is in the film [POINT BLANK] hardly matters. His blocklike snoutlike nose makes itself felt, also the silvery snake-like hair that doesn't look like hair, and the implacable, large-lipped mouth. Particular parts of his body and face are used like notes in a recurring musical score. His body stays stiff, vertical, very healthy and sun-burned, but he is not actually in the movie.

> [The] "whole movie-making system" [of Howard Hawks] seems a secret preoccupation with linking, a connections business involving people, plots, and eight-inch hat brims.

Zack, who starts THE STEEL HELMET as a helmet with a hole in it, a bit like a turtle until the helmet rises an inch off the stubbled field to show these meager, nasty eyes slowly shifting back and forth, casing the area, is like someone born on Torment Street between Malicious and Crude.

The visual shocks of recognition in these verbal renderings are not exhibits in a trial but items in an inventory, and Farber's most characteristic method is to pile these observations on top of one another, or juxtapose them in a disordered heap on the flat surface of a page, not string them together into linear narratives or arguments. To say that they go nowhere would miss the point; in point of fact they go everywhere, creating a busy and unwieldy sprawl that spills beyond the frame of whatever he happens to be discussing. (Donald Phelps's definitive essay on Farber, included in his collection *Covering Ground,* is called "Critic Going Everywhere.") For all their trailblazing—and Farber is the first American critic who took the trouble to discover what filmmakers like Hawks and Anthony Mann and Fuller and Michael Snow, among others, were actually doing—these perceptions could never serve to coax crowds into theaters (or dissuade them from going inside), which already places him well outside the tradition of American mainstream reviewing. They are equally ineffectual in proving points or settling debates, the aim of most academic writing. All they can really do is contribute to the swarm of ideas that buzz around movies, inside our heads.

His career as a critic spans thirty-five years—not nearly as long as his career as a painter, which already covers well over half a century and is still going strong, but slightly longer than his career as a carpenter (roughly 1938–1968). Born 20 February 1917 in a middle-class Jewish family in Douglas, Arizona, he started publishing a little before his twenty-fifth birthday when he was hired as *The New Republic*'s art critic in early 1942; within six weeks, he was writing their movie column as well, replacing Otis Ferguson after the latter was torpedoed on a tanker overseas. The art criticism, which continued sporadically until 1961, comprises forty-odd pieces; the movie criticism, much more voluminous, lasted at *The New Republic* for about five years, ending when Henry Wallace became editor-in-chief and Farber, already a conservative, quit in protest. He surfaced next in *The Nation,* where he continued for another five years, and in *Time,* where he only lasted six months, replacing his friend James Agee in both slots when the latter left for Hollywood. Subsequent extended (albeit much less regular) stints included *The New Leader* (1958–1959), *Cavalier* (1965–1967), *Artforum* (1967–1972), and Francis Coppola's short-lived *City Magazine* (1975), with key position papers published in between in *City Lights* ("Preston Sturges: Success in Movies," with W. S. Poster, 1955), *Commentary* ("Underground Films: A Bit of Male Truth," 1957), *Perspectives* ("Hard Sell Cinema," 1957), and *Film Culture* ("White Elephant Art vs. Termite Art," 1962). In 1968, the aforementioned

Donald Phelps published a 101-page collection of Farber's art and film criticism in his journal *For Now.* Two years later, Praeger published a larger collection of his film criticism, *Negative Space,* reprinted in paperback in 1974 as *Movies.* Starting around 1968, his criticism was written in collaboration with Patricia Patterson, another painter, whom he married in 1976, and between 1975 and 1977 a final burst of Farber–Patterson collaborations, including an extended interview with Richard Thompson, appeared in *Film Comment.* Then silence.

∎

Of all the forms of cultural shock that I've experienced, I think the most pronounced was my move from London to San Diego in early March 1977. More wrenching than my move from Alabama to Vermont in 1959—which caused my southern accent to evaporate within weeks after it became clear that I couldn't otherwise speak without inviting ridicule; more disorienting than my relocations from New York to Paris in 1969, Paris to London in 1974, New York to Hoboken in 1979. Part of the shock was returning to America after almost eight years abroad; another part was leaving a socialist society for the most right-wing community I've ever known. I found myself in La Jolla—the town where, as Raymond Chandler once put it, old people live with their parents. The smell of eucalyptus was overpowering, and the overall feel of the place was Arcadia West. American flags waved up and down the main street, and, after breakfast the morning after I arrived in a coffee shop decorated with Norman Rockwell paintings, a sweet-looking lady took my bill at the cash register and said, "Hold on, honey, while I ring this up on my Jewish organ."

Still, there was a good reason to be there. Back in London, working securely as a civil servant in a potentially permanent job, I began to worry that as a writer I was losing contact with American speech; I was growing homesick, looking for a way to negotiate my way back to the states and some version of my roots. After sending off a slew of inquiries to teachers in various film departments, one of them struck a geyser: Manny Farber, my favorite American film critic, whom I had never met face to face, sent back a wisecracking letter in vintage Farber prose that said he'd never imagined he could lure me away from London, but he needed a teaching replacement for the spring and fall quarters in the Department of Visual Arts at the University of California, San Diego. He described the local mesas and weather, alluded to some old Hollywood actors whose houses he jogged past in Del Mar, and said, in response to my remark about not having a driver's license, that I'd need to have a car. I phoned him and asked, "Is this Manny Farber?" "No, it's Abraham Lincoln," he barked back. A little later he intimated that there was "an outside chance" I could extend the job beyond two quarters, and I decided to take the gamble and make the leap. When I arrived a few months later, a little bit ahead of my forty-two cartons, four suitcases, filing cabinet, and tape recorder, it was a week after I had turned thirty-four, and two weeks after Manny had turned sixty.

When we met on campus, Manny—who bore a certain resemblance to Punch in Punch and Judy—hadn't realized until then that we'd never met before. Back in 1969, when we were both still living in New York, I'd written him asking to reprint two of his articles, on Preston Sturges and Godard, in an anthology I was editing, for $50 each. After receiving no reply I phoned him and got my first taste of his crusty wrath: "Fifty bucks? Do you know how many years Willy Poster and I worked on that Sturges piece?" Weeks later, just before I was due to move to Paris, I wrote him a sincere fan letter saying that I'd just read the Sturges article for the umpteenth time and couldn't imagine publishing the book without it—that my budget for fees was paltry but I'd double my offer to $100 for the Sturges. A few days later he phoned, quite friendly, accepting the offer. And that had been our only contact until I wrote him seven years later from London.

■

> The American painter approaches independent art—composition without subject interest—with the firmly efficient spirit of people who believe in "getting down to brass tacks." From Feininger's frosted use of kinetic design to Pollock's glum idolatry of automatic writing, strict obedience to the principle underlying an art style makes the work appear cold and persistent. The artist not only pushes one principle to the exclusion of all else, but the quick, largely decorative solving of each canvas unmasks the expedience and intensity of young Americans out to "succeed." Once his technique is mastered, he becomes an assembly belt turning out the same machine in varying colors, sizes, and shapes. Art schools now find students masterfully covering stretched mattress ticking with aluminum house paint—no model, no subject, no composition, and soon—"Look, Ma! No hands!"
>
> —*Farber in* The Nation, *17 February 1951*

It's sheer nonsense, of course, for Farber or anyone else to claim that he isn't an evaluative critic. Go back to those quotations about POINT BLANK, Hawks, Zack in THE STEEL HELMET, all of which are clearly appreciations—even if they're couched in the form of gruff witticisms, loving jabs. And if "criticism has nothing to do with hierarchies," what are the four key position papers cited above but passionate arguments on behalf of Sturges, "underground films," and termite art, polemics against "hard sell cinema" and white elephant art?

What makes Farber the most important American film critic, despite the fact that he has always been a minority taste, a critic for other critics? Among his major predecessors, I can think of only two: the underrated Harry Alan Potamkin, a Marxist intellectual and globetrotter of the 1920s and 1930s, and the overrated Otis Ferguson, a punchy slangmeister of the 1930s and 1940s. Among Farber's contemporaries were at least three friends and comrades-in-arms: Poster, Agee, and Warshow. Among his many disciples are Greg Ford, J. Hoberman, Donald Phelps, myself, Ronnie Scheib, and Duncan Shepard. (The latter followed Farber all the way out to San Diego from New York, where he reviews movies for the *San Diego Reader*.) And among those who came along a decade or so later than Farber are the two who wound up paving the main thoroughfares for others to follow in the 1960s and 1970s, Sarris and Kael.

Kael offered a role model—above all, in the intensity and clarity of her prose—but principally to those interested in "scoring." As valuable as she could be in some cases as a debunker, one rarely saw her expanding the options of the intellectual status quo; her role, on the contrary, was to make some intellectuals feel less guilty for shunning the challenges of difficult films. Farber was virtually discovering Michael Snow and welcoming the difficulties of Straub/Huillet, Rivette, Duras, and Akerman while Kael's kindergarten was happily and dutifully restricting itself to the intricacies of people like Peckinpah and De Palma.

Sarris started out as a significant role model himself—defending movies like 7 WOMEN, THE BIRDS, MURIEL, and GERTRUD against the philistines—but his decreasing passion for and even interest in such debates after the 1960s gradually made this option seem less and less viable. Like Farber, he had a journalistic weakness for puns and developed an evangelical mission to revise the canon, but unlike Kael or Farber, his root instincts weren't those of a spoiler. The main concerns of his reviews when he was most effective were usually mise en scène and relationships between men and women—a respectable agenda, but not one that often entailed any radical rethinking of what art was.

Farber's own major interests—iconography, acting, and realistic detail—weren't especially radical either, at least in themselves. What made him different, a trailblazer, was his writing, which resembled much of his painting by generating a text that, as Bill Krohn has put it, "can be entered at any point, without hierarchy, center, or horizon-line," entailing a "refusal to systematize" which often makes it "impossible to tell from the beginning of an essay on a film or a filmmaker where it is going to end up: There is no thesis, no antithesis, no possibility of synthesis, in part because the need to 'get it all in' works against the more traditional critical ambition to 'say everything' about a work by constructing a microcosmic model that includes, by definition, everything that *can* be said."

These comments come from Krohn's essay, unfortunately unpublished in English, about Farber's painting "My Budd"—a work deriving in part from

Farber's ruminations about Budd Boetticher. Later on, Krohn adds, "Among the notes I am struggling to integrate in this article is the uneasy question: 'Why does the big rock in the lower right quadrant look like a pickle?' It's doubtful that any kind of critical study can answer that kind of question, but Farber's essays make abundant use of these enigmatic details, which function as foreign bodies, parodies of critical remarks, banana peels for the argument." A soft-shoe dance with comic twists and bends, Farber's critical discourse abounds in pickles and pratfalls while invariably shooting for the moon—which suggests that his method is dialectical even if the content of his prose confounds the very notion of dialectics. If academic analysis is largely devoted to the dissolution and demystification of the mystery of art, Farber's serious jive is passionately dedicated to its survival and perpetuation. Beneath the braggadocio, many of the questions are those of a spiteful child about things like pickles.

■

When I arrived in La Jolla in early March, Manny was finishing winter quarter, and I attended his final lectures, given to about a hundred students. He gave a standup routine, performed without notes and delivered in extended snatches, like lengthy jazz solos, between successive reels of whatever movie he was showing. (The first was Ichikawa's AN ACTOR'S REVENGE. A few weeks earlier, he had shown Snow's RAMEAU'S NEPHEW . . . , and when a student complained about its intractability, Manny agreed: "It's like trying to find a friend in a stadium.") Discontinuous viewing was his preferred way of watching a movie, a method he shared with Godard; if a movie he really liked such as ORDET was being shown several times in the campus screening room over a given week, he'd turn up each time for a different reel or two—or maybe even for the same reels, whatever happened to be on.

This was around the same time that Manny gave me a portable typewriter he no longer used, a gift that automatically assumed symbolic and mythic reverberations for me. But it was hard to figure out how I could replace him as a lecturer, especially when my only previous teaching experience was freshman English for a handful of students on Long Island a decade before. It was even harder to decide what to do with a father figure, at a point in my life when I thought I had finally learned how to do without one. Having already spent over half my life away from Alabama, I regarded my own father as a benign presence in my life, but no longer a guide, advisor, or example in practical terms—at least not in the sense that he was those things for his own college students. Manny, however, seemed to radiate the most potent patriarchal presence of anyone within a fifty-mile radius, and it was difficult to resist being seduced by it—even though I was too formed by then to succumb to it entirely either, which made me both dependent and uneasy about my dependence. A year or so later, a mutual friend remarked to me that Manny had a bad habit of adopting people and then abandoning them, which was certainly true. During much of the time I lived in San Diego, he seemed to oscillate regularly and without warning between father, friend, and competitive Jewish sibling.

Manny assured me that lecturing would be a snap for me—just like writing, he said—but when he came to visit my second lecture, the only one he ever attended, I was far from hitting any sort of stride, and the students, who were asked to fill out evaluation forms, were far from enthusiastic. I even antagonized some of them with my manner and methods, and by the time the final student evaluations were handed in toward the end of the quarter, it was evident that I had flopped—not only in my lectures for undergraduates, but even (to a lesser extent) in my critical writing seminar for graduate students, where I was resented by some for my lack of smarts about How to Get Ahead in the Art World, which I was belatedly discovering was precisely the reason some of the students were in grad school. Indeed, there were times when this seemed to be what the whole department—largely composed of displaced New York artists—was chiefly concerned with. To put it bluntly, I was discovering for the first time how thoroughly the sixties in America were over. And I couldn't even pass a driving test.

Part of me, to be sure, was much too proud to care, but that only made things worse. Unlike Manny, I couldn't bridge the gap between writing and lecturing as if they were one and the same process, and couldn't or wouldn't find a standup manner for winning over a crowd. In the writing seminar, I was dismayed to find a lot of the students trying to write just like Manny, and proved less effectual than I wanted to be in helping them to find their own voices.

Meanwhile, my attempts to get a driver's license were all pathetic failures. Looking back at my appointment book for 1977, I can see that I probably spent more time taking driving lessons that I did watching movies, and each time I flunked the road test, it was for a different reason; once or twice I even flunked the written test as well. Although I could usually take a bus to campus, I was still helplessly dependent on others when it came to having any sort of social life, and Manny wasn't the only one who was getting fed up with my recalcitrance. (In mid-July—perhaps as a conciliatory gesture for having yelled at me in exasperation on the phone—he drove me all the way into downtown San Diego to take the written test. Then he got so fidgety waiting around for me that he asked me to take the bus back.)

Then there was the problem of Jean-Pierre Gorin, the former Godard collaborator who was one of Manny's closest buddies and until recently had been the other UCSD lecturer in film aesthetics. On a few days' notice, J-P had quit in the middle of winter quarter to fly to the Philippines to work on APOCALYPSE NOW—a job that proved to be less consequential than he had hoped—and then had come back to Del Mar. Not long after I had been phased out of the program, he had been phased back in, and we regarded each other more than a little warily. I resented what I regarded as the hard-sell, closet-intellectual demagoguery of his lecturing style and his concomitant reputation as a campus ladykiller, and he obviously felt threatened by my relationship with Manny; the air was thick with bad vibes and petty sibling rivalries.

Patricia, however, who was only a couple of years older than me, was fast becoming my best friend in San Diego—like the sister I always longed for and never had. I was beginning to suspect that part of what I responded to most in her and Manny's recent collaborations came from her influence, such as the gradual transition from praise to abuse in their extraordinary TAXI DRIVER essay ("The Power & the Gory," *Film Comment,* May–June 1976), culminating in a shock cut from skeptical analysis to a bolt of anger in the beginning of the second part: "What's really disgusting about TAXI DRIVER is not the multi-faced loner but the endless propaganda about the magic of guns." It's conceivable, of course, that Manny came up with that sentence—the sudden switch in tone certainly matches his method—but I don't recall any sort of anger about phallic gun worship in his earlier solo pieces; and given all the *noirs* he was celebrating, there were plenty of opportunities. It seemed, in any case, that a certain ideological sophistication and a stronger sense of social criticism had entered Manny's work around the same time that his collaborations with Patricia started, giving these pieces a certain moral density that were quite distinct from the macho celebrations of his earlier work. (If I had to define a basic psychosexual difference between Manny's movie predilections and mine, he, along with Kael, sees the medium as basically masculine, whereas I go looking in it for the feminine.)

We never got into political arguments, but our differences were making themselves felt. At one of our first meetings, Manny assigned me the job of inviting filmmakers to campus that spring, and when he suggested I include John Milius, I loftily replied that I wasn't willing to be associated with an outright fascist. If memory serves, he dropped the matter there, but in his interview with Richard Thompson, which was being conducted around the same time—actually started before I arrived in San Diego and completed a few weeks afterward—he includes a pointed commentary on a scene from Milius's THE WIND AND THE LION that I've always taken to be a reply of sorts to my London-bred intolerance. (Elsewhere in the same interview is an irritated response to Stephen Heath's *Screen* article, "Narrative Space," which I had just gotten Manny to read.)

Discussing THE DEER HUNTER with him a couple of years later, which I loathed and he rather liked—especially, as I recall, for the taboo-breaking singing of "God Bless America" by the major characters in the final scene—I asked how he felt about the dehumanized depiction of Vietcong soldiers as vicious insects. He conceded that maybe it was questionable to show the

Vietcong as being nothing like us, but no more so than the liberal approach, which would be to show them as being exactly like us. (On the whole, his social observations were nearly always iconographic; commenting on the differences between 1930s and 1970s movies, he once praised the treatment of people in the former by saying, "In the 30s, every shape was legitimate.")

Given my own impulses toward collective endeavors, largely inspired by my years abroad, I had hoped that some sort of collaborative writing project could be embarked on by Manny, Patricia, and myself; or, barring that, that we could at least critique one another's pieces while we were still working on them. But something in Manny—perhaps in Patricia as well—firmly resisted any proposals along these lines, even when we were working simultaneously on separate pieces for *Film Comment*. Their essay, to date the last critical piece published by either or both of them, was on JEANNE DIELMAN, which I felt obliquely tied to because of my own earlier writing about that film in "Edinburgh Encounters," one of my pieces that had most impressed them. My own essay, on Luc Moullet, is possibly the single piece of mine most influenced by Manny, even though Manny hadn't liked Moullet's LES CONTRE-BANDIÈRES one bit when I had screened it for him. Ironically, I recall that all three of us felt annoyed at being segregated and marginalized together in a section toward the back of *Film Comment* (November–December 1977) entitled "Beyond the New Wave."

One key difference (among others) between our respective pieces was our different positions about stars: JEANNE DIELMAN has a luminous star performance, by Delphine Seyrig, whereas the aesthetics of LES CONTREBANDIÈRES are virtually defined by its absence of stars and all that goes with them. Several years later, when Manny got a shelty puppy, he named it Jimmy, after Cagney. Indeed, I suspect that even his admiration for Straub/Huillet has something to do with their star presences.

■

A few other stars in the Farber canon: the heroes of Werner Herzog, the loft in WAVELENGTH, "Lee Marvin's Planter's Peanut Head," working-class domestic interiors, Barbara Stanwyck, Wellman, Godard, Fassbinder, "Stan and Ollie" (the title of a 1981 painting), "Rohmer's Knee" (ditto, 1982), Agee, Bresson's Mouchette, Peckinpah, John Wayne in THE MAN WHO SHOT LIBERTY VALANCE, William Demarest, James Stewart in Anthony Mann westerns, Wile E. Coyote, Jane Greer, Mexico. Over half of these are associated with violence and sadism.

■

By this time I had moved into a beautiful house overlooking a canyon in Del Mar, a mile or so from Manny and Patricia's house, which I was sharing with Louis Hock, a fellow teacher and filmmaker, and I was getting around by driving illegally, still without a license—a necessary recourse in order to get to my classes. As my teaching stint was drawing to a close, I had the unprecedented good fortune of learning that I would be receiving a $5,000 NEA grant, which would free me for a spell from having to worry about the rent, and receiving this news produced the first spark of an autobiographical book that quickly grew into *Moving Places*. I started working on this project as soon as fall quarter ended, and early in the next year, Louis and I were joined in our roomy house by Ray Durgnat, who had been hired at UCSD as my replacement—someone I had already admired, written about, and subsequently met and befriended in Europe a few years before, an exploratory critic whose methods suggest certain links with Manny's. As I recall mentioning to Brooks Riley, *Film Comment*'s assistant editor, we had all the makings of a full-fledged termite colony.

It was thanks to Ray that I finally passed a driving test in February 1978; shortly after passing his own first test, he drove me to the Department of Motor Vehicles in Oceanside, gave me a gentle pep talk, and even supplied me with a Valium. (A few hours later, after it grew dark, I talked him into going to see CITIZEN'S BAND, which we both liked, in a movie theater up the coast that had once been a church and still had pews to sit in.) Not long afterward, Ray and I and David Ehrenstein began collaborating on "Obscure Objects of Desire"—a discussion of nonnarrative for *Film Comment* that Manny and Patricia had helped to inspire, although we couldn't persuade them to participate in it.

Then, by the following spring, when I was far enough along in *Moving Places* to want to show a few portions of it to friends for comments, I sounded out Manny and got turned down. Patricia agreed, but eventually could make good on her promise only by coming over to my house on two successive afternoons and reading the pages in my presence. (When I had previously lent them to her, Manny had returned them to me with terse apologies about both of them being too busy.)

By then, however, my relations with Manny had grown much shakier. Ray had had to return to England in the middle of his second quarter, and I had been hired temporarily to take over his classes for a couple of weeks. Then, when the department chairman had asked me to continue teaching these courses for the remainder of the quarter, something in me finally rebelled against the feelings of rejection I had previously experienced, and I sent back a refusal, defiantly adding that I had too much contempt for the department. (I was thinking of many things at that point—including the fact that the faculty, at quarter's end, had even forgotten to rule on my former job application, obliging me to insist on their calling an additional meeting in order to make their ejection of me from the program official.) This response coincided with the opening of a major retrospective of Manny's paintings at the La Jolla Museum of Contemporary Art, which proved to be a highly tense affair for me in other respects. (A woman who lived far away, and had recently written me that she thought she loved me, turned up for the event without prior warning and proceeded to ignore me for most of the evening.) Manny was livid about my remark to the department, but I mainly learned about this from other people. Four days later I called a peace conference—the two of us met in neutral territory, at a Denny's—and did my best to bring about a reconciliation, with ambiguous results. About six weeks later—spurred by the generous offer of one of his former students, Carrie Rickey, to let me share her studio in SoHo as a flatmate—I moved to New York.

■

Autobiography plays a very ambiguous and uncertain role in Farber's work. Apart from some jokey asides—like a passing reference to the appearance of his nephew Jerry Farber in Orson Welles's MACBETH in his list of the top movies of 1950 for *The Nation* (13 January 1951)—personal references are scrupulously excluded from his criticism. Nonetheless, a good many of his paintings of the late 1970s and early 1980s are clearly autobiographical, such as "Birthplace: Douglas, Ariz." (1979), "Nix" (a vast and complex meditation on Sturges's comedies in relation to the minutiae of Farber's own life circa 1983), "For Fontaine Fox" (an homage to *Toonerville Trolley,* a comic strip from his childhood, 1983), and "Tuy was great" (about a visit to Spain in 1984). And in a copiously detailed, year by year "Biography" appended to at least two catalogues devoted to his art work, he is often personal to the point of being confessional. Here, for example, are four complete entries from the catalogue published by the Los Angeles Museum of Contemporary Art to accompany a massive Farber retrospective held between 12 November 1985 and 9 February 1986:

1932 Parents move to Vallejo, California to be closer to favorite son, Leslie, a pre-med student. Plays alto sax and some clarinet in another jazz orchestra, Kenny Clark's, and has brief celebrity as a halfback on football foundry high school team. Parents' dress store does robust business with prostitutes, a major profession in a thriving Navy city.

1949 Writes on art, jazz, furniture, and films for *The Nation* under books editor, Margaret Marshall, after stint clipping in the magazine's library. Takes over as *Time* film critic when Agee goes to Hollywood to write for John Huston. Lasts six months and is fired after a series of mediocre reviews. These include reviews of WHITE HEAT, THEY LIVE BY NIGHT, and Rossellini's GERMANY, YEAR ZERO.

1972 Starts incorporating snap lines and stepped-on lines made with paint soaked string within the interior of paint abstractions. Allied to small slabs of colored paper, the increased use of colored chalk, the aim is an increased density. Solo show: O. K. Harris, New York City; San Diego State University. First trip to Europe, spends two weeks at Venice Film Festival. Sees films by

Fassbinder and other young European directors, builds a "Radical Film" course around these experiences at UCSD. Two lectures at [Pacific] Film Archives on Straub and Fassbinder; a seminar at New York University, monitored by Annette Michelson, concerning Farber's switch in critical concern from the Hollywood action film to the experimentalists in New York and the radical directors outside the U.S.A. Meets filmmaker Jean-Pierre Gorin, who later joins UCSD faculty, becoming a sort of twin brain with Farber.

1982 Long interview with *Cahiers du Cinéma* editors and Jean-Pierre Gorin appears in April *Cahiers* with "A Dandy's Gesture" on magazine's cover. Accidentally torches Patricia's studio making coffee on cheap hot plate. Altercation with campus cop leads to incarceration in campus police station during fire; long court battle brings conviction for resisting arrest and forty hours teaching remedial writing to prefreshman students. Exhibits at Richard Bellamy's Oil and Steel and Diane Brown in Washington D.C. run concurrently.

In a footnote to an essay of mine about Farber's "movie paintings"—written in 1983 and published two years later, in *New Observations* #36—I noted that

> the relationship between autobiography and film criticism is both intricate and unavoidable, yet the rules of social etiquette governing this delicate connection—which require a suppression of autobiography in most marketplace criticism practiced by writers less well known than Pauline Kael or Gore Vidal—keep it in relative obscurity. Considering Farber's own precise sense of his position in relation to both film criticism and painting, it seems understandable that only the relative obscurity and hermeticism of his paintings would permit a comfortable adoption of the autobiographical mode; the relative exposure of his [film] writing, combined with its rhetorical strategies, make this tactic seem less tenable in print.

Considering the dialectic between exposure and concealment running through his work, it hardly seems surprising that he refused to appear in Gorin's second solo feature, ROUTINE PLEASURES, a film he very much likes, even though a good half of the film is directly about him.

With rare exceptions, Farber also avoids mentioning other film critics. (When he sarcastically quotes Robin Wood on ONLY ANGELS HAVE WINGS toward the end of his 1969 Hawks piece, the citation remains anonymous.) His only piece on another film critic that I'm aware of, a 1958 review of Agee's collected criticism, is one of the more balanced assessments of that critic that we have, but it also faults his late friend for using "other critics' enthusiasms" in the course of calling him "a master of critics' patter, the numbers racket, and the false bracket."

Perhaps the most sustained case against Farber as an "impressionistic" critic—the dirtiest of all academic adjectives in a post-*Screen* context—is made in Robin Wood's *Personal Views,* where a page and a half is devoted to the multiple errors about visual details in passages by Farber about TOUCH OF EVIL and WEEKEND in his introduction to *Negative Space,* followed by these remarks:

> The whole chapter, with its extraordinary associational processes, comes very close at times to stream-of-consciousness, and is worth looking up as an example of what you can get away with, with a bit of swagger. Such "impressionism" says as much about Farber's assumptions about his readers as it does about his own perceptions and his way of experiencing films. It is assumed that they will not know the films very well either, but will not feel this as much of a handicap in attending to discussions of them so vague as to be unchallengeable.

The last word seems to me a key one. If Farber's radical distance from what is commonly regarded as academic film study could be encapsulated in a single idea, this would be the notion that nothing he has to offer as a critic can be either verified or challenged. The same thing is true, of course, of Keats's "On First Looking Into Chapman's Homer," not to mention most of Agee's criticism (Warshow's is another matter), and if Agee's status among methodologically trained academics is almost as low as Farber's, this may ultimately say as much about the limitations of academically approved methodologies, theories, and principles of accuracy as it does about the limitations of Agee and Farber. The strengths of both writers are above all literary; it is merely a casualty of absentminded pigeonholing that classifies Agee as "literature" and Farber as something else. Indeed, it could be argued that Farber's prose at its best is even more vigorously—and rigorously—constructed than Agee's and in most cases is equally suited to perform the work of evocation, suggestion, analysis, and mimesis that it sets out to do.

By situating the movie on neither a screen nor a blackboard but inside a critic's overactive head, Farber obliges it to mingle with its immediate neighbors as well as some of its distant cousins, and what emerges from this mingling often has more to do with the world and its complexity—above all, *as we experience it*—than any close analysis of whether an actress was sucking her thumb or smoking a cigarette in a particular shot (one of Wood's examples). Faced with such an image, Faulkner might have theoretically gotten the detail wrong as well. But what he would have had to say about the image he wound up with might well have mattered more than whether it was accurate or not.

To write criticism that places itself beyond verification or challenge is to define criticism as an art, not a science, and to define that art *in terms of art* rather than scientifically. Exercised on its own terms, without reference to business or scholarship, such a practice defies the use of pull-quotes and advertising blurbs as much as term papers and dissertations; it usually becomes impossible, in fact, to appropriate or adapt it for any purposes other than its own. Refusing to reach for final conclusions about anything—the ultimate

aim of marketplace and university criticism alike—it can only revel and luxu-
riate in its own activity, hoping at best merely to keep up with rather than
master the art that it engages.

■

I'm trying to remember precisely and correctly the important things that
happened, but I can't be sure I'm always succeeding; memories play their
own tricks with these emotional residues, adding their own emphases and
sometimes subtracting anything that doesn't fit. Whatever happened, I know
that I never entirely got over a feeling of being rejected by Manny on some
level. Some of it came back again when he failed to offer any response to
Moving Places after it was published in 1980, eventually provoking a hurt,
angry note from me that I no longer remember clearly—except that I sent it
along with a piece on Straub/Huillet's FROM THE CLOUD TO THE RESISTANCE
that I had published in late 1982, which concluded with a tribute to him and
Patricia. This eventually prompted an apologetic call from him—perhaps
with Patricia's encouragement—in which he essentially said that it wasn't
that he didn't like the book, it's just that he liked my criticism more. He also
admitted to feeling that he'd spent so much of his life in flight from things I
was writing about, like Judaism and family, that it was difficult for him to
deal with such material. (I often wondered, in fact, what it had been like to be
born with a name like Emanuel.)

Years later, I felt twinges of the same rejection when he turned down my
offer of a free subscription to the *Chicago Reader*—but this time they were
only twinges. He said that now that he was devoting himself exclusively to
painting, reading about movies was no longer easy for him. Whatever he
meant and whatever the reason was, I accepted it. (It was probably the truth,
anyway; in the lower right white square of his 1991 painting *Seed, Field*,
written with some of the look and authority of a street sign, is the message,
"No film." To the best of my knowledge, the last time Manny worked on a
movie piece was in the late 1970s—on Syberberg's HITLER, A FILM FROM
GERMANY, which excited him quite a bit—but he never finished it. It's possible that his relative distance from the cities that showed many of the movies
he loved most, and a resulting feeling of remoteness from—and lack of mastery over—the "film scene" played a role in his eventual abandonment of
criticism.)

It's always easy to forget how shy he is, like so many tough, stoical types.
During my fall quarter at UCSD, I screened Sturges's CHRISTMAS IN JULY one
night at my house and invited him over. He was so overwhelmed by the experience that he left, speechless, after the first reel. I suggested later to him that
it seemed to me a movie about the Depression, even though it was released in
1940 and had a contemporary setting. Some time after that, while trying to
explain to me some apparent limitation of his own, he referred back to my

comment and said, "You know, I'm not someone who ever survived the Depression. It's not the sort of experience you ever really get over." Only weeks or months later did I discover, from someone else, that he had never seen this Sturges movie before that night—although he subsequently gave lectures about it more than once—and was too embarrassed to admit this to me.

It amazed me when he once told me that he regarded his dismissal from *Time* in 1949 as one of the great failures of his life, particularly because I doubt that he would have made much of a lasting impression on other critics had he remained there. (He seemed to agree with me, however, when I once cited his articles on Sturges, Walsh,* and TAXI DRIVER—none of which could have ever conceivably appeared in *Time*—as his three best pieces. Is it significant that all three are collaborations?) The dream of hitting the ultimate jackpot that is so central to CHRISTMAS IN JULY hovers over the energy of Manny's writing like a perpetual promise; yet in his life, I suspect, it has been closer to functioning like a permanent malediction. Condemned forever to traverse the marginal backwaters of art while hoping to break into the mainstream of entertainment, his achievement must seem like a mockery of his dreams—and vice versa, for that matter. His critical positioning—as important to his writing as his composition is to his painting—always paradoxically aims at a notion of bull's-eye that can exist only in a marketplace context where objects and ideas compete for our attention. He has been living this contradiction, it would seem, for the better part of his life—the contradiction of the realist bent on the construction of formal paradigms, the Horatio Alger who projects his starstruck dreams into the abstract relationship between a Tootsie Roll and a cherished movie. Brilliantly cluttered by the everyday flotsam of American culture—domestic knickknacks otherwise ignored by history and criticism alike—his writing and painting both express a love of the world as it's given that finally, perhaps even tragically, precludes any radical strategies for changing it.

Anyway, it's easy enough to forgive him now, because whatever else he did or didn't do, he invited me along with him on a two-day trip to Los Angeles in December 1977, only five days after I officially taught my last class in his department. I suppose it was his way of making up for not rehiring me, and it was a good way, a gentle way. I went along with him in his car to a slide lecture he gave about paintings at an art school. Shortly before his lecture was due to start, he suffered a sudden bout of stage fright that he confessed to me in the parking lot; he was mortified to discover that his socks didn't match, and I did my best to convince him that no one would notice—as no one did. After the lecture, we went to see THE AMERICAN FRIEND at the Los Feliz and spent the night in a beautiful house on a hill belonging to a

*"Raoul Walsh: 'He used to be a big shot,'" *Artforum* (November 1971), and *Sight and Sound* (Winter 1974/1975).

friend of his, a sculptor and his lawyer wife. The next day, I went around with him on numerous errands and visits to various friends and galleries; then, after we ate dinner with a mutual friend and went with her to see CLOSE EN-COUNTERS OF THE THIRD KIND at the Cinerama Dome, he drove with me back to Del Mar, and we talked the whole way. It was a warm and peaceful two days, and the two-hour drive back was especially pleasant, the best time I can remember spending with him.

The whole experience was like a throwback to Checking Up—a nightly ritual of my father in the 1940s and 1950s, practiced five nights a week, when he drove across the river from Florence to the movie theaters in Sheffield and Tuscumbia, collecting the final receipts of ticket sales from the cashiers after the last shows started, then driving back across the river to Florence again. It was a special privilege for me or my brothers to come along on this hour-long ride and talk, letting the night roll by.

I won't even tell you what Manny had to say to me about THE AMERICAN FRIEND and CLOSE ENCOUNTERS OF THE THIRD KIND on the way back to Del Mar; that's our secret.

—previously unpublished; written in 1993 for this volume

Part Two

Touchstones

Introduction

It seems to me that one of the most underrated elements in criticism is quite simply information—relevant facts deriving from research—and how this is imparted to the reader in relation to other elements. Thanks to the prestige of theory in academia and the equally valued role played by rhetoric in journalistic criticism, facts often seem to be held in relatively low esteem in critical writing nowadays, but as long as criticism aspires to be a vehicle for discovery, it seems to me that research should play a much larger role than it normally does. I bring this matter up because the value of the information imparted in all the pieces in this section seems to me inextricably tied to what I have to say about these films, and my analyses would be appreciably different without it—a factor that is probably most obvious when it comes to GERTRUD and OTHELLO.*

Sometimes information is simply a matter of observation. One of the critical commonplaces about THE SAGA OF ANATAHAN is that everything in the

---

*The review of the latter film—like the separate Welles essay in the next section—represents one of the many "spinoffs" of the long-term research that went into editing *This Is Orson Welles* by Welles and Peter Bogdanovich (HarperCollins, 1992). A few remarks about the "restored" OTHELLO have been revised and updated to incorporate facts gleaned from other sources after the piece was originally written. Two afterthoughts that I haven't been able to incorporate are my neglect of the role played by Alberto Barberis in composing the original OTHELLO score—about which I still have no information, apart from his screen credit—and the lamentable release version of Welles's unfinished DON QUIXOTE prepared by Jesus Franco, which I have since seen in both its Spanish and English versions. Regrettably, this is a hodgepodge that seems even more questionable than the "restored" OTHELLO, in sound as well as image—at least on the basis of the portions of the original edited footage that I saw in New York in 1988—but in the absence of information concerning how or why Franco made most of his choices, further analysis at this stage would be premature.

film with the exception of the ocean waves is artificial and created, and Sternberg has often been uncritically quoted as saying that the only thing he regretted in the film were these waves, precisely because they were not of his making. But to accept this statement is to ignore one of the key sequences in the film—the newsreel segment of Japanese soldiers returning home after the war—and to misconstrue the meaning of the artifice in the remainder of the film as a consequence.

The individual films discussed in this section don't constitute a definitive list of favorites. For the record, I cherish Dreyer's ORDET every bit as much as GERTRUD, and in many ways find the utopian poetry of Hawks's THE BIG SKY as stirring as the galvanic star power of GENTLEMEN PREFER BLONDES. For all its conceptual and emotional purity, I'm not at all sure that ANATAHAN deserves to be called Sternberg's best film. (Polemically speaking, some of my arguments on its behalf grew out of disagreements about it that I had with Manny Farber, Patricia Patterson, and Jean-Pierre Gorin in San Diego, where I was writing the piece; Manny, in particular, often cited THE DOCKS OF NEW YORK as the only Sternberg film he liked, and I can certainly see many qualities in it that are utterly foreign to the strengths of ANATAHAN.) Many other favorite films—AU HASARD BALTHAZAR; TIH MINH; L'ANNÉE DERNIÈRE À MARIENBAD; PLAYTIME; OUT 1; CHIMES AT MIDNIGHT; BREATHLESS; SUNRISE; HALLELUJAH I'M A BUM; THE GREAT CONSOLER; TOO EARLY, TOO LATE; STALKER; THE TIGER OF ESCHNAPUR and THE INDIAN TOMB; CITY LIGHTS and MONSIEUR VERDOUX; LA NUIT DU CARREFOUR and THE RULES OF THE GAME; TALE OF THE LATE CHRYSANTHEMUMS and SANSHO THE BAILIFF; LA RÉGION CENTRALE and YEELEN; among others—aren't examined in this section at all.

■

The review from *Monthly Film Bulletin* that begins this section—written when I was working as assistant editor under Richard Combs—is not exactly representative of the 135 reviews and features I wound up writing for the magazine, many of which were short reviews of softcore sex films and other forgettable items that Richard and I couldn't persuade any freelancers to cover. The job of the *Bulletin* was to run complete credits, detailed synopses, and reviews of every feature film released in England, along with a selection of the shorts—an agenda that has made it an indispensable reference source for many film scholars all over the world, because no other publication that has lasted as long has attempted anything comparable.

When I started work on the *Bulletin*, on issue number 488, it was in its forty-first year, and the entire staff of the magazine consisted of Richard and myself, working in an overcrowded office on 81 Dean Street down the hall from the equally tiny offices of Penelope Houston, which she shared with her secretary Sylvia Loeb, and David Wilson, her assistant editor on *Sight and Sound*. By the time I left almost two and a half years later, we had acquired a secretary (Sue Scott-Montcrieff) and had moved to a much larger office next door, which made things somewhat easier. But a substantial part of the work still consisted of researching and typing up credits, mainly of uninteresting films, a process that usually involved everything from looking up film titles on index cards at the BFI's invaluable Information Department to lugging the first or last reels of various films to the BFI from nearby distributors on Dean or Wardour streets in order to go over them on movieolas. (Sometimes we even had to persuade projectionists after screenings to let us try to decipher the credits from individual film frames without such equipment.) And because we also had to list the lengths of films in numbers of feet before *and* after censor cuts—usually relying on the figures we got from the censor board and from certain distributors, but otherwise measuring the prints ourselves when this information was unavailable—a large amount of our work consisted of physically handling many of the films we were cataloguing.

Perhaps the most significant change that took place in the magazine during that period, a change in which I played some part, was substituting informational features on the back page for a monthly chart that polled the leading newspaper reviewers on the current releases in the fashion of *Cahiers du Cinéma*'s "Conseil des dix" during the 1950s and 1960s—that is, with rankings of one to four stars, or "bullets" (in the shape of black dots) to represent antipathy. I can recall that Alexander Walker of the *Daily Telegraph*, one of these reviewers, was dead set against this change because he was convinced that the *Bulletin* was a hotbed of leftist biases—something he complained about on a regular basis—and believed the chart was one of the only features in the magazine that reflected a wider range of political sentiments. Indeed, one of the issues that always seemed to swirl around the *Bulletin* as a state-supported journal was the question of information versus opinion. Some readers felt we should stick to credits and synopses and omit the reviews, to which I usually replied that neither credits nor synopses were as "objective" as most people pretended, and that information was always highly selective as well as subjective. (It's a truism that official screen credits, especially in studio productions, can't always be trusted as the ultimate source of who did what on a film—key screenwriters often go unmentioned, to cite only one example—and it's equally evident that any synopsis subjectively privileges certain kinds of narrative information over other kinds.) With this in mind, the first back-page informational supplement, which I prepared myself, was a bibliography of interviews, scripts, and texts by Jean-Marie Straub and Danièle Huillet for the March 1976 issue, designed as a supplement to reviews of many of their films in the same issue. (Later, I did similar bibliographies for Jacques Rivette and Eric Rohmer.) If memory serves, the new feature didn't lead to any cancellations of subscriptions—unlike my decision to feature a still from Michael Snow's WAVELENGTH on the cover of the February 1975 issue, when I was briefly serving as deputy editor and decided to illustrate my own (belated) review of the film. And the informational supplements were later expanded and supplemented by critical articles some time after I returned to the states.

Ever since Penelope left *Sight and Sound* in late 1990, and the *Bulletin* became absorbed within the retooled *Sight and Sound* as a midsection in July 1991, still with Richard as editor (until his departure in late 1992), its continuing survival as an institution has become more precarious, especially now that *Sight and Sound* no longer has a guaranteed subscription list tied to membership in the BFI. (To commemorate the *Bulletin*'s last issue, its 687th, in April 1991, Richard selected an appropriately apocalyptic cover—a cataclysmic shootout that he ironically labeled "Redemption and resolution in THE GODFATHER PART III.")

During my own tenure at the BFI, as well as before and afterward, the two magazines had very separate identities. Sometimes justly and sometimes unjustly, *Sight and Sound* was regarded in Britain as the voice of the literary establishment—so much so that most other British film journals from *Movie* to *Screen* largely defined themselves in opposition to its values of good writing, gentility, individual critical voices, and Penelope's international tastes—a mixture of scrupulous editing and eclecticism that, all things considered, could be reasonably compared in certain respects to *The New Yorker* under the editorship of William Shawn. Whatever its limitations, I consider it the best film magazine in English I've ever written for, even if many of the pieces I wrote for Penelope largely reflected the influence of other magazines—including *Cahiers du Cinéma*, *Screen*, *Movie*, and *Film Comment*.

But the mythic and symbolic associations of the magazine within British film culture were so formidable that entire schools of thought within that culture were defined primarily by their opposition to it. Foremost among these schools was the BFI's Education Department, which published *Screen Education* and had significant links to *Screen*, and the uniqueness of my position in the Editorial Department at the time was the fact that I was the only one who fraternized on occasion with members of this other group. A good sense of how divided the two factions were becomes clear if one looks at all the bibliographies in *The Cinema Book*, edited by Pam Cook—the veritable Bible of the Education Department's *idées reçus* during this period—which systematically omit everything ever published in *Sight and Sound* as a matter of course. (My principal point of contention with the Education Department's philosophy was its dependence on film clips as the be-all and end-all of film education; I was often shocked to discover how many film teachers "taught" GENTLEMEN PREFER BLONDES, for instance, without having ever seen the entire movie.)

The *Bulletin*, by contrast, was never considered part of "the establishment" and was respected by many English critics who shunned *Sight and Sound*. As one token of this difference, I regarded it as something of a coup when I persuaded Ben Brewster, the editor of *Screen* at the time, to review Ozu's EARLY SPRING for the *Bulletin* in 1976. The fact that Ben had taught himself Japanese was enormously helpful in compiling the credits, but his unwillingness to compose a *Bulletin*-style synopsis, choosing instead to give a detailed account of every scene in the film—a refusal I felt some theoretical sympathy for, given my own lack of skill in this form of *Bulletin*ese—sadly prevented this experiment from having any sequels.

■

It seems worth noting that the first item in this section, as well as the last two, were written as a staff reviewer, whereas the pieces on ANATAHAN, GERTRUD, and GENTLEMEN PREFER BLONDES were all written as a freelancer. I bring this up because the latter three pieces came about through specific circumstances that probably wouldn't have existed if I had been a staff writer at the time. I wrote the ANATAHAN piece after booking the film for a course at University of California, San Diego; I was sharing a house at the time with Louis Hock, an experimental filmmaker who owned a 16-millimeter projector that he was able to hook up to my stereo. I wound up recording the sound track on audiocassettes (this was in 1977, before I knew about VCRs), a technique I was to employ even more systematically a little later on with ON MOONLIGHT BAY for my book *Moving Places*, and I'm sure my analysis would have been substantially different without this procedure. (Ed Dimendberg, my editor on this book, rightly points out that my account of the film's visuals is skimpy, to say the least.) What I hadn't realized at the time was that the version I was writing about, booked from Twyman Films, was a recent "restoration" of the film done by Sternberg's widow—a term I place in quotes because the new version involved a few visual and aural additions to the original. Some film scholars, Bernard Eisenschitz in particular, have raised objections to these additions, which consist of a few nude shots of the actress playing Keiko and some modifications in the sound mix. I haven't been able to research this matter independently, but it seems reasonable to assume that any posthumous "improvements" made on films like this one and on Welles's OTHELLO should be approached skeptically, though they rarely are by critics—myself included, in this case.

My article on GENTLEMEN PREFER BLONDES grew out of four particular sources: my fascination with the relationships between the songs in the movie, which dated back to notes taken during my days in Paris; my preoccupation with 1950s ideology, which had already been a major focus of *Moving Places*; my interest in Richard Dyer's remarks about Monroe's contradictory Lorelei Lee in his book *Stars*; and my piece on Barthes that is reprinted in the previous section. Originally, the Barthes piece was designed to be run with my translation of a brief, early piece by Barthes ("Au Cinemascope," originally published in *Les Lettres Nouvelles*, February 1954, and still unpublished in English). To my frustration, after *Sight and Sound* secured the rights to run this piece, they wound up omitting it due to lack of space; but because Barthes's three paragraphs seemed relevant to my ideas about GENTLEMEN PREFER BLONDES, I wound up recycling portions of them in this article two years later. In the course of all these transactions, I somehow managed to suppress a key childhood memory that reemerged long after this piece was published—a memory that serves to explain quite apart from my labyrinthine arguments why so many people associate this 1953 movie with CinemaScope. For an early CinemaScope test reel that I had actually seen at an exhibitors convention in Atlanta with my father that spring, one of the sequences shown was the "Diamonds Are a Girl's Best Friend" number *reshot* in that format. (Whether or not Hawks was around for this reshooting is something I've been unable to uncover.)

The piece in this section that required the most work and took the longest was the one on GERTRUD. This entailed acquiring and reading not only Drouzy's biography in French, but also a copy of the script in French that contained the suppressed intertitles, as well as much rummaging around in several libraries until I finally located the original play in French at the New York Public Library. The latter two discoveries were both related in part to certain quarrels I had with the chapter on GERTRUD in David Bordwell's fascinating and generally brilliant book on Dreyer. (The first of these quarrels was aired in a review of the book in *Film Comment*, written well before I discovered the play.)

Ironically, the impulse that first moved me to write about GERTRUD—no trace of which remains in the final piece—was a desire a decade earlier to respond to a point made about the very limited use of "reverse-field" cutting in the film by Noël Burch and Jorge Dana in their article "Propositions" (*Afterimage* [London], no. 5, Spring 1974). Burch and Dana observed that this form of cutting occurred only very early and very late in the film—when Gertrud tells her husband that she loves someone else and when she says goodbye to her friend Axel in the final scene. The point I wanted to argue was that this was the only time during the film that real communication took place between two people, which was why I thought Dreyer privileged the technique in this fashion. But by the time I finally got around to writing the piece, so many other concerns had intervened that I never got around to propounding my original argument.

When I first proposed this article to Penelope at *Sight and Sound*, she was dubious about there being anything more to say about GERTRUD, and I'm grateful to John Pym—who succeeded David Wilson as her assistant after succeeding me on the *Bulletin*—for changing her mind.

Another significant contrast in this section can be found in the pieces done for *Sight and Sound* and *Film Comment* and those done for a less specialized and more mainstream readership in the *Chicago Reader*. I tend to think that my belated requirement to communicate with people other than film buffs on this weekly (and, earlier, on *Soho News*) has helped my writing—especially at the *Reader*, where I've been edited much more, and where my editors, none of them hardcore film buffs, are always the first people I have to address.

Ozu's GOOD MORNING

OHAYO (GOOD MORNING)
Japan, 1959
Director: Yasujiro Ozu

Cert—U. *dist*—Cinegate. *p.c*—Shochiku/Ofuna. *p*—Shizuo Yama-
nouchi. *sc*—Yasujiro Ozu, Kogo Noda. *ph*—Yushun Atsuta. *col*—
Agfacolor. *ed*—Yoshiyasu Hamamura. *a.d*—Tatsuo Hamada. *m*—
Toshiro Mayuzumi. *l.p*—Chishu Ryu (*Keitaro Hayashi*), Kuniko
Miyake (*Tamiko Hayashi*), Yoshiko Kuga (*Setsuko Arita, Tamiko's
Sister*), Koji Shidara (*Minoru Hayashi, Older Son*), Masahiko Shi-
mazu (*Isamu Hayashi, Younger Son*), Keiji Sada (*Heichiro Fukui,
English Teacher*), Haruo Tanaka (*Pencil Salesman*), Haruko Sugi-
mura (*Mrs. Haraguchi*), Miyaguchi (*Mr. Haraguchi*), Eiko Miyoshi
(*Mrs. Haraguchi's Mother*), Eijiro Tono (*Tomizawa*), Teruko Nago-
ako (*Tomizawa's Wife*), Sadako Sawamura (*Mrs. Okubu*), Kyoko
Izum and Hasabe (*Couple with TV Set*), Toyo Takahashi. 8,460 ft.
94 mins. *Subtitles.*

In a Tokyo suburb, Minoru and Isamu Hayashi—aged thirteen and seven, respectively—play a game of pushing one another's forehead and farting with
their friends Zen Okubu and Kozo Haraguchi. The latter winds up defecating
instead and has to return home for a change of undershorts. Meanwhile, there
is some consternation about the disappearance of the local women's club dues,
and the fact that Mrs. Haraguchi, the treasurer, has recently bought a washing
machine is the cause of some suspicion, until the latter discovers that her
mother has absentmindedly put the dues aside. Minoru and Isamu are chastised by their mother Tamiko for watching television in a neighbor's house
instead of attending their English lesson; their English teacher, Heichiro, currently jobless, is given translation work by their aunt, Setsuko, while the
equally jobless Tomizawa drunkenly complains to their father Keitaro about
the difficulty of being retired by his company. Keitaro comes home to find his
sons fretting because of Tamiko's refusal to buy a television set; he tells them
they talk too much and grows angrier when Minoru insists that grown-ups do
the same, citing phrases like "Good morning" and "Fine day"; they retaliate
by taking a vow of silence. When they fail to greet Mrs. Haraguchi the next
day, she assumes this is because Tamiko is sore about the misplaced dues and
tells Mrs. Okubu that Tamiko holds grudges; Mrs. Okubu promptly returns a
bottle of beer and a bus ticket to Tamiko and warns Tomizawa's wife. Refusing to speak in school and unable to ask their parents for lunch money, Minoru and Isamu flee from home with rice and tea when their schoolteacher
turns up; the couple with the television have meanwhile moved away and

Tomizawa has started work as an electrical appliance salesman. Heichiro goes out looking for the boys and finally brings them home, where they find that Keitaro has bought a television from Tomizawa. Greeting Mrs. Haraguchi the next day, they join Zen and Kozo and resume their farting game; Kozo again has to return home. At the train station, Heichiro and Setsuko say "Good morning" to one another and discuss the weather and cloud formations; Kozo is chastised by his mother and his shorts are hung out to dry.

Devoted to both the profound necessity and the sublime silliness of gratuitous social interchange, OHAYO is a rather subtler and grander work than might appear at first. Commonly referred to as a remake of Ozu's silent masterpiece I WAS BORN, BUT . . . , it is as interesting for its differences as for its similarities. The focus of the earlier film is a family adapting to a new neighborhood by undergoing brutal social initiations: the father humiliates himself before his boss to get ahead while the sons are accepted by their peers only after humiliating a local bully. Shocked by the behavior of their father, who says that he has to demean himself in order to feed them, the sons retaliate by going on a hunger strike. In the lighter climate of OHAYO, twenty-seven years later, the setting is again middle-class Tokyo suburbia, but the central family is firmly settled, and serious problems—whether old age, unemployment, or ostracism—are principally reserved for their neighbors and friends. The sons' complaint this time is that their parents won't purchase a television set and that grown-ups talk too much; the form of their rebellion is refusing to speak. Significantly, it is the humiliations in the first film which provide much of the comedy, a subject assuming gravity only when it causes a rift between father and sons. But the more pervasive humor of OHAYO extends to the rebellion itself and all it engenders, as well as the various local intrigues surrounding it. Clearly one of Ozu's most commercially minded movies—with its stately, innocuous muzak of xylophone and strings recalling Tati backgrounds, a similar tendency to keep repeating gags with only slight variations, and a performance of pure ham (quite rare in an Ozu film) by the delightful Masahiko Shimazu as the younger brother—its intricacy becomes apparent only when one realizes that each detail intimately links up with every other. Rhythmically, this is expressed by the alternation of simply stated (if interlocking) miniplots with complex camera setups, less bound by narrative advancement, depicting the physical layout of the neighborhood itself: the perpendicular passageways between houses and the overhead road on the embankment behind brilliantly suggesting certain structures as well as strictures in a society of interdependent yet insulated busybodies. In a context where banal greetings among neighbors, schoolboy farting contests, and sweet nothings between a couple are treated as structural equivalents, and sliding doors and shot changes become integral facets of the same "architecture"—an interrelating complex of adjacent, autonomous units—the fascination is how even throwaway details become part of the design. A poster for THE DEFIANT ONES, for instance, alludes not only to the recalcitrant sons, but the sense of antagonistic parties chained together by circumstance that often seems to function just below the surface of the everyday pleasantries. A grandmother muttering gripes in between her prayers, a drunken Tomizawa coming home to the wrong house, the young scat-singing couple (at whose home the boys watch television, courting disapproval) being quietly hounded out of the community, a thoughtful Keitaro wondering if television will "produce 100 million idiots" or pondering his future retirement: all these moments are characteristically uninflected, and each goes straight to the heart of the film. Mainly designed to look as casual and as inconsequential as its title, GOOD MORNING gleefully embraces a world that I WAS BORN, BUT . . . can acknowledge only painfully. With a father figure at the center of its constellation—Chishu Ryu, as Keitaro—who is exempt from ridicule, it neither seeks nor finds any comparable reasons for serious doubts or despair. Yet thanks to the precision and consistency of the vision, Ozu can take up all the other grinning denizens of this discreetly closed world and pin their endearing absurdities neatly into place.

—*Monthly Film Bulletin*, no. 502, November 1975

Sound and unsound thinking. The problem is that we've scarcely begun to learn how to listen. It can't be mere coincidence that so many of the most exciting early sound features—DESERTER, ENTHUSIASM, THE GREAT CONSOLER, IVAN, LA NUIT DU CARREFOUR, THUNDERBOLT—are virtually inaccessible today, apart from rare archive screenings. More available touchstones, like BLACKMAIL and HER ONLY SON, are often just as flagrantly overlooked, or else—with certified classics such as THE BLUE ANGEL, M, and VAMPYR—chiefly reduced to their visual coefficients when they are analyzed in any depth.

The visual biases of auteurism have helped to amplify this neglect. It is difficult to get anything approximating the measures of CHIKAMATSU MONO-GATARI, GERTRUD, LANCELOT OF THE LAKE, PLAYTIME, or UNE SIMPLE HIS-TOIRE if plot, acting, and direction remain the only measuring rods. And con-fronted with a self-proclaimed testament of a central auteurist figure that depends more on sound than on image, auteurist criticism can only stop short and gawk:

> . . . Sternberg, in creating his last work, THE SAGA OF ANATAHAN, attempted much, and yet at the same time expressed himself with less clarity than in any of his earlier films. It is the work of an old man, of a supreme technician faced with facilities beneath his standards and a cast unequal to the pressures he placed on them.
>
> . . . But if one accepts Sternberg as a great artist of the cinema, it follows that ANATAHAN must be a work of definite, if obscure merit.
>
> —John Baxter

... Sternberg himself regards ANATAHAN as his best film, a judgment both
his defenders and detractors would probably reject. ... Sternberg's commentary, at times contrapuntal and at times apparently superfluous to the narrative,
would appeal only to specialists in his career.

—Andrew Sarris

In his own Sternberg study, Herman G. Weinberg performs the invaluable
service of reproducing the text of Sternberg's narration and bravely rallies to
the film's defense, although his arguments tend more toward hagiography
than criticism: "How many film records do we have of great directors' voices,
in which we can study their personalities through their voices? Why are not
ANATAHAN's critics grateful for this?" Fortunately, the closed universe of
ANATAHAN is a good deal wider than the aficionados' and specialists' circle,
where merit can remain definite but obscure only because it becomes answer-
able to a higher deity, such as director or "oeuvre."

John Grierson said of Sternberg: "When a director dies, he becomes a photographer." I would argue, in Sternberg's defense, that when a director dies,
he becomes a filmmaker. The industrial employee ended his career as a subsi-
dized artist, thereby bidding farewell to the industry critics; and it would be
better to come across THE SAGA OF ANATAHAN as a private message found in
a bottle, unsigned and labeled "To whom it may concern." Barring that possibility, it still demands to be examined through its own credentials. The only
interesting commentaries on the film that I know of are Sternberg's own, in
Fun in a Chinese Laundry, and Claude Ollier's remarkable (and untranslated)
"Une Aventure de la lumière" (*Cahiers du Cinéma,* no. 168). Some of the remarks below are indebted to each.

For latecomers.   THE SAGA OF ANATAHAN, made by Sternberg in his late
fifties, was financed by two Japanese producers and, as an opening title announces, shot in a studio constructed for that purpose in Kyoto. It has simultaneous Japanese dialogue delivered by actors and English narration recited
by Sternberg, along with diverse kinds of on- and off-screen music and a
highly selective series of sound effects. For its point of departure, it uses the
true story of a group of Japanese sailors who were shipwrecked on a tiny island in the Marianas, already inhabited by a man (Kusakabe) and woman
(Keiko), in 1944, and who refused to surrender to American forces until
seven years after the end of the war—by which time several of the men had
killed one another in fights over the woman. The film was released in 1953,
and, according to Sternberg, received badly almost everywhere, including
Japan.

Prerequisites.   A triumphant film about defeat, dealing with the effects
of time and competition in a context that places itself outside all time and all

competition, ANATAHAN establishes a multiple audiovisual web of artifice that becomes the precondition of its truth. To cope with it, auteurism has to invert its usual priorities. It must accept that the cornerstone of Sternberg's reputation, his visual obsessions (from Dietrich to nets to bric-a-brac to textures of fog and smoke) are denied their Hollywood upholsteries and either flattened to the point of parody, or, a formula that seems more accurate, x-rayed into a diagram that emphasizes their limitations while reducing their more seductive illusionist aspects. And apart from the dull procession of compositions with dead-center framing—most of it devoted to the kind of closeted Sternbergian space that makes the diverse areas on Anatahan resemble the interchangeable parts of a pipe organ—one has to contend with an unmemorable cast whose dialogue chiefly goes untranslated and most of whose members are nearly as undifferentiated as the studio trees sprayed with aluminum paint.

This is a lot to accept, particularly if one has learned to look at films cut into such disassociated sections as story, dialogue, acting, photography, sound, and sets—like a *Variety* reviewer or a butcher slicing up a carcass to price the relative worth of its separate parts. Yet if one can deal with it as a whole and living body with its own rules of functioning, the relative insubstantiality of the images becomes an important aspect of that body's strength. From one point of view, it is a formalism run amok, whose overall texture has become so flat, hard, and consistent that one is finally able to walk on it like a floor.

That's why any stills accompanying this article must inevitably lie about the film; they are little more than ornamental plates for the sounds to reverberate against—a site for contemplation, not enchantment. With your eyes shut, it couldn't possibly work. As with the "empty" shots of Place d'Italie near the end of Rivette's SPECTRE, there has to be a neutral *and* open visual representation in order for a structured fiction to take root in the spectator's mind (as opposed to on the screen); black leader would only seem like a hiccup. ANATAHAN's tangled white emptiness is better.

Most films ask us to walk over soundtracks that are as formally repetitive as ANATAHAN's frames, and we don't even question the process; we're happy to accept words, noises, and music as visual cues, but have trouble accepting images as sounding-boards. Not that Sternberg makes it easy. Depending, for most Western viewers, upon the *unintelligibility* of the Japanese dialogue to fulfill an abstract role in the film that is in some ways comparable to its visual texture, and purporting to speak *for* his characters as well as about them, he establishes a distance from his materials that many find inhuman. But this alienation is only the other side of Sternberg's intimacy with his subject and his audience, and the problems it creates are inseparable from the rare achievements it makes possible.

Anatahan, c'est moi.

> Since two o'clock yesterday afternoon . . . I have been writing Bovary. . . . It is a delicious thing to write, whether well or badly—to be no longer yourself but to move in an entire universe of your own creating. Today, for instance, man and woman, lover and beloved, I rode in a forest on an autumn afternoon under the yellow leaves, and I was also the horse, the leaves, the wind, the words my people spoke, even the red sun that made them half-shut their love-drowned eyes.
>
> —Letter of Gustave Flaubert to Louise Colet,
> 23 December 1853

> . . . M. Mauriac has put himself first. He has chosen divine omniscience and omnipotence. But novels are written *by* men and *for* men. In the eyes of God, Who cuts through appearances and goes beyond them, there is no novel, no art, for art thrives on appearances. God is not an artist. Neither is M. Mauriac.
>
> —Jean-Paul Sartre,
> "François Mauriac and Freedom"

One needn't try to reconcile these two quotations here. Each has something decisive to say about ANATAHAN, from the respective vantage points of artist and critic. There's no question that use of the first person plural and foreknowledge of future events in the narration ("And we were to be here seven long years") denies the characters any freedom; whether it denies *us* any freedom is another matter. As the only Sternberg film predicated on the absence of love, ANATAHAN focuses exclusively on male passion and its consequences, a subject that for Sternberg has never had much relation to freedom. But ANATAHAN, unlike earlier Sternberg, is more interested in examining this passion than in arousing it—thereby allowing the spectator an unprecedented amount of freedom.

Keiko.   Not only a character, but a sound worked through countless variations: cake-o, kay-ko, keck-ho, even key-ko when the shriller actors call out her name. The cuckoo, cock crow, and implicit cuckold of THE BLUE ANGEL are never far away; here the sound is linked aurally to the rattle of the shell-curtain that covers the entrance to Keiko's hut. *Kusakabe*—identified by Claude Ollier as Sternberg's surrogate until he dies, and the last of the dead men to appear in the final sequence—is also a four-syllable figure that rhythmically echoes certain phrases in the Okinawa folk song sung by the men and heard repeatedly in the film: *Anatahan* itself, though accented differently, has a related lilt. A pair of triplets moving up the scale in the score recurs as often as the printed dates, and the countless shots and sounds of waves, all of which help to make the film's abstraction of time as systematic as its reduction of space.

The narration's first person plural   is reportedly derived from a published account of the Anatahan incident by Michiro Maruyama,* the musician whose counterpart in the film fashions a stringed instrument (with which he accompanies the Okinawa folk song) out of the wreckage of a B-29—an act suggesting that he, too, is a Sternberg surrogate, for both men make music out of deadly foreign materials. This first-person narration shifts to the singular only twice, marking the disappearance of Keiko from the island ("Long ago, I heard her say that if she had wings she would fly home," as she waves both arms to signal an American vessel) and her phantom reappearance on a Japanese airfield in the final sequence ("And if I know anything at all about Keiko, she too must have been there," the last line in the film). But to complicate matters, Maruyama himself figures only once in the narration, when, like all the other individual characters, *he is referred to in the third person.*

Thus the "I" of ANATAHAN remains as ambiguously unplaced as the "we," which changes its referent every time a character dies or is mentioned in third person, and the spectator is obliged to readjust to this shifting space. Equally shifting is the relationship of these unstable pronouns to the visible events occurring before, during, or after the narrator's descriptions or translations. While we observe Keiko and three of the men inside her hut, we're told that "At all these events that began now, we were not present. We were not inside that hut. . . . Even had we been there, all our versions would differ." (Whose version, then, are we watching?) As we go on to witness the murders of two of the men, the narrator reports that "we can only guess" or "surmise" how each one took place, although, in the latter case, "two bullets buried deep in Nishio's back"—which we hear being fired, but don't see in the victim's woundless back—"helped us to guess correctly."

If we regard the commentary as our primary source of knowledge, what we see are only "guesses" about what happened; otherwise we must assume that, as writer-director-photographer, Sternberg is privy to information that he denies himself as narrator. Yet if we can also "guess correctly" about something "we can only surmise," what we see can only exist in some no-man's land between the two sides of this contradiction.

It is on this same *terrain vague* that we must respond to the Collected Wit and Wisdom of Sternberg, in his Statements About the Human Condition: "The difference between a child and grown-up is in the way the brain is in control of the emotions." "A good part of our life is spent in trying to gain the

---

*I've been unable to determine whether this account is available in English, but I *have* been able to locate the *Life* magazine article (16 July 1951) that originally inspired the film, where one discovers several details at variance with the plot: "Mrs. Kazuko Higa," the real-life model of Keiko, was ordered by Captain Ishida to marry a crew member who "soon died mysteriously"; five of the survivors discovered when they returned to Japan that their wives had remarried. The individual who refuses to surrender and leave the island with the others is presumably Sternberg's own invention.

esteem of others; to gain self-esteem, however, we waste little time." "The relationship between a man and a woman is based on emotions which often may not be understood by others—who in one way or another fumble just as much." In practical terms, the truth or falsity of any of these explanations is a function of the degree to which we can imaginatively inhabit any given conjuncture of data and interpretation, sound and image, in subjective rather than objective terms—how far, in short, we can occupy the narrator's "we." Without the extravagance of a Dietrich or a Hollywood studio, camp irony is no longer an available option; this time Sternberg means business. And, as he laconically notes in his autobiography, "It is most probably an error to assume that human beings will pay admission to inspect their own mistakes rather than the mistakes of others."

Formal divisions.   The nine-reel division of ANATAHAN in 35-millimeter corresponds to the nine distinct sections of narration. The usual two-reel division in 16-millimeter further helps to clarify the film's symmetry by counterposing the newsreel footage at the end of the first reel—depicting the return of Japanese troops at the end of the war—with the fictionalized homecoming of the Anatahan survivors at the end of the second. Emotionally and conceptually, these are the two peaks of the film, representing the respective extremes of "real" and "artificial" that are attained, and their interrelationship is underlined by the narration accompanying each. Sternberg's monotonous, deadpan delivery (a rare form of self-denial that fulfills his own theory of acting, supporting Elliott Stein's contention that Sternberg has secret affinities with Bresson) allows the music's emotional ascendance on these occasions to be as majestic as the Monteverdi *Magnificat* at the end of MOUCHETTE, whereas the words are empowered to live on their own meanings. These parallel "voices" and "narratives" are then fused by the wordless musical choir, which becomes audible in each case the moment that families are evoked, through a gradual rise of volume that creates a throbbing plurality of voices:

(1) (*Sounds of plane, then boat whistle over strings.*) But far away in Japan, our country had faced the reality of defeat. The Emperor had called the troops home. And millions streamed back—away from the nightmare of trying to conquer a world. Father and son—wife and husband—mothers (*harp glissando*), daughters—friends—(*Choir becomes audible over strings*) all those who feared they might never meet again. The men who had fought in vain came back home—though there were many that did not come back.

(2) (*Sounds of plane, then noisy crowd over strings.*) We were back in Japan—heroes to all but ourselves—(*Choir and strings rise in volume*) brother and sister were there—our friends were waiting—father and mother—our neighbors came. We saw our wives—our children—now seven years older—we would have to earn their affection all over again—we were home—at last. (*Sounds of wind and sea; music ceases.*) And if I know anything at all about Keiko—she too—must have been there. (*Wind continues over aural flashback*

of Okinawa folk song, rising in volume, followed by laughter and dialogue,
then a reprise of the song, slowly fading until strings take over the end title.)

The first homecoming   is the most audacious gesture of ANATAHAN. After restricting himself entirely to an artificial universe of representations, from toy boat and painted clouds to studio island, it dares to show us real Japanese soldiers in documentary footage returning to their homes and families, fusing private obsessions with objective history. As a cosmic statement of surreal equivalences that lies at the root of the film this is anticipated in THE SHANGHAI GESTURE by the slow dissolve of the casino over Ona Munson's face, which similarly blends the universal with the personal. What makes the conceit much more shocking, beautiful, and moving here is the fact that the *kinds* of representation involved are at infinitely greater odds with one another. If the tone of this sequence, like the last, can only be called religious, this may be because it requires the equivalent of religious faith to believe, with Sternberg, that sound alone can bridge these irreconcilable realms. In this respect, both sequences parallel the end of Dreyer's ORDET by performing miracles.

Second homecoming.   "This film is an attempt to photograph a thought," reads the opening title of Sternberg's first film—a project only fulfilled completely at the very end of his last. As each Anatahan survivor appears in turn behind a barrage of flashbulbs in foreground, in front of a giant rear-projection of a landed plane (in a studio approximation of a Japanese airstrip that looks phonier than anything else in the film), the narration conjures up still another "correct" surmise by proposing Keiko, who then appears as a phantom *in relation to* the phony set. This illusion within an illusion occurs solely on the pretext that Sternberg—speaking finally in his own person—imagines her there, and like a multiplication of two minus signs, this conjugation offers us, for the second time in the film, a purely documentary truth.

Then, after each survivor makes his appearance, in a parody of a curtain call—an ironic finale to Sternberg's lifelong denigration of actors—there is an aural flashback to the *Tsundara Bushi* sung on the island, beginning over Keiko's face. Each character who died on Anatahan emerges in turn from the darkness, walking directly toward the camera between reverse-angle close-ups of Keiko while the equally ghostly folk song fades in and out on the sound track. With this confrontation, the film finally arrives at a coexistence of tenses, identities, significations, and essences where the living and the dead, male and female, abstract and concrete, past and present, dreamer and dreamed can all speak together within the same discourse, on the same plane of artifice and truth, woven together into the contours of a single expression. With nowhere left to go, the film then cuts from Keiko's face to a mountain— not so much an equivalence as a full stop.

—*Film Comment*, January–February 1978

First Number: We're Just Two Little Girls from Little Rock

I don't believe in the kino-eye; I believe in the kino-fist.

—Sergei Eisenstein

Before even the credit titles can appear, Marilyn Monroe and Jane Russell arrive to a blast of music at screen center from behind a black curtain, in matching orange-red outfits that sizzle the screen—covered with spangles, topped with feathers—to look at one another, toss white ermines toward the camera and out of frame and sing robustly in unison. As electrifying as the opening of any Hollywood movie that comes to mind, this jazzy materialization so catches us by surprise that we are scarcely aware of the scene's fleeting modulations as the dynamic duo makes it through a single chorus. The black curtain changes to a lurid blue, then a loud purple; the two women twice exchange their positions on stage while gradually dancing down a few steps; and the complex flurry of gestures they make toward each other—all gracefully dovetailed into Jack Cole's deft choreography—makes the spectator feel assaulted by them as a team as well as individually: a double threat.

As awesome a demonstration of kino-fist strategies as anything in POTEM-KIN, this opening to GENTLEMEN PREFER BLONDES is just the first in a series of rude shocks. The second comes only moments later—after the credits have appeared over the same stage curtain and an offscreen choral version of "Diamonds Are a Girl's Best Friend" (in a passage of relative respite, during which we're shuttled through no less than seven more garish color changes)—when, after "Little Rock" resumes, the film cuts from Monroe singing solo to a reverse angle of a tuxedo-clad Tommy Noonan watching, waving, and wanly blowing a kiss from a cabaret table. The lumpy, passive, decisively unheroic presence of Noonan in the shot—as the film viewer's uninvited surrogate, as a neuter/neutral surface off which the dynamism of Monroe is allowed to ricochet—creates a dialectical montage of collision, like lightning striking a plateful of mush, as jolting in its way as the first apparition of Monroe and Russell.

Henceforth, all Howard Hawks's cards are on the table. The viewer is warned that the unbridled spectacle of his two female stars and the flabby repose of male reaction shots comprise the dialectical limits of this film's cartoon universe, and the only equals to be seen anywhere will be the two stars themselves. Indeed, in a world where competition and corruption are taken for granted, their noncompetitive friendship forms a united front that is the film's only moral center.

If we pause, finally, to consider the words of their song, the notion of spiritual kinship becomes even more striking when we realize that they're assuming precisely the same identity. They begin as "two little girls from Little Rock" who "lived on the wrong side of the tracks." But after Monroe takes over to describe how, after "someone" broke her heart in Little Rock and she "up and left the pieces there," she eventually drifted to New York with a more hardened view of men and what she wanted from them, Russell promptly becomes the "I" in the same narrative: "Now one of these days in my fancy clothes/I'm going back home to punch the nose," before they end in unison, "Of the one who broke my heart . . . in Little Rock."

In effect, though neither Lorelei Lee (Monroe) nor Dorothy Shaw (Russell) has yet been introduced as a character, the movie is already offering both as Lorelei the gold digger. If we check back to Anita Loos's 1925 flapper novel, which provided the original source material, written in the form of Lorelei's diary, we discover that she's the only one who comes from Little Rock, and her departure is precipitated specifically by shooting an unfaithful lover. Yet with a magical transmutation made possible by musicals, the movie Lorelei is accorded not only a softer center but a spiritual essence multiplied by two, and distributed equally to Dorothy.

Hawks is famous as the director who never once deigned to film a flashback, and the pasts with which he furnishes his characters before their screen appearances are generally scanty. Sometimes this involves an unhappy love affair, as in ONLY ANGELS HAVE WINGS and RIO BRAVO; here it is dispensed with as quickly as possible, vaguely to motivate Lorelei's gold digging, and then just as quickly dropped so that the rest of the movie can bask in the immanence of a continuous present tense. The thing to stress is that the absence of any narrative discontinuity between song and story makes the numbers a form of *being* for both characters rather than a form of acting; and within this being, Dorothy is quite willing to assume or share Lorelei's identity, without warning, explanation, or regret.

While Hawks's only pure musical might conceivably be the most popular of his movies today, critics on the whole tend to be confounded by it. Treated only marginally in books devoted to the director, it has received attention more recently from feminist writers, who often disagree about essential characteristics. For Maureen Turin ("Gentlemen Consume Blondes," *Wide Angle,* no. 1), it is sexist, racist, and colonialist; for Lucie Arbuthnot and Gail Seneca ("Text and Pre-Text: GENTLEMEN PREFER BLONDES," *Film Reader,* no. 5), it is jubilantly feminist and, at least by implication, proto-lesbian. Molly Haskell ("Howard Hawks," in *Cinema: A Critical Dictionary*), no less persuasively, finds it "as close to satire as Hawks's films ever get on the nature (and perversion) of sexual relations in America, particularly in the mammary-mad 50s."

Like the blind men grasping different parts of the elephant, each of these writers is on to something—which helps to explain why the movie manages to accommodate some of the viewpoints and fantasies of heterosexuals *and* homosexuals of both genders. If doubts remain (as with Robin Wood, Gerald Mast, Leland Pogue, and Donald Willis in their Hawks books), these mainly have to do with the lackluster male leads, Noonan and Elliott Reid. But Richard Dyer in *Stars* goes further and, in judicious detail, finds incoherence at the very heart of the film, in the figure of Lorelei as played by Monroe: "a quite massive disjunction" between the innocence of Monroe's image and the calculation of Lorelei's character: "This is not a question of Lorelei/Monroe being one thing one moment and another the next, but of her being simultaneously polar opposites."

Insofar as Lorelei/Monroe is perceived as an isolated character, Dyer's point is irrefutable. But seen as an integral function in a diabolical machine that also incorporates Russell, Noonan, and Reid, she projects a coherence and legibility that is as sharply defined as theirs. In fact, the movie's innate capacity to suggest readability and unreadability, feminism and sexism, optimism and pessimism, beauty and grotesquerie at one and the same time makes it the ideal capitalist product, malleable to every consumer need: a distillation of Hollywood which is also a parody of same, a calculated/innocent excess of effect which rewards characters and spectators equally so that everybody gets what they think they want.

This may help to explain why a striking number of contemporary viewers, Maureen Turin among them, misremember the film as being in CinemaScope, that standard-bearer of 1950s amplitude. Admittedly, it was released by Fox only a few months before the company unleashed CinemaScope with THE ROBE and HOW TO MARRY A MILLIONAIRE, the latter of which had both Monroe and a related theme. But one is tempted to add another reason for this error, which is aesthetic: that GENTLEMEN PREFER BLONDES has the overall effect of the process without actually using it. Try imagining, for instance, the final shot—Reid, Russell, Monroe, and Noonan all facing the camera and wedding altar, with plenty of space between them—and the format naturally imposes itself.

Second Number: Bye Bye Baby

The movie's plot—the exploits of Lorelei and Dorothy as they sail from New York to Paris and back again on the *Ile de Paris*—both elaborates on the essence of the five musical numbers and gives the viewer a chance to recover from the last while preparing for the next. Lorelei, single-mindedly in search of money, is sent to Paris with a letter of credit by her wealthy fiancé Gus (Noonan). Dorothy, single-mindedly in search of love (or sex), is given a free ride as Lorelei's chaperone, while Gus's skeptical father hires private detective Malone (Reid) to spy on Lorelei and report any indiscretions . . . While the stars board the liner, along with members of an Olympics team who immediately arouse Dorothy's interest, they repair to adjacent staterooms. Dorothy is joined by the relay team and others, Lorelei by Gus with parting gifts, and two versions of "Bye Bye Baby" soon get under way.

In Hawks's nonmusicals, songs usually figure to celebrate groups and allegiances that have recently formed: Jean Arthur and flyers in ONLY ANGELS HAVE WINGS, Barbara Stanwyck and nightclub patrons in BALL OF FIRE, Lauren Bacall and Hoagy Carmichael in TO HAVE AND HAVE NOT. Here the same process is at work, starting from the warmth that spreads between Dorothy and the relay team and radiating outward. But, oddly enough, Dorothy is again singing a song that makes sense only for Lorelei, who is saying goodbye to Gus. Dorothy has invited the team and their friends into her room for a party, and after taking a few dance turns with one athlete she starts to sing her euphoric farewell—irrationally—to several of them in turn, before they respond as a chorus and some of their women friends follow suit.

Perhaps these women are seeing off the team, which gives the male and female choruses, if not Dorothy, some reason for singing the song. But the scene immediately follows an "intimate" scene between Lorelei and Gus and seems to relate to them even more, although they are now absent from the shot. Lorelei's repeated use of "Daddy" as her pet name for Gus, delivered in Monroe's inimitable baby talk, makes her or Gus the "baby" of the subsequent song more than anyone else, although the sentiment gets weirdly displaced.

A plea for faithfulness couched in the paradoxical form of a spirited lullaby, the song would be wholly logical only if Gus sang it to Lorelei. But Lorelei has just subverted this theoretical possibility by teasing Gus that he "can be a pretty naughty boy sometimes," thereby turning the tables and forestalling any such charges on his part. And as soon as Dorothy and her party complete their two choruses, it is Lorelei who sprints Gus back to the privacy of the next cabin to sing a slower, more sultry version of the same tune.

Seeing Monroe really turn it on—tripping her finger up Gus's lapel, caressing his shoulder and forcing him to keep close eye contact with her while he blushes and blanches—one is irresistibly reminded of Chaplin with his female victims in MONSIEUR VERDOUX, confidently running glissandos up and down his own sexual narcissism. The exchange of sex (or its promise) for capital is equally brazen in both characters, and the fact that in each case it is being performed by a charismatic star—Chaplin near the end of his reign, Monroe at the virtual onset of hers—makes it register with a decidedly Brechtian aftertaste. (If Monroe and Chaplin are equally predators, the spectator surely qualifies as part of their prey.) Hawks is again using Gus as a cartoon stand-in for the leering spectator in the stalls, but by folding this unsettling equation into the middle of Dorothy's good-natured altruism, he removes the potential sting from the insult, confuses the issue.

Sure enough, as Lorelei is about to conclude her vamp version, Dorothy, now the delighted observer, slaps the wall to announce her presence, Lorelei returns the song to up-tempo, and the crowd joins in for a final chorus. The ship's bell rings, a voice calls out "All Ashore" and the whole happy company—Gus and Lorelei, Dorothy and party—race to the deck amid festive streamers. By the time Lorelei's voice briefly prevails over the others as she prepares to bestow on Gus a farewell kiss (accompanied, as usual, by cartoon sound effects to indicate his swooning response), her inspired if cold hypocrisy has fused indistinguishably with Dorothy's bland if warm sincerity, so that each becomes an untroubled facet of the other. Here and elsewhere, they jointly project a true image of artificiality or an artificial image of the truth— the two possibilities are collapsed into a single aggressive personality, looking for men.

If it seems that the lumpy male spectator has just been sent packing, this turns out to be only half true. Just as Dorothy is always ready to take over for Lorelei, so Detective Malone, as lumpy and unstarlike as Gus, is waiting on board to take over as male spectator surrogate. Like Dorothy, he is less identified with wealth, hence more "normal" in the film's terms. But the distinction is only superficial: for most of the movie, he protects the interest of Gus and his father as faithfully as Dorothy protects and defends Lorelei.

■

Never have two women gotten along together so well in a musical.

—*Norman Mailer*

Central to the achievement of GENTLEMEN PREFER BLONDES is the extraordinary rapport between Jane Russell and Marilyn Monroe, which constantly enhances the interaction between Dorothy and Lorelei. This notion of documentary imposed over fiction is related to Hawks's flair for instilling a re-laxed atmosphere on his sets. One recalls the real romance that developed be-tween Bacall and Bogart while shooting TO HAVE AND HAVE NOT, the grace-ful incorporation of Dean Martin's drinking in RIO BRAVO. In the latter film, John Wayne's acute embarrassment when faced with Angie Dickinson's un-derwear seems to express the discomfort of the actor as well as of the charac-ter. Indeed, apart from the flat villains in both films, one could argue that Walter Brennan is the only prominent actor in either who constructs a wholly fictional character; the others are treated more generally as house guests.

It is worth noting, therefore, that Monroe and Russell actually became friends while working on GENTLEMEN PREFER BLONDES—despite the fact that Russell was paid $200,000 for her part (and got top billing), while Monroe, on her Fox salary and not yet a star, got only $500 a week. Hawks once ex-plained their unusual "chemistry" as screen presences by describing Monroe as a fantasy and Russell as "real." *Mutatis mutandis*, this anticipates the strat-egy of Hawks enthusiast Jacques Rivette two decades later, in pairing the cartoon-like Juliet Berto with the more theatrically trained and earthbound Dominique Labourier in CÉLINE ET JULIE VONT EN BATEAU. (Not coinciden-tally, the two French actresses were already friends.) To understand the cu-rious logic of either film, the personality crossovers and theatrical imper-sonations, one ultimately has to see the two actresses as the dialectical yet compatible sides of a single female character, and all the men in the cast as variations on a single male character.

Third Number: Ain't There Anyone Here For Love?

As soon as the trip is under way, Lorelei, under the watchful eye of the eavesdropping Malone, checks the passenger list for "suitable" (i.e., rich) es-corts for Dorothy. "I want you to find happiness and stop having fun," she insists, objecting to Dorothy's current interest in the Olympics team. Dorothy proceeds to the indoor pool and gym where, surrounded by muscular athletes, she learns that they all have to be in bed by nine. A whistle summons them to their exercises and a male chorus begins to count to four to start them off. The number that follows reverses the premise of the last two by privileging the viewpoint of a female spectator, Dorothy, and isolating her from Lorelei.

A retreating camera exposes a screenful of bulging male flesh traversing the frame in various exercises, and Dorothy proceeds to deliver her up-tempo query/lament while threading her way through a labyrinth of indifferent bod-ies. For the most part, she seems as alienated from this dehumanized specta-cle as they are from her, and the few desultory glances she gives, whether skeptical or entreating, are all met by equivalent blank stares. In some early shots, one glimpses a group of female oglers and women in the pool, the lat-ter of whom Dorothy addresses; around the middle of the number, the camera isolates her in frontal close-up, underlining her apartness. But near the end, when she stoops near the edge of the pool so that athletes can dive over her, she gets knocked into the water, which quickly reintegrates her into the surrounding community. A group of men hoist her out and onto their shoulders; a waiter serves her a drink, and, as she finishes the song, she and the men have resumed friendly eye contact.

In short, her song passes through four forms of address—to other women, to herself, to the camera, to everyone—while implicitly addressing itself also to an offscreen Lorelei, whose infantile absorption in money seems equivalent to the loveless narcissism on display here. Yet the sheer physicality of this campy, materialist sequence is merely the culmination of a trait that has characterized the film so far: the cramming of massive bodies (or masses of bodies) into the frame. Practically every shot has featured the commanding bulk of the stars, the self-effacing (shy or secretive) bulk of the two male leads, and/or teeming crowds of extras, and the gym number is only clarifying this profusion of bodies by making it more blatant and functional. Trying to reconcile the contrary drives toward narcissism and friendship, the film uses these bodies along with diamonds (bulk versus glitter; warmth versus cold) as props in a philosophical debate between Dorothy and Lorelei which the mise en scène is continually expounding.

Fourth Number: When Love Goes Wrong, Nothing Goes Right

> If we can't empty his pockets between us, we're not worthy of the name Woman.
>
> *—Dorothy to Lorelei*

Despite the apparent equality established in the plot and the division of musical numbers, Dorothy plays second fiddle to Lorelei whenever money is around, which is most of the time. On ship, for instance, we're introduced to another pair of male spectator surrogates, both wealthy and smitten with Lorelei: Piggy (Charles Coburn), a childish septuagenarian, and Henry Spofford III (George Winslow), a mature toddler. Monroe and both actors are refugees from Hawks's 1952 MONKEY BUSINESS, a dark comedy about aging, and their roles here represent elaborations of their former cartoon-like characters. Piggy is even rendered via Lorelei's vision as a literal cartoon diamond—an image of sparkling, ageless stone superimposed over his ancient hogshead countenance.

While Dorothy falls for Malone, Lorelei gets Piggy to give her a diamond tiara belonging to his wife (the snooty Lady Beekman, the film's only villain). Their worlds collide when Malone takes a snapshot of Piggy embracing Lorelei and Dorothy discovers that he's a detective. This leads to the farcical retrieval of his film by both women, which occasions the line quoted above and ends with Malone stripped of his jacket and trousers and dispatched in a pink bathrobe . . . After a shopping spree in Paris, Dorothy and Lorelei are confronted by Malone, Lady Beekman, and a lawyer demanding the tiara back. Lorelei refuses, insisting it was a gift, and Malone alienates Dorothy further by getting Gus's father to cancel the letter of credit.

The movie's least effective, most conventional number comes when the heroines find themselves penniless in a Paris café. For once Dorothy, who starts the number, takes the upper hand in asserting its meaning, which is essentially social rather than narcissistic, with a crowd of working-class Parisians making up their sympathetic audience. Lorelei's problem with Gus hasn't yet been focused by his presence, so in effect her role in the song has more to do with her sympathy for Dorothy's romantic plight. Lorelei dominates only when there's money to be had: here there is none, so she briefly assumes Dorothy's populist identity—dilutes her sexuality with community values and uncharacteristically becomes "one of the people."

■

> Until now, the look of the spectator has been that of someone lying prone and buried, walled up in the darkness and receiving cinematic nourishment rather in the way that a patient is fed intravenously. Here . . . I am on an enormous balcony, I move effortlessly within the field's range, I freely pick out what interests me, in a word, I begin to be surrounded . . .
>
> —*Roland Barthes,*
> *"On CinemaScope," 1954*

Considering Barthes's quasi-Bazinian response to CinemaScope as a cinema of choice, the frequent misremembering of GENTLEMEN PREFER BLONDES as anamorphic suggests an unconscious perception of a movie whose "binocular vision" (Barthes's phrase in the article quoted) proposes two separate points of entry at almost every stage. Seen through Dorothy's lens, it is a world of warmth and good fellowship; from Lorelei's angle, it is a world of cold objects to be possessed. Superimposing both angles, Hawks creates a confusing yet reassuring panorama in which men who are cold fish desire to be possessed as warm objects, and women are friendly, narcissistic predators who bring this about. If we try to determine which woman is smarter, the film offers only contradictory signals. Lorelei spouts malapropisms and steals the tiara thoughtlessly, but is a brilliant strategist; Dorothy seems practical, but falls for a faceless lunk with no prospects and unconcernedly defends an amoral thief.

Barthes saw CinemaScope as the vehicle for an "ideal POTEMKIN, where you could finally join hands with the insurgents, share the same light, and experience the tragic [Odessa] steps in their fullest force . . . The balcony of

History is ready." In contrast to this, he bemoaned the Mythology of THE
ROBE, neglecting to note any incompatibility between one's ability to scan the
latter and the rapid montage making POTEMKIN possible. Insofar as the
"stretched-out frontality" of Monroe and Russell is seen only from the balcony of Mythology, the binocular vision of GENTLEMEN PREFER BLONDES is
no less incomplete. Add dialectics, class struggle, and the politics of spectacle as assault—three of the linchpins of POTEMKIN—and the picture becomes
fuller, more worthy of being seen from the balcony of History as well: a
1950s debate on the virtues of hoarding versus sharing. The film honors both,
but there's no question which it finds sexier—unless the sharing is strictly·be-
tween Lorelei and Dorothy, as in the first and last shots.

Fifth Number (and Reprise): Diamonds Are a Girl's Best Friend

The movie offers two climaxes, on a stage and in a courtroom, with a version of the song performed by each heroine. Both exhibit Hawks's unsenti-
mental fascination with excess, visible elsewhere in his handling of violence
(SCARFACE), death (THE BIG SLEEP, LAND OF THE PHARAOHS), youth and age
(MONKEY BUSINESS), as well as in the first and third numbers here. Lorelei's
version is the better remembered, for it voices her ultimate dark statement in
the most opulent manner possible; it is also Monroe's best-known number.
Framed by two encounters with Gus, and intercut with three shots of him at
his cabaret table, it comprises as much of a personal affront to him as "Bye
Bye Baby"; although this time, at least, it represents an honest one.

Green curtains part to reveal a flaming orange-red set (recalling the costumes in "Little Rock"), dominated by a chandelier bearing bound, smiling
women posed as statues holding candelabra; around them waltz couples in
formal dress. Lorelei, initially unnoticed in her pink evening dress, arrives at
screen center, dripping with diamonds, and repeats "No" in a mock aria to a
group of men clutching valentine hearts the same color as the decor, snapping
at them in turn with a black fan.

The sequence exults in grating contradictions. Lorelei is indirectly dismissing Dorothy along with men, by putting diamonds first, and her main
preoccupation is with the ravages of age: "Men grow cold as girls grow old,
and we all lose our charms in the end . . ." In another chorus, she implicitly
extols adultery, in sisterly fashion, to a group of women in pink around her—
interjecting "but get that ice or else no dice," which shatters the hint of
Dorothy's communal influence. The dehumanized world that surrounds her is
indeed the world of her glamorous imagination, gaudy but petrified, with a
grim, deathly profile of pained acquiescence.

In her last chorus, Lorelei snatches one of the diamond straps that the
corpselike gentlemen on stage are dutifully dangling and tosses it to Gus at

his table—rejecting and demanding diamonds in the same defiant gesture. Gus downs a drink, doesn't applaud the number, and when he appears backstage again he's ready to end their engagement. But to round off the reversal, Dorothy has by now persuaded Lorelei to go to work on Gus to extract the $15,000 needed to replace the missing tiara (which has mysteriously vanished), and Lorelei has already confessed, "I really do love Gus . . . there's not another millionaire in the world with such a gentle disposition." An expert calculator, Lorelei estimates that getting the money from Gus will take an hour and forty-five minutes, and while she ushers him in with "Daddy," Dorothy goes off with gendarmes to impersonate Lorelei in court.

She enters in ermines, flashes some leg to borrow time, and finally breaks into an impromptu "Diamonds"—stripping off her furs to reveal her flashy showgirl outfit and proceeding through a burlesque parody of Lorelei that's every bit as devastating as Lorelei's earlier self-parody. The men in the courtroom quickly change into a leering, clapping audience as she plays to each of them in turn, until the judge (Marcel Dalio) finally succeeds in restoring order. By that time, the vulgarity of her bump-and-grind and the reactions to it have tarnished Lorelei's appeal as decisively as Dorothy's expediency has compromised her own. In one fell swoop, Dorothy's social gift becomes demagoguery through Lorelei's influence, and justice promptly collapses.

The best and worst of both characters have played themselves out. All that remains is the return of the tiara (which Malone traces back to Piggy, after he quits his job to win back Dorothy) and Lorelei's conquest of Gus's father (Taylor Holmes, a wizened geezer out of Preston Sturges). Both scenes reduce the plot to a charade by giving us "logical" steps that lead in a perfect circle. The tiara gets ceremoniously passed from Piggy to Malone to Dorothy-as-Lorelei to judge to lawyer and back to Piggy again; and Lorelei uses the same technique on Gus's father that she has already practiced on Gus himself—while the question of how brainy she actually is gets passed through a few more contradictory, jokey exchanges.

Final Reprises: "Little Rock" and "Diamonds"

> Remember, honey, on your wedding day, it's all right to say yes.
>
> —*Dorothy to Lorelei*

Dressed in virginal white and carrying matching bouquets, Lorelei and Dorothy sing "Little Rock" with a revised conclusion as they grandly march down steps and the aisle to their grooms. While the camera pans from (1) Dorothy looking from her diamond ring to Malone to (2) Lorelei looking from her diamond ring to Gus and (3) back to Dorothy and Lorelei together, looking at us, a heavenly mixed chorus offscreen reminds us that "Square-cut or pear-shape, these rocks don't lose their shape"—implying that the disparate demands of humanism and capitalism, community and narcissism, can be finally met when the perfect circle becomes a wedding ring. But the last sly look of glancing complicity between Dorothy and Lorelei suggests that they have collectively sold us a bill of goods, an impossible object—a CinemaScope of the mind, a capitalist POTEMKIN.

—*Sight and Sound*, Winter 1984/1985

GERTRUD as Nonnarrative

The Desire for the Image

There are narrative and nonnarrative ways of summing up a life or conjuring a work of art, but when it comes to analyzing life or art in dramatic terms, it is usually the narrative method that wins hands down. Our news, fiction, and daily conversations all tend to take a story form, and our reflexes define that form as consecutive and causal—a chain of events moving in the direction of an inquiry, the solution of a riddle. Faced with a succession of film frames, our desire to impose a narrative is usually so strong that only the most ruthless and delicate of strategies can allow us to perceive anything else.

Carl Dreyer allows us to perceive something else, but never without a battle. The nonnarrative specter that haunts the narrative of GERTRUD (1964), contained in the figure of Gertrud herself, is threatened at every turn by dogs snapping at her heels—a narrative world of men with pasts and futures who stake a claim on her. But Gertrud, who lives only in a continuous present, persistent and changeless, eludes them all. And if she eludes us as well, this may be because our narrative equipment can read her only as a monotone—an arrested moment (as in painting) or a suspended moment (as in music) that can lead to no higher logic. Yet from the vantage point of her refusal to inquire, she has a lot to say to the men.

To arrive at the nonnarrative side of GERTRUD—the static essentials that no amount of narrative tide can wash away—it is useful to consider the life and art of Dreyer as well. We can begin, in fact, with the stories of two men and four women—Dreyer, Hjalmar Söderberg, Josephine Nilsson, Marie Dreyer, Maria von Platen, and Gertrud—only one of whom is fictional. Starting with these family plots, we can, I hope, reach those aspects of the film which eschew plot altogether.

GERTRUD as **Family Plot**

1889: Josephine Bernhardine Nilsson, thirty-three, pregnant, unmarried, and Swedish, who manages the household of a large farm in Carlsro, arrives in Copenhagen in mid-January. A couple of weeks later, she gives birth to a son. After the baby is passed from one foster home to another for the better part of a year, and spends a few weeks in an orphanage, Josephine returns to Copenhagen and places an ad in a newspaper claiming that the boy's father has left for America and looking to get him adopted.

Eventually the boy is taken in by a tram conductor and his wife. But when the Petersen family decides not to keep him, Josephine makes a third trip to Copenhagen in late August 1890, places another ad, and finally gets the boy adopted by a typesetter and his wife named Carl and Marie Dreyer, signing the necessary papers two months later. By this time, however, she has found herself pregnant again, perhaps by another man. In her seventh month, mid-January 1891, she desperately attempts to abort the child by taking a box and a half of matches, cutting off the heads and swallowing them, and suffers a hideous death from sulfur poisoning. A macabre autopsy is conducted in Stockholm by a team of doctors, and when it is finally concluded that her death was not suicide, she is buried in a churchyard.

The adopted son of Carl and Marie, named after his adoptive father, has a nonreligious upbringing. His older sister, Valbörg, was also born out of wedlock, when Marie was a teenager and before she met Carl, and throughout the younger Carl's childhood, Marie expresses her contempt for Josephine having abandoned her child. The boy grows up lonely, taciturn, and resentful; as he was to express it in a brief and rare autobiographical sketch written in the 1940s, he was adopted by a family who reminded him on every occasion that he should be aware of the nourishment he was receiving, and that, strictly speaking, he had no right to anything because his mother had deprived them of her support for him by arranging to die. (When Marie Dreyer herself dies, aged seventy-three, in 1937, he refuses to attend her funeral, saying she has already long been dead for him; he doesn't even want to hear her name spoken.)

He reveres and idealizes the image of his real mother, however, regarding her as a victim rather than a villainess. In 1908, shortly after his nineteenth birthday, he quits his post at the Great Northern Telegraph Company, leaves Denmark for the first time, and travels to Sweden to learn whatever he can about her. When he returns to Copenhagen three months later, he embarks on a career as a journalist.

1901: Maria von Platen, thirty-one, Swedish opera singer—who at nineteen had married a state official twenty-six years her senior, and who subsequently left him to join a bohemian milieu of artists in Stockholm—writes to the author Hjalmar Söderberg, expressing admiration for his work. A stormy affair develops between them and lasts for many years. Söderberg is tied by an unhappy marriage to an ailing wife; but when he finally succeeds in dissolving the marriage in the spring of 1906, he discovers that Maria has just been seduced by a young writer, Gustav Hellström, and has fallen in love with him. At a party, Söderberg hears Hellström bragging about his recent sexual exploits, Maria von Platen among them. Enraged and grief-stricken, Söderberg leaves Stockholm for Copenhagen and in the space of a month writes a play, largely based on this experience, entitled *Gertrud*.

1962: In the newspaper *Politiken*, Carl Dreyer, seventy-three—who has not made a feature in a decade, and who has been trying to finance one about Jesus for at least fifteen years—reads an article about a doctoral thesis published in Sweden which demonstrates that Söderberg's *Gertrud* was largely autobiographical. Back in the 1920s, Dreyer had thought of adapting *Gertrud* as well as Söderberg's novel *Dr. Glas*. Now his interest is sparked in particular by the information that Maria von Platen had grown up and spent both the first years of her marriage and the last years of her life in the same area where Josephine Nilsson lived. All at once, Dreyer hits on the notion of adding an epilogue to GERTRUD based on von Platen's last years, to be filmed on location at the very house where she lived—only ten miles from Carlsro, the site of his own conception.

After Dreyer finds a producer for the film, he contacts the present owners of Maria von Platen's house, pays them a visit, and writes to her family for permission to shoot there. But too many complications intervene and, as with his desire to shoot GERTRUD in color, he has to set this dream aside, finally agreeing to reconstruct some of the interiors in a studio.

The three narratives above are selectively paraphrased, after a fashion, from portions of Maurice Drouzy's *Carl Th. Dreyer né Nilsson* (Éditions du Cerf, 1982), the first Dreyer biography in any language. Collectively, they weave an intriguing mesh of motivations in relation to the cantankerous beauty and contradictory impact of Dreyer's late masterpiece and most controversial work—most of which is set in 1906, the year he left home. Seizing upon Dreyer's traumatic relationships to both his real and adoptive mothers as the key that unlocks the mysteries of his films, Drouzy writes a troubled biography that in many respects seems comparable to Donald Spoto's recent life of Hitchcock. And if his thesis is too monolithic to qualify as a convincing critical argument, it brings a flurry of fresh insights into many corners of Dreyer's life and work. At the least, it definitively lays to rest some of the misinformation found in most standard works (for example, Katz's *Film Encyclopedia*: "He was brought up by a strict Lutheran family . . .").

An intensely private filmmaker whose scripts were nearly all adaptations, Dreyer has never been regarded as an autobiographical artist, but the obsessional nature of his work has posed mysteries that critics have been trying to unravel for over half a century. (The assumption that Dreyer was a religious artist—suggested by his frequent recourse to religious subjects, but contradicted by virtually all the other information we have about him—is probably the most common method of filling in the blanks.) Without conclusively solving any of these mysteries, Drouzy allows us to speculate further about a good many matters: the persistent images of tortured and/or suffering women (in LEAVES FROM SATAN'S BOOK, MASTER OF THE HOUSE, PASSION OF JOAN OF ARC, VAMPYR, DAY OF WRATH, ORDET); the subject of Dreyer's first documentary (unwed mothers); the mistrust and lack of identification with all institutions, coupled with the theme of intolerance; his interest in adapting *Light in August* (which juxtaposes an ideal earth mother with a doomed, illegitimate orphan who can never know his true identity); his passionate feminism; and a great deal more.

For Drouzy, much of Dreyer's *oeuvre* reflects his attitudes toward his "true" and "false" mothers, and even some of the character names in his films are telling. Only Gertrud encompasses both the true *and* false mothers by figuring at once as monster and martyr—an intransigent purist like Dreyer himself.

Significantly, Dreyer acknowledged both aspects of Gertrud's character in various interviews, seeing her as stronger than all the male characters yet intolerant as well ("She can't accept anything that she doesn't feel herself"), adding that none of the men could possibly live up to her ideal. One could argue, in fact, that the entire tragic force of the film can be felt behind Dreyer's passionate ambivalence. Critics on the whole have been divided between regarding her as monstrous or sublime, fulfilled or self-deluded, victim or victor, but the film's curious achievement is to make her all these things at once, at every moment.

The perfection of Nina Pens Rode's performance, seldom remarked on, is very much a matter of its capacity to absorb these contradictions. Consider her cracked, fragile voice (which enters another realm entirely when she sings, a difference enhanced by the postdubbing of the music), her confident ironic smile, her girlish gestures around Erland (such as her pendulum-like swings toward and away from him when they sit together at their last meeting), her measured, parsimonious movements around a room. These disparate traits and others have a kaleidoscope effect quite distinct from Falconetti's more concentrated Jeanne d'Arc—an equally nonnarrative, nondeveloping character also conceived as a form of unwavering intensity.

GERTRUD as Adaptation

Disregarding the play for the moment, the film unfolds roughly as follows:

1. On the eve of his appointment as a cabinet minister, and immediately after a visit from his elderly mother, Gustav Kanning, a liberal, middle-aged lawyer living in Copenhagen, is told by his wife Gertrud that she no longer wants to continue their marriage. Under his questioning, she admits that she loves another man (whose identity she refuses to reveal) but has not yet slept with him. Before she leaves, ostensibly for the opera to see *Fidelio*, Gustav and Gertrud plan to attend a banquet honoring the fifty-year-old poet Gabriel Lidman, a former lover of Gertrud before she met Gustav, who is returning from abroad for the ceremony.

2. In a park, Gertrud meets the young composer and pianist Erland Jansson, a pampered *enfant terrible* who is the object of her love. After she tells him of her decision to leave her husband, and recalls in a flashback her previous visit to Erland's flat, when she sang one of his compositions, they leave together for his flat to make love. At her request, Erland plays one of his pieces while she undresses in the next room.

3. Alone in a carriage, on his way back from a board meeting, Gustav experiences a sudden desire to see Gertrud again (expressed in off-screen narration in past tense) and decides to meet her at the opera. He learns from an attendant that she has not been there all evening.

4. At the banquet for Gabriel Lidman, Gertrud develops a headache during her husband's speech and goes into the adjacent sitting room, where she is joined by her old friend Axel Nygren, visiting from Paris, who discusses with her free will and his psychiatric research there. Looking up at a tapestry on the wall, Gertrud is shocked to find a dream that she had previously described to Erland—being chased naked by a pack of dogs—virtually reproduced. When Axel leaves, she is joined by Gustav, agitated by her absence from the opera, her recent refusals to sleep with him, and her decision to leave him. Then, when he is called away by the Vice-Chancellor, she is joined by Gabriel, still in love with her, who reveals having attended a courtesan's party the night before—a party that Gertrud had begged Erland not to attend— where he heard Erland drunkenly boasting of his conquest of Gertrud. After Gabriel bursts into tears and leaves, Gustav returns with the Vice-Chancellor and asks Gertrud to sing for him, enlisting Erland as accompanist. While singing, Gertrud faints.

5. In the park, Gertrud meets Erland and urges him to run away with her, offering to support him. He refuses, confessing that he is committed to another older woman who helped him when he was penniless and is now pregnant by him. He suggests that Gertrud remain with Gustav and continue their affair, and invites her to return with him to his flat, but she refuses.

6. Back in the Kanning flat, Gabriel comes to call. While Gustav is out of the room, Gabriel begs Gertrud to live with him again, but she refuses, and recalls in a flashback how she left him in Rome years before after finding a note on his desk which said, "A woman's love and a man's work are in conflict from the beginning." After Gustav returns, Gertrud goes to phone Axel, saying that she's coming to Paris to attend lectures at the Sorbonne and wants to join his psychiatric research group. Before Gabriel leaves, Gustav announces that he has just accepted the post of cabinet minister. Then he pleads with Gertrud once again to remain with him, even if she continues her affair; but Gertrud insists that she's leaving alone, and does so.

7. Thirty or forty years later, Axel comes to visit Gertrud at her house in the country, where she lives alone. She tells Axel she has no regrets for the life she has led and returns all his letters of friendship to her, which he burns in the hearth. She reads him a poem she wrote when she was sixteen, which she describes as her "gospel of love," and mentions that she has already selected her grave site and the inscription, "Amor Omnia" (Love Is Everything). Axel leaves her after they have said goodbye for the last time.

Because Söderberg's play has never been available in English, non-Scandinavian Dreyer criticism generally has next to nothing to say about it. Fortunately, a French translation exists—published in *La Grande Review* in 1908—and it reveals that the film is anything but a close adaptation, even though most of the dialogue can be traced back to Söderberg. An elaborate series of cuts, additions, alterations, and transpositions preserves the main plot while markedly changing both the characters and parts of the story's meaning.

To cite only a few of the most conspicuous differences: in the original, Gertrud has had a child by Gustav who has died in infancy; Gabriel (a playwright, not a poet) has a Spanish wife; there are many references to the politics of the day, and the setting is Stockholm, not Copenhagen; Gustav's mother visits him not only in the first act but at the end of the third, after Gertrud's departure, and a subplot charts both her cultivation of young male singers and her failure to visit a poet, a former lover, on his deathbed.

Gertrud recounts the same dream with the dogs, but there is no tapestry to reproduce it. At the banquet, many additional characters figure, including a mysterious female "shadow" who appears before Gertrud in Strindbergian fashion to recite a short poem which, in the film, becomes her own "gospel of love" at sixteen. The "Amor Omnia" inscription is one that Gabriel recalls seeing with Gertrud one spring night on the grave of a stranger. Both flashbacks, Gustav's carriage ride and the love scene in Erland's flat are alluded to but not shown; when Gertrud breaks with Gabriel in Rome, he is suffering from writer's block—which motivates the note on his desk—and it is long after they have ceased living together.

All the characters in the play are somewhat coarser, their motivations less pure—especially Gabriel, who is more of a wastrel, and Gertrud, whose cruel streak and chatter make her distinctly less heroic. ("Do you want the brutal truth?" she asks Gabriel in the third act. "I could love you once more if you could make yourself thirty again.") Most important of all, Axel and everything he represents—friendship, psychoanalysis, a belief in free will—are nowhere to be seen; and when Gertrud leaves Gustav in the third act, it is not clear where she is going.

According to Dreyer, most of the epilogue is derived from a letter from Maria von Platen to John Landqvist. Without this letter as evidence, it is all too tempting to read both the epilogue and Axel and Gertrud's early involvement with psychoanalysis as a personal catalyst on Dreyer's part which transforms the meaning of everything else. Yet if we assume that his use of von Platen's life is as creatively selective as his reworking of Söderberg, it is hardly excessive to claim that he was interested in achieving something more than mere documentation. In broad terms, his major contribution to the play is a purification of Gertrud's character which places her well beyond the bitter misogyny of the original, privileges and extends both her constancy and her martyrdom over several decades, and infuses her with an ambiguity regarding the origin, endpoint, object, and nature of her obsession with love.

GERTRUD as Passage and Process

> If Dreyer's film . . . doesn't function formally as a dream, it nevertheless . . . prescribes an "oneiric" vocabulary: at once the *telling* of a dream and a session of *analysis*, an analysis in which the roles are ceaselessly changing; subjected to the flow, the regular tide of the long takes, the mesmeric passes of the incessant camera movements, the even monotone of the voices, the steadiness of the eyes—always turned aside, often parallel, towards us: a little above us—the strained immobility of the bodies, huddled in armchairs, on sofas behind which the other silently stands, fixed in ritual attitudes which make them no more than corridors for speech to pass through, gliding through a semi-obscurity arbitrarily punctuated with luminous zones into which the somnambulists emerge of their own accord . . .
>
> —*Jacques Rivette, 1969*

> The darkness has formed a pearl,
> The night has born a dream.
> Hidden, it will grow inside me,
> Blindingly white and tender.
>
> —*Second verse of Erland Jansson's
> "Serenade," sung by Gertrud*

A ghost sonata, GERTRUD summons up other obsessive and haunted memory films—THE MAGNIFICENT AMBERSONS, LOLA MONTÈS, LAST YEAR AT MARIENBAD, THE MAN WHO SHOT LIBERTY VALANCE, INDIA SONG—as well as phantoms of the films Dreyer wanted to make but couldn't during the last years of his life: MARIE STUART, MEDEA, LIGHT IN AUGUST, AS I LAY DYING, JESUS—all steps toward what he conceptualized as film tragedy.

Theorists are fond of noting that film and psychoanalysis started at about the same time, and the hypnotic nature of the medium runs parallel to the notion of projections on a dream screen. Dreyer's return to his origins, like Gertrud's eventual return to the town of her birth, thus suggests the origins of cinema as well as desire, and critics who have regarded GERTRUD as "out of date" are not entirely wrong: it is certainly out of its time. Intimately bound up with questions about identity and the self, it transforms a once contemporary play into a perpetually unfashionable, seemingly atemporal memory film that is as much concerned with echoes and overtones, auras and afterimages as with the remote and often inaccessible events that produce them.

The trance-like rhythm caught by Rivette, evocative of the psychoanalytic session, combines two simultaneous cognitive modes—"the *telling* of a dream and a session of *analysis*"—which invite identification and detachment alike. While presenting Gertrud to us in very much the way that she views (and remembers) herself, the film also allows us to see beyond her self-image, however narrow the world may be which circumscribes it.

This distance is more apparent in the prints of GERTRUD that mainly circulate today, missing the four rhymed intertitles which separated the three acts and epilogue in the original 1964 release version, all addressed by Gertrud to herself (and written for Dreyer by Grethe Risbjerg Thomsen, who also contributed the song lyrics). Whether Dreyer himself removed these titles is unclear, but he did voice some misgivings about them to Borge Trolle in *Kosmorama* ("They didn't quite fulfill the purpose I had for them"), while adding the intriguing suggestion that had the film been in color, they wouldn't have been necessary. Because these verses are difficult to come by today, it seems worth reproducing them in full (translated literally from the French version of the script, where they also appear without rhyme or meter):

1   You dreamt of a beloved hand
     That could break your chains.
     A sudden murmur shatters
     The silence of your joyless house.
     You leave now, your heart
     Overflowing with tenderness
     Toward your beautiful dream of happiness.

2   A new lucidity in your heart
     Has filled your life with warmth.

But your happiness is without peace.
Troubled, you keep watch over your love
Among all those people who ignore it.

3 Your dream is finished.
Only the truth remains.
Hard as stone,
To that you were always faithful.
Deep is your suffering, pure is your heart
While the night encircles you.

4 Spring and winter pass
Back in the town of your birth.
Here you are, alone and old
And far from your memories.
This one must know:
To be able to grow old gracefully
Only two things exist:
Love and death, nothing more.

Dreyer's films tend to pose themselves as *challenges* to belief rather than as beliefs that demand simple adoption, and this is a stumbling block for many spectators. The sainthood of Jeanne d'Arc, the supernatural postulates of VAMPYR, the acceptance of witchcraft at the end of DAY OF WRATH, and the miracle at the end of ORDET are all imposed on the plots as formal necessities; yet our inability to accept any of these facts wholeheartedly is central to the impact of these films. A comparable problem relates to the idealism and self-image of Gertrud, and considering the laughter that initially greeted the above verses, it seems possible that Dreyer decided they overwhelmed the more objective side of the film.

Whatever the reason for their absence today, there are many other instances of Gertrud's love as self-love—including the verse from Jansson's "Serenade" quoted above. Significantly, the water in the pond behind her and Erland forms a placid mirror to a stately line of trees at their first park meeting, a reflection broken by a drifting, riddled turbulence at the second. Like the mirror given to Gertrud by Gabriel (visible in the Kanning parlor) and the one given to her by Gustav (which remains off-screen), these surfaces all suggest portals of narcissism, judged and placed according to the self-image they throw back; and the ones tied to her love for Erland are solipsistic as well—nature reduced (or expanded) to the dimensions of her self-infatuation. "Strange woman," says Erland in his flat, shortly before they kiss. "Who are you?" "I'm many things. Dew which falls from the leaves. White clouds that pass aimlessly. I'm the moon. I'm the sky." Like the verses, these mirrors function as inner voices more than ornaments—images of the self as a self-enclosed universe.

By contrast, the fires that flicker through GERTRUD usually suggest potential fusions reaching beyond the self: the candles in Gustav's flat and the ones
flanking Gabriel's mirror in the Kanning parlor; the torches and candles at the
banquet; the burning hearth that shimmers behind Gabriel and Gertrud in the
third act and glows *between* Axel and Gertrud in the epilogue (while consum-
ing his letters to her); not to mention the incandescent sunlight that floods
both flashbacks and the epilogue. Yet by the end of the film, they have become mirrors too: "I feel as though I'm staring into a fire about to be extin-
guished," Gertrud says to Axel just before he leaves. The play's epigram,
transposed by Dreyer to a statement of Gabriel's recalled by Gertrud, is "I
believe in the pleasures of the flesh and the irremediable loneliness of the
soul." This dialectic between incandescent joining and dark isolation—like
the long bouts of inactivity separating the last four features in Dreyer's career—is harmonized like a treble and bass clef to compose the melody of
Gertrud's longing, metrically spaced in a no less dialectical fashion between
development and stasis.

GERTRUD as Nonnarrative

> Sometimes a conflict emerges between the desire for the image
> and the desire for the story which is, after all, in psychoanalytic
> terms, normal, since the first one expresses, beyond the codes of
> modernism, a specular fascination for the body (of the Mother),
> and the second, the return of the repressed narrative, and conse-
> quently the necessity to pay one's debt to the Father.
>
> —*Bérénice Reynaud**

> Look at me. Am I beautiful?
> No. But I have loved.
>
> Look at me. Am I young?
> No. But I have loved.
>
> Look at me. Do I live?
> No. But I have loved.
>
> —*Gertrud's "gospel of love,"*
> *written at the age of sixteen*

When Godard defended GERTRUD in the 1960s as "equal, in madness and
beauty, to the last works of Beethoven," one wonders whether he might have
been partly thinking of the question and answer written by Beethoven as an
epigraph to the finale of the last quartet (the corresponding musical passage
figures centrally in 2 OU 3 CHOSES QUE JE SAIS D'ELLE): "Muss es sein? Es

*"New York Independent Cinema," *Fuse* (Summer 1985).

muss sein!" (Must it be? It must be!). Poised evenly and unbearably between apologia and critique, GERTRUD can be said to perform the radical step of superimposing that query and response rather than placing them in sequence.

When we first see Axel, we learn from Gertrud that he has written a book on free will; in the epilogue, he presents her with a copy of a new book, on Racine. Gertrud, an atheist, believes in free will, unlike her father, "a sad fatalist" ("He thought that everything was predestined"), and believes, like Axel, that "to wish is to choose." Yet only a moment later, after Axel mentions studying "psychosis, neurosis, dreams, and symbols" in Paris, she discovers the wall tapestry behind her, a depiction of her recurring dream. Soon afterward, in separate scenes, Gabriel tells her that he "had to" inform her of Erland's indiscretion, and Erland tells her that he "had to" attend the courtesan's party. "*Had to,*" muses Gertrud. "That's the key word to everything." Positing the unconscious as tragic destiny, GERTRUD places narrative causality and free will in the same ambiguous category.

The earliest expression of Gertrud's identity, the poem cited above, comes in the epilogue, just before she tells Axel of the grave inscription she has chosen for herself, "Amor Omnia." The immediate juxtaposition of these framing badges (or shields) suggests that she has chosen her life, and lived it freely; yet what does this continuum say about her alleged past love for Gabriel and Erland? Having denied beauty, youth, and life itself for an earlier love, she seems to have condemned herself to a compulsive replaying of a fixed past, which implies that her preoccupation with love may be little more than a form of arrested adolescence. Might we not conjecture that Dreyer's preoccupation with his mother, fixed during his own adolescence, led him to a comparable nonnarrative impasse?

Throughout the film, this tension between freedom and obsession has been materially reproduced in a number of ways. Abrupt cuts to shots when the camera is already in motion (such as the rapid, rapturous track and pan accompanying Gertrud to her first rendezvous with Erland) convey at once the free flux of life and its sense of being achingly just out of reach; the suspension of direct sound for both the musical performances (Gertrud singing with Erland) and the off-screen, past-tense narration (Gustav in the carriage, Gertrud recounting both flashbacks) creates an otherworldly ambience that makes these passages seem to occur outside time. And just as the camera movements that follow the characters define a form of narrative suspension between the stretches of dialogue, the stationary setups recording the dialogue allow the words to take flight: continuous motion and continuous stasis are equally in evidence.

Depending upon their temperaments and predilections, critics have described the film as either full of or devoid of camera movements (rather than somewhere in between). Even a critic as sophisticated as David Bordwell, tied to an exclusively narrative model, can read GERTRUD only as an "empty film," interpreting nonnarrative as absence rather than as a different form of presence. But the obsessive desire for the image is as central to the meaning of GERTRUD as the habitual desire for the story, and the furious, unceasing tug of war between these desires is the very source of the film's tragic rhythm. Only Axel, who accepts Gertrud as she is, escapes this tension: her husband must inquire why she is leaving him, her former lover asks repeatedly why she left him, and her present lover can only ask himself whether he loves her. It is only with Axel that Gertrud can have a true conversation, and when she returns his letters and he cheerfully burns them, their joint action is to refuse a narrative together, deny any riddle to be solved.

Insofar as this gesture reflects on Dreyer, it is an autobiographical gesture that paradoxically rejects autobiography. Like Gertrud's selection of her gravestone, or the film's final shot of a closed door, it represents an effort to forestall any future Drouzys. Transfixed by a static image of his mother, Dreyer enters a nonnarrative realm that can be associated with both prebirth and death—a state that both precedes and follows any need to acknowledge his father, any necessity to tell a story, placing narrative within parentheses. A work of perpetual time travel, GERTRUD no less forcefully projects a suspended gaze and meditation on a frozen destiny, perfect yet appalling.

—*Sight and Sound*, Winter 1985/1986

THE MANCHURIAN CANDIDATE

──────────────────────────────── ★★★★

THE MANCHURIAN CANDIDATE
Directed by John Frankenheimer
Written by George Axelrod
With Frank Sinatra, Laurence Harvey, Janet Leigh, Angela
Lansbury, James Gregory, Leslie Parrish, John McGiver,
Khigh Dhiegh, and James Edwards

The first and only time I've seen a good 35-millimeter print of Carl Dreyer's 1944 masterpiece DAY OF WRATH was in Europe about a month ago. The film was being rereleased, along with Dreyer's 1925 MASTER OF THE HOUSE and his 1955 ORDET, at several small theaters in Paris, and the difference in seeing it in optimal conditions was incalculable. The carnal impact of the film's sound track, lighting, compositions, camera movements, and performances may be dimly evident in duped 16-millimeter prints and on video, but the overall effect is like that of viewing a great painting through several layers of gauze, or hearing a great symphony through earmuffs. By and large, this prophylactic experience is the only way our film heritage is preserved for most people in the United States—which is another way of saying that it isn't really preserved at all.

Why are major rereleases of old movies in spanking new prints—apart from Disney cartoon features, and the five Hitchcocks that resurfaced a few years back—such a rare occurrence in this country, and so common in France? (I'm not only thinking of Dreyer: the last times I saw new prints of THE SHOP AROUND THE CORNER and GENTLEMEN PREFER BLONDES were in Paris, too.) Perhaps Mary McCarthy was onto something when she noted that "the only really materialistic people I have ever met have been Europeans," and that "the strongest argument for the unmaterialistic character of American life is the fact that we tolerate conditions that are, from a materialistic point of view, intolerable." I doubt that the French are any smarter than us, but there's plenty of evidence that they know more about how to enjoy themselves: they can even find pleasure in art.

So it's an event of some importance that MGM/UA has decided to rerelease THE MANCHURIAN CANDIDATE, an uncommonly pleasurable (which includes exciting, unsettling, funny, provocative, and mind-boggling) black-and-white feature of 1962 that can only receive its maximal impact on a big screen. The pretext for this rerelease is that the movie has long been unavailable because its star, Frank Sinatra, purchased the rights in the early 1970s in order to keep the movie under wraps. At the suggestion of critic Richard Corliss, it was unearthed at the last New York Film Festival, and the enthusiastic responses to it convinced MGM/UA to give it a limited run in a few major cities.

There has been a lot of speculation about why Sinatra shelved the film in the first place. Most theories connect the move to his friendship with John F. Kennedy. When Arthur Krim—the former president of United Artists (UA), who was also the Democratic party's national finance chairman at the time—balked at making the film, which seemed to him too politically volatile, Sinatra persuaded Kennedy, a fan of the Richard Condon novel the script was based on, to intervene on behalf of the project. The subsequent Kennedy assassination may have triggered some feelings of guilt on Sinatra's part, for the film includes a political assassination (and Sinatra had already played a would-be presidential assassin in the 1954 thriller SUDDENLY); another motivation may have been his own later political shift from the left to the right.

It's a movie whose subversive, offbeat, and ambiguous overtones have never fully received their due, here or anywhere else. Ironically, while it is as "advanced" for its period as many of the films of the French New Wave—and qualifies as a kissing cousin of that movement, much as Michael Powell's 1960 PEEPING TOM did in England—it appears that the French critics missed the boat on this one entirely, perhaps in part because it couldn't be adequately accounted for in auteurist terms as "un film de John Frankenheimer." Critics as diverse as Andrew Sarris and Dwight Macdonald treated it with contempt in 1962, and even Pauline Kael, who was possibly the movie's biggest American champion, never devoted more than a few sentences to it. Despite a few appreciations in film journals, screenwriter and coproducer George Axelrod was probably at least half right when he noted in 1968 that "it went from failure to classic without ever passing through success"—a fate that also befell many of Orson Welles's best features, for reasons that may not be entirely coincidental.

Indeed, when I first saw the movie as a college sophomore, it was CITIZEN KANE that the film initially brought to mind. Not that it was as good, or that it represented a comparable directorial debut; Frankenheimer was riding high at the time, but he already had four features under his belt—two of them released the same year as THE MANCHURIAN CANDIDATE—after a prolific period as the best director of live television dramas for *Studio One* and *Playhouse 90* (which roughly paralleled Welles's earlier work as a stage and radio director).

What seemed most Wellesian about the movie were aspects of the camera, editing, and acting styles—including uses of chiaroscuro, wide angles, deep focus, shock cuts, and overlapping dialogue—as well as how mercurial and unpredictable the overall movement was. It started out as a war film, veered into political satire (with touches of Kazan-like family melodrama—complete with a David Amram score—and pseudodocumentary), and took on elements of paranoid science fiction, black comedy, suspenseful intrigue, and horror. After various side trips into straight action (an all-stops-out karate fight), existential psychodrama with arty trimmings, and alternately straight and parodic versions of lush Hollywood romance, it finally settled into the pacing of a thriller, before ending with a phony scene that exuded patently unfelt patriotic soap opera. Yet despite all these disconcerting mixtures and gear changes, the narrative remained fluid and gripping throughout.

Less Wellesian were the film's cavalier treatments of period and character. The film is set in 1952–1954, and a lampoon of Joseph McCarthy figures prominently in the plot, but hardly any effort is made to re-create the period. The handling of character—which seems largely predicated on the premise that a use of big-name stars enables an audience to slide over incongruities—is a good deal weirder. The initial meeting of Frank Sinatra and Janet Leigh on a train, for instance, provides one of the strangest examples of "meeting cute" on record:

Leigh: Maryland's a beautiful state.

Sinatra: This is Delaware.

Leigh: I know. I was one of the original Chinese workmen who laid the tracks on this stretch. But nonetheless, Maryland's a beautiful state. So is Ohio, for that matter.

Sinatra: [*a bit later*] Are you Arabic?

Leigh: No. Are *you* Arabic?

Sinatra: No.

Leigh: Let me put it another way. Are you married?

The fact that by the time of their second short meeting, Leigh has already returned her fiance's engagement ring and declared her unlimited devotion to Sinatra is handled just as blithely as the fact that Sinatra is portrayed as a voracious intellectual bookworm, or that Laurence Harvey plays an American with an unexplained English accent, or that Leslie Parrish, the other female romantic lead, who played Daisy Mae in the 1959 LI'L ABNER, and portrays a liberal senator's daughter here, is shown without any overt irony as a nearly equivalent sort of bimbo. In short, the movie plays on standard Hollywood clichés as if on a grand organ—delivering most of them deadpan, but mixing and altering them so adroitly that they often come out as surreal gibberish.

I haven't yet said anything about the movie's central plot, and because it depends on a good many twists and surprises, readers who haven't yet seen the film are invited to step off here and not come back until they have. The story exists in a sort of parallel universe inspired by paranoid right-wing fantasies of the period—including the notion that Russian and Chinese Communists are working jointly at a scheme to take over the United States via inside stooges and the theory that brainwashing techniques have developed to the point where prisoners can even be programmed to kill their own loved ones against their own conscious wills.

Two major instruments in this scheme are a captured U.S. officer (Laurence Harvey) and his stateside stepfather, an alcoholic, pea-brained, McCarthy-like demagogic senator who is controlled by Harvey's conniving and powerful mother (Angela Lansbury), who turns out to be an agent for the Reds. Harvey's hatred for his emasculating mother is an integral part of his brainwashing, keyed to the queen of diamonds in a pack of playing cards. We eventually learn that her hypnotic control over her son includes incest, and her desire for ultimate power is currently motivated less by Communism than by a desire to take revenge on her fellow Communists for brainwashing her son.

The dizzying complexities of this Freudian scenario, halfway between Greek tragedy and lurid comic book, are worked out brilliantly on the level of exposition, but they can't be subsumed under a responsible or coherent political position. (Elsewhere, Frankenheimer and Axelrod have both come across as liberals.) The politics of the movie are in fact a kind of shadow play, manipulated like the Hollywood clichés for the sake of jazzy effects, just as the characters function basically as dream figures. None of it begins to make sense on reflection as part of a coherent universe. But the remarkable achievement of Axelrod and Frankenheimer—who coproduced the movie, and seem to have worked with an unusual amount of freedom—is to use the characters and politics to set certain narrative mechanisms in motion, and to make us accept them as if they *were* both coherent and believable. And, as a significant side benefit, they expose the deceptive mechanisms of political and Hollywood mythmaking in general.

The film's method becomes most apparent in two matching tour de force set pieces, which occur almost consecutively fairly early in the film. Each scene is structured around a different kind of discontinuity and disorientation, and each makes an ironic commentary on the film as a whole by commenting on the deceptiveness of a particular kind of public spectacle.

The first set piece is a recurring nightmare dreamt by Sinatra's character, a former member of Harvey's captured patrol, which we gradually discover is the memory of a real event in Manchuria distorted by hypnotic suggestion—a public demonstration by a Chinese Pavlovian (Khigh Dhiegh) to his colleagues of the successful brainwashing of Harvey and his men, which culminates in Harvey murdering two of his own men under the Pavlovian's orders.

Meanwhile, the American soldiers onstage have been hypnotized and think they're attending a ladies' garden club meeting in New Jersey; a 360-degree pan around the lecture hall begins with this incongruous delusion, only to arrive at the real meeting before the end of the camera movement. Thereafter, the film cuts back and forth between and gradually merges the two parallel versions of the event, and the one disquieting constant in this sequence, apart from the continuity of the lecture itself, is our identification figures, the soldiers themselves—figures who are at once the focus of the spectacle and spectators themselves. The fact that they're all drugged and hypnotized makes them our surrogates in another way: they're passive spectators, unable to exert any control over the proceedings. The question of their moral responsibility for what is happening remains as troubling and as uncertain as our own relation to what we're seeing. (Later, this queasy ambivalence becomes concentrated on Harvey's career in the States as a brainwashed assassin: his powerlessness to affect or guide his own actions matches our own impotence as spectators.)

Sandwiched between this Manchurian set piece and its subsequent continuation (when a black soldier in the patrol, played by James Edwards, has the same nightmare, with black garden-club ladies replacing the white ones) is another public hearing, set in Washington, D.C., where Sinatra is again present, this time as a press secretary. The scene is a televised press conference given by a U.S. Cabinet member, which erupts into pandemonium when Harvey's stepfather (James Gregory) restages the witch-hunting debut of Joseph McCarthy by claiming to have a list in his hand of 207 "known" card-carrying Communists working for the Defense Department—a figure that later gets amended to 104, then 275, and finally 57.

Here the discontinuity of action and the spectator's disorientation is controlled by the television monitors transmitting the event—a personal touch of Frankenheimer's, with his extensive background in live television—which show the same events occurring simultaneously from different angles. Once again, spectacle and spectator become confused, although here spectatorship becomes anything but passive—the anger and aggression displayed on both sides give the scene the temperature of a near-riot.

Gregory and the Cabinet member are situated at opposite ends of the hall, with a crowd of reporters and technicians and television monitors, cameras, and other equipment between them, and Frankenheimer creates an intricate spatial confusion in his various ways of juggling and juxtaposing these elements. At one point, we see Lansbury, the power behind Gregory, hovering over his image in diverse frontal angles on one of the monitors in the foreground while Gregory himself is visible in profile in the background. (The predatory relation of Lansbury to her puppet husband recalls the famous shot in CITIZEN KANE of Agnes Moorehead calling out the window to her little boy in the snow, just as she's signing his life away to a banker. By replacing the window frame with a television monitor, the film points up how much Lansbury's control over events hinges on her control over media images.)

At another point, a different monitor closer to the stage alternately shows the Cabinet member, from a separate angle, and Gregory screaming back at him. Perhaps the most complete sense of disorientation is reached when Gregory is seen pointing his arm in one direction while a reverse angle of him on a monitor shows him pointing in the opposite direction—a prefiguration of the movie's eventual collapse of any distinction between the political left and right on the level of plot.

The unreliability of visual evidence and the tendency of appearances to deceive is the common element in these two set pieces, and a fundamental principle behind the film's paranoid scenario, which gradually—and literally, in the climactic chase sequence—describes the overall shape of a labyrinth. Carrying the same principle further, the movie confuses us emotionally and conceptually as well as visually by playing related tricks with dramatic and generic conventions. It's typical of the movie's playful use of diverse kinds of political and patriotic rhetoric that the climactic race to stop a political assassination in Madison Square Garden gets stalled interminably by a playing of the national anthem. Prior to this, after building up a great deal of sympathy for the father of Harvey's girlfriend—a courageous and principled liberal senator, played with a lot of charisma and poise by John McGiver—the film treats his cold-blooded murder as a kind of bad-taste, antiliberal joke: the bullet that kills him passes first through a milk carton in his hand, and before he drops dead, milk gushes out.

With an equal amount of perversity, Gregory is linked visually on at least three separate occasions to Abraham Lincoln; busts and portraits of Honest Abe are as plentiful in his and Lansbury's house as queens of diamonds are in the movie. And the sinister Chinese Pavlovian, with his quaint bourgeois taste and his habit of cracking corny jokes, is made to seem as cuddly as a Dickens eccentric. Visual and verbal non sequiturs abound: in perfect Sinatra-ese, Sinatra describes at one point having "a real swinger of a nightmare"; at a costume party, Lansbury is dressed as Mother Goose, and after Parrish comes dressed as the queen of diamonds, the movie goes out of its way to "explain" this as a totally outrageous coincidence.

The point about this latter absurdity is that Axelrod could quite easily have worked a logical explanation for this into the dialogue—the script is anything but lazy—but preferred to flaunt the contrivance here, as he does in the first two scenes between Leigh and Sinatra. (It's been many years since I've read Richard Condon's novel, but if memory serves, the calculated goofiness of such details is nearly always Axelrod's contribution. Although the original's plot is certainly baroque enough to begin with—and is even more explicit about such matters as the mother-and-son incest—the movie embroiders it further with a more irreverent style.) Going beyond mere excess, the movie gives some poignancy to Sinatra's line, "I could never figure out what that phrase meant, 'more or less'"; by the time the end title appears, most spectators won't be able to figure it out either.

Alternately using and ridiculing all the Hollywood-Pavlovian techniques at its disposal, THE MANCHURIAN CANDIDATE actually succeeds in making us care about its deliberately cardboard characters when it isn't pulling the rug out from under us in order to prove how easily we can be brainwashed, too. Lansbury and Harvey have never been better: the former, in particular, is pure sulfuric acid and brimstone, while the latter's feline priggishness eventually gives way to a moving sense of pain that can be found nowhere else in his work. The supposedly saner performances of Sinatra and Leigh are no less crucial in establishing our relation to the other two. As improbable as Sinatra and Leigh are, they function rather like Lockwood and Nelly Dean in *Wuthering Heights*—as "normal" lenses framing the mad incestuous couple, square witnesses obliging us to fill in the blind spots in their viewpoint, thereby participating in the demonic creation.

Exhilarating and often terrifying in its prodigal and gleeful invention, as well as its varied kinetic pleasures, the film is also sufficiently serious about its inspired mischief to give us a lot more to think about than any rollercoaster ride devised by Lucas or Spielberg. If 1988 Hollywood gives us a movie half as good as this one, we have quite a year in store.

—*Chicago Reader*, 11 March 1988

OTHELLO Goes Hollywood

OTHELLO
Directed and written by Orson Welles
With Orson Welles, Michael Mac Liammóir, Suzanne
Cloutier, Robert Coote, Fay Compton, Doris Dowling, and
Michael Laurence

Sustained until death at 70 by his fame as the prodigy with the baby face, Orson Welles always appeared to abide by words he put in the mouth of Citizen Kane: "There's only one person in the world to decide what I'm gonna do—and that's me."

—from a two-page magazine ad for the Dodge
Shadow that appeared last month under the heading
"Amazing Americans . . . a celebration of people
who have lifted our nation's pride"

I guess this describes the official Orson Welles we're all supposed to love and revere. The ad demonstrates how even the recalcitrance of a wasted and abused artist can wind up as a handy marketing tool. Chrysler, a corporation that never would have dreamed of sustaining, much less supporting, Welles as an artist when he was alive—and surely wouldn't pay a tenth of what this ad cost to help make his unseen legacy available today—proudly invites us to join it in celebrating his artistry. Clearly they're onto something: loads of money can be made sustaining our self-applause for recognizing Welles's genius. But let's not be too quick about defining what this genius consists of. If we aren't careful, we may wind up honoring something quite different from what he accomplished.

Indeed, part of what continues to be fascinating about the unruly genius of Welles, seven years after his death, is how much it confounds the norms of commercial movies and conventional artistic careers on every conceivable level. Explaining who he was and what he did is a task that has already confounded at least half a dozen ambitious biographers, because the ordinary definitions, categories, and patterns of understanding generally prove to be not only inadequate but downright misleading.

Take CITIZEN KANE. At least three books on the subject exist, and all three assume a priori that it's a Hollywood classic—an assumption that winds up determining almost everything these books have to say about it. But although it was made in and released by a Hollywood studio, it shatters so many Hollywood norms that it seems debatable whether it's best understood as a Hollywood picture like CASABLANCA or SINGIN' IN THE RAIN as opposed to, say, an independent feature that uses certain Hollywood facilities (which is arguably how it was considered before the books came along). Yet it's in the interests of the Hollywood propaganda machine—which operates 24 hours a day, 365 days a year, in every branch of media (and most branches of academia, where "classical Hollywood cinema" and "the genius of the system" are current fashionable buzz terms)—to silence that debate. Central to this self-protective agenda is proving that serious alternatives to Hollywood don't exist—ergo CITIZEN KANE was not an alternative but part of the mainstream.

This even became a concern when KANE was reissued in a "restored" version last year; actually the only changes were in the brightness of some shots, so that the opening newsreel wasn't as grainy and the projection room sequence wasn't as dark—both obvious efforts to bring the movie closer to Hollywood norms. (These changes were made by Robert Wise, a onetime Welles associate who collaborated on Hollywood "improvements" of Welles's work as far back as THE MAGNIFICENT AMBERSONS.)

For these and related reasons, Welles is almost invariably considered a Hollywood director—and sometimes a failed one because he directed only six studio pictures over nearly half a century. But the six represent only about a third of his completed movies and a fourth of his film output—even though, thanks to the nonstop publicity mills and their gospel of production values, they're vastly better known and distributed than all the others. You might say that a yellow brick road has been paved by the media to allow us to reach those six Hollywood movies in video stores and on television; but to make it to most of the others we still don't have dirt paths or even maps. When it comes to unreleased, unfinished independent features like DON QUIXOTE, THE DEEP, and THE OTHER SIDE OF THE WIND, we may have to wait many more years for someone to put up the money to make them available. (In the case of QUIXOTE, we may not have to wait as long. The Spanish government has already stepped forward, and a feature-length film carved out of Welles's dozen or so hours premieres in Barcelona this spring; most of the original material is now permanently housed at the Filmoteca Española in Madrid. But how long will we have to wait before American distributors or cable television show any interest?)

If we consider just the completed films over which Welles had final and complete artistic control, only KANE and the 1950s television pilot THE

FOUNTAIN OF YOUTH even begin to qualify as Hollywood products. All the others—OTHELLO, THE TRIAL, CHIMES AT MIDNIGHT, THE IMMORTAL STORY, THE MERCHANT OF VENICE, F FOR FAKE, FILMING OTHELLO, and a few other television works—qualify as independent.

OTHELLO was the first of these, and in many ways it remains the most important and exciting of them as well. It's more significant to Welles's work as a whole than KANE, because it leads to much more in his subsequent oeuvre—and its long absence from American screens has been a major obstacle for anyone wishing to understand that oeuvre. Originally designed as an Italian studio production in 1948, the movie underwent a radical conceptual transformation after the producer went bankrupt and Welles decided to finance it out of his own pocket. Other changes followed; when the costumes failed to arrive for the shooting of Iago's murder of Roderigo, Welles spontaneously decided to film the scene in a Turkish bath, which allowed him to go on working without the costumes.

Shooting it piecemeal at other diverse locations in Morocco and Italy between 1948 and 1951—with bouts of acting and investor-chasing to pay the bills—Welles literally reinvented and recast the rudiments of his style in relation to this new method of filmmaking, which he continued to develop over the remainder of his life. In place of the long takes of his Hollywood work, he fragmented shots into jagged crazy-quilt patterns and syncopated rhythms, often favoring jarring discontinuities in the editing over the dovetailing continuities of KANE and AMBERSONS. Without benefit of studio tracks or cranes, he opted for a rougher, more vertiginous form of camera mobility that was arguably more physical as well as intimate (as in the evocations of Othello's epilepsy). The abnormal distances between people artificially created on RKO soundstages for Kane's mansion were rediscovered, then explored and amplified, in the architecture of Moorish castles and a Portuguese cistern—and thereby put to vastly different uses, as were the low angles composed in relation to this architecture. (Even a studio movie like TOUCH OF EVIL is radically different in its uses of locations and disorienting sound direction and distance from what it might have been without the experience of OTHELLO.)

Without the resources of Hollywood sound equipment, Welles aimed for a rawness in such sound effects as crashing waves, colliding curtain rings, and echoing footsteps. Drawing from his prodigious radio experience (which entailed producing a weekly show for almost nine years as well as two previous years of acting), he partly compensated for his inferior equipment with subtle atmospheric effects dubbed in later and integrated with the music. Ciro Giorgini, who has been interviewing OTHELLO crew members for an Italian documentary, wrote me that one of the production assistants told him that Welles stroked the strings of a piano to achieve a sound effect for the opening sequence and ordered a *spinetta*, an old form of harmonium, from Florence for other effects.

OTHELLO originally had no nationality; it was assigned one—Moroccan—

only when this became a legal necessity at the 1952 Cannes Film Festival, where it shared the top prize with TWO CENTS WORTH OF HOPE. Though Welles periodically lost financial control over the film afterward, it was never, to my knowledge, significantly altered or recut by others. After he made his essay film FILMING OTHELLO in the 1970s for German television, he suggested that a stipulation for showing the two films together at festivals—which he hoped would happen—would be showing OTHELLO in a decent print.

This point seems worth emphasizing in order to counter the erroneous impression, created for advertising purposes, that OTHELLO was ever a "lost" film. Good 35-millimeter prints still exist abroad, and the film was "lost" here only in the sense that FILMING OTHELLO lamentably still is: for an unconscionable number of years it had no American distribution. In other words, out of sight, out of mind—and anything not for sale is out of sight.

Welles was never a good businessman or salesman, but this hardly accounts for the cool American response when United Artists belatedly released OTHELLO in the fall of 1955 and brought in only $40,000. Reviewers tended to compare it unfavorably to Laurence Olivier's Shakespeare films, finding OTHELLO amateurish and self-indulgent in relation to the polish and production values of HENRY V and HAMLET. In some ways this response only repeated and amplified the objections to Welles's MACBETH seven years earlier: that Welles had done violence to the Shakespeare text, indulged himself, and made many of the lines unclear.

The main reason why they were supposedly unclear in MACBETH was the Scots accents, and Welles was obliged to edit and redub a second, shortened version without them. In the process we lost the first ten-minute take in a released Hollywood movie, a year before Hitchcock's ROPE. (The original version is now available on video, ten-minute take and all, and the lines are perfectly clear.) The lack of clarity of many lines in OTHELLO was partly blamed on faulty lip sync, most of which has been eliminated thanks to the painstaking work done in Chicago on the new version, although much of this has involved stretching or compressing some of the original line deliveries in ways that inevitably tamper with the recorded performances. Frankly, I've always thought that both of these "problems" were partially excuses for people intimidated by Shakespeare or by Welles's refusal to approach the playwright on his knees. There was a widespread conviction back then that the best thing movies could possibly do was serve up Shakespeare straight. Another part of the problem undoubtedly came from the Hollywood propaganda machine, which was in some ways even more effective then in marginalizing independent work than it is today. But if we recall that the Latin root of "amateur" is *amare*, "to love," Welles's romantic, impractical, and passionate commitment to his own work—quite the opposite of Olivier's bloodless professionalism—was the real scandal. "Fear of completion" may have been the charge that dogged him for most of the rest of his career, but it was clearly fear of *in*completion that brought him to the end of this particular adventure.

I saw OTHELLO on television in Alabama in my early teens—by sheer luck, it was the first Welles *or* Shakespeare movie I ever encountered—and was blown away by its dizzying mise en scène, its creepy horror-movie atmosphere (including the dank Moorish locations and the near-somnambulism of Welles's underplayed performance), and the eerie and awesome power of the modernist score (still one of the best in movies). When I later read American "experts" on the subject—people such as drama critic Eric Bentley—I was shocked by their violent disagreement:

> A film bad from every point of view and for every public. Technically, it is gauche, the dialogue being all too obviously dubbed. It lacks popular appeal, as the story is neither simply nor skillfully told. To connoisseurs of Shakespeare, it can only be torture. . . . If Mr. Welles's failure as director is partial, as actor it is complete. . . . He never acts, he is photographed. . . . I don't know what *The Daily Worker* said, but it missed a trick if it didn't hold up Mr. Welles as a prize example of individualistic, bourgeois culture in decay. To which I suggest adding that the whole film is a precise example of formalistic decadence.

In retrospect, I think I can see now what made Welles's first unambiguously independent film an act of even more courage and defiance than CITIZEN KANE. In KANE he was bucking only Hollywood and Hearst; with OTHELLO he was defying both Hollywood and academicians—not to mention the whole institutional setup for picture making itself, as it was then dimly understood by Bentley and others. Properly speaking, he had entered the treacherous domain of the avant-garde—probably against his own conscious wishes—and a substantial portion of the American intelligentsia never forgave him for it. From then on, with the unique exception of TOUCH OF EVIL, he would continue to make features only with the support of European producers—and not very many of those. Then he died, and folks like the Chrysler people came along to explain how much we'd loved, appreciated, and *sustained* him all along.

Some people wonder today how a leftist like Welles managed to escape or elude the McCarthy witch-hunts and blacklists of the early 1950s. The answer is that he was abroad at the time, striking out on his own—and not coincidentally filming a tale of treachery and paranoid suspicions, of jealousy and betrayal that reflected some of the traumas back home. Maybe some leftists got the message all too well, whether they consciously admitted it or not, and resented Welles's bid for his own freedom while they were suffering humiliations in the states.

It may not have been until the 1970s that a sober assessment of the film as a Shakespeare adaptation was offered, in Jack J. Jorgens's excellent *Shakespeare on Film*:

> Welles's OTHELLO is one of the few Shakespeare films in which the images on the screen generate enough beauty, variety, and graphic power to stand compar-

ison with Shakespeare's poetic images. His visual images compensate for the inevitable loss of complexity and dramatic voltage accompanying heavy alterations in the text.

A later part of Jorgens's analysis is so acute that Welles quotes it in FILM-ING OTHELLO:

> The visual style . . . mirrors the marriage at the center of the play—not the idyllic marriage of Othello and Desdemona, but the perverse marriage of Othello and Iago. . . . If the film's grandeur, hyperbole, and simplicity are the Moor's, its dizzying perspectives and camera movements, tortured compositions, grotesque shadows, and insane distortions are Iago's, for he is the agent of chaos.

■

As you can see, I'm more than a little excited by the prospect of a movie as wonderful as OTHELLO getting a second chance in this country. If any doubts remain, these mainly have to do with differing opinions about what Welles's OTHELLO is—and what its "restoration" consists of.

When Francis Coppola proudly presented the "complete" NAPOLÉON of Abel Gance at Radio City Music Hall in 1981, an entire subplot was excised so that the screening wouldn't run past midnight and jack up the theater's operating costs. If I'm not mistaken, the same subplot is missing from the NAPOLÉON that's now shown on video and cable in the United States, but not from the versions shown in Europe. Thanks to the complicity or indifference of the American press, most Americans who've seen NAPOLÉON are completely unaware of this tampering. But considering that Coppola's name was much larger than Gance's in the ads—even though it was Kevin Brownlow who carried out the restoration—maybe they assume that it's Coppola's film anyway, to do with it as he wishes.

No such deception has been carried out in the restoration of Orson Welles's OTHELLO; all the shots and ninety-one minutes are present and accounted for. But the aesthetic and historical issues raised by this new version are by no means simple, and the degree to which they've been mystified, obfuscated, and distorted in the press is unfortunate, because very few people who've seen the film in its present state have known what they were getting. Thus I'm fully in agreement with *The New York Times*'s Vincent Canby, who reviewed "an expertly restored print that should help to rewrite cinema history"—though not, I suspect, in the way Canby intended. Because the press as a whole has been rewriting cinema history by misdescribing what we have in front of us, some precise clarification is in order.

I've known Michael Dawson, the local coproducer (with Arnie Saks) of the restoration, for almost four years, and thanks to him was able to meet Beatrice Welles-Smith—Welles's youngest daughter, who authorized the restoration—two years ago. In connection with my own research projects on Welles, Dawson and I have found many occasions to exchange information and thoughts; although our philosophy of film restoration is not the same, it's been a friendly disagreement. Dawson's approach is almost exclusively technological, and his aim has been to bring OTHELLO's sound track in line with current commercial norms. But I believe state-of-the-art technology should ultimately be subservient to historical research that pinpoints as much as possible what's being preserved, altered, or discarded. Significantly, though Dawson eventually discovered that at least two distinctly different Welles-edited versions of OTHELLO exist—the first premiered at Cannes and the second in New York—he researched this point only *after* the restoration of the second version was virtually complete. (Apart from the Library of Congress, for instance, no film archives anywhere in the world were ever consulted.)

In short, rather than concentrate on the film's history, Dawson concentrated on the technical challenges of the assignment—a job, I should add, that he and his collaborators have carried out most impressively, especially given the limited time and money they had. Yet no serious attempt was made to acquire the manuscript of the late Francesco Lavignino's score (though it exists and is preserved by his family—contrary to claims made in the *Chicago Tribune* and elsewhere). Instead, conductor Michael Pendowski was asked to annotate what he heard to the best of his ability and then rerecord the music with members of the Chicago Symphony and Lyric Opera. The "redoing" of the sound effects in stereo was carried out by others in the same fashion. (This is considerably different from how the *Village Voice* reviewer claimed it was done: "The musical score was remastered . . . it's a bit like encountering a grimy monument that's recently been sandblasted." But then practically no press account I've read has accurately or adequately described the work done.) Consequently, whereas the visual work on the negative conforms mainly to a dictionary definition of restoration, the sound work obviously doesn't— qualifying instead as a highly subjective reworking of some of the original materials, a postmodernist dream *inspired* by the original OTHELLO sound track.*

To make matters more complicated, the film's New York distributor, Julian Schlossberg—whose name is as prominent in some ads as Francis Coppola's was in some ads for NAPOLÉON—has altered some of the sound work done in Chicago. I won't even attempt to sort out who made which decisions, but I should stress that the protechnological, ahistorical approach adopted at the outset was not deviated from significantly. The underlying assumption appears to be that contemporary sound technology can only improve Welles's

---

*At a Welles conference in Rome organized by Ciro Giorgini in October 1992, which I attended, the first reels of three separate versions of OTHELLO, including the "restoration," were screened in succession in the presence of a daughter of Francesco Lavignino, who maintained on that occasion that Pendowski's version of the music was not her father's work. Unhappily, a version of this ersatz score has since been issued commercially in the United States with no acknowledgment of any discrepancy and no communication with Lavignino's family. (1993)

original work because he had inferior equipment to work with. My own assumption is that Welles's aesthetic decisions are impossible to isolate from what he had to work with—and that includes a single microphone when the score was first recorded. Hollywood buffs might judge these results substandard, but when you start to tamper with the original choices, it's hard to know where to stop. (You might as well reshoot CITIZEN KANE in 3-D or Cinerama on the theory that if those technologies had been available to Welles in 1940 he surely would have used them.)

There are multiple consequences to this approach. Although one could again quarrel with the brightness or darkness of particular shots (especially because Welles's own specifications, given in relation to a fine-grain print held by the Library of Congress, were ignored in the final release version), there's no question that the new OTHELLO looks magnificent in terms of overall clarity. It also sounds wonderful, particularly if you place clarity and texture of voice and musical instrument over other criteria (such as fidelity to Welles's original sound conception). Nearly all the dialogue is in sync now, which is clearly an improvement, and Welles's own voice has never sounded better. But in many crucial respects, it's no longer a sound track by Welles. At best, it's a sound track using or imitating some elements from the original film and not using or imitating others—and changing the relationships *between* those elements in the bargain. To put it bluntly, the new version looks and sounds like a different movie, and state-of-the-art equipment or not, a lesser one.

The atmospheric effects cited above (such as Welles stroking piano strings and the use of a *spinetta*) are of course missing, though I suppose it could be argued that they weren't sufficiently audible in the original to inspire imitation. My problem is that what the original sounds like is more a matter of personal interpretation than one of scientific analysis, and I'd rather trust Welles on this matter than Pendowski (who freely admitted to me he's not familiar with Lavignino's other work, which includes three other scores for Welles productions of Shakespeare). Even with the best will and mimicry in the world, most of the *precise* elements of the music and sound effects as supervised by Welles—specific performances, textures, and tonalities—are no longer part of the film. Neither, for that matter, is the chanting of Latin by monks in the funeral procession in the film's remarkable opening sequence—a prolonged hushed recitation that serves effectively both as a diminuendo after the music ends and as a tapering sound bridge to the silence that follows in both Welles-edited versions of the film. Why this major part of Welles's sound design has simply been deleted from the scene is anyone's guess, although I'm told that it may be restored in the video and laserdisc versions.*

Where Welles and his crew got the sound of their crashing waves straight from the Mediterranean, the Chicago crew uses Lake Michigan. Where La-

*It was. (1993)

vagnino's score at one point, according to Welles, used forty mandolins at once, Pendowski's approximation, according to Pendowski, never uses more than three or four. Moreover, Pendowski had nothing to do with the rerecording of the sound effects, and one could argue that one's sense in the original of music and sounds being aesthetically *integrated* is significantly reduced. The use of stereo adds further complications, involving many aesthetic choices Welles never had to make.

Interestingly enough, Welles had briefly explored the possibility of recording MACBETH—the film before OTHELLO, done entirely in a studio—in stereo, but I've found no clues about how he might have used it. Considering his eclecticism and originality, I seriously doubt that he would have followed the standard contemporary Hollywood practice of placing all the voices behind the screen and dispersing the sound effects and music through the other speakers, as has been done in this version. This has the effect of "normalizing" OTHELLO in a way analogous to the mainstreaming of KANE—making it conform to a current Hollywood model of correctness. Certainly the dynamic relationship between dialogue, music, and sound effects is profoundly altered from the OTHELLO I know and love; the percussive assault of the music in the opening sequence, for instance, is substantially reduced by virtue of being spread out like butter rather than brought to a sharp monaural point that pierces one's consciousness. The single most important aesthetic change that results from this—at least in my own subjective impressions—is that the film is no longer as spooky and creepy as it was; the spectral chill in its bones, which once made me think of NOSFERATU, has largely disappeared. (Then again, maybe if NOSFERATU were "sandblasted" and refurbished, it wouldn't remind me of NOSFERATU either.)

The original OTHELLO hasn't been destroyed (at least, not yet). It's simply being kept from the eyes and ears of Americans for business reasons, much as the longer version of Gance's NAPOLÉON is. With most of the dialogue now in sync, more of it can be understood now than ever before; Bentley's complaint that it is "all too obviously dubbed" still holds true, but to a lesser degree. Whether Europeans, who've never expressed discomfort with the original version, will welcome an "improved" one—albeit in a Welles cut that they may not have seen before—remains to be seen. But we should certainly rush out and see the new OTHELLO and marvel at everything Welles brought to it. Whether we should regard it as a model for restorations to come is quite another matter.

Part Three

Filmmakers

Introduction

I should begin here with a somewhat embarrassed confession about a methodology I have employed with increasing frequency, especially since the mid-1980s—the practice of recycling certain elements from my earlier criticism. On a purely practical level, it can of course be argued that very few people who read me in, say, the *Monthly Film Bulletin* in 1974 are likely to be following my weekly columns in the *Chicago Reader* two decades later, and that my pieces for *Soho News* in 1980 (to cite another random example) are not likely to have survived in the periodical collections of many libraries. But I still blush to admit that, in a hatchet job I performed on Donald Richie's book on Ozu for *Sight and Sound* in 1975, I sharply reproached Richie for re-using the same phrases about Ozu again and again in his own criticism. This was written at a relatively early stage in my own career when I imagined other film buffs like myself going to libraries and reading virtually everything in print on a given topic; I didn't really think through the implications of writing about the same films and filmmakers for different audiences in separate countries over many decades—as Richie had certainly already done at that point, and as I have subsequently done. Maybe we're both lazy, but it seems to me that the degree of purity I was expecting is both unreasonable and unrealistic, especially when it comes to freelance writers; Michel Ciment suggested as much in the pages of *Positif* when he commented adversely on my presumption.

To be fair to myself on this score, I usually don't plagiarize myself literally (as some writers are wont to do) when I carry out this practice but, rather, use something I've already written as a starting point or springboard—something to get my writer's crank in motion, as it were. (As an excellent cure for writer's block—at least if one is working on the same piece in more than one sitting—I can recommend starting each work day by either revising or simply retyping the final page of one's last work session, which often allows the momentum of one's previous efforts to carry one over the rough spots into fresh material.) In the case of my article on Raúl Ruiz in the next section, however, the material went through four stages or incarnations. It began as a relatively short piece written for the January 1985 *Monthly Film Bulletin*; then some elements from that piece were used in another short article commissioned by the Toronto Festival of Festivals for a bilingual booklet (English and French) devoted to a retrospective called "Ten to Watch." Then I did a much longer piece for volume 3 of *Cinematograph* in 1987, edited by my friend Christine Tamblyn—an annual publication of the San Francisco Cinematheque which encourages a certain amount of formal experimentation; and finally, I revised and updated this piece slightly for the January 1990 issue of Noah Forde's wonderfully eclectic and occasional Los Angeles film magazine, *Modern Times*, in the version reprinted here.

My second contribution to *Cinematograph*, written for volume 4, edited by Jeffrey Skoller—an issue devoted to nonfiction film—was "Orson Welles's Essay Films and Documentary Fictions: A Two-Part Speculation," probably the most formally playful of the articles in this section. As with the Ruiz piece, part of the reason for the formal play was an attempt at mimetic criticism—that is, an attempt to reproduce some of the formal and stylistic qualities of the work I'm describing (an ambition that can be found to varying degrees elsewhere in this collection, in pieces on Godard's criticism, Barthes, Farber, MÉLO, and Rivette, among others). But another part, I should confess, came from a more purely formalist and even capricious desire to follow certain arbitrary rules and patterns in creating a series of mirroring structures between the various sections of the piece. This is why, for instance, the first two sections begin with "two propositions" that are followed by two lists—the first list containing twelve items, the second containing twenty-four. Then, after two more sections dealing respectively with THE FOUNTAIN OF YOUTH and FILMING OTHELLO (each of which, I should add, represents recycled material—the first, an article written for the 1986 National Video Festival catalog; the second, program notes written for New York's Film Forum in 1987), the last two sections and the final section devoted to footnotes are all built around lists containing eight items each. If a thematic excuse for this exercise is needed, I suppose it could be argued that the mirror structures have bearing on both the arbitrary nature of separating fiction and nonfiction that affects film criticism in general (and some Welles criticism in particular) and the sense of formal play that I find in much of Welles's work.

■

"Work and Play in the House of Fiction," my last major effort written in Paris before I moved to London, is the result of my obsession with two of

Jacques Rivette's films, OUT 1: SPECTRE and CELINE AND JULIE GO BOATING, which I had been seeing, reseeing, and compulsively discussing in Paris with my best friends at the time—Eduardo de Gregorio (Rivette's screenwriter during this period, who worked on CELINE AND JULIE), Gilbert Adair, and Lauren Sedofsky—for most of that year. With Gilbert and Lauren, I had just interviewed Rivette in my Left Bank apartment for *Film Comment*, and I had greatly benefited from being able to attend several private screenings of the work print of CELINE AND JULIE and many showings of OUT 1: SPECTRE during its brief commercial run at Studio Gît-le-coeur.* I had not, however, attended the only public screening of the 760-minute work print OUT 1: NOLI ME TANGERE in Le Havre three years earlier, and another fifteen years would pass before I was finally able to see the film—to my mind Rivette's greatest—in a finished (i.e., fully processed) print, at the Rotterdam Film Festival in early 1989. Apart from the fact that forty-five minutes of the sound track were still unlocated at this stage, this was the film's world premiere, and its presentation at Rotterdam was one of the last great efforts of Hubert Bals, the festival's director, who had died the previous July. But, sad to say, my eventual catching up with this masterpiece occurred during a period that can only be described as postcinematic: only two other people stuck it out for the entire screening (it was shown over two or three days, as the consecutive reels arrived from France), and even after the film later resurfaced on French and German television as an eight-episode serial and in other European venues, it was almost entirely ignored. Not even *Cahiers du Cinéma* could be bothered to write about it, though it strikes me as being *the* key film about the 1960s. Apparently we'll have to wait for a more aesthetically and historically enlightened era for the film to be discovered and appreciated for its staggering achievement.

■

The inclusion of one personal memoir (about Tati) in this section raises the wider question of what role this kind of material can or should play in criticism. The value of knowing something about an artist's intentions as well as various forms of production, preproduction, and postproduction information has to be weighed against the potential danger of such material supplanting criticism entirely and becoming indistinguishable from publicity— the "infotainment" syndrome and the cult of personality where intentionality (whether that of the artist or the publicist) reigns supreme and the groupie mindset is seldom far away. In the establishment of auteurism during the late

---

*As further signs of my Rivette mania, the following year, thanks to Eduardo, I twice flew from London to France to watch several days of the shooting of the next two Rivette films— DUELLE in Paris and NOROÎT in Brittany. My last sustained work in London was editing a collection of Rivette texts and interviews for the BFI and organizing a "Rivette in Context" season at the National Film Theatre; two years later, in New York, I presented a revised version of this season with Jackie Raynal at the Bleecker Street Cinema.

1960s and early 1970s, the role played by interviews with directors—in the pages of such magazines as *Cahiers du Cinéma, Positif,* and *Movie,* as well as in such books as Truffaut's *Hitchcock* and Peter Bogdanovich's interviews with Hitchcock, Hawks, Lang, and Ford—was perhaps even more influential than the role played by reviews and critical essays.

I'm very much of two minds about this issue. As is obvious from this book so far, my criticism tends to be highly partisan and even promotional when it comes to certain filmmakers I support. Part of what pushes me in this direction, however, is a desire to be heard at all against the onslaught of mainstream media promotion and hype that dominates our film discourse—and dominated it long before the relatively recent rise of infotainment. In other words, against the argument that Godard is his own best publicist and that his spiels are therefore inappropriate as critical tools in evaluating his work, one has to consider the fact that the massive amounts and reaches of publicity accorded to much less interesting and talented filmmakers have lulled most critics into docile acquiescence, which suggests that "mere" publicity for the work, ideas, and even personality of Godard constitutes a critical and even polemical act in such a climate. Considering both the extent to which all "coverage" is promotional in one way or another and the monstrous inequities that exist whenever money is concerned (which is virtually always when it comes to film), I've never considered it to be an ethical problem in promoting relatively unpopular or unknown work over relatively popular and well-known work, because most of the mechanisms that promote popularity and knowledge in movies have nothing whatsoever to do with critical values.*

As one extreme example of these mechanisms, let me cite the curious case of my dealings with the Chicago office of Warner Brothers, which did not invite me to any of its press screenings for nearly three years—the only local film company that has ever behaved in such a fashion, and one whose policy in this matter was initially confirmed and protected on the highest multinational levels of Warner Communications. The reason for this blackballing was an incident that occurred in early 1991. A local film critic called one day to reschedule a lunch date because he wanted to attend a screening of NEW JACK CITY that had just been set up. I hadn't been invited to the screening, and when I asked my friend if he thought I could attend it myself, he suggested I call Warners' local publicist, but asked me not to reveal who had told me about the screening, which was supposed to be a secret. The publicist, a Warners employee since the late 1950s, is known among Chicago film critics for his sensitivity about such matters, but I decided it wouldn't hurt to ask. I was sadly mistaken.

---

*After my piece on KING LEAR appeared in 1988, I received a note from Tom Luddy, the producer, informing me that he'd sent the piece to Godard, who told him to tell me that he really liked it. Considering Godard's customary reticence on such matters, I can think of few compliments that I've treasured more.

When I phoned the publicist was out, so I asked his assistant if I could attend, and she didn't imagine there would be any problem. About an hour later, however, my phone rang, and when I picked it up the publicist began screaming at me and demanding to know who had told me about the NEW JACK CITY screening. I said I didn't remember, and when he persisted in badgering me I came up with the name of one of the most prominent local critics—not the one who had told me, but one who I thought was least likely to be hurt by being named. "You're lying!" the publicist screamed, and went on to explain why he knew I was lying before hanging up on me. A few minutes later he rang up again and screamed at me some more. I told him I had only called in the first place to ask if I could attend the screening, and if he didn't want me to come, I wouldn't. He said he didn't want me to and hung up again; my name was promptly removed from the invitational list for Warners screenings. A few weeks afterward, I recounted the above story in my *Reader* column about GUILTY BY SUSPICION, a Warners feature about the Hollywood blacklist (see "Guilty by Omission" in part 5), not merely as a relatively trivial example of how it felt to be blacklisted, but also as a sort of mea culpa regarding my own unheroic behavior in the incident—the fact that my first impulse was to lie to the publicist rather than openly defy him, as I did later. About two years after this column appeared (as well as a subsequent and relatively uninformed story in *Variety* about the original incident), the chairman of the National Society of Film Critics wrote a friendly letter to the publicist on my behalf, mentioning in passing that my paper had a circulation of about a third of a million. About a year afterward, in early 1994, after both the chairman and Michael Wilmington of the *Chicago Tribune* made further appeals to Warners' west coast office on my behalf, I was finally invited to Warners screenings again. (Prior to that, I still saw and reviewed some Warners films, usually a week or more after other reviewers, but wound up missing more of their movies than those of any other major studio.)

The point of such an aberrant anecdote is that, in spite of the eccentricity of the Warners publicist—who clearly valued his own satisfaction in this matter over the curiosity of my 330,000 or so readers—it really isn't so aberrant after all. From my own experience both as a critic and as an occasional observer of the film industry, I would say that this industry operates to a surprising degree on just such arbitrary peccadilloes and demonstrations of personal power, exercised more for their own sake on many occasions than for the sake of any higher principles—including even business principles. The rise and fall of many reputations within this scheme—and I'm thinking now of people like stars and directors rather than publicists or critics—often seem determined by these ferocious yet arbitrary hobbyhorses, which carry the force of law once they're extended beyond studios and their publicity machines and into the critical discourse itself. The spectacle of seeing these matters helping to determine in many cases what the rest of the country thinks about various movies and people is both comical and monstrous, but, I would venture to say, it happens on some level or another in the world of movies every day of the week, simply because the film industry itself—which, practically speaking, includes the press—is an organism largely made up of thwarted bureaucrats who dream of exercising *some* kind of power any way they possibly can, regardless of its ultimate meaning or consequences. Whether the final decision is that of a producer, director, distributor, publicist, exhibitor, or journalist-reviewer, the degree to which irrational impulses ultimately hold sway in certain matters should never be underestimated.

■

An issue somewhat related to the matter of interviews with directors is the question of whether a critic can or should write about the work of his own friends—and, to broach a related question, whether a film critic should allow himself or herself to become friends with filmmakers in general. Some of my more serious colleagues have studiously endeavored (with mixed results) to avoid such friendships and the potential conflicts of interest they could give rise to. In my own case, I happen to be friends with a good many filmmakers that I (usually) support, although most of these—such as Sara Driver, Sam Fuller, Jon Jost, Mark Rappaport, Raúl Ruiz, Peter Thompson, and Leslie Thornton—are filmmakers I initially supported before I ever became friends with them. (For the record, the only piece in this book written *after* I became friends with the filmmaker in question is the one on Fuller's WHITE DOG.) One of my best friends, however, is an English experimental filmmaker, Peter Gidal, whose films I've rarely supported in print and have even on occasion attacked, although I find some of his theoretical positions interesting even when I disagree with them. Relatively early in my career, I nearly lost one friend, Eduardo de Gregorio, because of my failure to write about his first feature, SÉRAIL, when it showed at the Edinburgh Film Festival. Since then, I've generally been luckier and more successful in negotiating such matters, which are seldom easy.

■

My review of MÉLO represented something of a test case for me at the *Reader* because it ran to eighteen typed pages in manuscript. Michael Lenehan, the editor, responded that many readers probably wouldn't get to the end of this piece and that I shouldn't make a habit of writing reviews this long; but he generously agreed to run it without cuts. I don't know in fact how many readers got to the end of the review, but I was gratified to discover that MÉLO wound up having a longer and more successful run in Chicago than it did in New York or Los Angeles. Much of this was undoubtedly due to Dave Kehr's highly favorable review in the *Chicago Tribune*, but I'd like to imagine that my piece played some small role in this process as well.

Since I've been at the *Reader*, I've had nine different editors at one point or another. (The choice of who edits me each week usually depends on the amount of other work she or he has at the time.) After I turn in each column, I'm shown the editor's major changes and queries and allowed to respond to them—a process of negotiation that always involves contesting certain changes, accepting others, and arriving at mutual solutions or compromises in still other cases. As I've discovered in my own endeavors in editing the prose of Truffaut, Welles, and Bogdanovich, the best editing is usually the kind the reader is least aware of, though the supreme masters of this game—who within my experience are probably Penelope Houston and Michael Lenehan—sometimes manage to minimize the awareness of the writer as well. (Conversely, the worst editors are those who render one's prose unrecognizable; one of these effectively kept me from writing for *Film Comment* for years.)

Work and Play in the House of Fiction

On Jacques Rivette

In the spring of 1970, Jacques Rivette shot about thirty hours of improvisation with over three dozen actors. Out of this massive and extremely open-ended material have emerged two films, both of which contrive to subvert the traditional moviegoing experience at its roots. OUT 1, lasting twelve hours and forty minutes, has been screened publicly only once (at Le Havre, 9–10 September 1971) and remains for all practical purposes an invisible, legendary work. (Its subtitle, significantly, is NOLI ME TANGERE.) SPECTRE, which Rivette spent the better part of a year editing out of the first film—running 255 minutes, or roughly a third as long—was released in Paris earlier this year. And during the interval between the editing of SPECTRE and its release, Rivette shot and edited a third film, CÉLINE ET JULIE VONT EN BATEAU, 195 minutes in length, which surfaced in Cannes last May.

The differences between SPECTRE and CÉLINE ET JULIE VONT EN BATEAU are considerable: they are respectively the director's "heaviest" film and his "lightest," probably the least and most accessible of his six features to date. Both of them clearly situate Rivette in the forefront of narrative innovation in contemporary French cinema, exhibiting a sophistication about the entire fiction-making process that seems to go well beyond the recent efforts of his peers. On a narrative level, one might say that they resume a line of development abandoned by Resnais after LAST YEAR AT MARIENBAD and MURIEL, and by Godard after 2 OR 3 THINGS I KNOW ABOUT HER and MADE IN U.S.A.

To have fused many of the concerns of these separate lines of inquiry is remarkable enough. What is more remarkable still is that Rivette has extended them, into the outer reaches of a terrain that the following notes can only attempt to sketch.

1

[Ornette Coleman's *Free Jazz*] causes earache the first time
through, especially for those new to Coleman's music. The second
time, its cacophony lessens and its complex balances and counter-
balances begin to take effect. The third time, layer upon layer of
pleasing configurations—rhythmic, melodic, contrapuntal, tonal—
becomes visible. The fourth or fifth listening, one swims readily
along, about ten feet down, breathing the music like air.

—Whitney Balliett, "Abstract," in
Dinosaurs in the Morning

If there is something comforting—religious, if you want—about
paranoia, there is still also anti-paranoia, where nothing is connected to anything, a condition not many of us can bear for long.

—Thomas Pynchon, Gravity's Rainbow

The organizing principle adopted by Rivette in shooting the raw material
of OUT 1 and SPECTRE was the notion of a *complot* (plot, conspiracy) derived
from Balzac's *Histoire des treize*, where thirteen individuals occupying different sectors of French society form a secret alliance to consolidate their
power. Consciously setting out to make a critique of the conspiratorial *zeit-
geist* of his first feature, PARIS NOUS APPARTIENT, Rivette also used this principle to arrange meetings and confrontations between his actors, each of whom
was invited to invent and improvise his own character in relation to the overall intrigue.

It should be noted that repeated viewings of SPECTRE help to clarify not its
"plot" but its formal organization. The analogy suggested above between
Rivette and Coleman is far more relevant, however, to the notion of *performance*. Much like Coleman's thirty-eight-minute venture into group improvisation with seven other musicians, SPECTRE's surface is dictated by accom-
modations, combinations, and clashes brought about by contrasting styles of
"playing." The textures run the gamut from the purely cinematic skills of
Jean-Pierre Léaud and Juliet Berto to the stage-bound techniques of Françoise Fabian; from the nervousness of Michel Lonsdale to the placidity of
Jacques Doniol-Valcroze; from the reticence of Bulle Ogier to the garrulity of
Bernadette Lafont.

For Coleman as for Rivette, the thematic material is kept to a minimum
and mainly used as an expedient—a launching pad to propel each solo player
into a "statement" of his own that elicits responses from the others. Apart from
the brief ensemble passages written by Coleman, there is no composer behind
Free Jazz, hence no composition; the primary role of Coleman as leader is to
assemble players and establish a point of departure for their improvising.

Rivette's role in SPECTRE is similar, with the crucial difference that he edits and rearranges the material afterward, assembling shots as well as players. And the assembly is one that works *against* the notion of continuity: sustained meaning, the province of an *auteur*, is deliberately withheld—from the audience as well as the actors. Consequently, it is hardly surprising that the "13" in SPECTRE never reveals itself as anything more than a chimera. By the time the film is two-thirds over, it is evident that the *complot* is a pipe dream that never got off the ground, an idea once discussed among thirteen individuals that apparently went no further. Aside from the efforts of certain characters (mainly Lonsdale and Fabian) to keep its real or hypothetical existence hidden, and the attempts or threats of others (Léaud, Berto, Ogier) to "expose" it, the "13" never once assumes a recognizable shape—in the dialogue or on the screen.

SPECTRE begins by pretending to tell us four separate stories at once. We watch two theater groups rehearsing *Prometheus Bound* (directed by Lonsdale) and *Seven Against Thebes* (a collective), and also observe Léaud and Berto—two rather crazed and curious loners, each of whom tricks strangers in cafés out of money. (Léaud impersonates a deaf-mute; Berto usually starts by flirting.) For the first thirty-five shots—ten of them black-and-white stills accompanied by an electronic hum—Rivette cuts between these four autonomous units, establishing no plot connections. The only links set up are occasional formal repetitions: a scene echoed by a subsequent still, two pans in separate shots of Léaud and Berto in their rooms. Even within each unit, many shots are either "too long" or "too short" to be conventionally assimilable as narrative. Rivette often cuts in the middle of a sentence or a movement, and the missing pieces are not always recuperated. Conversely, a shot in which Léaud's concierge reminds him to leave his key ends irrelevantly with her walking away from the camera and sitting down at a table to write. Like some of the cryptic stills punctuating later portions of the film, such a diversion proposes—without ever substantiating—yet another supplementary fiction.

Then almost miraculously, in the thirty-sixth shot, two of the four "plots" are brought together: Léaud is suddenly handed a slip of paper by a member of the theater collective. On it is typed a seemingly coded message which he sets out to decipher, along with a subsequent message he receives, following clues provided by references to Balzac and "The Hunting of the Snark" (the former gracefully explained by Eric Rohmer in a cameo role). And when Léaud's deductions eventually lead him to a hippy boutique called "l'Angle du hasard," the "plot" appreciably thickens: the boutique is run by Ogier, whom we later discover is a friend of both Lonsdale and Michèle Moretti, another member of the collective; and all three are members of the alleged "13."

Meanwhile, Berto, the fourth narrative strand, has been making some unwitting connections of her own. After stealing letters from the flat of Doniol-

Valcroze (another one of the "13," along with his wife, Françoise Fabian) for the purpose of possible blackmail, she dons a wig and arranges a meeting with Fabian: an incongruous match suggesting Mickey Rooney versus Rohmer's Maud. Then, when she fails to collect money, she turns up at the boutique to try the same ploy with Ogier.

This second encounter marks the fusion of all four "plots," and occurs just before the film's intermission. It is the only time Berto and Léaud ever cross paths (they are the only important characters who never meet), and the spectator may well feel at this point that he is finally being led out of chaos. But the second half of SPECTRE, after drawing the four strands together more tightly, proceeds to unravel them again; and the final hour leaves us as much in the dark as we were in the first.

Indeed, the delivery of the first message to Léaud is totally gratuitous, an act that is never explained, and most of the other "connections" are brought about by equally expedient contrivances. In a country house occupied at various times by Lafont, Lonsdale, Ogier, and Moretti, Rivette parodies the very notion of "hidden meaning" in a subtler way, by making sure that a single nondescript bust with no acknowledged relation to the "plot" is visible in every room. It even crops up in the locked room possibly inhabited by Igor, Ogier's missing husband, a room she enters only near the end of the film. Obviously the bust is a joke; but why is it there? To suggest a *complot*. And according to the tactics of SPECTRE, suggesting a *complot* is at once an absurdity and a necessity: it leads us nowhere except forward.

■

Complot, in short, becomes the motivation behind a series of transparent gestures: spectres of action playing over a void. We watch actors playing at identity and meaning the way that children do, with many of the games leading to dead ends or stalemates, some exhausting themselves before they arrive anywhere, and still others creating solid roles and actions that dance briefly in the theater of the mind before dissolving into something else. Nothing remains fixed, and everything becomes ominous. Relentlessly investigated by Léaud and blindly exploited by Berto, the spectre of the "13" reactivates the paranoia of its would-be members, mainly increasing the distances between them. Other crises intervene (a stranger runs off with the money of an actor in the collective; Ogier threatens to publish the intercepted letters); fear begets fear; both theater groups disperse; Ogier and Moretti are last seen driving off to meet the perpetually missing Igor; and Berto and Léaud are each returned to their isolation. Repeated "empty" shots of Place d'Italie in the final reel—chilling mixtures of Ozu-like emptiness with Langian terror—embody this growing sense of void, which ultimately widens to swallow up everything else in the film.

Much as *folie à deux* figures centrally in L'AMOUR FOU and CÉLINE ET

JULIE VONT EN BATEAU, failed *folie à deux* gradually becomes the very essence of SPECTRE. The inability to "connect" reveals itself as part and parcel of the incapacity to sustain fictions, a failure registering most poignantly in the relationship of Ogier and Léaud, which begins with mutual attraction and ends in estrangement. Of all the "two-part inventions" in SPECTRE, theirs is the richest in shifting tensions, and the growing rift is brilliantly underlined by the staging of their scenes in the boutique—particularly when they're stationed in adjoining rooms on opposite sides of the screen, each vying in a different way for our attention. This spatial tension reaches its climax in their last scene together, on the street, when Ogier forcibly breaks away and Léaud mimes the invisible barrier between them by pushing at it in agonized desperation, finally wandering in a diagonal trajectory out of the frame while blowing a dissonant wail on his harmonica.

"It didn't work," he feebly confesses in the film's final shot, after repeatedly trying to make his Eiffel tower trinket swing back and forth exactly thirteen times. Speaking for the audience and the other actors/characters as well as for Rivette and himself, he is testifying to the impossibility of a sustained pattern or meaning. On the deepest level, he is expressing an anguished agnosticism toward *all* fiction, directing a frightened stare into the face of intractable reality.

An infernal machine programmed to arouse narrative expectations in order to frustrate them, begin stories in order to contradict or cancel them, SPECTRE cruelly exposes the artifices of cinematic fiction by revealing many of the precise ways that they play on our reflexes. The scenes of violence that figure in the second half—Ogier's murder of a messenger (played by the film's producer!) and the brutal beating of Berto by a leather jacket named Marlon (Jean-François Stévenin)—are especially disturbing in this respect. They perform the ritualistic role of supplying "action" and "excitement" at junctures when we probably feel that they're most sorely needed, yet the reasons for these actions are so enigmatic that they fulfill no other visible function.

Even more than Rivette's other features, SPECTRE is built around a series of profound contradictions. Its apparent subject and substance is group effort, yet what it finally conveys is entropy and isolation. The extraordinary freedom of the shooting is counteracted by the aggressive constraint of the montage. One could reproach the film for having either "too little" or "too much"— a paradox reflected in the title, which suggests all colors (spectrum) as well as none (the transparency of a ghost). Without proposing any sort of influence, it is interesting to compare the title of *Gravity's Rainbow*, another recent work oscillating between form and formlessness, plotting and chaos, a compulsive desire to control the world and an equally strong desire to leave it alone—a novel, in fact, that proceeds to tie and untie its strands with a similar duplicity of purpose and diffusion of focus.

Before editing SPECTRE, Rivette spoke in a *Le Monde* interview of wanting to make it "not a digest of the long version, but another film having its own logic: closer to a puzzle or a crossword game, playing less on affectivity and more on rhymes or oppositions, ruptures or connections, caesuras or censorships." But it is a game that one submits to rather than plays, for it offers no chances of winning. One can sit before it as though at a tribunal—facing an Inquisition that repeatedly asks "Why?"—or one can watch it like network television, and ignore the contradictions as if they were commercial breaks, viewing it all as pure spectacle. Or—likelier still, alas—one can get caught between these two possibilities, and intermittently become bored. A do-it-yourself kit, SPECTRE has no singular experience to convey, but a set of raw materials. Like Léaud in the film, we can concoct plenty of formulas out of them. A submerged history of the splinterings and disaffections of *Cahiers du Cinéma* after 1968? A film as steeped in silences as certain works by Webern? A semi-Sadean exposure of a lot of personal traits that actors generally seek to hide, particularly uncertainty and fear? Or a flight into the unknown seeking no "success" or predetermined destination, only adventure?

SPECTRE isn't easy going for anyone, nor was it intended to be. Leaving its audience and its actors each suspended over a void, it offers itself as a dead-end experiment that can be neither emulated nor repeated—although it certainly will be learned from for years to come. Going further in self-annihilating narrative than any director before him, Rivette has burned up all the ground beneath his feet.

2

All in the golden afternoon
    Full leisurely we glide;
For both our oars, with little skill,
    By little arms are plied,
While little hands make vain pretence
    Our wanderings to guide.

—Alice in Wonderland

Without, the frost, the blinding snow,
    The storm wind's moody madness—
Within, the firelight's ruddy glow
    And childhood's nest of gladness.
The magic words shall hold thee fast:
Thou shalt not heed the raving blast.

—Through the Looking Glass

CÉLINE ET JULIE VONT EN BATEAU is like a picnic thrown on one of the sections of this charred terrain: a Mad Tea Party with a colorful crazy-quilt tablecloth, loony guests, inspired after-dinner games, and plenty of sweets to eat. Try to catch hold of it and it hurtles ahead like the White Rabbit, and down into a nostalgic burrow where dreams and memory play. More than any other Rivette work, it is about the cinema—what it's like to watch and what it's like to create. Unlike LA NUIT AMÉRICAINE, it pursued this subject only by analogy and through evocation.

Ostensibly, the film is about Julie (Dominique Labourier), a librarian with a taste for magic books and Tarot cards, and Céline (Juliet Berto), a cabaret magician whom she first encounters hurrying past her in the opening scene. The initial setting is Montmartre, and the central action comprises the daily visits paid in turn by each girl to a haunted house, from which she emerges looking ravished and stunned, with a piece of candy on her tongue and no memory of what transpired inside—until she eats the candy, which affords an immediate (if scrambled) playback of a Victorian melodrama featuring a little girl named Madlyn, her widower father Olivier (Barbet Schroeder, the movie's producer), two scheming ladies named Camille (Bulle Ogier) and Sophie (Marie-France Pisier), and Miss Angèle, Madlyn's nurse, who is played alternately by Céline or Julie.

To encapsulate the film's point of departure in two overcrowded sentences is to point up its outlandishness, but not the spirited fluidity with which it is made to happen on a screen. As Rivette has indicated, the candy plays an analogous role to the use of Balzac in SPECTRE—a narrative mechanism designed to permit passageway between separate fictional worlds. But while the separate worlds of SPECTRE tend to contradict or cancel one another, the double plot of CÉLINE ET JULIE does precisely the reverse: the two girls in Montmartre clearly *generate* the story in the house, just as surely as the strange happenings there spawn and enrich the antics of their life outside. And if the skepticism toward fiction in SPECTRE leads to transparent actions playing over a void, CÉLINE ET JULIE is like a game of catch played over the same void, with the ball tossed back and forth remaining solid as long as it is kept in motion.

The presence of another, contiguous world lying just beyond the visible one is established in the opening shot. We watch Julie idly smoking on a park bench, and hear an off-screen rasping noise that seems momentarily threatening because it is still undefined. (The next shot reveals that she is drawing a circle on the ground with her foot.) Everything that follows works toward a related impression: Julie's red magic book, wind in the trees, the voices of unseen children, a cat darting from one bench to another before alighting gracefully on the ground and waiting—all create a mood of pregnant pause and magical suspension in which anything at all might happen . . .

At which point Céline appears, trailing sunglasses, a scarf, and a wrap behind her. And as Julie takes off in pursuit, we have already embarked on an adventure that goes beyond the boundaries of everyday logic. For the chase is no ordinary event at all—with Céline ever so firmly leading Julie on, and both girls frequently slowing their flight down to a leisurely stroll. The direct sound punctuating their path through a very picturesque Montmartre is occasionally overlaid by incidental piano music. (Rouch spiced with a dash of Minnelli?) Even the precise documentary *look* of their journey is casually subverted by certain controlled and flamboyant details, like a steady recurrence of the color red—and more important, the beginning of a series of doublings, such as the fact that each girl takes off her shoes at a different stage in the pursuit.

Doubling is indeed an essential part of the film's structure, figuring between the two plots as well as between the two girls. Shortly after the chase, in the library where Julie works, we find the screen split between the girls in unacknowledged proximity (recalling scenes of Léaud and Ogier in SPECTRE): in the background, Céline traces her hand in a children's book with a red Magic Marker, while in the foreground Julie makes red fingerprints with an inking pad. Much later, the traumatic climax of the story in the haunted house shows Madlyn smothered in bed, with the mark of a bloody hand imprinted on her pillow; and the cast of a red hand is one of the many playthings bandied about in Julie's flat. One might say, in short, that in the course of the film all four women are caught literally red-handed in the act of plotting.

After the library scene, we find Julie back in the park (the children visible this time), where she chants a magic spell, closes her eyes, and the camera cuts—to Julie again in long shot. Then she returns to her flat, encounters Céline on the stairs, and ushers her in to let her take a shower and to bandage her bloody knee. (Both *these* acts are later "doubled": Julie takes a shower, and Miss Angèle attends to a wound on Camille's hand.) Céline launches at once into one of her preposterous tall tales, about tigers and pygmies, and soon after she alludes to a mysterious house, Julie begins to help by supplying some of the details. ("And the women—were they dark or fair?" "Both. Dark and fair.")

And the next morning, before Julie sets off for the house in question, it is she and not Céline who comes up with the address. (To confound causality further, a snapshot of the house is subsequently discovered in Julie's trunk.) Similarly, it is Céline who turns up to meet Gilou, Julie's absurdly romantic boyfriend from Brittany—a rather pathetic figure who apparently needs to be dispensed with in order to clear the way for Olivier, his novelistic counterpart, who boasts a comparably Heathcliffian profile. Offhandedly exchanging roles and lives as well as clothes, each heroine sets off for the house on alternate days, to be admitted into—and then, just as mysteriously, ejected from—the fiction inside. Along with the relationship between the girls, this experience has implied erotic overtones: a sort of narrative rape that can be recollected only in tranquillity with the aid of the candy, usually by both girls together, in achronological MARIENBAD-like fragments.

As they suck on the sweets in Julie's flat and react to the fractured replays

of this nineteenth-century pastiche, they explicitly become movie spectators—laughing, shrieking, yawning, musing, and dreamily extemporizing on
whatever they see. (This "film-within-a-film" even has a title of its own,
PHANTOM LADIES OVER PARIS, which appears in the main credits.) The screen
transforms itself into a mirror, their laughter and amazement fuse with ours,
and in the netherworld between film and spectator, dreaming and waking, a
collaborative enterprise of creating spectacle as well as watching it begins to
take shape. Recalled like shards of a dream, the inner plot requires creative
participation in order to become legible, and we assist in this act of completion along with the girls.

At the center of this splendidly murky intrigue are Camille and Sophie,
each plotting against the other with poisoned candy or flowers to murder
Madlyn, and thereby become eligible to marry Olivier, who made a vow to
his late wife not to remarry as long as their daughter lives. Camille, a somewhat faded daisy of the Blanche DuBois species, is glimpsed fluttering down
a staircase or appearing in portals like Camilla Horn in Murnau's FAUST, ut-
tering crazed lines like "I'm leaving you the roses because of their thorns"
and—when Miss Angèle is removing flowers from Madlyn's room—"Why
this violence?" Sophie, an elegant enigma who hides pieces of candy in a
small cupboard, plays games with Madlyn and inexplicably gasps at the sight
of the flower she draws.

Each time the events are recalled, the plot is "advanced" or complicated a
bit more. But it doesn't take on its most ghoulish aspects until the girls decide
to enter the house together. This time, the pallor of the other principals is a
ghostly greasepaint white—recalling the cold cream on Céline's face in the
cabaret dressing room—and when Camille cuts her hand on a broken wine-
glass, she bleeds a ghastly blue. The entire intrigue becomes a frozen theatrical tableau, as Céline and Julie in their giddy waking states project their girlish games into and around the gloomy proceedings—blowing their lines as
they take turns enacting Miss Angèle, clamorously mocking the behavior of
the ghosts (or beautifully parodying Olivier's narcissism in a "mirror" dumb-
show); in general, behaving like some insane derivation of Abbott and Cos-
tello having improbably stumbled into a tale by Henry James.

The confrontation is as unsettling and mind-bending as a comic nightmare
out of Buñuel, but it ends in exorcism. Céline and Julie escape from the
house with Madlyn, shifting the balance between the two plots; and all three,
finding themselves back in Julie's flat, decide to embark on a boat ride.
Gliding down a placid river like fugitives from a Renoir film, they come upon
the immobile figures of Olivier, Sophie, and Camille, drifting past in another
boat. Reassembled more symmetrically, the fictions diverge to go their separate ways; and we cut to Céline on the self-same park bench, opening her eyes
to spy Julie hurrying past. The doubles are doubled, the circle is complete;

and we're left with the inquisitive stare and implied Cheshire grin of a mysterious cat.

■

Once again, Rivette is playing on a contrast of acting styles—chiefly the animated cartoon comportment of Berto (in her richest performance to date) and the theatrical aggressiveness of Labourier. Improvisation still dictates much of the overall texture, but it is conducted within much narrower limits than in SPECTRE, closer to a "jazz chart" than an open-ended experiment like Coleman's.

The *ambiance* is rather like a retrospective of old *Cahiers* favorites: movie memories reflected as formal diagrams of the appreciations of certain directors by Rivette and many of his colleagues in the 1950s. Thus the elaborate doublings of shots and characters seem partially derived from the discovery of such structures in Hitchcock by Truffaut and Godard (although it is Hitchcock with the causality removed); the retreats into childhood in Hawks's MONKEY BUSINESS and the wild dream-creations of Tashlin's ARTISTS AND MODELS are reproduced in spirit, if not in letter; and other enthusiasms of that period abound, from Mizoguchi and Rossellini to Nicholas Ray and Cocteau.

Indeed, one of the more pleasing aspects of CÉLINE ET JULIE is the way that it clarifies and helps to redefine much of the cinema that inspired it. A recent Paris revival of GENTLEMEN PREFER BLONDES offers a perfect case in point. Seeing this fifties musical again after CÉLINE ET JULIE reveals how even the garish cartoon-like simplicity of one of Hawks's more bloated efforts can accommodate a formal play of exchanges between the leading ladies that is far from simple—the implacable reality of Jane Russell and the sheer mythos of Marilyn coexisting, colliding, connecting, communicating, setting up contrasts, reversals, and fusions with one another beneath and through the established musical comedy conventions. CÉLINE ET JULIE, by exploring some of the same parameters in a quite different context, illuminates the potential richness of such a film behind its various commercial disguises, throwing up a rich and ravishing jewel box of possibilities.

Consider again the relationship of Berto and Labourier: the "unreal" plastic inventiveness of the former, the assertive psychodrama of the latter. Pointing up the differences, the doublings insure that each fulfills the other's roles, immediately creating sparks and frictions—as in Labourier's powerful (if ear-curdling) cabaret number, which quickly gravitates into an assault on the audience (like Russell's courtroom impersonation of Monroe in BLONDES), simultaneously releasing and bearing witness to much of the competitive tension that her performance has previously accumulated.

All Rivette's features might be regarded as different kinds of horror films; CÉLINE ET JULIE VONT EN BATEAU is his first horror-comedy. The anxiety and despair of PARIS NOUS APPARTIENT and LA RELIGIEUSE, L'AMOUR FOU and SPECTRE seem relatively absent, yet they perpetually hover just beyond the edges of the frames. We still have no privileged base of "reality" to set against the fictions, each of which is as outrageous as the other; and along with Borges, we can't really say whether it's a man dreaming he's a butterfly or a butterfly dreaming he's a man—although we may feel, in either case, that he and we are just on the verge of waking. It's a sham, of course—as a spectator complains of Céline's magic act, before being forcibly evicted from the cabaret—but a sublimely delicious one. As long as the separate fictions interpenetrate, we can stay balanced on Rivette's precarious tightrope, and don't have to worry about a net not being there to catch us if we fall. Improvising along with the actors, we look straight ahead and join in the crazy fun, trying to forget that beneath us lies the frightening knowledge of SPECTRE—that terrible certainty of a long drop that knows no bottom at all.

—*Sight and Sound*, Autumn 1974

The Tyranny of Sensitivity

John Cassavetes, Filmmaker and Actor
Museum of Modern Art, 20 June–11 July

Nineteen years ago, when I was a high school senior making one of those boring, difficult adolescent transitions—from being a social outcast in my hometown in the Deep South to being a social outcast as a southerner at a New England prep school—I had the good fortune to discover John Cassavetes's SHADOWS at the New Embassy at Broadway and 46th. It was near the beginning of my spring vacation, which meant that I could return to this movie again and again, during the same week or so when I was getting my first looks at BREATHLESS, THE RULES OF THE GAME, ROOM AT THE TOP, SPARTACUS, THE MISFITS, and TAKE A GIANT STEP.

Art in our time, Harold Rosenberg once wrote, appeals either to other artists or "to introverted adolescents, to people in crises of metamorphosis, a small-town girl who has met an intellectual, a husband forced to give up drinking, a business man who feels spiritually falsified, all these being, like the audience of artists, more attentive to themselves than to the work." And D. W. Griffith, Annette Michelson once reminded us, was a contemporary of Picasso. So it shouldn't be all that curious to see simultaneous retrospectives of two artists, Picasso and Cassavetes (a contemporary of Jackson Pollock), at MOMA this month.

Back in 1961, in a $40,000 movie called SHADOWS, there was a warmth in what happened between people that could bring me close to tears. Part of this was an incestual warmth between siblings—played by Hugh Hurd, Lelia Goldoni, and Ben Carruthers—that reminded me of J. D. Salinger's Glass family, another team of neurotic actors. But it was a warmth that went further (and was more radical, I thought) by being interracial as well as incestual, and it had none of the hard crust of Salinger's *New Yorker* upper-class snobbery.

There was also Charles Mingus's lovely, plaintive jazz score, offering a similarly unbridled emotional nuzzle. I soon grew to cherish every sign of vulnerability that the movie wore on its tattered sleeve—even the misspelling of "saxophone" in the opening credits, or the much-discussed closing title ("The film you have just seen was an improvisation"), accompanied by a Shafi Hadi sax solo, which appeared over Carruthers walking aimlessly past the old Colony Record Shop on 49th, not far from Birdland.

■

These signs of vulnerability ranged from effective/cornball Method riffs—like Tony Ray pausing just a beat between two words in his seduction of Lelia ("You've got the softest lips I've ever . . . felt")—to more subtle stuff between a would-be nightclub crooner (Hurd) and his would-be manager (Rupert Crosse), so delicately and sweetly nuanced that it became a veritable lesson in ways that people could behave decently toward one another. (If a certain amount of crude, anti-intellectual bullying turned up in other sequences, this could easily be overlooked.)

I was such a good pupil that the following year, when I was a freshman at New York University (NYU), I went all the way to the Brooklyn Paramount to get my first look at Cassavetes's second film, TOO LATE BLUES, made in Hollywood. A flawed, mawkish, and fitfully beautiful film about jazz musicians with Bobby Darin, Stella Stevens, and the unforgettable Everett Chambers, it was getting lambasted by practically every critic in sight, yet still had some improbable powerful moments—both musical and actorly—in the midst of all its bathos. And a year later, I saw Cassavetes's other abortive Hollywood project, A CHILD IS WAITING, back in my hometown.

Five more years passed before FACES premiered at the New York Film Festival. If, as one of Rosenberg's introverted adolescents, I was mainly attentive to SHADOWS for all the things it said about me, I'm sure that many other, differently oriented spectators were seized by Cassavetes's first commercial hit in precisely the same way. Despite the loss of the jazz motif in Cassavetes's subsequent work, the new crop of buffs—like me in 1961 and 1962—were all too happy to confuse "freedom" and "reality" with whatever had been socially repressed in them. And so it has gone, with diverse peaks and valleys, in the five features directed by Cassavetes since FACES: HUSBANDS, MINNIE AND MOSKOWITZ, A WOMAN UNDER THE INFLUENCE, THE KILLING OF A CHINESE BOOKIE, and OPENING NIGHT.

■

As Picasso has his blue and pink periods, Cassavetes as a director can be said to have his jazz and Gena Rowlands periods—the latter cycle encompassing everything from A CHILD IS WAITING to OPENING NIGHT except for HUSBANDS and THE KILLING OF A CHINESE BOOKIE, the only films not featuring Cassavetes's talented wife. As an actor, he seems to have only one period, black and white, although he's usually most effective as a straight villain—think of ROSEMARY'S BABY and THE FURY. The latter film and Elaine May's abrasively brilliant MIKEY AND NICKY are two unfortunate omissions in the museum's season, which otherwise seems satisfyingly full: all nine of his directed films, and as many independent samples of his career as an actor (including some television work).

In their very different ways, HUSBANDS and THE KILLING OF A CHINESE BOOKIE show Cassavetes at his most freakishly mannerist. The loutish, self-ingratiated misogyny in the former was so offensive to me when I saw it several years ago that it threatened to make me swear off Cassavetes forever. (Earlier this year, reading Saul Bellow's *Humboldt's Gift*, I was unpleasantly reminded of HUSBANDS, threatening to swear off Bellow forever.) Softer and more charismatic, THE KILLING OF A CHINESE BOOKIE is an unexpected genre film that, even more unexpectedly, turns out to be a kind of personal testament, a film that movingly sums up Cassavetes's sloppy, lovable, stupid brand of humanity and cinema—underlined by hero Ben Gazzara's theme song, "I Can't Give You Anything But Love"—as succinctly as THE TESTAMENT OF ORPHEUS sums up Cocteau's.

What are we ever going to do with a temperament as brutally obstinate, as sprawling and unwieldy, as Cassavetes's except turn it into a Rorschach test for our own passionate forms of vanity, a sounding-brass for the tyranny of our own precious sensitivity? Yet like any obsessive fisherman who casts his nets wide—a Whitman, O'Neill, Pollock, Mingus or any other stammering, hollering counterpart—he occasionally comes up with some pretty fancy catches. His latest film, OPENING NIGHT—the first Cassavetes film about an actor, with a virtuoso performance by Rowlands—pushes forward a kind of frenzied psychodrama already set forth by A WOMAN UNDER THE INFLUENCE, which, in turn, repeats a narrative event—a woman attempting suicide in a man's presence—already seen in TOO LATE BLUES and FACES.

For many critics, the height of absurdity in TOO LATE BLUES is reached when Bobby Darin forces Stella Stevens's face into a sink after such an attempt, and there is a sudden cut to her face under the faucet as seen from the vantage point of the sink drain. Cassavetes's refusal to tear away from an actress's face at a crucial moment, regardless of all the technical gaucheries and jeers that this will cost him, is largely what his awful, irritating integrity is all about. Tons of it can be seen in MOMA's retrospective.

—*Soho News*, 18 June 1980

Love Films

A Cassavetes Retrospective

I have noticed that people who were loved or felt they were loved seemed to lead fuller, happier lives. All of my own work in theater and film has been concerned with varying themes of this love.

A Woman of Mystery has to do with an unexplored segment of our society, referred to as the homeless, bag ladies, winos, bums—labels that are much easier for the public to deal with than the individual.

It has been difficult to explore this particular woman of mystery. She is not only homeless (if homeless means without the comfort of love) but she is nameless, without the practical application of social security, or any other identity. Alone, she clings to her baggages on the street.

Our heroine enters into a series of encounters that challenge her isolation, her inability to communicate. A young woman passerby seems to feel that this woman with the suitcases is the reincarnation of her dead mother. An emotional dismissal of the younger woman causes the woman's memory to play tricks on her. A young man seems to touch unexplained dependency in her and a clerk at a travel bureau gets dangerously close to exchanging love.

Change continues as the woman comes forward, attempting sociability. But, in the end, normal feelings of affection are too difficult to return to. The woman has been permanently disabled by the long discontinuance of feelings of love.

These are John Cassavetes's program notes to his last realized work—an awesome three-act play starring Gena Rowlands and Carol Kane that he wrote and directed, and that I was lucky enough to see. It was performed in a small theater in Beverly Hills for two weeks during the summer of 1987; considering the size of the auditorium, I can't imagine many people saw it. It was obviously a production done for love rather than money, and its treatment of the homeless couldn't be described as an act of either condescension or abstract piety. Terrifyingly human, tragic, and mysterious, it revolved around both the heroine's lost identity—literally, her lack of definition—and the difficulty others, including the audience, had making contact with her. Actual street people—including some musicians, a standup comic, and a poet—came onstage and performed during the intermissions, and at no point did the actors seem out of step with them.

Basic questions about love, identity, and definition are at the root of all of Cassavetes's work as a filmmaker, and it somehow seems appropriate that the sharpest, starkest posing of those questions came at the very beginning and at the very end of his career. In his groundbreaking first feature, SHADOWS (1959), these questions center on two brothers and a sister who live together in Manhattan. The older brother, a dark-skinned black named Hugh (Hugh Hurd), is the only one of the three who has a pretty clear sense of who he is, even though this happens to be a pretty terrible (though serious) nightclub crooner. His lighter-skinned younger siblings, Ben (Ben Carruthers) and Lelia (Lelia Goldoni), are much less centered, in part because they both "pass" for white; Ben "passes" consciously, Lelia apparently unwittingly, and neither can be said to have a fully fixed identity. After Lelia loses her virginity to a young white seducer, he escorts her home, where he's taken aback when he sees her greet Hugh as her brother. In one fell swoop her sense of self is devastated by her seducer's shock and discomfort. Virtually none of this is discussed or "explained" in the dialogue; apart from a fleeting reference by Hugh to "a problem of the races," the entire drama is played out in the faces and behavior of the actors, with a subtlety and sensitivity that still bring me to tears every time I see the film.

SHADOWS started out as an improvisation on this scene in Cassavetes's New York acting workshop. Talk-show host Jean Shepherd happened to be visiting and was so impressed that he invited Cassavetes onto his late-night show, *Night People*, during which Cassavetes brashly proposed that interested listeners send in one dollar apiece to finance a film; $2,500 was collected within a week. After raising additional funds, Cassavetes shot a free-form, hour-long feature that was screened three times at midnight, for no admission, to about two thousand people, and that was declared a masterpiece of the "New American Cinema" by critic Jonas Mekas. But Cassavetes failed to find a distributor, so he shot eight additional scenes and edited a new 85-minute version that had more conventional continuity and narrative structure; it opened in 1961 and is the only version of SHADOWS that survives today (though Mekas, for one, regards it as inferior to the original). The two versions cost a total of $40,000, and together they launched a revolution in American independent film that is still going on.

Lured to Hollywood by a studio contract, Cassavetes directed two more pictures with mixed results, TOO LATE BLUES (1961) and A CHILD IS WAITING

(1963); the second of these was so altered by producer Stanley Kramer that Cassavetes virtually disowned it. Returning to maverick independence with a vengeance, he next made FACES (1968), the success of which led to two more studio deals (HUSBANDS and MINNIE AND MOSKOWITZ) over which he had full control and final cut. They were followed by three features he distributed himself: A WOMAN UNDER THE INFLUENCE (1975), THE KILLING OF A CHINESE BOOKIE (1976, rereleased in a shorter version in 1978), and OPENING NIGHT (1978); only the first of these was a commercial success—the other two were resounding commercial failures and barely circulated. Then came two features done for other companies, GLORIA (1980) and LOVE STREAMS (1984), which did somewhat better, but not well enough to finance any more pictures. (An abortive experience taking over the direction of BIG TROUBLE [1986], a comedy that was already in production and was subsequently recut by the producer, doesn't really qualify as part of the Cassavetes oeuvre.) The remainder of Cassavetes's "independent" activity was his small-scale theater work in Los Angeles: *East/West Game*, which he wrote and directed in 1980; three more plays in 1981, two of which were written by Ted Allan (including *Love Streams*, the basis of Cassavetes's last film); and *A Woman of Mystery* in 1987.

■

Tragically but predictably, now that John Cassavetes is dead it's become possible, even fashionable, to like his movies again. Indeed, I suspect that the five-week retrospective starting tonight at the Music Box—encompassing all the features Cassavetes owned—will be much better attended than was the Film Center's retrospective five years ago. With the exception of LOVE STREAMS, all of his major works are being shown, and there are no finer works in the American independent narrative cinema.

This belated recognition means that his work is only a fraction of the size it could have been if critics and audiences had been more attuned to what he was up to. Speaking for myself as well as for most of my colleagues, we were usually wrong about Cassavetes—even when we wrote in support of his work, which wasn't often enough. Admittedly, he didn't help us out much, being one of the least articulate of major filmmakers when it came to describing the methodology and meanings of his work; his lack of clarity or eloquence made him resemble one of his characters. But in general we were defeated by the task of verbalizing essentially nonverbal film experiences.

We assumed, quite wrongly, that Cassavetes was a primitive realist who depended mainly on improvisation from his actors, but he was neither primitive nor a realist in any usual sense, and most of the dialogue in his movies was written by him. We often assumed that the dialogue was improvised because it sounded spontaneous, and we often assumed that the stories and characters were supposed to be "realistic" because the shooting style gave the films a documentary look. These false impressions were undoubtedly furthered by the fact that SHADOWS declared itself to be an "improvisation" in its final credits (mainly, it seems, because the actors generated some of the dialogue) and aimed for a kind of verisimilitude in relation to its milieu (not always successfully, as an awkwardly conceived "literary" party reveals). In addition, FACES, by concentrating on certain forms of middle-class behavior that had been overlooked by Hollywood—particularly the compulsive laughter that grew out of sexual embarrassment—made it seem realistic to many people when it came out in 1968. Comparable elements cropped up in HUSBANDS, MINNIE AND MOSKOWITZ, and A WOMAN UNDER THE INFLUENCE, but it can be argued that by the mid-1970s Cassavetes had shifted almost entirely into a mythological universe controlled more by notions about genre (THE KILLING OF A CHINESE BOOKIE and GLORIA) and personality (OPENING NIGHT and LOVE STREAMS) than by superficial concerns with social accuracy. Most critics, still stuck in their earlier formulations, tended to be baffled by this development, though a closer look at some of the earlier works might have revealed what was in store.

The central location of FACES—the home of a middle-class couple in a state of crisis—was the house that Cassavetes, Gena Rowlands, and their children lived in; it was used again as the central location in LOVE STREAMS. No effort seems to have been made to redecorate or refurnish it to suit the tastes of the middle-class couple in FACES, and nothing about it—neither the art and signed photographs framed on the walls nor the books on the shelves—rings true for these characters. Such indifference to setting is not a virtue, but given the film's concentration on the actors' faces, it can't really be considered a serious flaw; Cassavetes clearly regarded it as irrelevant or at least secondary.

FACES opens with a private screening of a film in the office of the hero (John Marley), an insurance executive, who is surrounded by business associates. The lights in the screening room fade and the credits for FACES appear, implying that these people are watching the movie that follows, a movie about themselves. But the remainder of the film never alludes to this screening, and if we don't emerge from the film totally confused, we probably conclude that the film the business associates saw wasn't FACES but an industrial short or some commercial relating to insurance.

The title heroine in the galvanizing A WOMAN UNDER THE INFLUENCE, a working-class housewife and mother played by Gena Rowlands, has a serious nervous breakdown and is committed to an institution for six months. There's a large party at her house to welcome her back when she's released, but not once is it suggested that her devoted husband (Peter Falk), their kids, or any of her friends or other relatives has been to visit her during her half year away.

Comparable distractions and irrelevancies crop up in most of the other movies, and they can't be wished away. But in order to understand what Cassavetes is doing, one has to get beyond them. His cinema is centered almost

exclusively on actors and scenes; questions about settings, events, and dura-
tions between scenes, and most of the other forms of narrative glue and "filling" (or "stuffing") that we expect from fiction films to establish the characters and their milieus are generally given short shrift. Disdaining exposition,
Cassavetes's movies generally plunge us into the world of their characters
without the usual signposts and road maps, forcing us to flounder for a while
along with the characters. Existentially speaking, his movies are about what
they show and what we see and hear, not about theoretical or actual "background" material that takes place between or beyond the shots. But to accept
this principle, we have to adjust the expectations we bring to most films.

Another potential obstacle needs to be brought up. In spite of—or should I
say because of?—their radical humanism, Cassavetes's films are not "politically correct." According to David E. James in *Allegories of Cinema: American Film in the Sixties*, the casting of a white actress in the part of Lelia
in SHADOWS constitutes an ethical and aesthetic cop-out that invalidates the
drama; given the beauty and power of Lelia Goldoni's performance, I must
confess this argument made me want to throw James's book against the wall.
However, the brutality with which women are often treated in HUSBANDS—
which the film's bullying macho ambience often seems to endorse (or at least
tolerate) more than criticize—turned me against Cassavetes for a number of
years, and I still haven't resolved whether this description of the film qualifies
as a misreading. (Peter Bogdanovich, for one, has defended HUSBANDS as "the
first, and in many ways still the most trenchant and honest, American look at
the overwhelming alienation and homelessness which the hypocritical sexual
revolution was by then [1970] leaving in its wake.") Conversely, THE KILL-
ING OF A CHINESE BOOKIE, which I've always cherished as Cassavetes's testament—an ironic self-portrait starring Ben Gazzara as Cosmo Vitelli, the pathetic, lamebrained, and defeated (yet indefatigably stylish, courageous, and
noble) owner of a Los Angeles strip joint—has been denounced by a feminist
friend of mine as the worst kind of patriarchal and sexist sentimental slop. And
from the point of view of political correctness, I suppose she could be right.
I doubt, however, that she could make the same argument about GLORIA—a
joyously subversive reworking of the gangster film that is arguably as feminist as THELMA AND LOUISE.

If, however, we consider the stranglehold that "political correctness" of various persuasions currently has on the media—fostering attitudes that would
probably make a movie like SHADOWS impossible to finance today—I think
Cassavetes's work warrants a closer look. The complete absence of villains
and the touching celebration of various kinds of human sweetness and affection—exemplified by such wonderful characters as Hugh's manager (Rupert
Crosse) in SHADOWS, a disco hustler (Seymour Cassel) in FACES, and even
Cosmo Vitelli in THE KILLING OF A CHINESE BOOKIE—has a great deal to do
with what keeps his films vital and powerful. If Cassavetes's radical human-

ism challenges some of our cherished notions about appropriate role models, perhaps that challenge makes it even more valuable in the long run. For all their hectoring anti-intellectualism, his movies are frequently object lessons in how we might behave more decently and caringly toward one another.

■

Although Cassavetes has been one of the most influential of all American independents—having marked the works of directors as different as Bog-danovich, Jean Eustache, Jean-Luc Godard (who has dedicated two works to him), Henry Jaglom, Elaine May, Rob Nilsson, Maurice Pialat, Jacques Rivette, and Martin Scorsese, among many others—I can think of only one other American independent writer-director-actor who is conceptually comparable to him: Orson Welles. Considering the extreme disparity between these directors in terms of visual and cultural style, a connection may seem unlikely, but it actually runs quite deep. And it isn't surprising to hear that Welles and Cassavetes were great admirers of each other's work.

Having just completed the editing for publication of a book-length interview with Welles, I've been struck by the degree to which Welles considered the actor rather than the director to be the key figure in filmmaking—an attitude Cassavetes clearly shared. It might even be said that "acting" was the subject of all of their films—not merely because of their passionate interest in actors, but also because their view of human nature and behavior had a lot to do with performance and the notion that everyone is an actor. (Both directors often recruited their actors from highly unlikely places. The extraordinary Lynn Carlin, for example, was working as a secretary for the then-unknown Robert Altman—and had been hired briefly to type the original script of FACES—when Cassavetes recruited her to be the film's lead.)

For Cassavetes, acting is merely a heightened form of the social activity we all pursue in our various transactions with the world. This idea is the literal concern of OPENING NIGHT, which focuses on the crises experienced by a troubled stage actress (Gena Rowlands) and the other actors (including Cassavetes) she performs with; but it's no less important in the role-playing highlighted in his other films. Consider the carefully manufactured facades of most of the leading characters in SHADOWS, FACES, A WOMAN UNDER THE INFLUENCE (especially the title heroine), and THE KILLING OF A CHINESE BOOKIE—and the confusions and clarifications about their identities that arise when those facades are chipped away—and you have the essential subjects of all four films.

The martyrdom of Cassavetes—like that of Welles before him—seems to be the obligatory price exacted in this country for working outside the methods and assumptions of the industry. (Both directors, significantly, have received much more recognition for their independent efforts abroad than in this country.) This martyrdom also has something to do with the "scandal" of caring more about the work itself than about the financial reward to be gained from it. What probably elicited the most scorn in Hollywood, where both men lived, was their willingness to subsidize their own low-budget productions with the money made from their more routine work as actors—something both were usually forced to do in order to make movies at all.

We're still living with the legacy of that martyrdom, and it's difficult to calculate the size of our loss. (What kind of film culture would we have today if we had as many movies by Welles and Cassavetes as we have by Woody Allen? The very notion staggers the imagination.) Fortunately, the size and power of what we have is still enormous. And now that we have the evidence of Cassavetes's genius again before us—films that have far too long been unavailable and neglected—we owe it to ourselves to discover what his art and vision were all about.

—*Chicago Reader*, 20 September 1991

The Death of Hulot

It was about ten years ago, in late November 1972, that I first took the No. 163 bus from Porte de Champerret in Paris to Jacques Tati's office in la Garenne-Colombes, just around the corner from an unassuming street known as Rue de Plaisance. With his assistant Marie-France Siegler—a French-American in her thirties who, like me, hailed from Alabama, and had set up this interview—Tati occupied two offices in a modern building whose suburban neighborhood bore visible traces of both the contrasting *quartiers* in MON ONCLE: the chummy old lower-middle-to-working-class district where an unemployed Hulot lives, and the sterile, newly built upper-to-middle-class subdivision where his "successful" brother lives.

The modern building, fronted by a glass door with a disc-shaped brass knob, was no less suggestive of PLAYTIME, and Tati's office contained other familiar emblems, such as the same synthetic black chairs. In fact, about the period of MON ONCLE (1958), his production company had commanded the entire floor; he had restricted himself to two modest rooms only after investing and then losing practically everything he had on PLAYTIME (1967), his most expensive film, the masterpiece that wrecked his career. And the previous year, 1971, he had released TRAFIC, an attempt to salvage his career. He was sixty-four when I first met him, although he hadn't made his first film as a director until he was practically forty.

It was easy enough to be liked by Tati. All one had to do was say that PLAYTIME was one's favorite film (which was true), that it had actually changed one's way of looking at people and things in cities (also true), and after almost two hours of pleasant interview in English—most of it later published in the May–June 1973 *Film Comment*—he was half-seriously assuring me that if I ever needed a place to stay, I could sleep in his office. (My hair was longer in those days; that and my lack of fluency in French may have led him to assume that I might not have had a place of my own in Paris.) At the same time, it was possible to see more than one side of his mood that afternoon: an hour later, while having a drink with Marie-France in the bistro on the ground floor of the same building, I saw her boss angrily stride in, beet-red, and chasten her in French for not being around when she was needed. He was not an easy man, nor was he having an easy time of it.

Becoming friendly with Marie-France through our shared Alabama backgrounds, approximate ages, and enthusiasm for Tati, I wound up writing an English commentary for a 16-millimeter short she had made called LA DERNIÈRE NUIT DES HALLES. (A onetime mime student whose life had been profoundly affected by MON ONCLE, as much through her identification with its social protest as through her fascination with its technique, she shared with Tati a notion of the simple and everyday as a continuous circus, and her tender and sentimental farewell to Paris's fruit and vegetable market was really a film about the circus closing down.) After that we had stayed sporadically in touch, and in early January she called me with the mind-boggling news that Tati was interested in working with me on the script of his next film, a project about television called CONFUSION. And for much of the remainder of that month, on an almost daily basis, I was going out to la Garenne-Colombes to do precisely that.

■

I was flattered, even awed, but also rather bewildered: apart from my sympathy as a critic and interviewer, what possible use did Tati have for an American writer*—a use, moreover, for which he was willing to pay me? As I had discovered in our interview, he was a completely nonverbal sort; a man whose mime-like habits made his body language and vocal sound effects closer to the sound of his "voice" than actual speech. He thought with his body, and it wasn't at all clear to me how I could contribute meaningfully to that process.

Understanding was gradual, and came only from the actual practice of our afternoons together. In a way, E. M. Forster's "How do I know what I mean until I see what I say?" could be translated into the question repeatedly posed by Tati's body language, which was central to his method—namely, "How do I know what I think until I see what I do?" And in order to see what he did, he needed a spectator, another set of eyes and ears, someone to respond to his gags and improvisations. It's a method many comics follow; where I suspect

---

*It's intriguing to note that in *Sight and Sound*'s recent Top Ten poll (Autumn 1982), the two critics apart from myself who list PLAYTIME, Gilbert Adair and Vincent Canby, are both English-speaking, as are the two others who list CÉLINE ET JULIE VONT EN BATEAU (David Thomson and Robin Wood)—another French comedy about the joys and perils of spectatorship.

it differed most for Tati was in his compulsion to reproduce in his body as much of the image and sound as was humanly possible, playing all the characters and props that figured in the action.

A cinematic raconteur, Tati possessed a talent for evoking the formal impact of a shot with his voice and body which is shared, to my knowledge, only by Kevin Brownlow and Sam Fuller—two other wild men quite capable of leaping about and squawking, if necessary, to illustrate what a particular moment of film might be like. For Brownlow, it is a favorite film moment remembered and savored (most often through vocal inflections); for Fuller, it is a crazed conceptual notion that his pulp imagination and cheap energy turn into some variant of Godardian aggression. But for Tati—taller, more legato and loping in demeanor—it was always a gesture that came from life, not art. Neither a cinéphile nor (by and large) a director for cinéphiles, Tati lacked the polemical stance regarding the rest of cinema that characterizes Bresson, although he had a similar dislike for professional actors. (In defense of the costly sets of PLAYTIME, he would argue, "They're not more expensive than Sophia Loren.")

He wasn't an intellectual or someone who read much—although, among film critics, he was unstinting in his praise of Bazin and Sadoul. During one of our first sessions, while I was still trying to figure out why he had hired me, I ventured that, because the principal subject of CONFUSION was television, it might perhaps be worth thinking some about, say, Marshall McLuhan. The suggestion brought blank stares from Tati as well as from Marie-France. After a brief explanation of McLuhan's reputation and influence in the States at the time—so pronounced, I recall, that during my grad school days in the mid-1960s, there was an undergraduate course in existentialism at the State University of New York at Stony Brook which used *Understanding Media* as its sole textbook—it quickly became clear that they weren't interested in the slightest.

No less doomed was any extended effort to discuss other people's films. The current favorite of Tati and Marie-France when I was working for them was HAROLD AND MAUDE. At various times, he expressed admiration for Keaton and Kubrick (as well as for Woody Allen's BANANAS), but never went into any detail. When I suggested at one point that he see Buñuel's LE CHARME DISCRET DE LA BOURGEOISIE, he could only muse about who this Buñuel fellow was. Wasn't he the chap who made a film—he forgot the title—strongly influenced by JOUR DE FÊTE?

The way our work proceeded always depended on his moods, and each afternoon was different. After the first week or so, I was lent a copy of the treatment he had already prepared in French for CONFUSION, chiefly a description of various situations and gags involving Hulot set either in a television studio or out on various news sites and/or shooting locations. Much of this was satire about the phony clamor of American television (the bilingual title was as deliberate as the *franglais* of PLAYTIME and TRAFIC), which Tati had already spoken about in our interview. "When you see people on American television, the way they speak and move and wear their clothes (they all have wigs, you can see them)—nothing is real. That's why what they create isn't warm, or natural. When you see all that cream they put in the commercials—I watched from 9 A.M. to 11:30 and I saw only cream, everywhere: cream on the bread, cream on the shoes, cream on the face, cream on the potatoes, cream to be dirty—chocolate cream, that looks like I don't know what. At 12:30 I had an opportunity for lunch and I said, 'Really, I'm not joking, I can't eat.'"

For a while, I used to fantasize ways that Tati could extend his multiple focal points through his uses of television—such as Hulot repeated countless times on various television sets in a window, or monitors in a studio. But mainly it was a matter of talking, looking, and listening. Some days, when what he called his Slavic side predominated (he had a Russian father called Tatischeff), a cloud of melancholia would seem to descend over him, and it would become hard to work. Sometimes he would take down his large scrapbooks devoted to the production of PLAYTIME and linger over photographs of the sets.

■

Tati always trusted children more than adults. Animals could elicit a lot of attention and respect, too: I recall him performing for somebody's dog in a restaurant for a good ten minutes, evidently more concerned with the dog's responses to his antics than with those of any human onlookers. One time he recounted screening PLAYTIME privately for a small group of film industry bigshots, one of whom had to bring along his little girl because he couldn't get a babysitter, a fact for which he apologized profusely. Then, after the film started, she did something truly unforgivable: every time there was a gag, she would giggle, causing her nervous father to turn around and shush her. It was a story recounted, of course, by Tati playing alternately the little girl and her father, oscillating between delight and horror with a regularity suggesting ping pong.

"The birth of the reader must be ransomed by the death of the author," Roland Barthes wrote in the 1960s. "I think PLAYTIME is revolutionary in spite of Tati," Jacques Rivette said during the same decade. "The film completely overshadowed the creator." "PLAYTIME is nobody," Tati more instinctively said to me during our interview. Yet, as it became increasingly clear to me, the birth of Tati the director had to be ransomed by the death of Hulot the performer. It was an existential crisis of the first order, and his career never quite recovered from it. People who never heard of Tati loved Hulot, whereas Tati personally was sick and tired of Hulot, a character originally invented for only one film, and which the public refused to let him abandon, rather as Conan Doyle's reading public refused to let him dispose of Sherlock Holmes.

Hulot remained Tati's bread and butter, but it was this same lunar presence who stood between him and his desire to be a director. Not like Chaplin, who merely regarded direction as the placement of his performance, but quite the reverse: a vision that democratized the holy fool so that he/she occupied every corner of the frame, every character and object and sound, no longer the emperor of a privileged space.

Hulot as star got in the way of all that. This was true even in LES VA-CANCES DE MONSIEUR HULOT, where Tati discovered that he could evoke Hulot without his actual presence; the rattle and sputter of his off-screen car sufficed. It is equally the point of all the false Hulots in PLAYTIME, who form a sort of chain of being between Hulot himself and all the nondescript bumblers in the audience. One lookalike drops his umbrella in the background of a shot at Orly, distracting us from the arriving party of female American tourists; another behaves at a gadget exhibit in a boorish manner that gets the real Hulot in trouble; a third presents a going-away gift from Hulot to Barbara, the film's heroine, which Hulot can't deliver himself. The absolute equivalence of real and false Hulots is basic to the film's ethics and aesthetics, which deplore the kinds of space created by stars, whether human or architectural.

It was a singular experience to accompany Tati to the bistro downstairs for lunch—a recognizable miniature version of the Royal Garden Restaurant in PLAYTIME. His behavior there would seesaw almost dialectically between observation and clowning: the way another customer moved would amuse or delight him and he would duplicate the gesture immediately, with a manic glee that was unnerving if you happened to be the one he was copying. One afternoon, arriving for work, I checked the restaurant for Tati and Marie-France, went upstairs and found the office doors locked, and then returned to the restaurant only to discover that a few feet from my very nose, near the entrance, sat the two of them at a table, hugely diverted by my bemusement, waiting for me to discover them. Becoming part of a Tati gag was inevitable if you hung around him, but it always became part of a dialectic when the copied version was transmitted back to you. It was the same way, I'm told, that he directed performances in his films: imitate the funny way that someone walked, then ask him or her to imitate his imitation.

The physicality of Tati's comedy is intimately involved with the love and hatred it can elicit from spectators, in part according to the ways that they relate to their own physicality and that of their immediate environments. The world he depicts is a peculiar one consisting of public events viewed from private perspectives (a touching example from JOUR DE FÊTE: the village postman's horrified look at discovering via a newsreel how mail is delivered in America), a central theme of modernism that actually places Tati in the unexpected company of Joyce and Eisenstein (as well as Duras, Godard, Rivette, and Straub/Huillet, among closer contemporaries who revere his work). In the second half of PLAYTIME, Tati achieved through intuitive genius a network of polyphonic complexities such as Eisenstein and the others arrived at mainly by conscious design.

If the connection sounds farfetched, think of the intricate trajectories of diverse characters and objects through a single day and city in *Ulysses* and PLAYTIME, or the striking anticipation of the latter in THE GLASS HOUSE—a favorite unrealized project of Eisenstein's described in some detail in Jay Leyda and Zina Voynow's recent and very beautiful *Eisenstein at Work* (Pantheon Books/The Museum of Modern Art, 1982). As Ted Perry usefully summarizes in his introduction:

> One of the clearest examples of how polyphony could serve as the generative idea for an entire film occurs in the notes and sketches which Eisenstein made for a never-realized enterprise entitled THE GLASS HOUSE. The undertaking drew its inspiration from a number of different sources: the visit to the new glass wonder which was the Berlin Hessler Hotel, some knowledge of Zamaytin's novel entitled *We,* and Frank Lloyd Wright's plans for a glass skyscraper. As early as 1926 and as late as 1947 Eisenstein made notes and sketches for the project. He was fascinated with the visual possibilities of seeing multiple actions in different parts of a glass house where opaque objects, such as rugs, would interrupt the line of sight and serve as compositional devices. Of utmost interest was the possibility that the same shot, or scene, could contain not only an action but also people, on the other side of the glass walls, seeing and reacting to the action. Eisenstein's term for such a film, stereoscopic, referred not only to the three-dimensional quality of the image but also, and more importantly, to the simultaneous interplay of the subjective and the objective. Instead of a shot of an event alternating with a shot of people's reaction, the objective event and the subjective reaction would take place within the same image.
>
> No wonder Eisenstein could write on February 15, 1928, "On Saturday received *Ulysses,* the Bible of the new cinema" [. . .]

■

The American release of PLAYTIME, six years after its completion, occurred around the time I was working for Tati, when he had no control over the shortened 35-millimeter version being shown. By then, he also had no control over (or revenues from) the widespread distribution of many of his films in 16-millimeter in the United States. Apart from knowing that he was bankrupt and that pirated dupes of PLAYTIME seemed to be proliferating everywhere, I never had any clear sense of all his financial difficulties. The last time I saw him, on a brief visit to Paris from London in February 1977, he was about to leave for Switzerland to show the original 70-millimeter, 151-minute version of PLAYTIME, which I've never seen; he invited me to come along, but my schedule made it impossible. He still owned the only complete 70-millimeter version, but I later heard, rightly or wrongly, that he had had to give that up too when the rights to all his films were auctioned off.

I don't know if he ever understood what hit him; I'm not at all sure that I do, either. Our meetings were discontinued when he became ill, and before our last meeting in 1977, I can recall seeing him again only when he showed PARADE at the London Film Festival in December 1975. A year earlier, at a Paris Left Bank cinema, during my first look at PARADE, I found myself, to my embarrassment, weeping uncontrollably. It was a circus show he had videotaped in Sweden and transferred to film. A friend at the time who despised Tati had told me it was pathetic, and I felt that it was almost like what seeing Griffith's THE SEARCH must have been like in 1931—beautiful for what it was, yet excruciating in relation to what one knew its director wanted to do and was capable of doing.

In retrospect, though, it has grown in importance for me. It has none of the bitterness that intermittently mars TRAFIC (a more compromised work in its inception, because its commercial viability required the star presence of Hulot), and equates spectator and performer more decisively. One can also appreciate the relief with which Tati finally abandons his nemesis here, returning to the pantomimes that initially launched him in the music halls, about which Colette marveled, "He has created at the same time the player, the ball, and the racket; the boxer and his opponent; the bicycle and its rider. His powers of suggestion are those of a great artist."

By the time I saw PARADE again in London, this much was clear to me; it remains to be seen for most other people, who eight years later have still never heard of the film. I remember telling Marie-France how much I liked PARADE, and the unbridled pleasure that broke out on Tati's face when she reported this to him a few moments later. His bad health was more visible by then, but he was big and powerful for a Frenchman, and he hung on for seven years more. From time to time, one would hear rumors in the press about CONFUSION being reanimated as a project, but the financing never came together. He clearly had reached the end.

Yet the true death of Hulot, as far as I'm concerned, occurred not in late 1982, when Tati died, but in early 1973, at the most fruitful of all our afternoon sessions. If memory serves, it was also the last. Tati was musing about how he'd like to start off CONFUSION with something truly outrageous: have the screen grow dark, for instance, so that kids in the audience would start whistling (he promptly imitated them); make it look as though the film broke or caught fire or . . . *or what about killing off Hulot, once and for all?* Suddenly Tati got up from his desk—he always thought best on his feet—and started pacing about his little cubicle, blocking out a scene. Yes, they would be transmitting something like a live soap opera or melodrama from a television studio, and real bullets would accidentally be inserted in a prop gun instead of blanks. Hulot would be a studio technician; or, even better, an innocent bystander who was there for some other reason and stopped to watch this live performance, and when one hammy actor pulls out his pistol to blast another hammy actor, he misses and instead shoots dead an out-of-frame Hulot.

Consternation in the studio; they can't stop the action because this is live, the show must go on. So the melodrama continues while the crew frantically conspires to remove Hulot's corpse without the television cameras picking it up; meanwhile, the actors have to keep stepping discreetly over his body while continuing their dialogue every time they have to cross the set. It was a brilliant, hilarious improvisation in which at least five interlocking things were occurring at once (including, of course, the television monitors that showed the oddly strained drama in progress); Tati was playing all of them, including the Hulot corpse, and had me helpless, in stitches.

After a while he calmed down and returned to his chair. "The only trouble is," he said, "I'll never raise the money to make a movie that starts off with a scene like that." The finality of that made him grow somber again, and after toying with a few more conventional gag ideas, he sank back into his Slavic gloom and looked out the window for a while. Then he smiled and said we'd done enough work for the day, and I took the bus back to Paris.

—*Sight and Sound*, Spring 1983

Orson Welles's Essay Films and Documentary Fictions

A Two-Part Speculation

> I want to give the audience a hint of a scene. No
> more than that. Give them too much and they won't
> contribute anything themselves. Give them just a
> suggestion and you get them working with you.
> That's what gives the theatre meaning: when
> it becomes a social act.
>
> —*Orson Welles, quoted in* Collier's,
> *29 January 1938*

Two propositions:

1. One of the most progressive forms of cinema is the film in which fiction and nonfiction merge, trade places, become interchangeable.

2. One of the most reactionary forms of cinema is the film in which fiction and nonfiction merge, trade places, become interchangeable.

How can both of these statements be true—as, in fact, I believe they are? In the final analysis, the issue is an ethical one. In support of 2, there are docudramas that use spurious means to grant bogus authenticity to fiction (MISSISSIPPI BURNING is a good example), and documentaries that employ fictional devices in order to lie more effectively (to cite two very different examples: the studio retakes in Leni Riefenstahl's TRIUMPH OF THE WILL, which are well documented in Albert Speer's *Inside the Third Reich*, and Mick Jagger pretending to watch footage of a killing on a movieola near the end of GIMME SHELTER, which we know is a false and contrived scene from the cameraman of that sequence, Alan Raymond).

In support of 1, there are masterpieces collapsing, combining, and/or juxtaposing fiction and nonfiction in order to facilitate and broaden a filmmaker's grasp on a subject in the interests of truth. This is a highly subjective matter, of course, but a few of my own key touchstones in this category would be:

1. Josef von Sternberg's THE SAGA OF ANATAHAN (1953)

2. Alain Resnais and Marguerite Duras's HIROSHIMA, MON AMOUR (1959)

3. Jean-Marie Straub and Danièle Huillet's THE BRIDEGROOM, THE CO-MEDIENNE, AND THE PIMP (1968)

4. Jacques Rivette's OUT 1: NOLI ME TANGERE (1971)
5. Orson Welles's F FOR FAKE (1973)
6. Jacques Tati's PARADE (1973)
7. Jean-Luc Godard's ICI ET AILLEURS (1974)
8. Chris Marker's SANS SOLEIL (1982)
9. Françoise Romand's MIX-UP (1985)
10. Râúl Ruiz's MAMMAME (1987)
11. Joris Ivens and Marceline Loridan's A TALE OF THE WIND (1988)
12. Leslie Thornton's PEGGY AND FRED IN HELL (still in progress)

■

Two propositions:

1. *All of Orson Welles's film and television work can be divided into two categories, fiction and nonfiction.*
2. *All of Orson Welles's film and television work can be divided into two categories, stories and essays.*

This leads us into certain semantic problems from the outset: stories, after all, can be fictional or nonfictional, and essays can make use of fiction as well as nonfiction. Then there is the equally vexing question of how we define a "work" by Orson Welles, which has been addressed in some detail by James Naremore[1]: if we include only works that were both completed and publicly shown, we narrow our scope considerably, but if we decide to broaden our list, we invariably come up with a different set of problems.

Let us try to make do with four separate lists, all of them necessarily somewhat tentative and incomplete, none of which includes the (now lost) films done by Welles as interludes in many of his stage productions, but still comprising two dozen works in all:

(a) *nonfiction or essay films by Welles that were completed and shown:*

CITIZEN KANE *(trailer, circa 1940)*

THE ORSON WELLES SKETCHBOOK *(BBC-TV, 1955, six 15-minute programs)*

AROUND THE WORLD WITH ORSON WELLES *(ITA-TV, 1955, six 26-minute programs)*

NELLA TERRA DI DON CHISIOTTE (IN THE LAND OF DON QUIXOTE) *(RAI, 1964, nine 30-minute programs)*

F FOR FAKE *(film, 1973)*

FILMING OTHELLO *(film, 1978)*

(b) *nonfiction or essay films by Welles that were completed but not publicly shown:*

condensed first act of Wilde's The Importance of Being Earnest *and last scene of Shakespeare's* Henry IV *(filmed record of performance in Munich, 1950)*

ORSON WELLES AND PEOPLE *(independently produced television pilot about the life of Alexandre Dumas, 27 minutes, circa 1956)*

PORTRAIT OF GINA *(ABC, 1958)*

SPYING IN VIENNA *(sketch done for unshown CBS television special,* Orson's Bag, *1969)*

F FOR FAKE *(trailer, 1976, 9 minutes)*

(c) nonfiction or essay films that were started but not completed:

IT'S ALL TRUE *(film, 1942)*

MOBY DICK—REHEARSED *(film record of London stage performance, 1955)*

THE DOMINICI AFFAIR *(program for* Around the World with Orson Welles *television series, 1955)*

THE MAGIC SHOW *(film record of magic performance without camera tricks, 1969–1985)*

FILMING THE TRIAL *(film, circa early 1980s)*

(d) fiction films of Orson Welles that utilize documentary, pseudodocumentary, or essayistic elements:

CITIZEN KANE *(1941; pseudodocumentary* News on the March *segment)*

THE MAGNIFICENT AMBERSONS *(1942; essayistic narration)*

THE STRANGER *(1946; documentary footage of concentration camps)*

MR. ARKADIN *(1955; pseudodocumentary prologue)*

DON QUIXOTE *(1955–1985, unfinished; essayistic narration)*

THE FOUNTAIN OF YOUTH *(television pilot, 1956; essayistic narration)*

CHIMES AT MIDNIGHT *(1966; essayistic narration from* Holinshed's Chronicles*)*

THE OTHER SIDE OF THE WIND *(1970–?, unfinished; pseudodocumentary form throughout)*

■

The process-oriented methods that permitted at least four Welles features and a number of short works to be left unfinished are easier to understand than they would be if we adopted the mental habits of producers, which is exactly what more and more critics today seem to be doing; but that is no comfort to those of us eager to understand, and eager as critics always are to have the last word, which we are not about to have with this filmmaker. At least our direction, as always, is laid out for us: as long as one frame of film by the greatest filmmaker of the modern era is moldering in vaults, our work is not done. It is the last challenge, and the biggest joke, of an oeuvre that has always had more designs on us than we could ever have on it.

—*Bill Krohn,* Cahiers du Cinéma, *1986*[2]

Any investigative foray into the legacy of Welles that is undertaken today, including this one, has to be at once historical research and an exercise in science fiction. With a substantial part of Welles's work still unavailable to us, each "new" work has to serve double duty as a fresh chapter in his tangled oeuvre and as an additional skeleton key for unlocking some of the mysteries in his other works, visible and invisible alike. In the case of FILMING OTHELLO—the last feature of his to have been completed and shown publicly before his death in 1985—we have an additional complication of confronting an extended meditation on an earlier Welles feature that is currently unavailable in the United States (although this situation may change in the near future: Welles's youngest daughter Beatrice, who has inherited the American rights to OTHELLO, is currently planning to rerelease the film, and, as I write, Michael Dawson is in the process of restoring the film for this purpose). But while this meditation of FILMING OTHELLO is clearly no substitute for the 1952 OTHELLO it describes, it is a fascinating enough essay in its own right.

FILMING OTHELLO was planned as the first in a series of films in which Welles would reexamine some of his earlier works; the second in the series, which he had already started (again, with cinematographer Gary Graver), was devoted to THE TRIAL. Why did he choose these films rather than, say, CITIZEN KANE or TOUCH OF EVIL? Partially, it seems, because these were the two of his released features on which he had final cut which were most governed by chance and the financial vicissitudes which required last-minute changes and improvisations. Indeed, both films were initially designed to be shot in studios and then had to be completely redesigned in relation to found locations once the initial financing evaporated. And both films outline the radical change in Welles's aesthetics that accompanied this readjustment—the realization that if he wanted to make films his own way, as he had once before been able to do only on KANE, he would have to do them differently.

OTHELLO, in particular, inaugurates the whole "second manner" of Welles's film career, which might be called the *bricolage* or *caméra-stylo* manner (in contrast to the studio shooting that dominates nearly all of his 1940s work)— a manner that persists with only a few exceptions (i.e., TOUCH OF EVIL) to the end of his life. Because Welles found himself periodically running out of money during the shooting of OTHELLO—obliging him to go off and act in commercial films in order to raise the money to continue—he found himself adopting a number of new strategies in order to make his stop-and-start procedures more viable. Some of the major characteristics of his second manner include the spirit of *bricolage* (the most famous instance in OTHELLO being the restaging of the killing of Roderigo in a Turkish bath after the costumes for the scene failed to show up), the increasing importance of editing over camera movement (largely due to the loss of such studio equipment as tracks and cranes), the increasing use of doubles (for actors and locations alike), a certain loss in sound depth, and Welles's growing tendency to dub other actors' voices himself—all characteristics that tended to increase the spatial disorientation of the viewer and minimize the long takes of Welles's earlier work.

Conceivably the most modest of all the films in the Wellesian canon (unless one counts the nine-part television series IN THE LAND OF DON QUIXOTE done for RAI in 1964, a conventional and relatively uninteresting "home movie" travelogue), in budget as well as aspiration, FILMING OTHELLO can itself be read as a kind of shotgun marriage between chance and control. In contrast to both Welles's carefully composed monologues beside a movieola and an impromptu question-and-answer session in Boston is the "dialogue" with Michael Mac Liammóir and Hilton Edwards over lunch which forcibly combines these modes: on the one hand, three colleagues ruminating about Shakespeare's play around a table; on the other, isolated and carefully composed shots of a conversing Welles seated at another table—clearly inserted later, though with no attempt to disguise the mismatches of sound as well as image. (Earlier examples of this doggedly "unprofessional" technique can be found in the 1958 television film PORTRAIT OF GINA, cited above—a rambling personal essay about Gina Lollobrigida and pin-ups in Italy which was made for and rejected by CBS in 1958, and which is conceivably as full of digressions as this parenthesis. The checkered history of this particular *film maudit*, moreover, has plenty of mismatched discontinuities of its own: almost eighteen years after Welles left it behind in his hotel room in Paris, it was rediscovered by chance in a storage area in the mid-1980s; after a lengthy excerpt was shown on French television—the only portion I've been able to see—the film was screened in its entirety at the Venice Film Festival before promptly vanishing again, reportedly due to legal objections from Lollobrigida.) According to Gary Graver, these mismatches can partially be explained by the fact that several years passed between the lunch with Mac Liammóir and Edwards and the inserted shots of Welles, and the film stock that was used for the former was no longer being made when Welles came to shoot the latter. Even here, however, the apparent dialectic between an impromptu documentary method and a more "composed" form of discourse is not as clear-cut as it may first appear: Welles's allusion at one point during the lunch to a woman's remark made between takes foregrounds that this "documentary" is far from random, while the gist of his inserted remarks blends smoothly with the logical flow of the discussion.

If many of Welles's late films gravitate toward the essay film ("The essay does not date," he remarked in a 1982 interview, "because it represents the author's contribution, however modest, to the moment at which it was made."), it should be kept in mind that the forms of essay and documentary are inscribed in his fictional work from the beginning, even before he turned to movies. (The news bulletins in his famous 1938 *War of the Worlds* radio broadcast are the most obvious example, but a careful examination of his other work in radio and theater during the 1930s would surely turn up others.) More specifically, it is the ambiguous merging of fact and fiction which engages Welles the most—providing the basic principle behind his DON QUIXOTE (to judge at least from the forty-five minutes or so that I've seen, which plant Cervantes's fictional characters in a documentary version of contemporary Spain), becoming the very subject of F FOR FAKE, and actually forming more of the texture of FILMING OTHELLO than Welles's candor as a monologuist might at first suggest. For most of what we see of OTHELLO in FILMING OTHELLO is not excerpts preserved intact but an intricate re-editing of the original material—the scrambled shards of a dream of OTHELLO, oddly akin to the dreamlike prologue of KANE, rather than the film itself. Apart from the precredits funeral sequence that opens OTHELLO and FILMING OTHELLO alike, the footage is re-edited and shown silent over Welles's 1978 commentary, giving a complex and ironic twist to Welles's remarks about "quoting or misquoting" critical comments by Jack Jorgens and André Bazin about OTHELLO.

Creatively misquoting his own film at the same time that he misquotes his critics, Welles thus continues his projects of candid concealment and continuous revision which have already made his filmmaking career as labyrinthine and as mysterious as it is. And transposing some of the same giddy continuity of OTHELLO whereby Iago crosses continents "in the middle of a spoken phrase" and the separate thrusts in a skirmish between Roderigo and Cassio occur a thousand miles apart, Welles reshuffles and reorders much of the material in his own commentary, and revises the performances of himself and Mac Liammóir by reciting some of the same speeches—performing a creative dance around an object that is never allowed to remain fixed and static. Such work-in-progress, with both the subject and the object of the discussion in a perpetual state of becoming, seems only fitting as a contribution to an oeuvre which, as Bill Krohn points out above, refuses to allow us the last word, even while it actively and generously invites our participation.

■

The position of power enjoyed by the storyteller/essayist/narrator in much of Welles's work is more than a simple or seamless technique; considering the multiple and complex changes that are wrung from this position, it deserves to be treated as a preoccupation of the work itself, a notion of media as mirror whereby the performer paradoxically becomes the spectator of himself, the drama at hand providing the individual lens for his latest exercise in self-

scrutiny. It is a narcissism always mediated and/or contested by a moral inquiry: HEART OF DARKNESS, *Welles's first Hollywood project, revolved around the notion of playing both Marlow (off-screen narrator and first-person camera) and Kurtz (on-screen demagogue/villain)—that is, witness as well as subject.*[3] *From* KANE *through* TOUCH OF EVIL, *the Welles character that we see on screen is never as moral (virtuous or truthful) as the Welles persona who might be telling the story off-screen—even if, as in* THE LADY FROM SHANGHAI, *the Welles character is narrating his own story (and thereby registers as a sadder and wiser version of the Michael O'Hara that we see).*[4]

In THE FOUNTAIN OF YOUTH, *Welles's first television pilot—an adaptation of John Collier's short story "Youth from Vienna" that begins as an essay on the subject of narcissism—the dialectic is given a new pattern. For once, the narrating Welles persona is intermittently visible as well as audible; he begins the show, in effect, as a slide show lecturer, and reappears periodically to remind us of his privileged position. But as he basks in both his fictive power to give his static slides motion and his essayistic authority to freeze his characters again in order to digress about Narcissus or Ponce de Leon, the visibility of his manipulation undermines certain aspects of his narrative authority, turning his fiction into a documentary about himself (much as* FILMING OTHELLO *begins as a documentary about the actual* OTHELLO, *and partially winds up as a documentary about a re-edited, hence fictional,* OTHELLO). *By speaking for the characters as well as about them—literally lip-synching Joi Lansing, Dan Tobin, and Rick Jason, his three stars, at certain junctures to mock their role as puppets—his moral fallibility (that is to say, his narcissism) becomes identified with theirs, and the implicit nastiness of Welles's amused, glacial detachment consciously boomerangs.*

It seems fairly likely that ORSON WELLES AND PEOPLE—*Welles's second unsold television pilot, made after* THE FOUNTAIN OF YOUTH *and before* TOUCH OF EVIL—*is a lost work that will never be recovered. According to Fletcher Markle, a good friend of Welles during this period who is one of the few people to have seen it, it was a pilot about the Dumas family, done for a half-hour biographical series that would in theory eventually include such disparate figures as Winston Churchill and P. T. Barnum; Welles financed it himself on a minuscule budget, using the $5,000 he had been paid for appearing (paradoxically, as himself) and performing part of a magic act on* I LOVE LUCY, *and the entire thing was shot in a single day, in "a cheap, non-union 16mm studio—a converted garage, as I recall, somewhere off Hollywood Boulevard," with Welles as narrator, armed with "masses of period photos and drawings of Dumas and the Paris of his day" that were "blown up for use on the insert stand."*[5] *One imagines that it might have been a somewhat elaborated version of the simple talking-head format of* THE ORSON WELLES SKETCHBOOK, *a British television series done a year or so earlier, just as* IN THE LAND OF DON QUIXOTE *can be regarded as a close cousin of the British* *television series* AROUND THE WORLD WITH ORSON WELLES *(to judge from the single episode I've seen in the latter—a chat with Kenneth Tynan about bullfighting, shot in Spain). Like* PORTRAIT OF GINA, *it seems likely that most or all of these television works, with the striking exception of* THE FOUNTAIN OF YOUTH, *qualify as ephemera, but they are significant insofar as they represent the seeds or offshoots of more important works—much as the methodology of* F FOR FAKE *can already be seen in embryo in* PORTRAIT OF GINA, *for instance.*

■

The two major documentary forays of Welles on film, standing roughly at opposite ends of his film career, are IT'S ALL TRUE (1942) and F FOR FAKE (1973), two projects whose very titles together express a dialectical relationship to the documentary. The first of these, which occasioned the disastrous turning-point in Welles's Hollywood career away from creative control and studio support, was in some respects as ambitious as CITIZEN KANE and THE MAGNIFICENT AMBERSONS in its conception. But for many years, some of the facts about this work have been repeatedly misrepresented in books about Welles, so a brief description of the project is in order.

Originally planned at RKO as a collection of sketches on diverse North American subjects—including a history of jazz, a love story about Italian immigrants, and a Robert Flaherty tale about the friendship between a Mexican boy and a bull—IT'S ALL TRUE quickly turned into a film about Latin America when Nelson Rockefeller, Coordinator of the Office of Inter-American Affairs and RKO board member, appointed Welles as Good Will Ambassador to Brazil in late 1941. Welles was encouraged to speed up the production of both THE MAGNIFICENT AMBERSONS and JOURNEY INTO FEAR so that he could arrive in Rio in time to shoot the Carnival for a history of the samba. The Mexico episode, which Norman Foster had already started shooting in September 1941, was temporarily suspended so that Foster could direct JOURNEY INTO FEAR, and Welles was assured by RKO that he could complete the editing of AMBERSONS in Rio. Welles also planned episodes about the conquest of Peru and another Brazilian episode re-creating the journey of four Northeastern fishermen, or *jangadeiros*, on a raft from Fortaleza to Rio (over 1,500 miles) to petition the Brazilian president for social benefits. All four episodes seem to have been conceived somewhat after Flaherty's documentary methods—that is, a mixture of genuine documentary with re-creations. Unfortunately, RKO failed to honor its promises about AMBERSONS (Welles was not able to do the final cutting), and the leader of the *jangadeiros* accidentally drowned during the re-creation of their journey to Rio. RKO had meanwhile gone through a massive reorganization during Welles's absence, and the film was abruptly called off and shelved after Welles had shot a great deal of footage. (Welles made many subsequent unsuccessful efforts to buy back the footage and complete the film after his return to the United States.)

Paradoxically, it wasn't until many years after the release of F FOR FAKE that enough information about IT'S ALL TRUE came to light to make a limited critical assessment of this project possible. This information came in two parts. First came the discovery in the mid-1980s of about two-thirds of the unedited material shot by Welles in Fortaleza at the very end of his Brazilian sojourn, with a silent Mitchell camera and a skeleton crew of five (cameraman George Fanto and his assistant Reginaldo Calmon, Richard and Elizabeth Wilson, and Shifra Haran)—material which possibly represents the most ambitious footage shot by Welles in Brazil, most of which had never been seen (even by Welles) or even processed prior to its relatively recent discovery. (Samples of this footage are visible in Richard Wilson's 1986 short FOUR MEN ON A RAFT, which he is still hoping to expand into a feature.) Then came the revelatory research carried out in both Brazil and the United States by Robert Stam and others[6]—research which is still in progress, but which has already yielded some fascinating discoveries. Drawing on an array of Hollywood and Brazilian documents, including the research conducted and commissioned by Welles at the time, Stam persuasively argues, for instance, that most of the complaints about Welles's profligacy in Brazil can be attributed to his radical problack stance, including the fact that he enjoyed the company and collaboration of blacks, as well as his insistence on featuring nonwhites as the central characters in both of the film's Brazilian episodes. Based on this reading, which Stam explores in detail, one is encouraged by Stam to reread most disapproving biographical accounts of Welles's "Brazilian episode," especially those of Charles Higham and John Russell Taylor, as unconsciously but unmistakably racist. (It should be noted, incidentally, that the style of photography in the Fortaleza rushes bears certain relationships to the visual styles and rhetoric of both Flaherty and Dovzhenko; variations in this style can be found in both OTHELLO—also shot by Fanto—and certain passages in DON QUIXOTE.)

Certainly the ideological issues raised by Welles's encounters with Hollywood are rich in unexplored subtexts, from the relatively recent canonization of CITIZEN KANE as a safe Hollywood classic to the widespread hostility expressed by American critics toward Welles for the remainder of his life because he failed to match up to industry standards, yielding him a "failure" after KANE in the eyes of the middlebrow press.[7] If the progressive lucidity of Stam's research, converting fiction into fact, helps to clarify to what degree the radical political thrust of Welles's work as a whole—on radio and in theater as well as in film—has been either ignored or actively concealed by most Welles research, it is worth examining briefly another kind of routine obfuscation in academic film studies that has helped along some of the same process: converting fact into fiction.

It is almost an axiom in contemporary academic film theory that the fewer films one has seen or knows about, the better and clearer the academic mind is in following its own theoretical bents. As a French cinéphile, Gilles Deleuze is rather atypical in this respect, as the numerous film titles cited in both *Cinéma 1: L'image-mouvement* and *Cinéma 2: L'image-temps* demonstrate. Although he is not always meticulous, he at least gives some evidence that he usually knows something about what he is discussing. This is less true, alas, of many of his readers, including the English translators of *Cinéma 2: L'image-temps*, and thanks to the weird collusion of Deleuze, his proofreaders, the aforementioned translators, and *their* proofreaders, *Cinéma 2: The Time-Image* (University of Minnesota Press, 1989) offers detailed commentary on a good many nonexistent films—a Borgesian bounty that inadvertently echoes all the fake masterpieces that are created, exhibited, and discussed in F FOR FAKE.

Among the many intriguing items found in the index are Mankiewicz's THE BLOODHOUND, Minnelli's THE PERFECT WIFE, Donen's PAJAMA PICNIC, Ophüls's HOUSE OF PLEASURE, Murnau's THE LAST MAN (not to be confused with THE LAST LAUGH, which is listed separately), Straub's RESISTENZA, a CABINET OF DR. CALIGARI directed by Fritz Lang (which also crops up in Peter Gidal's recent *Materialist Film*, giving it further credence), and even a Marguerite Duras Western (DESTRY SHE SAID).

In the case of Welles, this has the rather grotesque consequence of collapsing IT'S ALL TRUE and F FOR FAKE into the same film (although, to complicate matters further, they are listed separately in the index). The French title of F FOR FAKE is VERITÉS ET MENSONGES; Deleuze—who is, after all, only a film theorist—calls it VERITÉS ET ILLUSIONS; and his translators, apparently finding at least half of both titles problematical, solve this difficulty by calling it IT'S ALL TRUE. (They have also faithfully preserved all of the misspellings and typos in the French edition, so that two of Welles's leading costars in F FOR FAKE—Elmyr de Hory and Oja Kodar—are now Elmer and Kadar.)

Collapsing the distinctions between truth and fiction in more ways than one, Deleuze's semigibberish text in English about Welles in *The Time-Image*, mixing titles, mauling names, and inverting the order of sequences in F FOR FAKE, creates a mad, tantalizing weave that is positively Wellesian (the bracketed comments in italics are my own):

> . . . a becoming, an irreducible multiplicity, characters or forms are now valid only as transformations of each other. And this is the diabolical trio of THE LADY FROM SHANGHAI, the strange relay-characters of Mr. Arkadin [*sic*], the chain which unites those in TOUCH OF EVIL, the unlimited transformation of those in THE TRIAL, the journey of the false which constantly passes through the king, his son, and Falstaff, all three imposters and usurpers in some way, culminating in the scene where the roles are exchanged. It is finally the great series of IT'S ALL TRUE, which is the manifesto for all of Welles's work, and his reflection on cinema. F for Falstaff, but above all *F for fake*.

. . . the great series of Welles, the story that is continually being modified, may be summed up as follows:

1. "presentation of Oja Kadar, whom all men turn to look at in the street"; 2. "presentation of Welles as conjuror" [*Deleuze has inverted the order of sequences here*]; 3. presentation of the journalist, author of a book about a forger of paintings, but also of false memoirs of Hughes, the millionaire forger with a multiplicity of doubles, whom we do not know if he has himself harmed the journalist [*why no more inverted commas, and why no more coherent syntax?*]; 4. conversation or exchange between the journalist and the forger of paintings; 5. intervention of Welles who assures that, for an hour, the viewer will neither see nor hear anything else false [*again, out of sequence*]; 6. Welles recounts his life, and reflects on man in front of Chartres Cathedral; 7. Oja Kadar's affair with Picasso at the end of which Welles arrives to say that the hour has passed and the affair was invented in every respect; 8. Welles wishes his audience a good evening.

■

F FOR FAKE remains one of Welles's most controversial works insofar as for many spectators, including some Welles enthusiasts, it is not really a "Welles film" at all. (To clarify Deleuze's garbled description a little, the film, visibly narrated by Welles in a manner that suggests at times both THE FOUNTAIN OF YOUTH *and* FILMING OTHELLO, *is mainly concerned with art forger Elmyr de Hory, Clifford Irving—who wrote a book about de Hory called* Fake *before be successfully forged Howard Hughes's autobiography—and diverse elements of fakery in Welles's own past, such as his* War of the Worlds *broadcast and his own entry into professional acting in Dublin . . . not counting several hoaxes and digressions of its own.)*

There has even, ironically enough, been some confusion regarding the authorship of F FOR FAKE, *as there has been with* FILMING OTHELLO *(occasioning, in the case of the latter film, one of the few gaffes in the updated edition of Naremore's* The Magic World of Orson Welles, *the best critical study of Welles in any language). Simply because Welles refuses to include what are generally thought to be "typically Wellesian" shots in* F FOR FAKE—*a deliberate ploy, one learns, from his extended interview with Bill Krohn in 1982,[8] and a strategy that can also be found somewhat less systematically in* THE IMMORTAL STORY *(1968) and (for contextual reasons)* THE OTHER SIDE OF THE WIND—*viewers who insist that they know who Welles is better than Welles does himself wind up feeling that they've been sold a bill of goods. The legend of Welles has always had much more potency for many people than the reality and, in more ways than one,* F FOR FAKE *seems to have been both inspired by this paradox and structured around it.*

One of the first "tricks" (or ruses, or fakes) in F FOR FAKE *occurs during the opening credits sequence, a few minutes into the film—a complex découpage with very musical articulations and transitions between and within shots, all to the strains of Michel Legrand's theme song. The following titles appear in the following forms:*

1. *"François Reichenbach presents" (painted in red with a brush against a white background, the brush painting the last letter just as we cut to);*

2. *"?" (painted in white with a brush on a movieola screen that has just shown a flying saucer atomize a building, followed by a freeze-frame of the explosion—a clip in black and white from the film* EARTH VS. FLYING SAUCERS—*and followed by the shot going out of focus);*

3. *"about Fakes" (coming into focus and shown already painted on a label on a film can; several more film cans clatter on top of it, the top can saying);*

4. *"a film by Orson Welles" (shown already painted on a label on a film can; the camera pans to the left to a stack of adjacent multicolored film cans and moves up to);*

5. *"WITH THE/COLLABORATION/OF CERTAIN" (shown already painted on the sides of three separate film cans; the camera moves up to);*

6. *"EXPERT/PRACTIONERS" (shown already painted on the sides of two separate film cans; the camera moves up to);*

7. *"and INTRODUCING" (shown already painted on the side of one film can; the camera moves up to);*

8. *"OJA KODAR" (shown already painted twice on two separate film cans; the camera moves up to frame the top version in the center).*

One of the first questions raised by this assembly—and the only one which I intend to address here—concerns the word "practioners." No such word exists in the English language; it cannot be found, at least, in any of my dictionaries. Yet because of the speed with which we read it (the hand or the film frame is quicker than the eye), most of us assume that the word is probably "practitioners." We read it, in other words, as if it makes sense.

Does this qualify as a typo like one of those in the "Deleuze text" quoted above? Hardly. Appearing only four shots after an allusion to Welles's War of the Worlds *hoax on radio, the first of his major pseudodocumentaries, it is one of the earliest signs in the film that our own gullibility is this film's principal subject. Gullibility, after all, is only just another form of imagination, and the imagination of the audience remains the essential tool in Welles's box of tricks throughout his career—the central factor that makes everything else possible. What we think is what we get, and what we think is not so much what we see as what we think we see.*

Notes

1. "Between Works and Texts," *The Magic World of Orson Welles*, rev. ed. (Southern Methodist University Press, 1989).
2. Special Orson Welles issue, *Cahiers du Cinéma*, hors série (1986).
3. It should be stressed, however, that Welles's plan to play Kurtz wavered, unlike his determination to play Marlow. As he expressed this uncertainty in separate conversations with Peter Bogdanovich in 1969 (for an interview book scheduled for publication by HarperCollins in 1992) and myself in 1972 (for an article, "The Voice and the Eye," published in *Film Comment,* November–December 1972), he contemplated playing Kurtz only because he was unable to find anyone else for the part. This same ambivalence is reflected in the fact that he assigned the Kurtz role to Ray Collins the first time he presented *Heart of Darkness* on the radio, and played the part himself the second time.
4. It should be noted, however, that Welles's narration in both THE LADY FROM SHANGHAI (1946) and MACBETH (1949) was occasioned by the recutting of his original versions; in neither case was it part of the original conception. ("A director," Welles was fond of saying, "is someone who presides over accidents.")
5. Letter to the author, 10 February 1987.
6. See, in particular, Stam's "Orson Welles, Brazil, and the Power of Blackness," as well as articles by Catherine Benamou and Susan Ryan in *Persistence of Vision* (special Welles issue), no. 7 (1989).
7. A further exploration of this subject can be found in my own reply to an article by Robin Bates in *Cinema Journal* 26, no. 4 (Summer 1987).
8. Special Orson Welles issue, *Cahiers du Cinéma*, hors série (1986).

—*Cinematograph*, vol. 4, 1991

The Importance of Being Perverse

Godard's KING LEAR

KING LEAR
Directed and written by Jean-Luc Godard
With Peter Sellars, Burgess Meredith, Jean-Luc Godard,
Molly Ringwald, Norman Mailer, Kate Miller,
Léos Carax, and Woody Allen

Jean-Luc Godard's latest monkey wrench aimed at the Cinematic Apparatus—that multifaceted, impregnable institution that regulates the production, distribution, exhibition, promotion, consumption, and discussion of movies—goes a lot further than most of its predecessors in creatively obfuscating most of the issues it raises. Admittedly, HAIL MARY caused quite a ruckus on its own, but mainly among people who never saw the film. KING LEAR, which I calculate to be Godard's thirty-fourth feature to date, has the peculiar effect of making everyone connected with it in any shape or form—director, actors, producers, distributors, exhibitors, spectators, critics—look, and presumably feel, rather silly. For better and for worse, it puts us all on the spot; as Roland Barthes once wrote of Pier Paolo Pasolini's SALO, it prevents us from redeeming ourselves.

From its birth, a table-napkin contract signed by Godard and producer Menahem Golan of Cannon Films at the Cannes Film Festival in 1985, to its disastrous world premiere at Cannes two years later, the project has always seemed farfetched and unreal, even as a hypothesis. From its inception, the film might be regarded as the packaging principle gone haywire; while the original package never quite made it to the screen—script by Norman Mailer, who would also play Lear; Woody Allen as the Fool—enough vestiges of it remain to prove that Godard has essentially honored, or at least parodied, the dottiness of the initial concept. He even starts the film off with a real phone conversation between himself and Golan, with the producer urging him to finish the film in time for Cannes: "Where *is* this film? We have talked about it, promoted it; so where is it?" Now that one can actually see the movie in a theater, it *remains* partially hypothetical, alas, because commerce has effec-

tively and summarily ruled out its most striking attribute. Having been fortunate enough to have seen KING LEAR at film festivals in Toronto and Rotterdam, I can testify that it has the most remarkable use of Dolby sound I have
ever heard in a film. So far, however, to the best of my knowledge, the film
has been shown in Dolby almost nowhere else, so you'll have to take my word
for it. The Music Box, which is showing the film locally in a limited one-
week engagement, has stereo speakers, but while it's probably the loveliest
movie theater of the 1920s still operating in Chicago and has a sound system
that is quite adequate for most things, the multiple separations needed for
Godard's split, staggered and overlapping channels—which play a variety of
tricks with distance, space, depth, and layered aural textures—simply aren't
there.

So the popular Hollywood-fostered myth that the best film technology
equals or guarantees the best art, pernicious enough to begin with, is given
the brutal force of law by commerce. The conventional, simplistic uses of
Dolby are the only kinds we can hear in theaters; ergo, they must be the best.
Conversely, the dazzling contrapuntal sound work of Godard here (and, to a
lesser extent, in the two-track Dolby of his DETECTIVE) can't be heard; ergo,
it can't be the best. Consequently, the film's disruption of the Cinematic Apparatus extends to the local rating system; if its sound track were fully audible, I would give it four stars rather than three.

After a flurry of alternate titles flashes on the screen (*Fear and Loathing, A
Study, An Approach, A Clearing, No Thing*), we get two successive takes of a
scene with Norman Mailer and his daughter Kate Miller playing themselves
in a hotel suite, discussing the script he has just written for the film—a Mafia
version of *King Lear* known as *Don Learo*—and momentarily interrupted by
the first of many screeching off-screen seagulls. Then Godard begins to nar-
rate off-screen in a raspy, grumpy voice how the "great writer" left the film
with his daughter after a display of "star behavior." (Mailer's own account of
the split, seconded by associate producer Tom Luddy, is that he would have
gladly delivered Godard's dialogue if it hadn't been assigned to a character
named Norman Mailer; apparently it touched on a theme of incest between
himself and his daughter.)

With Mailer and Miller both out of the way, the film turns next to American stage director Peter Sellars, who introduces himself off-screen as William
Shakespeare Jr. the Fifth, and roughly describes his job as restoring what he
can of his ancestor's plays after a massive cultural memory loss was brought
about by Chernobyl. Wandering around the town of Nyon, Switzerland (where
all of the film is set), with some of the dreamy dopiness Godard would have
assigned to Jean-Pierre Léaud in the 1960s, he encounters a new Lear and
Cordelia, played by Burgess Meredith and Molly Ringwald, in a fancy restaurant. As the film proceeds in fits and starts from there, we get snatches
of Shakespeare's *Lear*, snatches of what appears to be Mailer's *Don Learo*,

and snatches of what appears to be an earlier unrealized Godard project, *The Story*, about Jewish gangsters Bugsy Siegel and Meyer Lansky in Las Vegas. (*Three Journeys into King Lear*, as one printed title puts it. But does "King Lear" in this case refer to the play, the character, or the Cannon Films project?)

Like many of Godard's films, KING LEAR has a situation and a group of characters rather than a plot, and a series of fresh beginnings rather than a development. "This was after Chernobyl," intones William Shakespeare Jr. the Fifth. "We live in a time in which movies and art do not exist; they have to be reinvented." Photographs of filmmakers—Cocteau, Bresson, Pasolini, Visconti, Lang, Tati, Welles—are introduced at various points, presumably as *aides-mémoires*. When Godard himself appears in the flesh, as Shakespeare Jr.'s guru, he is called Professor Pluggy, speaking semicoherently out of one side of his mouth, accurately described in the movie's press book as a "Swiss Rasta Wizard with patch-cord dredlocks." Portions of Shakespeare's *Lear* fitfully recur (as when Lear receives telexes of fealty from Regan and Goneril, while the loving Cordelia pledges only "nothing," or rather, as the film stubbornly and obsessively repeats it, "no thing"); Pluggy is visited in both a mixing room and a screening room; a copy of Virginia Woolf's *The Waves* is bandied about, the novel's closing passage is quoted, and Edgar (French filmmaker Léos Carax) is assigned a wife named Virginia who "isn't there"; great works of art (by Gustave Doré and Tex Avery, among others) are quoted, some of them lit by candles; a shoebox model of a screening room is illuminated by a sparkler: another printed title informs us that this is "a film shot in the back"; Woody Allen briefly appears as the Fool, aka "Mr. Alien," in an editing room where a needle and thread are used to stitch pieces of film together.

"From a director of genius, a film which is, frankly, a mess," wrote Richard Roud in *Sight and Sound* last summer. Certain other critics were so aghast that their reviews rivaled the film in perversity and incoherence; more than one, for instance, claimed that Godard had obviously never read the play—a curious claim considering how much of the play is used and chewed over. And even many of the more sympathetic critics seemed to suffer from various kinds of post-Chernobyl amnesia: the supposedly hip and knowledgeable *Cahiers du Cinéma*, apparently forgetting Burgess Meredith's distinguished and varied past as an actor for Renoir, Lubitsch, and Preminger, as well as a writer and director, identified him simply as the trainer in ROCKY and ROCKY II; the *Village Voice* and its vigilant fact checkers, apparently forgetting Godard's ONE PLUS ONE, BRITISH SOUNDS, LETTER TO JANE, and his unfinished ONE A.M., identified KING LEAR as his first movie in English. One serious film critic seriously relayed to me her conviction that Godard's method of editing KING LEAR was to throw the celluloid in the air and see where it landed.

The point of all these critical aberrations is that, like the perverse fate of the film's sound track, the movie's cantankerousness actually seems to encourage them. In other words, as an assault on the Cinematic Apparatus, it actively works to make the critical community, including Godard's hardiest defenders, virtually tongue-tied. For a filmmaker whose gadfly relationship to dominant cinema has remained virtually constant for three decades, Godard is of course expected to be unexpected. But the relative narrative coherence of SAUVE QUI PEUT (LA VIE), FIRST NAME: CARMEN, DETECTIVE, and HAIL MARY may have lulled some viewers, Golan included, into expecting the kind of coherence (wrongly) associated with certain classic titles.

When I saw KING LEAR last year in Toronto, it struck me as being Godard's most exciting film since PASSION—his last feature, incidentally, where narrative *in*coherence reigned supreme—because of its prodigious and beautiful sound track. As important as words and sounds always are in Godard, this is possibly the only time that they truly overpower his images (considering Meredith's magnificent line readings of Shakespeare as well as all the other elements in the shifting aural textures, a tonal range extending from seagull squawks and pig grunts to electronically slowed-down human speech and choral music); the shots are certainly attractive, but their relative lack of distinction for a Godard film actually seems functional in relation to the richness of the sound track.

Without Dolby, some of the film's shortcomings become more apparent—such as its nervous habit of repeating and reshuffling shots and titles, a familiar Godardian reflex that by now suggests a tired jazzman falling back on an old lick in order to stall for time. But the strength that remains, which is principally destructive, is the film's dialectical relationship to most of the other movies that we see, its capacity to make their most time-honored conventions seem tedious, shopworn, and unnecessary. This originality often seems to be driven by hatred and anger, emotions that are undervalued in more cowardly periods such as the present, just as they were probably overvalued twenty years ago. It is a source of energy that remains crucial to much of the avant-garde, epitomized by a line spoken by a character in William Gass's story "In the Heart of the Heart of the Country": "I want to rise so high that when I shit I won't miss anybody."

For Godard, it's a legitimate source of pride that he won't film anything to illustrate a scriptwriter's point or provide continuity; his disdain for ordinary filmmaking practice becomes a creative challenge, and, in terms of his limited capacities for storytelling, a calculated risk. The previous Godard film that KING LEAR most resembles—the insufferable WIND FROM THE EAST (1970), prized by many academic armchair radicals for its simplistic and "teachable" theoretical schemata—also confronts narrative from a nonnarrative position, but with some important differences. Even at his most absurdist, as in LEAR, Godard has a lot more knowledge at his disposal sixteen years later—in knowing how to film nature, appreciate or ponder an actor or a text, light a shot, or simply fill a moment with sound, color, shape, and movement. What he seems to have less of—in the absence of his former cinéphilia and Marxism—is a pretext for getting from one of these moments to the next.

If Picasso's various periods as an artist are often identified by separate colors, Godard's periods might be linked to different styles of self-portraiture. From the beginning of BREATHLESS (1959) to the "end of cinema" title concluding WEEKEND (1967), it was Godard the film critic and the all-purpose sage. Godard #2, who lasted roughly from May 1968 through the mid-1970s, was a political/theoretical rebuke to his predecessor, working principally in 16-millimeter and in collaboration with others (first with Jean-Pierre Gorin and the Dziga Vertov Group, then with Anne-Marie Miéville at their short-lived studio, Sonimage, in Grenoble). Godard #3, who began around the time that Godard moved with Miéville back to his native Switzerland, also marked a return to more commercial considerations (i.e., stars and stories—which Godard #2 had mainly abandoned) and a more concerted move toward placing himself in his work—either literally, as an actor, or autobiographically, as in SAUVE QUI PEUT (LA VIE) or PASSION, where actors stand in for him.

Properly speaking, as an actor, Godard #3 has A and B versions: the abrasive, crotchety, boorish Godard who figures in FIRST NAME: CARMEN, MEETIN' WA (his taped 1985 interview with Woody Allen), and KING LEAR; and the more benign, elder statesman persona who appears in SOIGNE TA DROITE (his most recent feature) and some of his more recent interviews and television appearances. The fact that 3A and 3B are consecutive suggests that Godard may be beginning to mellow, but the difference may also have something to do with money and power. Just as the theme of prostitution has cropped up frequently in his work, but only when he shoots in 35-millimeter, Godard the curmudgeon seems likelier to emerge when he has to share space with bankable stars.

There's a minor tradition, however, detectable in some of Cannon Films' more artistic productions that KING LEAR certainly belongs to—what might be called the uncompromised/personal home-movie tradition. John Cassavetes's LOVE STREAMS and Norman Mailer's TOUGH GUYS DON'T DANCE are the two most distinguished examples that come to mind, both using their writer-director's homes as their central locations, and both so supremely personal on the level of style that every passing inflection—from incidental uses of music to line deliveries to camera angles to editing rhythms—expresses the personality of the creator. (One wonders if Râúl Ruiz's forthcoming TREASURE ISLAND for Cannon will have some of this quality.)

KING LEAR isn't literally set in Godard's home, but according to my atlas, it's no more than a few miles away. More importantly, it registers as a personal work in a way that most of his recent features do not. One isolated thematic example of this can be gleaned from a recent interview—that the shoe-box model of a screening room duplicates a toy cinema that Anne-Marie

Miéville built for herself when she was eight years old. The point of this detail isn't to argue that we all need a skeleton key to the film, which Godard's or Miéville's personal life supplies, but to suggest that many of its meanings are too hermetic *by design* to fall within our grasp.

In fact, one might argue that the film's deliberate elusiveness can be traced back to a particular reading of Shakespeare's *Lear*—specifically, the refusal of Cordelia to declare her love for her father, a king relinquishing his power, which sets the whole tragedy in motion. Unlike Goneril and Regan, her sisters, who comply with the old man's demand that they convert whatever love they might claim to have for him into a commodity, a public display of "proof," Cordelia—who later proves to be his *only* faithful and loving daughter—can only declare, "Nothing," which leads him to disinherit her. This "nothing," which Godard's film pointedly represents as "no thing," points to the refusal to become a commodity, to function as an object—a refusal which, as I have tried to show, is basic to the film's strategies, and relates to more than just a refusal to behave like a normal, "consumable" product. Theoretically and practically, a film that is "no thing" threatens and challenges the functioning of the Cinematic Apparatus itself. Indeed, as Golan himself expresses the dilemma, "Where *is* this film?" Like Lear, we all wind up disinheriting it, much preferring the comfortable lies of a Goneril or a Regan.

Consider, for instance, the movie's stars, its principal bankable assets: Molly Ringwald and Woody Allen for starters, Mailer, Sellars, Meredith, and Godard himself after that. In order to use the first two of these, and possibly some of the others, Godard had to agree not to use their names in the advertising. Moreover, he uses most of them in a way that contradicts their status as stars: Sellars is assigned the Woody Allen schlemiel part while Woody gets a few lines of Shakespeare but no laughs at all; Ringwald is framed and lit in a manner that makes her virtually interchangeable with Isabelle Huppert in PASSION; Godard makes his own barks and mumbles border on incoherence. Only the nearly forgotten Burgess Meredith is permitted some of his former eloquence.

In a related fashion, whatever might turn the film into "a Shakespeare play," "a Mailer script," "a story," or even "a Godard film" in the usual sense is purposefully subverted. The film aspires, like Cordelia, to be (and to say) "no thing," to exist and to function as a nonobject: ungraspable, intractable, unconsumable. For a movie that is concerned, like Shakespeare's play, with ultimate essences rather than fleeting satisfactions, it is an aspiration that has an unimpeachable logic.

—*Chicago Reader*, 8 April 1988

Alain Resnais and MÉLO

---★★★★

MÉLO
Directed by Alain Resnais
Written by Henry Bernstein
With André Dussollier, Sabine Azema, Pierre Arditi,
and Fanny Ardant

The exquisite art of MÉLO, like the art of Alain Resnais in general, bears a certain resemblance to sculpture: it needs to be seen from several different vantage points if one is to fully appreciate its shapeliness and the powerful multiplicity of its meanings. The following selection of vantage points can't pretend to be exhaustive; at best, it presents only a few starting points for sounding the bottomless depths of this deceptively simple movie. The first six points are provided by the film's title and the names listed in the heading above. The last four—theater, mise en scène, symmetry, and mystery—offer more general and abstract perspectives.

1. MÉLO. The title is an abbreviation for *mélodrame* or melodrama, which derive from the Greek word *melos*, music, and the French word *drame*, drama. What do we usually mean by melodrama? "Sensational dramatic piece with violent appeals to emotions" and "extravagantly theatrical play in which action and plot predominate over characterization" are two relevant dictionary definitions, among others. The earlier meaning is drama with music.

All three of the major characters in MÉLO are musicians, and many of the film's most intense passages occur when they are either performing music (usually together) or recollecting earlier performances. Resnais has consciously extended this principle by "scoring" and "conducting" the dialogue as if it were itself music. The two longest and most mesmerizing cadenzas in the film are monologues contained in single shots, accompanied by nearly continuous camera movement and subtle lighting changes.

In the first, near the beginning, Marcel Blanc (André Dussollier) recounts to his old music-conservatory chum Pierre Belcroix (Pierre Arditi) and Pierre's wife Romaine (Sabine Azema) a story that seeks to explain why years ago he

190

gave up hoping for a love of total trust. On tour in Havana with his mistress Hélène, he played Bach's Third Violin Sonata at a concert, addressing it and his emotions directly to her in the front row—only to discover her exchanging glances with a stranger several seats away, a gesture that she lied about later when he questioned her about it.

In the second cadenza, near the end, a few years after the suicide of Romaine—who began a brief, secret affair with Marcel the day after he delivered the above-mentioned monologue—her husband and Marcel's friend, Pierre, recites to Marcel by heart the letter that she wrote to him before drowning herself in the Seine.

The musicality of both of these monologues is intensified by very slow camera movements—beginning in both cases with Pierre and ending on Marcel—and by changes in lighting that occur along the way, changes that have no realistic causes but serve dramatic ends. The first camera movement drifts from left to right behind Pierre and Romaine—who (like the camera) are facing Marcel at the other end of a table—before moving into a close-up of Marcel. The successive configurations on the screen during this remarkable lengthy take are as follows: Marcel-Pierre-Romaine; Pierre-Marcel-Romaine; Romaine-Marcel; and Marcel alone. This series is a "musical" prefiguration, as it were, of the drama as a whole as seen from Marcel's viewpoint; the story begins with Marcel set apart from the married couple, continues with Marcel intervening between them, and then focuses on Romaine and Marcel together, before concluding with Marcel alone. In the second cadenza, while Romaine's suicide letter is being recited by Pierre, the camera traverses the increasingly dark stretch of empty space between Pierre and Marcel, until it finally arrives at Marcel's tear-stained face. The darkness "stands in" for the missing Romaine.

The importance of music is apparent in MÉLO before a single note is played or a single word is spoken. The film opens with a stylish art deco theater program for Henry Bernstein's play *Mélo* as it would have been presented in Paris when the play opened on 11 March 1929, except that the names and oval portraits of the actors and director—whom we see as the pages are slowly turned, while we hear the off-screen murmur of an opening-night audience—are those of the film MÉLO. Then, after we read on the last page, "9:30 P.M., June 1926, in Montrouge on the outskirts of Paris," we see a painting of a red theater curtain while we hear the traditional raps against the floor which begin a French stage performance, and there is a lap dissolve to Pierre knocking out his pipe in a continuation of the same raps—in the backyard of his house with Marcel and Romaine at the end of a pleasant meal. The percussive sound of this knocking succinctly prepares us for the musicality of the dialogue, and the dialogue about music.

2. *Alain Resnais.* Barring only the octogenarian Robert Bresson, who may never shoot again, Resnais is incontestably the greatest living French

filmmaker, and quite possibly the French director who has been most frequently *and* unjustly maligned in this country. Despite the fact that he has substantially revised his form and style for each of his eleven features to date, working with a total of eight separate writers, his films share an emotional purity, a visual elegance, and a rhythmic grace that together constitute a recognizable signature. And his central preoccupations—memory, loss, love, death, and desire—have remained more or less constant. The problems he has posed for American aesthetes appear to have been equally constant.

The standard (and unwarranted) objection to Resnais in this country—that he's all form and no content, or, alternately, all technique and no feeling—can be heard from many of his alleged defenders as well as many of his overt attackers. "Resnais knows all about beauty," Susan Sontag conceded at the end of her 1963 review of MURIEL, his third feature. "But his films lack tonicity and vigor, directness of address. They are cautious, somehow, overburdened and synthetic. They do not go to the end, either of the idea or of the emotion which inspires them, which all great art must do."

Twenty-five years later, although one can certainly single out Resnais features that are flawed (JE T'AIME, JE T'AIME, L'AMOUR À MORT) or relatively minor (STAVISKY, LA VIE EST UN ROMAN) or both (LA GUERRE EST FINIE), only two of Sontag's complaints seem to hold up: Resnais' films are all synthetic, and they lack directness of address. The same could be said for the collected fiction of Henry James, William Faulkner, and Jorge Luis Borges.

Actually, I think what bothers many American critics about Resnais is that he scares and confuses them: LAST YEAR AT MARIENBAD has got to be one of the scariest and most confusing movies ever made, and many have never forgiven Resnais (and Alain Robbe-Grillet, his scriptwriter) for the radical upset it caused here in the early 1960s. The fact that Resnais tells stories *and* experiments with form expels him from the avant-garde and mainstream alike. He's an avid fan of "Dick Tracy" and Stephen Sondheim, but intimidated Americans have wrongly made him out to be some forbidding kind of French intellectual. Maybe what they can't stand is his delicacy: "Even at its best," writes a smirking capsule writer in *The New Yorker*, "MÉLO isn't much more than a classy dinner-theatre production—without the dinner." The pregnant pause in that leaden one-liner, with its scantily covered guffaw showing through, is the opposite of the finesse that Resnais brings to his smallest gestures as a director. But French artists who can be funny without farting are not likely to make it onto videocassette, and classy dinner-theater *with* the dinner (e.g., MY DINNER WITH ANDRÉ) is more in line with *The New Yorker*'s taste.

Other confusions for critics: Resnais is an intensely personal director who never writes his own scripts, although his role as an instigator and editor of scripts has never been properly evaluated. (MÉLO is the only feature he's filmed that was not written expressly for him—playwright Henry Bernstein died in 1953—and although Resnais modestly takes no script credit, the movie runs for about an hour less than the original play.) As a post-Surrealist, Resnais has a certain affinity with writers who launch certain works for the sake of taking on particular challenges. Much as Georges Perec wrote *La disparition* in order to prove that he could write a novel without using the letter *e*, Resnais chose to film *Mélo* partially to prove that a supposedly dated and unproducible playwright, one who was once all the rage and whom Resnais loved as a teenager, could be brought back to life again.

Actually, the precise origins of this film are a little more complex—and arbitrary—than that. For some time, Resnais had been working with the Czech novelist Milan Kundera on a contemporary script that would be relatively expensive to produce. Not wanting to remain inactive while the money was being raised, he started to look around for another project. Fanny Ardant suggested doing a play, and added, "You're always talking about Henry Bernstein"—apparently confusing this name with Leonard Bernstein, whose theories about musical structure fascinated Resnais. In short, what transpired was a kind of Surrealist accident, in which the conjunction of the title *Mélo* with the name Leonard Bernstein may have helped to suggest certain aspects of Resnais' approach to the material. (This form of creative indirection may be what confuses some American critics the most. But the method of trusting one's unconscious and arriving at the personal *through* indirection has had many distinguished literary precedents, from *Madame Bovary* to *Impressions of Africa* to *Finnegans Wake*.)

3. *Henry Bernstein (1876–1953)*. Among many other things, MÉLO is a profound history lesson, and part of the lesson it imparts involves the completely eclipsed reputation of the play's author. Thirty of his plays opened in Paris between 1900 and 1952, over half of them at Bernstein's own theater, and according to critic Claude Beylie, virtually none of them except for the last two was a flop. Yet his work has suffered an almost total blackout in the thirty-five years since his death. (Resnais, who was only seven when *Mélo* opened in 1929—with Charles Boyer as Marcel and Gaby Morlay as Romaine—never saw the original production, which ran for some five hundred performances, but he attended ten of Bernstein's subsequent plays over the years and read most of the others.)

Perhaps the most dated aspect of Bernstein's work for contemporary French tastes can be summed up in one word: psychology. As Resnais has pointed out, the three leading characters in MÉLO are all neurotics; and the compulsive rhythms and obsessional themes in their dialogue might be described as the point at which Bernstein's fascination with their psychology meets Resnais' interest in music. In the 1929 theater program for *Mélo*, Bernstein wrote that he regarded the play as "the most complete expression of my thought and sensibility" and "a synthesis of all the themes that I have become attentive to"; the role played by music in sublimating (as much as expressing) the extreme emotions of the characters and their repressed psychological states surely has a lot to do with this synthesis.

4. *André Dussollier (Marcel)*. Expressing and exposing contradictory layers in the same character seems to be a specialty for this remarkable actor. It may not be evident in his film debut as a hapless and naive sociologist in Truffaut's SUCH A GORGEOUS KID LIKE ME (1973), but it is fully in flower in Rohmer's LE BEAU MARIAGE (1982), where he plays an attractive young lawyer whom the heroine (Béatrice Romand) barely knows but is determined to marry. Dussollier only puts in four appearances in Rohmer's film, none of them very extended, but the reality and complexity he brings to his simple part are awesome. His performance is at once an impersonation of a conceited yet polite pretty boy, an objective commentary on this type of individual, and a series of mitigating notations on the man that make it impossible to polish him off simply or superficially. Rohmer's script is deliberately constructed so that we never learn a lot about this character; Dussollier's uncommon achievement is to take this elusive figure, whom the heroine flagrantly misreads, and suggest volumes without allowing us to arrive at a cozy moral attitude toward him *or* a "finished" portrait of who he actually is.

In MÉLO, Dussollier's Marcel Blanc (whose last name is appropriate) is constructed on certain related principles. The character is hardly the same—Marcel is a sensitive musician, not a hotshot lawyer, and although he conveys a similar impression of being a rather glib ladies' man and bon vivant, his style is a good deal more passive/aggressive. The dramatic curve that leads from the story of his lover's lie in the first act to his own lie in the third (to Pierre, about his involvement with Romaine) never gives us a fully rounded character to grasp, and Dussollier again uses this limitation to his fullest advantage. Once again, we have to collaborate with him in order to construct his character, and part of Dussollier's brilliance is his capacity to ensure that we don't jump to any easy conclusions as we apply the finishing touches.

5. *Sabine Azema (Romaine)*. The giddy affectations of Romaine, nicknamed Maniche by Pierre, constitute a stumbling block for some viewers of MÉLO, because the character as presented by the actress Sabine Azema is not always easy to take. But Romaine, the hub of an adulterous love triangle who is eventually driven batty by her devotion to Pierre and passion for Marcel, is a character defined by such emotional extremes that it would probably be a betrayal of the material for any actress to play her *un*abrasively. The despair and confusion that lead her to try poisoning Pierre before she finally drowns herself instead is at the heart of what makes this play both powerful in its own terms and profoundly unfashionable in ours.

The "cuteness" of Romaine, which Azema seizes and plays to the hilt, is one of the characteristics that a conventional contemporary adaptation would probably minimize. But Resnais and Azema seem interested in the way that the character is buffeted back and forth between the men like a giggling and decorative beanbag; making her something of a Freudian hysteric to boot, the film places her emotional maelstrom at the center of its focus, and Azema's frenetic performance is precisely what places the spectator in an emotional bind: one is forced to become either emotionally implicated in her turmoil, as audiences of the original stage production presumably were, or to reject the experience entirely. The most common form of this rejection is, of course, laughter—a sure sign of emotional fear or panic, triggered in this case by Resnais' absolute refusal to suggest any overtones of nostalgia or camp (which forces some spectators to import or manufacture their own). In a way, this scariness is the reverse of the scariness of MARIENBAD, where nostalgia and camp of various kinds give the film's deadpan surface a decidedly macabre edge. But as MÉLO pungently demonstrates, facing decisions in the past without the placebos of simplification is potentially just as terrifying to an audience as confronting decisions in the present.

6. *Pierre Arditi (Pierre) and Fanny Ardant (Christiane)*. The quartet of Dussollier, Azema, Arditi, and Ardant appeared in Resnais' two previous films, LA VIE EST UN ROMAN and L'AMOUR À MORT—movies whose exposure in the United States has been so limited that the above classification of them as "relatively minor" and "flawed," respectively, should be regarded as interim judgments at best. (Most of Resnais' films improve greatly with repeated viewings; after three or four looks at MÉLO over the past year, I feel I'm only beginning to make its acquaintance, but there's no question that each time it grows considerably.) The fact that Resnais has used these four actors three times in a row, and quite differently each time, can be interpreted two ways: as another example of the arbitrariness of his initial premises, or, conversely, as one aspect of the firmness and confidence of his technique, which partially depends on working with actors whose capacities are well known to him. Considering the extraordinary ensemble acting in MÉLO, which was shot in a little over three weeks, it is worth remarking that this work was preceded by another three weeks of rehearsals.

The casting here has a number of other implications. Arditi and Azema played a married couple as well in the somewhat Bergmanesque L'AMOUR À MORT, but there it was Arditi who died (only momentarily, before coming back to life), and at the beginning of the film rather than toward the end. Ardant's role in MÉLO, as Christiane—Romaine's cousin, who eventually marries Pierre after Romaine's death—is much briefer than her previous roles in Resnais films, but, as Resnais himself has noted, the fact that it's Ardant tells us in advance that the role is important. For as we discover in her longest scene—a conversation with a priest at the beginning of act three—she is the only character who seems to know everything that's going on: not only the clandestine affair of Romaine and Marcel (which Pierre later suspects, but never knows about for sure), but also Romaine's anguished attempt to poison Pierre, which neither Pierre nor Marcel ever learns about (although it's the most direct cause of her suicide).

The infantile side of Pierre's character, impressively caught by Arditi, is contained in Romaine's pet name for him, Pierrot, just as his pet name for her, Maniche, seems to point to her own infantilism. It is finally their mutual infantilism rather than their shared love of music (which her affair with Marcel complicates) that draws them together, more like siblings in some respects than like man and wife. When Pierre is suffering from her poison (unknowingly) and begs her to join him in playing a Brahms sonata—a piece he used to play with Marcel at the music conservatory, and which they begin to play together again at the play's final curtain—she refuses, but when he asks her to perform a series of somersaults for him, she happily complies. (Last year, Arditi and Azema both won Césars—the French equivalent of Oscars—for their performances in MÉLO.)

The fact that Romaine is unable to have a child with Pierre while Christiane subsequently can and does (as Romaine predicts) may be related to this infantilism—that is, Romaine becomes the child that she can't have. Christiane, by contrast, relates to Pierre like a mother, while Marcel's relation to Romaine is rather like that of a father (their first "date," in effect, is a "music lesson"). And in the final playing of the Brahms sonata by Marcel and Pierre, it might be said that, emotionally speaking, each of the men has come to represent Romaine for the other.

7. *Theater.* It's hard to know whether Resnais has a developed theory about theater and film—in fact, it's hard to regard him as a theoretician at all—but in practice, he proceeds in MÉLO as if film and theater were kissing cousins rather than natural enemies or mutually exclusive options. Like Cocteau in LES PARENTS TERRIBLES and Ichikawa in AN ACTOR'S REVENGE, he makes the theatrical cinematic, and the cinematic theatrical. By never letting us forget that we're watching a play, he allows us to yield the maximum from the fact that we're watching a movie.

Resnais' respect for the theatricality of the original is perhaps most apparent in the opening scene, set in Pierre and Romaine's garden toward the end of their evening with Marcel. Here Resnais rigorously avoids showing us the "fourth wall"—the wall "through" which we would see the action if we were watching a play—and Jacques Saulnier's lovely set includes all the artificial elements we would expect to find on a stage: twinkling stars, moon, an intricately lit background that offers a theatrically realistic impression of distant buildings in the neighborhood, and so on. And the lengthy takes, long enough at times to recall Hitchcock's ROPE, heighten the theatrical effect further with their respect for real time.

The theater's respect for real time, however, is customarily reserved for on-stage rather than off-stage action. Toward the end of this garden scene, for example, Marcel leaves for his car, accompanied by Pierre, and then, off-stage and off-screen, discovers that he has forgotten to deliver some roses that he brought for Romaine; he gives the flowers to Pierre, who returns to the garden and presents them to Romaine. Following theatrical convention, these off-stage events transpire much more quickly than they possibly could in real time, and by keeping his camera glued to the garden set, Resnais makes us acutely aware of this discrepancy. Later, in the second act, the minuscule interval that passes between the time Christiane calls for a doctor and the moment he arrives is made even more ludicrously apparent. The play's status as play is constantly thrown into relief by Resnais' apparent refusal to "adapt" it; he even focuses on a red theater curtain between acts.

This drawing of our attention to the artificiality of conventions—what the Russian Formalists refer to as "baring the device"—might seem, according to our generally unconscious adoption of those conventions, to be a way of distracting us from the characters and plot. But in practice this isn't really the case; instead the practice creates a series of different perspectives on the same material—a cubist or sculptural effect that actually allows us more possible points of entry. As a parallel example of this phenomenon, consider Sterne's novel *Tristram Shandy*—a favorite example of the Russian Formalists, because it "bares the device" at every turn, in every conceivable way, from the numbering of pages and chapters to the functions of the authorial voice. Yet at no point does this diminish the three-dimensionality of its characters and fictional world; if anything, Sterne's diverse high jinks only reinforce the solidity of Uncle Toby and Shandy Green.

In any case, Resnais' emphasis on theatrical convention is fairly systematic, but not programmatic: that is, he comes up with a number of ingenious solutions for handling theatrical space without mechanically repeating his procedures. One claustrophobic sequence in a nightclub, for example, shows the action exclusively in a mirror. And while, if memory serves, Pierre and Romaine's bedroom seems, like their garden, to be shown without a fourth wall, the living room of Marcel's flat seems to be shown from a greater number of perspectives—so many, in fact, that each new scene set there seems to redefine its space.

8. *Mise en scène.* The French word for "direction," which means literally "placing on the stage," was decked out with hyphens as "mise-en-scène" by Andrew Sarris in the early 1960s—around the same time that he began writing about "auteur theory"—and has been burdened with mystical connotations ever since. French theorist and filmmaker Alexandre Astruc defined it as "a means of transforming the world into a spectacle given primarily to oneself," but Sarris went much further: "Dare I come out and say what I think it to be is an élan of the soul?"

The question seems worth bringing up because "mise en scène" is the credit Resnais assigns himself at the beginning of MÉLO, as opposed to the more modest "réalisation" (realization) or the less modest "un film de . . ." (a film by . . .), both of which are more common. In the case of MÉLO, I think mise en scène can be said to mean all of the following: adaptation of the play into a script (which includes a great deal of condensation; citing Cocteau's description of his own 1921 "contraction" of *Antigone*, Resnais compares it to photographing Greece from an airplane); choosing actors and crew; supervising the selection of costumes and the construction of sets; directing the actors; selecting camera angles and lenses, and determining if, where, and how the camera moves, and how the lighting changes, with the help of the cinematographer (Charlie Van Damme); working with the composer of the original music (Philippe-Gérard); and doing the final edit. In short, quite a bit more than the function of "mise-en-scène" assigned by Sarris to Hollywood contract directors.

My earlier suggestion that Resnais' handling of lighting and camera movements in conjunction with speech resembles the scoring and conducting of music finds its strongest example in the opening scene. To return to the virtuoso extended take, during which Marcel tells Pierre and Romaine about the disillusionment he suffered while performing a Bach sonata at a concert in Havana—a crucial moment in the plot, because this later seems to be the precise moment at which Romaine falls in love with Marcel, setting the whole chain of melodramatic events in motion—Resnais' masterful mise en scène contrives to give us the effect of a flashback without once cutting away from the characters in the present and the sounds in the garden.

How does he do this? Two of the major elements in Marcel's story are the music he is playing at the concert and his nervous concern about the attention of his mistress Hélène in the audience. Resnais's slow camera movement—which moves first behind Pierre and Romaine, and then toward Marcel—helps us to conjure up both of these elements. The steady movement of the camera becomes the steady flow of the sonata, and Marcel's agitated scanning of the concert audience for his mistress's face becomes the camera scanning past Pierre and Romaine while Marcel is addressing them.

As stated earlier, the various "stations" of the camera and configurations of the characters during this sequence prefigure Marcel's subjective experience of the entire drama to come. So the complex achievement of Resnais' mise en scène in this shot is to superimpose three separate tenses and experiences at once—the subjective past (Marcel's monologue), the objective present (Marcel telling the anecdote to Pierre and Romaine), and the subjective future (Marcel's perception of his affair with Romaine)—and to do so in a manner that is simple, fluid, and mesmerizing, quite the reverse of what Sontag refers to as "overburdened" in his earlier features, which also aim at constructing multiple tenses.

9. *Symmetry*. The construction of Bernstein's play depends on a great many substitutions and displacements; Resnais' adaptation helps to throw

them into relief by treating the symmetries like the repetitions and variations of musical motifs.

The main examples of this that come to mind concern two sonatas and a series of lies. In the first scene, Pierre discusses his love for Brahms's Sonata for Violin and Piano in G Major, which is the main piece that he and Romaine play together, and which reminds him of his youth with Marcel at the conservatory. Later, Marcel recalls his performance of Bach's Sonata for Violin in C Major in Havana.

The second scene, a secret meeting between Romaine and Marcel at the latter's Paris flat, begins as they're playing the last measures of the Brahms sonata, and ends as Marcel begins to perform the Bach. In the second act, during the attempted poisoning, Pierre tries to convince Romaine to play the Brahms sonata with him—a piece that, years later, Marcel agrees to play with him at the end of the third act.

In a similar instance of symmetry, Marcel's detailed and elaborate lie to Pierre in the final scene—that Romaine loved only her husband and remained faithful to him, and that his own tears are caused by a current lover and unresolved relationship—forms a complex and ambiguous rhyme effect with the lie told to him by his mistress Hélène in Havana. In between these two poles, Romaine tells elaborate and multiple lies to Pierre, and a priest urges Christiane to conceal the truth about Romaine from Pierre. The constellation of all these lies provides a universe of moral relativity that makes us much less confident about the wrongness of lying than Marcel is in the opening scene. Although lying ends a relationship of love and trust with Hélène, it effectively preserves one with Pierre, as well as Pierre's memory of his relationship with Romaine.

10. *Mystery.* This moral ambiguity is merely one facet of a voluptuous mysteriousness that envelops MÉLO as a whole: its characters, its plot, its period, its meanings. For every artificial detail, there is a corresponding element of authenticity and truth: the "artificial" theater program containing the names and faces of Azema, Ardant, Arditi, Dussollier, Bernstein, and Resnais has the same art deco cover as the "real" theater program of 1929; the studio set of Marcel's flat contains real artworks by Juan Gris and Henri Laurens rather than reproductions (for the sake of the actors, according to Resnais). The complex dialogue created by the film—a dialogue between the style of the 1920s and the content of the 1980s—ultimately makes us just as much aware of the content of the 1920s and the style of the 1980s. (MÉLO is certainly a film of the 1980s rather than an antique, but it may take us another twenty years to determine why and how.)

Our usual view of the past, as filtered through nostalgia and other forms of ideological reduction and simplification, is glimpsed as if through the wrong end of a telescope. (A model for this shrinkage is provided by Main Street, U.S.A. in Disneyland and Disney World, where every brick, shingle, window, and gas-lamp is five-eighths the normal size—allowing every pint-sized customer to conclude glibly that the present is much larger than the past.) By making the past as vast, as complex, and as luminously real as the present—perhaps even more so, if one considers the depleted view of the present offered by most movies—MÉLO suddenly puts us in touch with how remote and self-serving our usual bite-size portions of history are, and how much remains to be discovered and rediscovered.

How much do we finally know about Romaine and why she commits suicide? According to what the plot implies, the moment that she falls in love with Marcel and the moment that she decides to kill herself are both moments that we *see*; yet she remains mainly a closed book to us. When she arranges for a musical session at Marcel's flat, and takes steps to conceal this rendezvous from Pierre, we may conclude along with Marcel that she wants to sleep with him. But when Marcel caustically says to her, "You sleep with everybody, don't you?" and she replies, "What's it to you?" are we to conclude from this that she *does* sleep around? If so, who and where are her other lovers?

If she loves Marcel so much that she's willing to leave Pierre for him, and if she loves Pierre so much that she can't bring herself to leave him (which is seemingly why she resorts to poison), why is her only suicide letter—which incidentally explains none of these things—written to Pierre and not to Marcel? And does Pierre really believe Marcel's lie at the end, or does he merely pretend to because his friend is so stubborn about maintaining it?

Much of the mysterious beauty of MÉLO circulates around such questions. Like the beauty and mystery of the music itself, the film moves progressively deeper into feelings and understandings, not to arrive at a single, fixed destination, but to implicate us in the very process of that unveiling, and in the very textures of that density. This is a masterpiece that uses as its point of departure the most hackneyed and familiar of melodramatic plots—the adulterous triangle and the attempted murder—and then makes it all seem brand new.

—*Chicago Reader*, 15 April 1988

Part Four

Provocations

Introduction

This is the most rebellious and contentious section of the book, and because of this, some readers will regard it as the least practical or viable. Before you make up your own mind about this, however, I'd like to ask you to examine precisely what you mean by "practical" and "viable." Do you mean most likely to change the world, or do you mean most likely to affect the majority? If in fact you believe that the likeliest way to change the world *is* invariably to affect the majority, then it might be beneficial to look at that premise a little more closely and see if it always holds up.

Speaking from my own experience, the times when I've reached the greatest number of readers at once—writing features in the pages of magazines like *Elle* and *Omni*—are the times when my point of view has had the least amount of effect. How do I know this? I can't exactly prove it, but a writer's sense of his or her impact comes from feedback, and I've had virtually no feedback at all on the pieces I've written for mass-market magazines.

It might be argued that my contributions to *Elle* and *Omni* have been too brief and occasional to carry much significance. What, then, of my regular stints on *Oui* (1974–1975) and *American Film* (1979–1980), my principal means of self-support the year before I moved from Paris to London and during the last stages of my work on *Moving Places*, respectively? In both cases, where I was often accorded more leeway than I had at *Elle* and *Omni*, the discernible impact of my pieces was again almost nil. This is not to say that I necessarily regarded my assignments for these magazines as hackwork. (Truthfully, sometimes I did and other times I didn't.) Either way, whether the editorial changes made in my copy were negligible or substantial, the published results, in my opinion, never carried much weight—which is why none of these pieces is included in this collection. (Theoretically, this *could* have turned out differently. My piece on Barthes in the first section, for instance, was originally commissioned by *American Film* and wound up in *Sight and Sound* only because the *American Film* editor decided against running it.)

As the result of such experiences, I usually feel that it's better to affect a few people very strongly than to affect a lot of people superficially. This is fundamentally at odds with the numbers game that permeates much of American thought—the assumption that not only can everyone be president, but anyone who doesn't try to become one is a damned fool. A few friends and relatives, for instance, believe that my job as a film critic for the *Chicago Reader* is "good" only in the sense that some day it might lead to something *really* "good," like being film critic for *The New Yorker*, when my response to this is that many of the pieces I've written for the *Reader*—which are fundamentally the pieces I've wanted to write—could never have been written for *The New Yorker*. In fact, when it comes to prestigious and powerful institutions like *The New York Times*, I wonder how much individuality really counts in the long run: Vincent Canby may be less square than Bosley Crowther, his long-term predecessor, but the *Times* is so much stronger than either of them that whoever gets the job of film critic there is likely to wind up writing with the same values and in the same way for the same audience, in the long run.

Admittedly, sometimes a fact or opinion can have weight and influence only *after* it becomes mass-market. I'm happy to report that a direct consequence of "OTHELLO Goes Hollywood"—written for the *Chicago Reader* and reprinted in part 2—is that the monks' chants that were removed from the film's opening scene in the so-called "restored" version were themselves restored to this version on video and laserdisc. I suspect, however, that this happened largely because my observation was picked up by a few national writers, such as Todd McCarthy in *Daily Variety*; if it had remained only in the *Reader*, it may have had no lasting effect.

To greater or lesser extents, the pieces in this section argue on behalf of minority positions that I don't expect most readers to share or adopt. This may sound defeatist to some, but only if consensus criticism of the sort that is commonly practiced is viewed as the ideal. In the case of my defense of HARDLY WORKING, it's worth noting that Jerry Lewis himself has called it his worst film—an opinion I disagree with—and that the movie has been eliminated from some retrospectives of his work, perhaps at his own request.

Speaking for myself, the critics who generally affect me the most aren't necessarily the ones I most agree with or with whom I most identify. Contrary to the rising popularity of both tribalism and "targeting" on a worldwide level—which would dictate, if I were to go along with it, that I assiduously search out middle-aged heterosexual southern Jewish film critics to read and befriend—I can't see much profit in looking exclusively for duplications of one's own positions, however comforting and validating it may be at times to find them. Although some compatibility of opinions obviously helps one to form a feeling of trust for some reviewers, it's rare that a feeling of total accord on a given subject will stimulate any further thought; more often its effect is to stop a line of thinking dead in its tracks.

■

It probably isn't coincidental that this section is the one containing most *Soho News* pieces, because the year and a half when I was writing regularly for this small-time alternative to the *Village Voice*—starting in May 1980 and concluding in November 1981—is the period when my writing was most contentious as well as combative. Apart from serving as film reviewer for that weekly (most often, alternating with Veronica Geng as the first-string critic), I had my only regular stint to date as a book reviewer (see bibliography)—a kind of work I regret I haven't had subsequent opportunities to do except sporadically. It's a period that overlapped with the publication of *Moving Places* in fall 1980—a formative experience that undoubtedly made me more assertive, especially once it became clear to me that the attention I had hoped the book would get was not forthcoming.

The premium placed on physical space in Manhattan has always seemed to me to have a lot to do with the way that people treat one another on that island. In fact, every stage of my stint at the *Soho News* seemed to reflect that fact. I was initially brought in as a writer at the suggestion of Richard Corliss—the paper's former first-string film critic, who had just left for *Time*— and the first suggestion of the arts editor, Tracy Young, was that I be used to cover experimental films as a way of forcing out another critic, who had been covering that beat on the paper for some time. During that same period, I should add, instances of what I considered to be that critic's arrogance and intolerance had already prompted two sarcastic letters from me that had both been published. But even though this critic struck me as embodying, along with some more valuable qualities, the epitome of provincial New York turf mentality, I made it clear to Tracy at the outset that I didn't see how it was necessary to force her out of the paper—surely there was room for both of us. So she stayed on; but when Tracy offered her the same invitation in reverse a year and a half later—reviewing experimental films as a way of forcing me out—she took it without blinking. (The turning point came when Tracy insisted that this critic would be perfectly capable of writing an "unbiased" review of a feature by her former husband, which I incidentally liked more than she did; I still recall my bitter amusement over the resulting piece, which failed to mention the film's lead actress—the director's current wife—even once.)

In between those two events, I must confess that Tracy granted me more freedom than any other editor has before or since, with the possible exception of Corliss at *Film Comment*. She wound up publishing nearly all of the seventy or so pieces I wrote for her, usually with minimal editing, and the one portion of a piece she rejected (after provisionally approving it in principle)—in praise of a film that at that point had failed to receive any public showings in New York, Straub/Huillet's FROM THE CLOUD TO THE RESISTANCE—was understandable given the consumerist nature of the paper's art section.*

Why Tracy eventually changed her mind about me and forced me out of the paper is not a matter that has ever been explained to me—nor was it a matter I felt I could ever ask her about. Indeed, the way I learned that I was no longer working for the paper—practically my only means of support at the time—was discovering that I could no longer reach her on the phone at her office. When I finally called her at home—she had given me her unlisted number months before—her only clarification was to tell me I was fired and to ask me not to call that number again.

Despite the lack of any explanation, I can think of at least two factors that probably played some role in my dismissal. One was the fact that the paper itself was in the process of going under and didn't last very long after I left. And another, I strongly suspect, was the cumulative effects of my combativeness in print. This included some sarcasm about South African gold mines being involved in the sponsoring of a festival of British films (which may have been especially imprudent given the Afrikaner ownership of the *Soho News* at the time); an attack on the New York Film Festival for refusing to invite me to any of its parties for three years in a row—particularly galling after I had sacrificed most of a holiday in order to oblige Corliss by writing a piece for *Film Comment* about their opening night film (A WEDDING)—which prompted an angry letter from Richard in the following issue, accusing me of

---

*The piece as a whole, entitled "Transcendental Cuisine," made its polemical point by interrupting my reviews of the usual weekly trash to talk about a movie that my readers couldn't see, which I had just shown in a course I was teaching at NYU. Tracy kept the trash reviews and discarded the rest, although over a year afterward, at the suggestion of Straub himself, I included the original piece, complete with the trash reviews, in an extensive monograph I edited to accompany a Straub/Huillet retrospective at the Public Theater. When I tried to reprint this piece in my book *Film: The Front Line 1983* (Arden Press, 1983), my editor, Fred Ramey, refused to let me reprint the trash reviews in the middle of the piece, with the result that my comments in the book proved to be as truncated as those in *Soho News*—once again because of the dictates of consumerism.

An even more sobering lesson in consumerism and rigid formats came when I discovered that both *The New Yorker* and the *Village Voice* were unwilling even to acknowledge in their listings that the Straub/Huillet retrospective included eleven important films by other filmmakers selected by Straub and Huillet—one of them, incidentally, a feature that was receiving its U.S. premiere (Luc Moullet's A GIRL IS A GUN). Typically, a letter of complaint about this to the *Voice* went unprinted, which shouldn't have surprised me: few New York publications will print any letters criticizing their editorial positions.

both paranoia and ingratitude; and, what may have been the coup de grâce, a prominently featured article, "Playing Oneself," which was essentially an argument for the ethical superiority of LIGHTNING OVER WATER over MY DINNER WITH ANDRÉ—and which contained a key sentence about the writer and costar of the latter film, Wallace Shawn, which later was quoted in *Esquire*: "I've known Wally Shawn intermittently over a 22-year period, and he's just about as nice as anyone can possibly be to someone he regards as a social inferior."

When Wally and I had been classmates at boarding school, he had been the only other student there who had asked to read my first novel. But when it came to getting his responses, I had to go around to his family apartment to see if he was there rather than phone him, because he refused to give me his phone number—a privilege he accorded then only to classmates he regarded as his social equals. Knowing that Tracy worshiped at the shrine of *The New Yorker*, whose editor in those days was Wally's father (an immensely kind and courteous man, I should add, who'd never shown to me any of Wally's cruelty)—and that Wally himself, who had reluctantly agreed to let me interview him (but only if he brought along André Gregory, his costar), had tried in vain afterward to get the paper to run another piece about his film—leads me to reflect on how blatantly I was playing with fire. For whatever it's worth, I still don't think that anything I wrote in the piece was unfair or unethical— my personal biases in the matter were established at the outset, and part of my motivation was defending Wim Wenders against some unfair charges that had been lodged against LIGHTNING OVER WATER elsewhere. But the fact that I was broaching at all the matter of Wally's privileged status at *The New York Times*—which had mercilessly trashed Wenders's film, as it would later trash his subsequent THE STATE OF THINGS even more unfairly—was clearly violating a sacrosanct taboo.

It's hard for me to evaluate this fearlessness and recklessness a dozen years later, since I'm no longer temperamentally disposed to wage such battles on the same terms today, but the ugliness of the social climate I was swimming through at the time certainly played a part in my rage. As one indication of this climate, I can recall a phone conversation I had with an editor at *American Film* in 1980, over a year before I left *Soho News*, which he opened by saying that he was sorry to hear I'd been fired. After I revealed to him that he was mistaken, he wouldn't tell me who his source for this misinformation was, but after a bit of detective work, I was able to uncover both the source and the basis for the story. The source was another critic whom I had regarded up to that point as one of my closest and most loyal friends. The basis was that still another critic, a protégé of Pauline Kael's who was eager to have my job, had heard that Pauline was having lunch with Tracy, and had let his eagerness and imagination run amok—telling another Kael protégé I'd already been fired and he'd already been hired, or words to that effect. I never learned the full extent of this chain reaction, but the "news" of the second protégé eventually reached my friend, who then informed not me but a magazine editor we both knew in Washington, D.C., about it. I should add that everyone involved in this little intrigue with the exception of myself—the editor, my friend, both protégés, and my informant—are today nationally known figures who write for highly respected publications with many millions of readers.

To me, the whole story represents the world of New York film critics in a nutshell and may help to account for the less measured tone adopted in some of my writing from this period. It also helps to explain why I don't harbor many regrets about no longer working in New York. By the time I moved to the west coast in 1983, I virtually felt I'd been run out of town on a rail. Many colleagues were even refusing to say hello to me on the street, though it's hard for me to see even today how my gadfly instincts had done their careers any appreciable harm. Fortunately, I still had a good many friends in the city; in fact, I continue to have more friends in New York than anywhere else in the world—but not the sort of professional contacts that would make me readily employable there.

Reflecting back on all the critical things I've had to say in this book about the New York film world, I should stress that many of the same problems may be even more prevalent in relation to theater. Ultimately these problems should be viewed as sociological rather than as the personal failings of individuals. The pertinent question is not why people who wish to get ahead in New York are obliged to flatter and whitewash those in positions in power, because clearly this situation exists everywhere else to some extent. What needs to be asked is why this is so much *more* the case in New York than it is elsewhere, with the result that intellectual candor in some areas becomes virtually impossible without unpleasant social consequences. I suspect that some critics would differ with me on this point, but I believe it is so much a fact of life that most New York critics have internalized it, and the few who haven't will know exactly what I'm talking about. If Georgia Brown in the *Village Voice* dares to question some of the bloc-voting of the New York Film Critics Circle or make fun of David Denby for declaring that even God would be frightened by JFK, she can undoubtedly expect to be treated like a pariah in some quarters for such unthinkable impertinence and rudeness—which is perfectly okay to display toward out-of-towners and filmmakers, but not toward one's more prominent colleagues (which can include programmers as well as critics). All things considered, it would be far easier to dismiss the entire European left in the pages of an alternative weekly—no one will penalize you for the presumption (and it's been done before)—than it would be to make fun of the silly notions of a single local media honcho.

In my introduction to part 1, I noted my initial surprise that individuals a lot more powerful than myself could be so unforgiving about any criticisms made of their work. Perhaps New York's peculiar restraints and self-censorships offer a partial explanation. If any intellectual challenge to those in power is deemed inadmissible to the "free" exchange of ideas, this surely can't help the confidence of these people in the long run, because they know their safety from such challenge is achieved only through an atmosphere of repression. No wonder they're so touchy.

Jerry Lewis's HARDLY WORKING

My dream scenario runs roughly like this: J. D. Salinger finally relents and allows Jerry Lewis to direct a film based on *The Catcher in the Rye* ("Salinger's sister told me if anyone would get it from him it would be me," Lewis remarked in a 1977 interview), and civilization as we know it collapses. In the ensuing sociocultural upheaval occasioned by this deconstruction of two critical reputations, anarchy reigns supreme: mad dogs roam the street, *The New Yorker* shrivels to a cinder out of acute, well-mannered embarrassment; and all those distinguished gray eminences in my profession who fear and loathe Lewis for what he says about their own bodies and social discomforts—some of whom shrink in terror from Tati for the same reasons—run screaming off to the Hamptons and Berkshires to write their own fiction, never to return.

As long as such a personal fulfillment fails to materialize, I guess you might say I'm hardly working. So is the cinema today, at least the kind I care about. Most serious European cinema is virtually banned in this country; major work in the 1970s by Akerman, Bresson, Duras, Godard, Rivette, Ruiz, Straub/Huillet, and Tati—which is allowed to occupy at least a small part of the intellectual life of Paris or London—scarcely exists even as hearsay on these shores. (After all, it might threaten the self-confidence of our tastemakers if they had to wrestle with anything more taxing than the shopping-mall goods of a Coppola or a Gaumont.) And it takes about a year from the time the latest Jerry Lewis movie (his first to be released in a decade) opens abroad to the time it straggles into trendy Manhattan, in a version twenty-odd minutes shorter.

Even the excitement of a new Michael Snow film, PRESENTS, that I was able to see in Toronto last month, and will be appearing here shortly, has to be confined strictly to a ghetto. It's clearly not challenging enough to most critics, who are still sweating over the intricacies of Paul Mazursky and Robert Benton. (Snow's name isn't even listed in the over seven thousand entries of Ephraim Katz's 1979 *The Film Encyclopedia*.) Truffaut discovered this box office secret years ago: your degree of seriousness and complexity is often gauged by your capacity to deal exclusively with the middle class. HARDLY WORKING—which deals with the working class and unemployment, and speaks directly to the racially, culturally, and economically disenfranchised (to judge by the delighted audiences I've been seeing it with)—doesn't rate on this scale at all.

■

A passionate Jerry Lewis fan since age seven (at MY FRIEND IRMA in 1950), I followed him religiously through his vehicles with Dean Martin in the 1950s. As I grew older, critics and friends started to teach me all the ways (and reasons why) I should dislike and be repelled by him; most of this had to do with either embarrassment or the unabashed artificiality of his public manner—an "education" that lasted through most of the 1960s. Then, for about the first half of the 1970s, I was lucky enough to be living in Paris—a freer, looser, and richer town than this one in certain respects—where I was able to resee a lot of Lewis's best films (all of them directed by either Lewis or his mentor, Frank Tashlin) and read some of the very interesting local criticism about him.

"Lewis is the only one making courageous films in Hollywood today," Godard remarked in 1967. More recently, on Dick Cavett's program last fall, Godard spoke wisely and well about the honesty of Lewis's film and its title, and he is absolutely right. Barring only Godard's own ICI ET AILLEURS and Wajda's MAN OF MARBLE, HARDLY WORKING is the most politically honest film I've seen this year. As a key document of the Reagan era, it is the only one to date I can even begin to identify with.

It is also unbearable, beautiful, terrible, wonderful, stupid, brilliant, awful, shocking, inept, and even very funny for various alternating stretches, much as Godard can be. The opening precredits montage, speeding us through a kind of refresher course in Lewis's 1960s work, is really comparable only to the beginning of TOUT VA BIEN. On a conventional level, it "hardly works" at all.

As in THE BELLBOY (1960), Lewis's first directed feature—also done in Florida locations on a minuscule budget—the gags follow a pattern of almost rigorous discontinuity: just one idea after another, each one stranger than the last. Thus the movie develops more on a thematic level (Lewis as a radically destructive force in the real world) than on a narrative one (an unemployed circus clown tries to hold a steady job). Directorially, it is perhaps his most mannerist film, particularly in its reaction shots, as mannerist as SEXTETTE or

RED LINE 7000 or ERASERHEAD. Pictorially, it is as much about aging as the last westerns of Hawks. (Lewis's face has never been half as interesting before.) Viscerally, it is as painfully direct about lost stamina as MAD WEDNESDAY or A KING IN NEW YORK, and not merely where Lewis is concerned: the sad, weary features of Harold J. Stone also compose a memorable site.

Like Salinger's best work ("Raise High the Roof Beam, Carpenters," not *Catcher*), HARDLY WORKING is about being inordinately hated as well as disproportionately loved, by one's self as well as by others—Lewis's objective situation. "I'm really happy I met you, Bo," the obligatory heroine (Deanna Lund) says to him; "You're happy you met *him*?" smirks her little boy—in the same tone of voice that a Fox publicist asked me, "You want to see this movie *again*?"

It's logical enough that Lewis parodies SATURDAY NIGHT FEVER—for what is Travolta's dancing in that movie but an autistic Lewis fantasy made socially acceptable?—but it's Lewis's peculiar form of honesty to show the fantasy deflated at once. "An inability to lie carried to the point of tragedy," Raymond Bellour's description of the last films of Fritz Lang, applies in spades here—even to some of the more grotesque details, such as Lewis wearing his expensive jewelry throughout, despite the fact that his character is either out of work or employed in menial jobs. When, toward the end of his stint as a postman, he arranges for a police escort to come along on his route, it's obviously a police escort accompanying a celebrity through a Florida suburb. (Snow, Godard, and Lewis are a lot closer than is generally supposed: all three are interested in *fields* rather than plots and often use autobiography to furnish their conceptual constructs, e.g., the exhaustion of space as action in PRESENTS, LE GAI SAVOIR, and HARDLY WORKING.)

Whole sections of this film are plastered up to their eyeballs in product plugs, from Budweiser to Goodyear, and Lewis makes no effort whatsoever to hide this practice, recalling his candor about plugs in chapter 13 of his book *The Total Filmmaker*. The movie seems profoundly Jewish—in its relations to food (a wonderful, excruciating donut-sampling scene in Stone's office) and to victimization, its Florida locations, its sexism, its playful sense of fantasy. Lewis's character Bo collapses into Lewis himself in so many different ways that the total effect is that of a personal, materialist documentary—as someone once called Sternberg's ANATAHAN, "My Heart Laid Bare." ("They must need clowns," Bo's sister tells him consolingly after the circus closes. "Sure, honey," Bo replies, "but who wants to get into politics?")

In the final analysis, solipsistically and in terms of solipsism's disastrous consequences, Jerry Lewis *is* America, and both are hardly working. So it's hardly surprising that this is a movie that tells more truth than any of us is entirely ready to bear.

DOOMED LOVE
The Masterpiece You Missed

How can I persuade you that the best new movie I've seen this year, the only one conceivably tinged with greatness, is a voluptuous four-and-a-half-hour Portuguese costume melodrama, shot in 16-millimeter? Obviously I can't. So rather than make you feel guilty about missing a masterpiece—as a couple of my friends managed to do when it was at MOMA last spring—let me assume at the outset that you will miss DOOMED LOVE all ten times that it shows at the Public between May 26 and June 14. Bearing this in mind, the following notes are an account of what you missed, are currently missing, or will miss.

1. If it's confusing and misleading for some to call DOOMED LOVE an avant-garde film, this seems mainly because of the widespread working assumption that "avant-garde" is a social category above and beyond an aesthetic one. As industry-oriented critics like Kael and Sarris are frequently reminding us (the former obliquely, the latter unabashedly), the crucial professional issue is not what movies we go to as critics but what parties, junkets, festivals, universities, grants, and other circuits of power we have easy access to—not what we see but what we *have* is our calling card, whereas "taste" is largely a rationalization for the personal erotics of self-gratification, cooperation, conflict, and flattery founded on such a system of exchange.

From this standpoint, calling DOOMED LOVE avant-garde might be tantamount to signing its death warrant. Indeed, it might even be worse than that, because avant-gardists as a group aren't even likely to claim the body at the morgue afterward. Practically speaking, in a philistine New York context, the film lacks both a launching pad *and* a burial ground; yet like any irritating, yammering masterpiece it somehow manages to create its own space for breathing and existing. Spoil-sports who insist on acknowledging and humoring it could do a lot worse than consult Carlos Clarens's perceptive interview with the seventy-three-year-old writer-director Manoel de Oliveira in the May–June *Film Comment*.

2. Adapted from a famous nineteenth-century Portuguese novel of the same title by Camilo Castelo Branco, DOOMED LOVE is a veritable workshop of ideas about the incestuous relationship between novels and movies, and the diverse possibilities of literary adaptations. (In this respect, GREED is an obvious precursor.) Most of the so-called avant-garde aspects of the film derive directly from this meditation and problem, whereby each scene becomes the filmic solution to a literary challenge. They are aspects, in other words, that need to be examined existentially, in terms related to the inner needs of the work—means for expressing an otherwise inaccessible content—not games specifically designed to tease or torment mainstream critics who are insulted by movies that attempt more than CAVEMAN.

Vocabulary is part of the problem here. One set of words about films exists for people who see them, another set for people who make them, and a third for the academics who study them. Assigning any or all of these sets to DOOMED LOVE is like copying down those celebrated descriptions given by several blind men who've been groping the same elephant. Put all these accounts together and you still don't have a single functioning mammal. The best new films always confound the old definitions, anyway. Much of the time, de Oliveira is using mise en scène and off-screen narration to create two-part expositional structures (e.g., a WAVELENGTH-like camera movement up to a window while the narrator reflects on the fates of the characters), each part tailored to the other.

3. At the center of the process of literary adaptation underlining DOOMED LOVE is a dialectic between the seen and the imagined, the perceived and the unperceived. Early on, there's a strangely literal fleshing out of a literary image: "The marriage of Venus and Vulcan obsessed him," says the narrator of a character, and, sure enough, we see a blonde in a loin cloth with similarly garbed attendants and a bearded Vulcan with a hammer. (As de Oliveira clarifies in the Clarens interview, there are actually two narrators. One of them, female, forecasts the future—rather like Mariana, one of the leading characters.)

Intricate dovetailings of narration and dialogue produce some elegant displacements and overlaps in and on the sound track. When the heroine's father shouts at her in close-up, the sound of his voice ceases at the precise moment that the male narrator announces that the (off-screen) daughter doesn't hear him because she's left the room. Much later, the imprisoned hero responds *in person* to the narrator's off-screen report of Mariana's blacksmith father's announcement (visible but not heard) that *his* daughter is delirious—a scene much easier to follow than to describe. Here the collision of the two narrative conventions, far from dismantling the scene, gives it a kind of layered density—an effect that's amplified by the gradual accumulation of objects and furniture in the hero's cell, which seems to make the space grow deeper at the same time that it inches its way closer toward an ordinary domestic interior.

4. A vest-pocket period spectacular set in the late eighteenth and early nineteenth centuries, DOOMED LOVE has clear affinities with such low-budget epics of obsessive energy as Sam Fuller's PARK ROW, Werner Schroeter's EIKA KATAPA, Kevin Brownlow and Andrew Mollo's WINSTANLEY, and Hans-Jürgen Syberberg's HITLER, A FILM FROM GERMANY. Following an aesthetics of economy that reduces spectacle to a shadow-dance of the mind—an abstraction of love rather than a glitzy substitute display (the Hollywood solution, despite a sunset or two worthy of Technicolor Selznick)—de Oliveira's long takes are often positioned in front of clearly (and sometimes beautifully) painted backdrops, and intermittently orchestrated in relation to a percussive contemporary score (by João Paes).

The first shot in part 2 of the movie, after the intermission, is a static red-tinted landscape (mountains, sky) that modulates to the tone of light brick as day breaks and church bells start to ring. There's a cut to the camera prowling around a courtyard where the hero, Simao (António Sequeira Lopes), is seated while the pealing continues—a rhythmic idea picked up by Paes's score until a woman rings a doorbell and the music stops. Shortly afterward, in the same pivotal scene, Simao commits a crime of honor—shooting a rival who happens to be the cousin of his beloved Tereza (Cristina Hauser)—which seals his fate for the rest of the film and all eternity, whichever comes first. (Like Romeo and Juliet, the teenage couple come from feuding noble families.)

5. A considerable portion of the plot consists of the epistolary romance between Simao and Tereza, conducted (*a*), in part 1, while he's secretly convalescing from a gunshot wound in the home of a blacksmith whose daughter, the devoted Mariana (Elsa Wallencamp), takes care of him (like Lancelot in Escalot), and Tereza is sequestered in a convent, and (*b*), in part 2, while he's serving a voluntary prison term for killing the cousin, having refused any appeal, and Tereza herself has become bedridden with a wicked Camillean cough.

In both (*a*) and (*b*), elaborate subterfuges are of course necessary to keep the correspondence going. As in the protracted agonies of separation that structure the plot of PETER IBBETSON, the couple never gets it on—when he's shipping off to India as a convict, she dies while waving a distant farewell to him from a balcony—and the whole narrative leading up to this becomes galvanized into an explication of what's keeping the couple apart in separate shots, as well as a formal explanation of what's binding these shots together. Personally, I found every stage of this process absolutely absorbing.

Mulishly persistent in their devoted renunciations, their obsession with medieval codes of chivalrous duty, Simao and Tereza are equaled only by the sacrificial Mariana, as self-effacing as Melanie in GONE WITH THE WIND. "When I see I'm not needed, I'll end my life," she flatly declares to Simao, around the same time she's sailing off with him on the prison ship. True to her word, she leaps into the sea only a matter of seconds after she's overseen his own burial; significantly, the two events occur within the same shot. If the theme of martyrdom evokes Carl Dreyer, it's worth noting that de Oliveira has had a lifelong struggle in getting his few features made that seems comparable to Dreyer's cosmic difficulties. (In a filmmaking career spanning half a century, his seventh feature to date, FRANCISCA, just surfaced in Cannes.)

6. The consistently inventive mise en scène of DOOMED LOVE can't be adequately summarized here, but a few more generalizations and examples may be in order. The use of both long shots and long takes is masterly; an early instance of the two together—in which the camera, accompanied by Handel, pans from a discreet distance with Tereza as she scurries through an autumnal forest, then returns to Simao sitting on a log—is simply breathtaking. (A bit earlier, in a lush interior, actors seem to freeze as in MARIENBAD or INDIA SONG, becoming distilled essences in a mural.) As the characters and situations—that is, our perceptions of them—grow, the camera often moves in closer during certain long takes, as if following the defensible assumption that intimacy and emotions have to be *earned* before they can be shared or shown. (Elliott Stein has aptly compared the film's paring-down principles to Bresson's.)

Along with Mark Rappaport (an early enthusiast of DOOMED LOVE, whose somewhat related efforts in IMPOSTERS can still be seen on weekends in the Bleecker's James Agee Room through mid-June), de Oliveira probably does about as much with mirrors as Hitchcock and Ophüls do with staircases. But part of his own game is to relate this usage to his very elaborate play with windows and open doorways, and in certain cases deliberately confuse us about what we're actually watching. In one memorable shot, Tereza's father, facing left in fuzzy close-up, addresses Tereza, who's facing us in a clear-focus medium shot; by the end of the scene, both characters are facing the camera, until he turns around and she, now walking away, is shown to be a mirror reflection.

7. The title DOOMED LOVE can be taken as a definition of acute cinéphilia—the same fatal disease that infected Dreyer ("What is film to you?" an interviewer asked him in 1950; "My only great passion," he replied)—and what this elicits and engenders. Ironically, it seems to work less well as a description of the lives of Simao, Tereza, and Mariana—all three of whom seem so busily, engagedly preoccupied with their all-consuming obsessions with one another that it's hard to regard either them or their love as "doomed" in any way. In a sense, the whole force of the film can be felt behind the tension of that contradiction, whereby cells of confinement eventually become banal domestic interiors and obsessions turn into everyday commonplaces. It's a staple of fiction probably dating back to *Clarissa,* a genre convention in which getting it on equals either ending or else somehow violating the plot. François

Truffaut—whose TWO ENGLISH GIRLS, THE STORY OF ADELE H., and THE GREEN ROOM can all be regarded as faltering (if poignant), formally bashful, conceptually timid steps in the direction of defining a grand literary passion that only DOOMED LOVE succeeds fully in articulating—has been trying to make this movie most of his life.

Watching this classically wrought example of controlled madness for 270 minutes, in the small auditorium of the Public's Little Theater—a black-walled vault that used to house the "Invisible Cinema" designed by Peter Kubelka for Anthology Film Archives a decade ago, all ninety seats shuttered or blinkered to screen out all social distractions (a perfect way to see LA RÉGION CENTRALE, but lousy for Buster Keaton)—I was reminded once again of the battles between narrative and nonnarrative cinema that used to be waged in this room. (Today the battles are over, the warring tribes shipped off to separate schools or summer camps, and a mongrel like DOOMED LOVE, doomed by its own integrity, has to walk the night without the sponsorship of either ghetto.)

Seen in terms of Freud and Barthes, the conflicts I'm talking about were largely Oedipal versus pre-Oedipal impulses, *plaisir* versus *jouissance*, pursuit of plot versus a polymorphous-perverse grabbing after everything else (at least within hailing distance of an infant's fist). Staging yet another shotgun marriage between these warring families in every spectator, at every moment, for existential rather than socially expedient reasons, DOOMED LOVE is heavy and long with its curling, curving linear plot, yet rich in the sort of meditations (and concentrated meditativeness) that can usually take place only around stasis. What a pity that you didn't get to see it.

—*Soho News*, 3 June 1981

As the most gifted and congenial by far of the New Hollywood tyros, Steven Spielberg may be the only consummate master of the post-television movie spectacular—the blockbuster that's diced out into bite-size narrative units like Chicken McNuggets (every structural hint of bone or body part processed out of existence, every juicy piece a separate unique experience, designed to vanish without a trace). Aspiring to the condition of continuous action as if that were a delirious state of grace—borne aloft by superbly timed jolts and impossibly narrow escapes, usually in three- to five-minute setpiece doses— RAIDERS OF THE LOST ARK all but bypasses character and logic for a string of stunning rides through separate portions of Disneyland, one right after the other, each one a visceral treat.

Valuing speed over sense, the movie is too energetically rushed to allow itself any detours into lyricism. It's a surprising turn of events for the director of CLOSE ENCOUNTERS OF THE THIRD KIND, but the box office blues of 1941 must have led Spielberg to some second thoughts about how to bring an audience to its knees—back to the lessons of JAWS, in other words, with the additional commercial support of George Lucas (who produced and collaborated with Philip Kaufman on the original story). Consequently, even when God puts in an appearance toward the end of this globetrotting adventure—a fiery, vengeful Old Testament God playing yang to the yin of the benign aliens in CLOSE ENCOUNTERS—He doesn't get to stick around any longer than a television commercial.

I'll never forget the queasy experience I had one Sunday afternoon last year, in the front row of a crowded midtown theater, watching the grisly elevator murder in DRESSED TO KILL at the same time that the man who created it, Brian De Palma, was a couple of seats away, watching me and others react to it (and leaving the theater as soon as the sequence was over). The curious thing about his gaze, as I recall it, was that it conveyed a lot of pride and satisfaction, yet none of it was directed at the screen.

It's a gaze I remembered more than once while responding in a similarly helpless way to the merciless mechanics of RAIDERS OF THE LOST ARK—and not merely because Spielberg and Lucas are also decadent disciples of Hitchcockian storyboard construction in which The Sequence becomes the whole raison d'être of filmmaking. It was also related to the dawning realization that the real continuity and characters of their movies can be truly located *only* in their audience responses—not in any autonomous evidence up on the screen, which is bound to be relatively uneven and riddled with gaps (e.g., how does the hero get to the Mediterranean island on a Nazi submarine?).

Consider Karen Allen here, a likable, resourceful actress who gets used like one of those convertible stage units in a play full of short scenes. First she's established (in a drinking bout) as one of the boys, then as some perfunctory variant of the mannish woman (Joan Crawford as Vienna in JOHNNY GUITAR) running a Nepalese saloon, then as a fluttery sort of captive heroine who clearly *isn't* one of the boys, then as a background prop; whatever a given scene requires, she dutifully becomes. The same principle holds (more or less) for everyone and everything else in the movie, from hero Indiana Jones (Harrison Ford) to villain Beloq (Paul Freeman) to the Ark of the Covenant to somebody's pet monkey. Try to summon up a composite image anywhere, a feeling or idea that you can salvage when the movie's over, and you're mainly stuck with an arsenal of disconnected poses and disposable functions.

There's a lot of confusion around—most of it to the advantage of banks—about the status of this blunderbuss approach in relation to art. Its effectiveness as dazzling entertainment is harder to quarrel with; I was glued to my seat, and even the monotonous lack of variation in the pacing (as in 1941) has something soothing about it. But the creepy presumption of most criticism nowadays is not only that it's possible to be a Serious Artist while wielding megabucks, but that it's often necessary to wield these lofty budgets in order to be considered "seriously" at all. Around the time of the release of STAR WARS, it was widely reported that Lucas intended to make only avant-garde films in the future. Such a story seemed preposterous then, and I find it even harder to swallow it now. Lucas lacks the *freedom* to make avant-garde films—assuming that freedom is ultimately a matter of mental space more than budget. Most people, I know, assume the reverse of this—such is the myth that keeps those industry wheels turning—but few highly budgeted directors have ever seemed like exceptionally free individuals to me.

So maybe the real auteur of RAIDERS OF THE LOST ARK is neither Spielberg nor Lucas—however brilliant each may be in his separate functions—but the money that plays with them and us, the money that calls all the shots.

Combining the dogged desire of Lucas to be pulpier than Sax Rohmer in this 1936 white supremacist archeological romp (while combining all the world's most important religious myths on the head of a pin and simultaneously whistling Dixie) with the mystical awe and propulsive storytelling of Spielberg, the movie has a certain economic relation to art, like 1941, that might be called Teenager's Revenge.

How deeply are we expected to get involved in a plot about the fabled Ark of the Covenant which doesn't feature a single Jew, with Arab (i.e., proto-Iranian) and Nazi villains galore? RAIDERS somehow contrives to convert the Great Whatsit of KISS ME DEADLY (nuclear death in Pandora's Box) into the 10 Commandments of Cecil B. De Mille, without ever convincing us that either has the moral weight of Cheech & Chong's roach clip, or the 15 Commandments of Mel Brooks in HISTORY OF THE WORLD, PART I.* It mainly locates its few tokens of crunchy transcendence in its audience's unconscious and its promo campaign. On the screen, it sticks more practically and nihilistically to the short-range task of being a "rattling good yarn"—one, indeed, that rattles and hisses at you in sensuous Dolby while boldly slinging you from one outrageously suspenseful snake pit to another. Before the movie's scarcely begun, Indiana Jones is being chased by a giant bowling ball of a boulder through a Peruvian cave that's otherwise characterized by tarantulas, treasures, diverse death-traps, and cave-ins.

"I am a shadow reflection of you," Freeman says coolly to Ford at one point, alerting those academics who might want to brood seriously over this enjoyable nonsense. The Ark itself is a McGuffin-prop lifted from DAVID AND BATHSHEBA, a Gregory Peck vehicle of thirty summers ago. As I see it, the Great Whatsit here is really nothing more than the proverbial Magic of Movies—the only subject Spielberg/Lucas seem equipped to tackle head-on, in tandem with the usual dull concentration on the nature of power trips (which is what turned APOCALYPSE NOW from a film about Vietnam into a film about being a director, and what makes the last shot of RAIDERS a clear steal from CITIZEN KANE).

In a way, the opening dissolve from the Paramount logo to an actual mountain peak tells us all we need to know. By the time we arrive at the climactic narrative striptease on a mountaintop, we see death pour out of the Ark like a lethal dose of projector light, spilling out hologram-like figures which emerge from the emulsion only to turn ugly and start zapping the Nazis dead. Faces melt fabulously (in the snazziest of all the flashy special effects) as the Nazis are being cremated; the heavens part to suck up all the cinders and then neatly close shut again, like a zipper.

But the most thrilling moment of sexual release for the audience I saw

---

*I was originally reviewing UP IN SMOKE (a Cheech & Chong comedy) as well as the Brooks movie—and Andrew Noren's CHARMED PARTICLES—in the same column. (1993)

RAIDERS with was the humorously delayed decision of Jones, much earlier, to shoot a fancy sword-swishing Arab with his gun rather than bother with his whip. Its offhand genocidal message comes very close to being the only one that New Hollywood (from TAXI DRIVER to STAR WARS to APOCALYPSE NOW to DRESSED TO KILL) can find beyond its own pretty, bejeweled navel—a pithy suggestion, derived from Conrad's Kurtz in *Heart of Darkness*, that simply says, "Exterminate the brutes."

—*Soho News*, 10 June 1981

Mapping the Territory of Râúl Ruiz

Preface

The sheer *otherness* of Râúl Ruiz in a North American context has a lot to do with the peculiarities of funding in European state-operated television that make different kinds of work possible. The eccentric filmmaker in the United States or Canada who wants to make marginal films usually has to adopt the badge or shield of a school or genre—art film, avant-garde film, punk film, feminist film, documentary, or academic theory film—in order to get funding at one end, distribution, promotion, and criticism at the other. Ruiz, however, needs only to accept the institutional framework of state television— which offers, as he puts it, *holes to be filled*—and he automatically acquires a commission *and* an audience without having to settle on any binding affiliation or label beyond the open-ended rubric of "culture" or "education." Consequently, the sheer existence of Ruiz's massive, varied work constitutes a genuine affront to the capitalist definitions of experiment governing our own culture. An obsessive tinkering into possibilities that successfully evades most of the ghetto classifications we assign to marginal works, the Ruiz oeuvre strikes us as "too much" or "too little" precisely because we can't comfortably file it away—even if it arguably constructs on occasion a new European ghetto of its own.

For all their differences every Ruiz film or tape seems to combine some aspect of the laboratory and the playpen, usually redefining what we mean by "serious" and "unserious" in the process. Half *bricoleur*, half *enfant terrible*, Ruiz recalls the exemplary careers of Godard and Warhol, not only through the sheer size of his output but also through the unsettling combination of

222

professionalism and amateurishness. Next to Godard's you-can-put-anything-in-a-film and Warhol's anyone-is-an-actor credos—to which one might add Jacques Rivette's dissolution of the distinction between good and bad acting by positing that everything an actor does is interesting—Ruiz's strategy of subverting his adopted formats from within creates a parallel form of mock seriousness where almost anything can be said or done with relative impunity. By shifting the rules of the game, all four filmmakers have outlined a new route toward freedom and productivity.

To understand how Ruiz has arrived at such a position, one must first consider where he comes from. A Chilean born in 1941 in Puerto Montt who studied theology and law (perhaps the two subjects most governed by institutions), he significantly made his first serious foray into the arts via institutional funding—a Rockefeller grant that allowed him to write over a hundred plays between 1956 and 1962. A good many years later, many of these plays would form the basis of several of his screenplays. After writing a couple of unrealized film scripts, he attended film school in Santa Fé, Argentina, for a year, eventually rebelling against the dogma "that it was the duty of every human being in Latin America to make documentary films" by quitting in 1967 to embark on an ambitious feature in Buenos Aires, loosely inspired by a Daphne du Maurier novel, which was never finished. (Like many of Ruiz's Chilean works, it is a lost work in more ways than one; the whereabouts of the only print are currently unknown.)

Then Ruiz wrote and directed TRES TRISTES TIGRES (1968), adapted from a play by Alejandro Sieveking—a film with no relation to G. Cabrera Infante's epic Cuban novel of the same title—and won the Locarno Film Festival's *grand prix* with it in 1969, although it was seen by only thirty thousand or so spectators in Chile. Judging from various interviews, the film has a neorealist subject—the marginal Chilean lower and middle class, according to one interviewer—but a somewhat self-reflexive style influenced by the *nouvelle vague* which played on camera/actor relationships: a 28-millimeter lens was used exclusively, the actors' awareness of the (mainly handheld) camera was emphasized rather than discouraged, and Ruiz notes "an attempt to tackle the embarrassment of Mexican melodrama by a kind of inversion, as if the camera were in the opposite position, showing the secondary characters, extras waiting for the big scene to take place." (See the interview with Ian Christie and Malcolm Coad in *Afterimage*, no. 10, Autumn 1981.)[1]

Next came an abortive collaboration on a Chilean/American coproduction (QUE HACER?, 1970) which Ruiz now dismisses, and a 16-millimeter feature suggested by Franz Kafka's "In the Penal Colony" (LA COLONIA PENAL, 1971), which is somewhat more substantial, although it survives only in a truncated version. (Dealing with an island whose main industry is the *manufacturing* of news and whose language is "completely invented," the film anticipates the metaphysical conceits of such later films as LA TOIT DE LA BALEINE.) This was followed by Ruiz's first television commission, NADIE DIJO NADA (1971)—a free adaptation of a Max Beerbohm story for Italy's RAI which he managed to complete under budget, thus enabling him to make his next two features: the hour-long L'EXPROPIACION (1972) and the nearly four-hour EL REALISMO SOCIALISTA (1973). Over the same two years, Ruiz made three shorts for Chilean television, a feature based on a best seller (*Palomita Blanca*, "a kind of *Love Story* . . . read by one million people, which is 10 percent of the Chilean population") which was subsequently cut and banned for export, an hour-long documentary about the numerous young girls auditioning for the lead part in PALOMITA BLANCA, and an additional short. Then came the military coup of September 1973, and with it Ruiz's exile: he moved to Paris in February 1974.

Since then, he has gradually come into his own and into international prominence as a writer-director in almost continual production thanks to state television commissions in France, Germany, Holland, and Portugal—and, more recently, his job as codirector of the Maison de la Culture of Le Havre with Jean-Luc Fargier, which allows him in effect to coproduce his own films and produce films by other filmmakers—yielding a flurry of activity that has particularly increased in the 1980s, and now includes directing theater, building films around other cultural events (e.g., the visit of Jean-Claude Gallotta's dance group to Le Havre in MAMMAME), and producing such films as Manoel de Oliveira's MON CAS. His first prestigious European film, L'HYPOTHÈSE D'UN TABLEAU VOLÉ (1978)—unless one counts the more difficult and esoteric LA VOCATION SUSPENDUE, made the previous year, which won the first prize at the 1978 San Remo Film Festival—helped to establish the Borgesian side of his reputation by positing a playful metaphysical system as the basis of his fantasy and suggesting a subtle camp irony lurking behind the taste for academic pedagogy, fanciful English storytellers (from Coleridge to Carroll to Stevenson to Chesterton), and notions of narrative as impenetrable labyrinth.

This literary aspect of Ruiz would seem to place him within hailing distance of the European art film, but the camp mockery of the latter's forms of seriousness, consistency, and craft invariably prevent this snug identification from taking hold. (The affinity noted by many critics with low-budget Welles films such as MR. ARKADIN and THE IMMORTAL STORY may come closer to the mark, at least regarding transgressive camera angles, compulsive globetrotting, flashbacks and other fabulist forms of address, and "irresponsible" production values.) To greater or lesser extents, all Ruiz works are closet comedies bent on undercutting whatever forms of solemnity threaten to congeal discourse into predictable patterns of illusion-making, ideology, editorializing, and/or generic complacency. But apart from certain shorts like COLLOQUE DE CHIENS and QUERELLE DE JARDINS, none of them is an overt comedy either, so that the relative security of *that* genre is no less remote.

It's partially the strategy of this political exile to elude categorical imperatives; to be categorized, after all, is the first step toward being labeled an undesirable. From this standpoint, the flippant whimsy of Ruiz is comparable to the irony of Nabokov, which holds many of his meanings perpetually in check. With everything theoretically open to contradiction and assault, most generalizations about Ruiz—probably this one included—have to be approached with some caution and skepticism. Writing from the vantage point of an American over five thousand miles from Paris who has managed to glimpse little more than a tip of the iceberg, mainly during short visits abroad—twenty-five features and seven shorts,[2] all but three of them non-Chilean and post-1973, seven of which (COLLOQUE DE CHIENS, LA TOIT DE LA BALEINE, LES TROIS COURONNES DU MATELOT, DES GRANDS ÉVÉNEMENTS ET DES GENS ORDINAIRES, LA VILLE DES PIRATES, MÉMOIRE DES APPARENCES, and MAMMAME) I've managed to see more than once—I hope that the notes that follow are at least true to the hypothetical filmmaker I've constructed.

■

According to the mathematician Pierre Rosenstiel, the "wise Ariadne" method consists of backtracking after exploring each new corridor. That way, it is known, and then it is the turn of another. By contrast, crazy Ariadne explores as much as possible and only backtracks as a last resort. These two attitudes are coherent and make it possible to resolve the labyrinth. Every traveler may be considered myopic. He cannot see further than the horizon. The map is the means of enlarging one's field of vision. Thus the map of the maze destroys the maze at a stroke. The map suppresses the labyrinth. The history of cartography is therefore the business of labyrinth destruction, as was known five thousand years ago. A labyrinth is resolved—one also says "beaten"—when each corridor has been used once and only once in each direction.

From one point of view, at least, any attempt to chart the breadth and unity of Ruiz's works in film and video threatens to become a betrayal of that work. If the map suppresses the labyrinth, it is always possible that the cultish desire to possess Ruiz's oeuvre as a coherent entity works against many of Ruiz's own strategies. An anti-auteurist par excellence, Ruiz proceeds partially by subterfuge and anonymity, addressing many of his works to an audience whose responsiveness is largely predicated on *not* knowing who he is or even precisely what he is up to. To a certain degree, Douglas Sirk operated on such a principle in Hollywood during the 1950s, making the social and aesthetic experiences of his films of that period qualitatively and quantitatively different from the experiences they have afforded Sirk critics in the 1970s and 1980s—few of whom have acknowledged or dealt with this striking discrepancy.

Take for instance the contemporary French television audience that the two-part, 100-minute PETIT MANUEL D'HISTOIRE DE FRANCE was designed for, who saw it transmitted in the series *Rue des archives* on successive weeks in late September 1979. A videotape compilation of French history "from our ancestors the Gauls . . . to the invention of cinema," it proceeds exclusively through quotation, comprising an audio-visual equivalent to the sort of work Walter Benjamin once dreamed of producing. Clips from former French television programs and series depicting French history are accompanied by the voices of French schoolchildren reading from primary school textbooks that date from 1903, 1929, 1956, and 1968. Frankly fictionalized depictions of events derived from plays are interspersed with more nonfictional "re-creations," and some of the juxtapositions are spatial as well as temporal, for the programs make frequent use of split-screen diptychs. To keep the chronology straight and the format educational, the date of a given event often appears in the upper right corner of the frame; and in keeping with the French auteurist consciousness that tends to see each representation as an individual creation, subtitles periodically identify each clip with a title and one or more auteurs.

The subversive aspect of SHORT HISTORY OF FRANCE mainly has to do with the overall proliferation of representations, whereby the same actor might turn up portraying two or more characters in periods that are centuries apart, and Joan of Arc is successively presented to us via Shaw (*Saint Joan*), Meunier (*Jeanne et ses Juges*), and Claudel (*Jeanne au Bûcher*). This leads to a subtle tone of self-parody, amplified in part by the faltering or mechanical deliveries of some of the off-screen children, which gradually undermines the very notion of history which the series is presumably designed to perpetuate—a sly sense of derision that only comes to the fore when Ruiz finally gets to Napoleon and uses what is apparently the series' only film clip, a frenetic rapid montage from Gance's NAPOLÉON. To hammer his point home, Ruiz immediately follows this clip with an equally rapid montage of his own, running through earlier parts of the program—a helter-skelter slag heap of near-subliminal flashes, one shot per era, which effectively reduces all of French history to a hysterical flood of incoherent clichés. Then the program calmly reverts to business as usual, and the *reductio ad absurdum* principle remains as an implicit echo rather than as an explicit strategy. Having made his momentary assault, Ruiz fades back into the woodwork, resumes his anonymity, and indeed the only overt sign of the program's double edge to come at the end appears to be entirely fortuitous, when the following legend appears on the screen: "La prochaine semaine: La vie est un spectacle." ("Next week: Life is a spectacle.")

But SHORT HISTORY OF FRANCE represents only one side of the Ruizian dialectic. No less characteristic are two fiction features shot on the same Portuguese island in 1983, LA VILLE DES PIRATES and POINT DE FUITE. If SHORT HISTORY OF FRANCE is essentially defined by its institutional and educational framework, these two films are characterized no less strikingly by their virtual lack of classification, genre, or motivation apart from pure stylistic play. The first two Ruiz features that I happened to see, they are oddly alike in their steadfast refusal to cater to the ostensible consumer demands of arthouse patrons. They are *irresponsible* works in the fullest sense of that term—not merely in their dogged marginality, but also in their refusal to aspire to the rigor or consistency of masterpieces, their total unwillingness to marshal their forces in any single, concerted direction. Indirectly yet decisively, they ridicule the activity of artmaking itself.

> First hypothesis: it's an old map and perhaps the city has changed. The map lags behind the territory. It is partly inaccurate.
> Second hypothesis: the map is prospective. It serves as a model for development. It is in advance of the territory. The city does not yet resemble the map.
> Third hypothesis: the city has been destroyed by a cataclysm and has been rebuilt in accordance with several maps. These present the characteristics described in the first two hypotheses. The inaccuracies are compounded. So one must envisage the construction of a perfect map.
> First proposition: the perfect map would be on the scale of one to one. It would be as big as the territory. Direction signs and road nameplates can be seen as a timid endeavor to create this perfect map, which would make it possible to do without a map.
> Second proposition: the perfect map would be the sum of all possible routes, memorized on a videodisc, which would reproduce them as required in a visual form. This perfect map would render inestimable services to the army, tourist agencies, and all sorts of travelers.

My own credentials for mapping Ruiz, as suggested earlier, are limited by the fact that the only Chilean features I've seen to which his name is connected are the 1970 QUE HACER?, made jointly with Saul Landau, James Becket, Nina Serrano, and Billy Yahraus, which he currently disowns, and THE PENAL COLONY, which is no longer complete. Judging from most accounts of his early films, they seem to be interesting but "pre-Ruizian" to the degree that they are Chilean or Latin American in subject, hence regional—if we understand that "Ruiz" in this context is less a biological entity than a particular point of convergence between different levels of culture, and a lack of fixed identity or allegiances which make work as mercurial as the PETIT MANUEL, LA VILLE DES PIRATES, and POINT DE FUITE possible. This is essentially the condition of the exile which Ruiz has shared since 1974, and the subject of the first film he shot after leaving Chile as a political refugee: DIÁLOGO DE EXILADOS (DIALOGUE OF EXILES, 1974), made in Paris. Rightly or wrongly, it is here that the Ruiz I am mainly discussing is born.

Starting with a quote from Brecht which asserts that immigrants make the best dialecticians, DIALOGUE OF EXILES proceeds in a manner that is sufficiently dialectical to estrange many Chilean and non-Chilean viewers alike.

As Ruiz pointed out in a 1975 interview, this approach led to certain political misunderstandings as well as to a diffused narrative which presented other difficulties. But it also created certain analytical possibilities:

> It is a film with a story: a group of exiles takes a hostage to prevent him from singing. Around this I developed a narrative which works against the usual pyramid of direction in normal commercial cinema, with its main protagonist and secondary characters. Here different characters are to the fore at different times and the mise en scène works to eliminate the pyramid, as I play on the contrast between rigorous direction and the natural informality of dialogue and acting. The union of these rather contradictory elements creates a certain potential, a capacity for analysis.

With an ambience suggesting PARIS NOUS APPARTIENT and early Robert Kramer (people seated around tables in small flats), and a dramatic rhythm structured around arrivals and departures (with doors and windows central pivots in the mise en scène), this feature manages to dissipate much of the tension generated by its central premise (a fascist emigré Chilean singer who increasingly irritates the Chileans helping him out) through its shifting narrative focus. This yields an interesting ambiguity of approach—making it, as Ruiz points out, a political film which eschews both propaganda and spectacle—but a less than compelling plot. (Among the cast are Argentinian emigré director Edgardo Cozarinsky and Valeria Sarmiento, Ruiz's wife and editor on most of his films since the early 1970s—and, starting with NOTRE MARIAGE in 1984, a director in her own right.) At the same time, the film remains fluid enough to contain a dream sequence set in Santiago—albeit one confined to a single blue-tinted shot. What seems most apparent is the trait already discussed in reference to the subsequent LA VILLE DES PIRATES and POINT DE FUITE: a refusal to cater to any particular audience, marginal *or* mainstream—or, put differently, a willingness to explore certain areas without any apparent compulsion to be commercially packageable.

> On this scale, two maps start to diverge. The map about to disappear is called the mental map. It is the image of a known territory. It is made up of habits, memories, feelings. It is the familiar universe of spaces commonly frequented. The other is a paper map, which represents a little-known or unknown territory. Scientists claim that we only see what we know. We must therefore conclude that the paper map is all-powerful.

A critical quandary: If Ruiz isn't an auteur, how does one deal with the obsessive repetition of certain themes in otherwise disparate works? The idea of a corpse hacked up into several pieces which are then hidden in separate places figures in at least three works made over a six-year period. In UTOPIA (aka MENSCH VERSTREUT UND WELT VERKEHBT), a ZDF (German television) commission that was itself dismembered by one-third to its present length of one hour, it provides the central plot premise; two years later, it recurs as an important incident in the parodic/melodramatic short COLLOQUE DE CHIENS; and in 1981, it figures as a passing detail in the dialogue of one of the initial episodes of LE BORGNE, an independently made metaphysical serial—shot privately over weekends by Ruiz with the assistance of friends and television technicians—which is apparently still unfinished.

A possible solution to this quandary: metaphorically speaking, the corpse in question may be Ruiz's own status and identity as an auteur, which commercial, political, national, and institutional categories have torn asunder and buried in diverse locations—making Ruiz critics a bit like police inspectors. In UTOPIA, also known as THE SCATTERED BODY AND THE WORLD UPSIDE DOWN, two traveling salesmen in Honduras are looking for pieces of the body of a lost friend and, according to Ruiz, each piece suggests "an isolated aspect of utopia." Is auteurism for Ruiz an unattainable utopian ideal, given the diversity of his projects and commissions, or an idealist illusion to be shunned? The work as a whole poses this dilemma without conclusively resolving it.

"For Ruiz," writes David Ehrenstein in *Film: The Front Line 1984* (Arden Press, 1984), "film is a form of anti-religion—a free zone capable of producing perpetual disbelief." Perhaps part of the reason for this position is the mercurial nature of his production, which often turns expediency into an aesthetic and/or metaphysical position. To cite one extreme instance of this, POINT DE FUITE (VANISHING POINT) arose in part out of a dare that Ruiz surpass Fassbinder's record of shooting seventy-odd camera setups nonstop; without bothering about retakes, Ruiz inched that record well into the eighties. Shot with damaged stock and wearing its shoddiness like a crown, the film oscillates (like LA TOIT DE LA BALEINE) between half a dozen languages, mainly atonal English and monotonal French, and drives one slightly batty with its portentous central gambling metaphor (poker games between three variously bandaged men), its seemingly irrelevant jazz drums on the sound track, and the capacity of each line reading to make the petulant dialogue (someone's ex-wife left the United States "because she couldn't stand the chicken there") sound even less likely than it reads. But the frustrated spectator who insists on locating some apparent raison d'être for the project may ultimately have to settle for the rather gratuitous dare cited above. The perverse fascination of this impulse—cinema for the sheer hell of it—is that, unlike most other forms of "bad" filmmaking valorized by the all-devouring cinematic apparatus, VANISHING POINT cannot be absorbed or justified—that is, consumed—according to any principles of transcendence (unless, perhaps, one postulates it as a very esoteric form of camp). Consequently, it is somewhat misleading—if initially provocative—to describe Ruiz as "the Edgar G. Ulmer of the art film," as various critics have done. For one thing, the fact that VANISHING POINT exists only as an unprocessed workprint—and is not likely to become anything else in the foreseeable future—only emphasizes the degree to which it is commercially unexploitable in a way that no Ulmer film ever is, at least to my knowledge.[3]

To cite Ehrenstein again, "By working cheaply, quickly, and quasi-anonymously on projects that are by and large made to order, Ruiz puts himself in the position (from a production point of view) of an Edgar G. Ulmer. In point of fact, if 'art' cinema has taken the place once occupied by the 'B' film, then Ruiz is certainly Ulmer's heir." One must bear in mind, however, that the conditions that periodically allowed Ulmer to prosper in B-films probably exist now only in European television, where there are "holes to be filled" as there once were in the second-feature category. As an "art" film director, however, Ruiz seems to occupy a position that is a good deal more precarious, despite his prolific output. The only "art" feature of his to have had a relatively wide international exposure, LES TROIS COURONNES DU MATELOT (1983),[4] has not fared very well outside of Paris—largely, one feels, because its cocky eclecticism is difficult to absorb without any understanding of Ruiz as a multifaceted phenomenon (and one whom, like Godard in the 1960s, is undoubtedly more interesting for his work as a whole than for any single "masterpiece"). To my mind, despite the film's dazzling employment of wide-angle, deep-focus color photography (intermittently suggesting a comic book version of Welles) and many arresting and disturbing surrealist conceits, THE THREE CROWNS OF THE SAILOR has a certain formalistic dryness that may have made it a less than ideal introduction to Ruiz's work for viewers on this side of the Atlantic. At least this was apparently the case for the North American audiences who encountered it, mainly at festivals, in 1984—and whose mainly hostile responses, combined with the hostility or indifference of all but a few North American film critics, make the possibility of a Ruiz market on this continent extremely unlikely, at least in the immediate future. (Another liability may have been a certain acerbic macho/misogynous undertone tied to the film's sailor milieu, along with an antirealistic geographical vagueness that equally links the film to Fassbinder's QUERELLE—a film that gave North American critics an equal amount of trouble.)

The problem is, it is difficult to come up with any single Ruiz feature that can be cited as a potential Open Sesame that might turn him into a marketable commodity. My own five favorites at the moment—LA TOIT DE LA BALEINE (1981), LA VILLE DES PIRATES (1983), MANUEL À L'ÎLE DES MERVEILLES (1984), MAMMAME (1985), and MÉMOIRE DES APPARENCES (1986)—all have a richly textured density that recommends them as intellectual fantasies and sensual treats, but none of them can boast a narrative line that sustains interest on its own terms throughout.

To take them up briefly in turn: THE ROOF OF THE WHALE, the one with the most pronounced ideological/political/polemical thrust, deals brilliantly with the plight of an anthropologist trying to learn the language of an obscure

Patagonian Indian tribe whose last surviving members he has discovered. Beautifully and inventively shot in color by Henri Alekan, the film proceeds less as narrative or as drama than as a prodigious stream of visual, verbal, and conceptual ideas centering around this theme. The performances are either minimal to the point of indifference or deliberately curtailed (so that, for instance, Willecke Van Ammelrooy, who plays the anthropologist's wife, appears to have learned her speeches in English phonetically) and, despite periodic bursts of portentous music, suspense exists only on a purely formal level.

Two sample narrative ideas, neither of which lead anywhere in particular: in a weird parody of Lacanian psychoanalysis, the anthropologist's child—a creature of indeterminate gender—becomes pregnant after gazing into a mirror; as an apparent gloss on this event, his or her mother remarks that poetry is dangerous because "metaphors become a religion, and religion is the opiate of the masses." At another point, one of the Indians—who by this time are steeped in Western culture—argues with the other that the relative merits of Beethoven and Mozart are really a matter of which composer has the better album covers. . . . At one level a parody of contemporary Western man's remoteness from the pre-industrial Third World, the film is no less a comedy about the anthropological peculiarities of his own tribal customs, intellectual and otherwise. But this theme in turn is intermittently interrupted or at least complicated by purely visual explorations in color, composition, perspective, texture, and camera placement which pursue the language theme through formal metaphors. Putatively a science fiction film set in the future, the film is so blithely unconcerned with fulfilling any genre expectations in relation to this fact that yet another potential audience is summarily expelled, or at best ignored.

CITY OF PIRATES, perhaps the most visually ravishing of Ruiz's works in 35-millimeter, has been evocatively encapsulated by Gilbert Adair in the summer 1984 *Sight and Sound*:

> Here the cinema virtually renounces its role as a recording medium. Nevertheless, in style of the endlessly shifting filters, reverse photography, visual tricks, etc., there remains an *image de base* (contrary to the technological jigsaw puzzles of Hollywood science fiction), therefore an effect of reality. A "double-bill" of two discrete narratives, concerning a cherubic infant killer and a neurotic Norman Bates-like loner: when, as the second plot develops, one has all but forgotten the first, it brusquely resurfaces. The color is the closest I have ever seen to '40s Kalmus Technicolor, as though nature itself had been made-up.

Bursting with shocking and poetic surrealist conceits, the film seems to embody the poetic recipe proposed in Godard's MADE IN U.S.A.—"Walt Disney plus blood"—while running through its arsenal of astonishing lab effects (painterly long shots of the island, brimming with magical light), unsettling fantasy notions (a man's face casually discovered under a pile of vegetables in a suitcase; the neurotic loner playing catch with himself), and uncanny spatial displacements (including "impossible" reverse angles where the camera appears to be lodged under a low glass table or inside a character's mouth). Yet as an exercise in storytelling, it can easily be seen as either overblown or undernourished: for all its beauty, it refuses to tailor its effects to the demands of "professional" storytelling.

MANUEL ON THE ISLAND OF WONDERS is a French/Portuguese television coproduction shot in 16-millimeter and made up of three 50-minute episodes. (More recently it has resurfaced as a single, reduced 130-minute feature, LES DESTINS DE MANOEL, which I haven't seen.) The first episode offers a narrative roundelay of recurring images and incidents whereby the eponymous hero aged seven meets himself aged thirteen and gets a forecast of future events. The second has Manuel exchanging bodies with an adult woodcutter, whereas the third relocates him in an aunt's haunted house and pivots around a children's party with Carrollian overtones.

Seen as a whole, the film's storyline is gradually formalized through mantric repetitions and subsequent narrative suspensions until the characters and settings eventually become slaves of a dream logic that converts them into nonnarrative archetypes and emblems—pure spectacle without the Oedipal trappings of plot. Like CITY OF PIRATES, it qualifies as a "children's adventure story" only insofar as it functions as a story at all—which is to say, only intermittently and superficially. Thus it seems highly appropriate that the cycle of episodes culminates in the extended children's party, which is dominated by a sort of polymorphous perversity of the imagination—an infantile pleasure that all but abolishes the ordinary cause and effect of storytelling. The effect may be mesmerizing to a viewer on Ruiz's wavelength, but it can only confound a spectator demanding a coherent synopsis.

Circulating under the title LIFE IS A DREAM in the United States, MÉMOIRE DES APPARENCES grew directly out of Ruiz's stage production of Calderon's seventeenth-century Spanish play *La Vida Es Sueño*, which had recently been retranslated into French by Jean-Louis Schefer. The film was shot between the premiere of this production at the Avignon Theater Festival in August 1986 and its transfer to Le Havre three months later. Actually, Calderon wrote two plays with the same title forty years apart, comprising respectively "profane" and "sacred" versions of the same drama; Ruiz's stage and film versions draw extracts from both, but greater emphasis is given to the former and better known of the two. In the film, a member of the Chilean underground resistance once used these texts as a mnemonic device to memorize the names and addresses of fellow resistance members; ten years later at a provincial cinema which is presumably showing a film of the play, he attempts to recall this information.

To complicate matters, the snatches of the film that we see comprise a survey of disparate popular film genres: film noir, space opera, bourgeois melodrama, swashbuckler, and so forth. And the theater auditorium itself becomes another dream world where a police station is located behind the screen, birds pass over or below the seats, and a model train—a familiar Ruiz motif in the early 1980s—runs by. An attempt to conflate Spanish baroque with the Chilean left, and both with grade-Z movie conventions, the film may well be Ruiz's most intellectually dense effort to date—probably longer than it needs to be, like CITY OF PIRATES, but bristling with unkempt energy.

By contrast, MAMMAME, which runs only about half as long, confronts the issue of adaptation—in this case, a dance piece performed by Jean-Claude Gallotta's nine-member group—on a shot by shot basis. Although the *fictional* coordinates of the film-within-a-film in MÉMOIRE DES APPARENCES undergo constant permutations, the *spatial* coordinates in MAMMAME similarly undergo a process of continual revision. (All that remains constant, in effect, are the body of Calderon's texts and the bodies of Gallotta's dancers.) Accompanied by a wordless patter of utterances from the dancers (which happily eliminates any need for subtitles), recorded in direct sound, this plotless dance, bursting with minidramas, begins on an artificially controlled theater stage and ends in nature on a seaside location. In between, the major anchor used to "ground" the spectator in the shifting décor is the ground and gravity itself, with a Wellesian employment of wide angles and deep focus often emphasizing the weight and mass of bodies in contrast to the endless mutable overhead space. One imagines that the absence of both plot and verbal language would universalize Ruiz's visual talents for a much wider audience, but so far, apart from a few limited screenings in the United States, this remarkable work—perhaps the closest thing to a masterpiece that Ruiz has made—remains unseen, untested, and unknown in the larger world where a movie like THE RED SHOES functions.

Even a Cocteauvian gem like HYPOTHESIS OF A STOLEN PAINTING, which functioned partly as Ruiz's calling-card in Europe, dissatisfies many arthouse expectations with its odd running time of sixty-six minutes (about the same length as MAMMAME) and its even odder educational television format. At the other end of the spectrum, one finds work as difficult and/or intractable as LA COLONIA PENAL, LA VOCATION SUSPENDUE (1977), LE BORGNE, POINT DE FUITE, and MÉMOIRE DES APPARENCES. And somewhere in between come the various television documentaries, aimed at a separate audience, which deftly negotiate between more conventional viewer expectations and diverse strategies of subversion—most of which are too localized or tied to specific events to allow for any easy transatlantic export.

Ruiz's most recent features at the time of writing, LA CHOUETTE AVEUGLE and LE PROFESSEUR TARANNE (both 1987), both show a certain running down of inspiration and suggest a temporary exhaustion.[5] The former and more

interesting of the two develops some of the ideas in MÉMOIRE DES AP-
PARENCES (including the use of a similar provincial movie theater); the latter
is a minimalist exercise in adaptation, rather like the 1984 DANS UN MIROIR,
with a rotating cast of nine actors playing the eponymous professor in Arthur
Adamov's play.

As a restless skeptic and prolific ideas-man who periodically raises the
question of what is or isn't necessary in a film, Ruiz frequently recalls the example of Godard in the 1960s. The surrealist dislocation of locations—such
as the standing in of Holland for Patagonia in THE ROOF OF THE WHALE—
can probably be traced back to ALPHAVILLE, whereas the interrogation of
documentary methods in the untransmitted INA (French television) film DES
GRANDS ÉVÉNEMENTS ET DES GENS ORDINAIRES (OF GREAT EVENTS AND ORDI-
NARY PEOPLE, 1979) conjures up recollections of MASCULINE–FEMININE and
2 OR 3 THINGS I KNOW ABOUT HER (as well as Chris Marker's LE JOLI MAI).
What begins as investigative reporting on Ruiz's own district of Paris during
the elections winds up as an investigation of the documentary form itself.

An off-screen narrator periodically disrupts the "information flow" with
pointed, self-conscious remarks: "We could pan over the courtyard. Some
credits might appear"; "Keep the pauses, to give a feeling of everyday life . . .
Leave in the pauses, to show that everyday life is rhetoric"; "Complete the
space by means of reverse shots"; "How many hesitations in behavior are
necessary to create the effect of the everyday? Between four and seven per
idea expressed. What intervals should separate one idea from another? Between two and seven seconds." And one line in particular, which conjures up
the ghost of the buried corpse theme: "The subject of the film is the dispersal,
the documentary's tendency to lose itself in detail." To which one should add
that all Ruiz's films tend to lose themselves in detail, as a matter of course.

> A map may be called inaccurate when one cannot find in the territory that
> which appears on the map. Inaccurate maps are valuable aids. They enable you
> to discover what you do not expect to find, take your desires for realities. They
> also make it possible constantly to make new maps.

Viewed as a tool for mapmaking, Ruiz's filmography constitutes a scholar's nightmare. Apart from the titles already mentioned are numerous films
and videotapes made in Europe, including LA TERRITOIRE (an abortive feature
made in Portugal in 1981), BÉRÉNICE and LA PRÉSENCE RÉELLE (both more
recent), and countless shorts and television programs. There is the additional
problem of shorter and longer versions of the same works: apart from the examples of UTOPIA and MANUEL already cited, Ian Christie reports in a recent
Monthly Film Bulletin,

> THE PENAL COLONY reaches Britain after a series of adventures too complex to
> detail here, in a version that lacks all credit titles and which may be some seven

minutes short. In this state, which is almost certainly the best achievable, it is not a film to be approached without some contextual information.

Concentrate on a single film in a single version, and the obstacles to cartography may seem just as daunting—whether these be the various languages spoken in THE ROOF OF THE WHALE or VANISHING POINT, the deformations of images and sound in LES DIVISIONS DE LA NATURE (an untransmitted French television documentary of 1978 about the Château de Chambord), the abrupt changes of tone in CITY OF PIRATES, the narrative overload of COLLOQUE DE CHIENS, or the interweaving of two "films" and time frames in LA VOCATION SUSPENDUE.

Even in the delightful LE JEU DE L'OIE (1980), "a didactic fiction about cartography" made for French television to promote a map exhibition at the Centre Pompidou in Paris—a Borgesian metaphysical fantasy whose hero progressively discovers that France is a lifesize board game—one has to deal with tatty special effects of Edward D. Wood Jr. caliber, along with the brilliant conceits *and* two separate off-screen narrators, male and female. (It is the latter of these who recites all the unattributed texts about maps found in this essay.)

If one gets a disquieting overall sense in Ruiz's work of a prodigal invention deprived of any holding center—save for irony, erudition, imagination, cunning, and exile—one should not conclude from this that everything in a Ruiz film is equally open to question. One of the enquiries that is pointedly absent from OF GREAT EVENTS AND ORDINARY PEOPLE is any sign of recognition on Ruiz's part that, with only two or three exceptions, the Paris neighborhood he is investigating is seen as almost exclusively male. (In general, as suggested in the case of THE THREE CROWNS OF THE SAILOR, the Ruiz oeuvre is infused with a Latin machismo that seems less open to ridicule than most other matters of life, death, and narrative with which he deals.)

At the outset of LE JEU DE L'OIE, the troubled hero (Patrick Bonitzer)—who is found to be vomiting out dice on one occasion, and shaken *as* dice by an enormous hand on another—discovers that "he is the victim of the worst kind of nightmare, the didactic nightmare." Some form of didacticism seems evident in every Ruiz project but, as with Borges, it is a didacticism that often parodies itself and becomes camp, yielding precisely the kind of nightmare that ensues when, through a delirium of literalism, thought becomes flesh and the universe becomes a brain dreaming of thoughts yet unborn.

But however much Ruiz may be involved with a Borgesian (or Rousselian) metaphysics of this sort, like the exiled Argentine directors Eduardo de Gregorio and Edgardo Cozarinsky he is involved with a leftist orientation of these labyrinths. His fantasies never trace perfect circles and return the viewer to a comfortable armchair equivalent of the status quo (a recurring trait that links Borges to Lewis Carroll), but invariably set off in treacherous directions without return tickets, challenging spectators to follow as long as they dare. A 360-degree pan in OF GREAT EVENTS AND ORDINARY PEOPLE which begins around a theoretical discussion about documentary among *Cahiers du Cinéma* critics abruptly continues outside their offices and into the street, threading theory and practice into the same arbitrary trajectory. ("The film creates the events to be seen," notes Bonitzer, before the camera lingers didactically over his difficulties in lighting a cigar.) Like the life-size maps behind Bonitzer inside a fake airplane in LE JEU DE L'OIE, or the Lacanian parody in THE ROOF OF THE WHALE, didacticism is merely another reference point in a decidedly unstable universe, ever ready to become institutionalized and therefore real. "The narrator should say something during this pause," notes the narrator during a pause midway through GREAT EVENTS, and of course, by doing so, he amply fills up the space.

> The return to the landscape makes it possible to ask a delicate question. If the map is a representation of the landscape or territory, what is the territory? It is quite clear that the territory is the sum of all the maps, the result of an infinite addition. Or, conversely, the territory is what is left when one removes the whole tissue of lines, drawings, symbols and colors which covers it. Its existence becomes doubtful.

Notes

1. Since writing the above, I was able to see this film at the San Sebastian Film Festival in 1988. It's worth noting that for all the film's "pre-Ruizian" qualities, the taste for eccentric and "impossible" camera angles is already fully in place.

2. For the opportunity to see this work, I am especially grateful to two institutions that have been vital to the recognition of Ruiz's importance in Europe: the Rotterdam Film Festival and the British Film Institute, whose interest in Ruiz was spearheaded by the late Hubert Bals and by Ian Christie, respectively. Thanks are also due to several institutions and individuals in the United States and Canada: Piers Handling at the Toronto Festival of Festivals (who commissioned an earlier version of this essay for a 1985 Ruiz retrospective), Deirde Mahoney and Jean Vallier at New York's Alliance Française (who, together with Jordi Torrent of Exit Art, presented another Ruiz retrospective in 1987), Wendy Lidell at The International Film Circuit, and Richard Peña at the Film Center of the Art Institute of Chicago.

For additional assistance in matters Ruizian, the reader is referred to the following sources in French and English: *Afterimage* (London, Autumn 1981), *Cahiers du Cinéma* (March 1983), *Positif* (December 1983), *Ten to Watch: Ten Filmmakers for the Future* (Festival of Festivals catalogue, 1985), *Râúl Ruiz: Works For and About French TV* (Exit Art catalogue, 1987), *The Cutting Edge* (International Film Circuit catalogue, 1987–1988), and Christine Buci-Glucksmann and Fabrice Revault d'Allonnes's *Raoul Ruiz* (Editions Dis Voir, 1987), the first book about Ruiz in any language.

3. It's always refreshing to be proved wrong in Ruizian matters. Since the above passage was written, VANISHING POINT has been sold to and broadcast on German television.

4. This was written in the mid-1980s. Since then, HYPOTHESIS OF A STOLEN PAINT-ING had a brief run in New York at the Bleecker Street Cinema in late 1987, along with COLLOQUE DE CHIENS, where it was abruptly killed by uncomprehending re-views, including an especially churlish one in the *Village Voice*. Around the same time, however, without acquiring distributors, MÉMOIRE DES APPARENCES and MAM-MAME received several showings in the United States, and on the whole fared much better with audiences as well as critics.

5. By contrast, the more recent TOUS LES NUAGES SONT DES HORLOGES and L'AUTEL DE L'AMITIÉ, both shown in Rotterdam in early 1989, are somewhat livelier.

An earlier version of this essay appeared in
Cinematograph, *vol. 3, 1987, published by*
The San Francisco Cinematheque

—Modern Times, *January 1990*

Notes Toward the Devaluation of Woody Allen

"Why are the French so crazy about Jerry Lewis?" is a recurring question posed by film buffs in the United States, but, sad to say, it is almost invariably asked rhetorically. When Dick Cavett tried it out several years ago on Jean-Luc Godard, one of Lewis's biggest defenders, it quickly became apparent that Cavett had no interest in hearing an answer, and he immediately changed the subject as soon as Godard began to provide one. Nevertheless it's a question worth posing seriously, along with a few related ones—even at the risk of courting disbelief and giving offense.

Why are American intellectuals so contemptuous of Jerry Lewis and so crazy about Woody Allen? Apart from such obvious differences as the fact that Allen cites Kierkegaard and Lewis doesn't, what is it that gives Allen such an exalted cultural status in this country, and Lewis virtually no cultural status at all? (Charlie Chaplin cited Schopenhauer in MONSIEUR VERDOUX, but surely that isn't the reason why we continue to honor him.) If we agree that there's more to intellectual legitimacy than name-dropping, what is it in Allen's work as a comic Jewish writer-director-performer that earns him that legitimacy—a legitimacy that is denied to, among others, Elaine May and both Mel and Albert Brooks?

The issue isn't simply one of respect, but one of identification and outright infatuation. The implication is that a good many of Allen's fans view his comic persona in very much the same way that they like to view themselves. If movies in general owe much of their appeal to their capacity to function as Narcissus pools, offering glamorous and streamlined identification figures to authenticate our most treasured self-images, film comedy tends to heighten this tendency in physical terms, so that it would hardly be an exaggeration to state that how we respond to such figures as Chaplin, Buster Keaton, Harry Langdon, Harold Lloyd, Jacques Tati, Lewis, and Allen has something to do with how we feel about our own bodies.

As a comic writer, Allen is easily the equal of Robert Benchley, George S. Kaufman, and S. J. Perelman, and conceivably within hailing distance of James Thurber. As a performer, it is largely his lack of actorly presence—his badge of authenticity—that endears him to the world at large. His self-hatred and lack of physicality may make him an unlikely love object, yet nothing is more reassuring about his persona than the acute sense of failure that he brings to every activity, making every small victory, every flicker of warmth or hope into an inspirational triumph.

As a writer-performer-persona, he is probably as personal as it is possible for someone in his position to be. But as a director and filmmaker, even after nineteen features, he remains strangely unformed and unrealized—not a creator of forms or even a distinctive stylist who can exist independently of his models. This can be seen not only in his use of Sven Nykvist, Ingmar Bergman's cinematographer, on several of his pictures (usually to create a clinically antiseptic look that evokes Scandinavian seriousness), but also in the visible derivations of Bergman's CRIES AND WHISPERS in INTERIORS, SMILES OF A SUMMER NIGHT in A MIDSUMMER NIGHT'S SEX COMEDY, and WILD STRAWBERRIES in ANOTHER WOMAN; of Fellini's $8\frac{1}{2}$ in STARDUST MEMORIES and AMARCORD in RADIO DAYS; and of Fellini's episode in BOCCACCIO '70 in Allen's episode (OEDIPUS WRECKS) in NEW YORK STORIES, among other examples. Even in ZELIG, one of his more original conceptions, the periodic statements by Jewish intellectuals playing themselves—Saul Bellow, Bruno Bettelheim, Irving Howe, Susan Sontag—are used in a way that makes them clearly indebted to the statements of the "witnesses" in Warren Beatty's REDS, which was released two years earlier. (The validation of ZELIG's fictional world offered by "real" intellectual celebrities, paralleled by the appearance of Marshall McLuhan in ANNIE HALL, is of course quite different from the dialectical function of the witnesses in REDS, who remain unidentified, but the appropriation of Beatty's technique is again characteristic.)

Most often these borrowings, when they're noticed, are rationalized in the press as "homages"; yet arguably they reveal the same sort of aesthetic immaturity that a beginning writer shows by imitating, say, Hemingway or Faulkner. Imitation can be a sincere form of flattery, and there's no doubting the sincerity of Allen's Bergman and Fellini worship. But beyond a certain point there's a question of whether this kind of emulation is being used as a tool for fresh discoveries or as an expedient substitute for such discoveries—a shield labeled "Art" that's intended to intimidate nonbelievers.

There's a world of difference between the *application* of film models by a Jean-Luc Godard or a Jacques Rivette, which offers critical insights into a particular film or director (such as the compressed references to MONSIEUR

VERDOUX and PSYCHO in Godard's WEEKEND, which point up the links made between murder and capitalism in both earlier films), and the simple transposition of a look or manner employed by Allen. Perhaps if Allen's cinematic frames of reference were wider—taking in, say, Carl Dreyer as well as Bergman, and Roberto Rossellini as well as Fellini—his appropriations might not seem so willful and automatic. One reason why Rivette's creative uses of Fritz Lang and Jean Renoir seem much more fruitful is that neither of these filmmakers is tied exclusively to a single country or culture. The styles of Bergman and Fellini, by contrast, are linked indigenously to the respective cultures of Sweden and Italy, so what point is there in transposing these styles to an exclusively New York milieu? Yet Allen is often treated in the press as if he were even more important than the directors he copies.

■

In an illuminating book about film editing called *When the Shooting Stops . . . the Cutting Begins*, Ralph Rosenblum describes in detail how he substantially reworked Allen's unformed and scattershot rough cuts on half a dozen early features—even successfully demanding that Allen shoot new endings to TAKE THE MONEY AND RUN, BANANAS, SLEEPER, and LOVE AND DEATH, and transforming a self-centered smorgasbord called ANHEDONIA ("the inability to experience pleasure") into a graceful romantic comedy called ANNIE HALL. Although Rosenblum no longer edits Allen's pictures, perhaps as a consequence of writing this book, Thierry de Navacelle's more recent *Woody Allen on Location*, a diary of the shooting of RADIO DAYS which includes in parallel columns the original script and the first "cutting continuity," amply shows that as recently as 1987 there was still a yawning abyss between Allen's conceptions and what wound up on the screen. Part of this appears to be a judicious pruning of compulsive morbidity: TAKE THE MONEY AND RUN originally ended with the bloody annihilation of its hero, whereas RADIO DAYS originally began with awkward radio coverage of the drowning of a Houdini type in an underwater stunt. But an equally important part of the problem seems to be that Allen usually starts with a literary conception rather than a filmic one. As he pointed out to Godard in a videotaped interview conducted in 1986, he regards the intertitles in HANNAH AND HER SISTERS as a literary device (as words), whereas Godard uses them in his own films as a cinematic device (as shots).

Obviously there's nothing wrong with this in itself; the American literary cinema has few sustained talents to call its own, and there's no doubt Allen's talents as a writer enhance that cinema in certain respects. Nor can Allen really be blamed for the inordinate claims made for his movies by Vincent Canby and others; his own remarks about his pictures tend to be much more modest. One also respects his passion and seriousness in speaking out against colorization and his refusal to let his only film in CinemaScope, MANHATTAN, be scaled down to the ratio of the television screen by losing its left and right borders—something that neither Bernardo Bertolucci nor Steven Spielberg has been able to accomplish with the video and television versions of THE LAST EMPEROR and EMPIRE OF THE SUN, for example.

But one still needs to ask why Allen has been nominated and all but elected our foremost "artistic" filmmaker and the poet laureate of our collective uncertainties in so many circles, most of them upscale and middlebrow. What does he do for this audience that is deemed so essential and irreplaceable? To what extent is his stature a progressive factor in our film culture, and to what extent is it reactionary? How much does his status as an intellectual filmmaker represent genuine intellectual inquiry, and how much does it suggest something closer to the reverse—a representation of intellectuals for nonintellectuals and even anti-intellectuals that serves to satisfy curiosity about intellectual concerns without any sort of intellectual challenge?

Why are the French so crazy about Jerry Lewis? Well, for one thing, some of them see him as being very much like America: infantile, hysterical, uncontrolled, giddy, uninhibited, tacky, energetic, inarticulate, obnoxious, sentimental, overbearing, socially and sexually maladjusted, and all over the place. (By contrast, at least on the surface, Allen is adolescent, neurotic, controlled, whiny, inhibited, preppy, lethargic, articulate, cynical, wormy, socially and sexually maladjusted, and confined.) It's not so much a matter of necessarily loving all these qualities as it is envying or admiring or identifying with some of them, and being horrified by others—a sort of compressed model of the love-hate that many French people feel toward America as a fantasy object. I suspect that what many French people experience as the overcultivated constraints of their culture finds a welcome release in Lewis's explosiveness and ungainliness, and their taste for freewheeling fantasy is partially met by Lewis's remoteness from realism—the sheer wildness of his ideas as a writer-director, and the deconstructive habits such as the vulgar modernism that he shares with Mel Brooks, which periodically reminds us in various self-referential ways that we're watching a film. (At one point in the mid-1960s, Godard described Lewis as "the only free man working in Hollywood.")

None of this, however, should be regarded as monolithic or exclusive regarding French tastes: the French also happen to be crazy about Woody Allen. But it's worth remarking that the French are less prone than we are to regard Allen as any sort of improvement on or substitute for European art-film directors. The essence of any taste is largely a matter of what it excludes as well as what it includes, and the ascendancy of Woody Allen as an art-film director in the United States coincides with a steady drop in interest in foreign-language art films. We can count on every Allen film being readily available in one form or another all over the United States, but not every film by Bergman or Fellini (whose last feature, INTERVISTA, has never been released here); in the cases of Antonioni, Godard, and Alain Resnais, *most* of their last several films remain unavailable in the United States.

■

Allen is far from being the only comic director who thinks verbally more than visually; the same is true of Mel Brooks, and an overall orientation toward the word rather than the image may have something to do with the nature of Judaism as an oral culture. When someone in Brooks's HISTORY OF THE WORLD, PART I remarks, "The streets are crawling with soldiers," one knows in advance that Brooks will have to follow this with a non sequitur visual equivalent—giving the word and voice primacy, literally making it flesh by spelling it out in rebus form. "Death was greeted with a certain amount of awe," intones narrator Orson Welles near the start of the same film, and everyone standing around in the perfunctory, instantly forgettable shot who isn't supposed to be a corpse goes "Awwwww—." Saying as well as spraying it, chewing and spewing words until they overspill and start to fill in some of the cracks left by the illustrative images, Brooks's characters and their shticks go much farther into literalism than Allen's do, to the degree that they often make consecutive, coherent narratives impossible, adhering to the more freeform structures of standup routines. (For the record, Allen's uncharacteristic first feature in 1966, WHAT'S UP, TIGER LILY?, was as wild and deconstructive as anything by Brooks or Lewis.)

Allen, by contrast, depends mainly on stories with naturalistic underpinnings; whatever the stylistic varnish given to any particular film, the form more often than not is relatively conventional (which helps to account for what makes his movies relatively accessible). But Allen's heroes remain fundamentally standup personalities, and what is most often funny about them is their wisecracks. This tendency is tied, in any case, to the increasing formal problem in Allen's work of integrating his comic, actorly persona with his more serious aspirations as a narrative filmmaker. His last several comic films have proposed different solutions for injecting Woody into a plot: incorporating him into mock newsreels (and uncharacteristically depriving him of a voice) in ZELIG, bringing him back as a sympathetic romantic hero in BROADWAY DANNY ROSE and as a Kafkaesque hero in OEDIPUS WRECKS (in NEW YORK STORIES), using Mia Farrow as a partial Woody substitute in both THE PURPLE ROSE OF CAIRO and RADIO DAYS, using Dianne Wiest as a female Woody in HANNAH AND HER SISTERS and RADIO DAYS, and isolating him like a bacteria in the parallel plots of both HANNAH AND HER SISTERS and CRIMES AND MISDEMEANORS.

A better sense of how Allen handles these problems of language and persona can be deduced by comparing his strategies with those of Chaplin, Tati, and Lewis. For Chaplin, speech brings about a transformation of the Tramp at the end of THE GREAT DICTATOR, and then his elimination from all the subsequent films. Tati's Monsieur Hulot, initially designed to appear only in MR. HULOT'S HOLIDAY, is furnished with a wealthy sister and nephew in MON ONCLE, multiplied and universalized by various lookalikes (to prove that we are all potential Hulots) in PLAYTIME, brought back in desperation as the central hero of TRAFIC after the commercial disaster of the former film, and finally abandoned with relief in PARADE. In all these films, speech is overheard more than heard, and sound is generally used to complement and punctuate (rather than illustrate) the images. Lewis in his own films—although doing little to alter his character (apart from adjusting to the effects of aging)—accompanies his bodily deformations with deformations of language, creating a kind of spastic Jabberwocky at moments of hysteria to reflect his gangling physical instability.

Like Allen, these figures can be regarded as autobiographical artists in the deepest sense, their gags springing directly from their own lives and experiences. (This might seem less obvious with Lewis, but it's worth noting that his last feature, CRACKING UP, has slapstick sequences alluding to both his open-heart surgery and his near-suicide.) All three can also be said to be animated by a conflict between narcissism and self-hatred in relation to their comic personae. Where they differ crucially from Allen is in the degree to which they express this conflict dialectically. Rather than work both sides of the street, as Allen does, they usually maintain enough distance from their own characters to allow audiences to have a critical perspective on them. Allen, by contrast, is too close to Woody to allow us this detachment; his task is to seduce us into sharing his character's confusions and ambivalences without being able to sort them out. (After all, Woody can't sort them out, so why should we?) And rather than propose an artistic solution to a personal conflict as Chaplin, Tati, or Lewis do, he offers a kind of aesthetic smoke screen designed to keep us from realizing that the conflict isn't being squarely faced.

■

Intellectuals and anti-intellectuals, liberals and conservatives, can all walk away from Allen's movies feeling that their own worldviews have been corroborated and illustrated because no issue is ever forced to a point of crisis—a few potshots in every possible direction usually suffice. The gag in ANNIE HALL about *Dissent* and *Commentary* merging into *Dysentery* has something for everybody: readers of both journals feel grateful for this uncharacteristic form of recognition in a commercial movie; people who feel distaste for the intellectualism associated with both publications are rewarded; and even those who might bristle at the political incompatibility of the two magazines are likely to be amused by the pun.

CRIMES AND MISDEMEANORS offers another case in point. A film that professes to address the rampant amorality and self-interest of the 1980s gives us an ophthalmologist (Martin Landau) who arranges to murder his mistress and gets away with it and a socially concerned documentary filmmaker (Allen) who isn't rewarded for his good intentions. But both characters seem equally motivated by self-interest, and we are asked to care much more about Allen's character as a fall guy than about the murdered mistress (Anjelica Huston). Landau's masochism about his initial feelings of guilt are matched by Allen's masochism about being a loser. There is a lack of ironic distance on this aspect of both characters, and if the film is genuinely attacking self-interest, it is seriously handicapped by being unable to see beyond it.

A major distinction here is social context. Chaplin and Tati offer characters whose main problem is coping with the world; Lewis and Allen's characters, however, are concerned with both coping and scoring, and the importance of scoring—greater in Allen's case than in Lewis's—implies a different relationship to the society in question. Scoring is the aim of the extrovert hungering for society's approval and applause; and for all their apparent maladjustments, Allen's heroes already belong fully and integrally to the society they wish to succeed in. They never suggest total outcasts, as Lewis's heroes often do.

One thing that makes both Chaplin and Tati profound social critics is the fact that their characters' difficulties in coping with society lead to a consideration of society's difficulties in coping with them. Lewis carries over some of this process (see, for instance, THE NUTTY PROFESSOR), but Allen virtually abandons it. Apart from the loving self-deprecations, and the daring jibes against his audiences in STARDUST MEMORIES, his social critique seldom gets beyond the range of one-liners, whereas the obsession with success and scoring usually implies that it is the oddball individual and not the society that needs to make adjustments.

One of the most disturbing facts about contemporary American life is its rejection of the concept of victims; the current synonym for "victim" is "loser." When Allen's character in CRIMES AND MISDEMEANORS is listening to his sister describe her humiliation at the hands of a sadist after answering a classified ad, Allen's horrified responses are telegraphed to the audience as invitations to cruel and derisive laughter, not pity. This is a curious ploy in a film that professes to be protesting the erosion of moral and ethical values, but one that is consistent with Allen's usual methods, because it's much easier to laugh at a loser than at a victim.

Evenly matching the dichotomy between Winners and Losers in Allen's films is the dichotomy between Insiders and Outsiders. Allen generally places one foot in each camp—looking with contempt at Insiders (Alan Alda's television producer in CRIMES AND MISDEMEANORS) from an Outsider's position, but also looking with contempt at Outsiders (the movie fans in STARDUST MEMORIES) from a privileged Insider's position. In RADIO DAYS, the warm superiority assumed by the narrator (Woody again) toward his family and the abject inferiority felt by Sally (Mia Farrow) toward radio stars (before she becomes one herself) are cut from the same cloth. Suffusing both realms with nostalgia while taking swipes at each side from the other, Allen refuses to commit himself wholly to either group or even to own up to that refusal—a decision that would shape and delimit the scope of his gags and allow them to work together. By shifting allegiances, he can make all the characters lovable or fair game whenever he wants. A higher laugh quotient is attained by this process, but a much fuzzier moral perspective, because complacent vanity and a lack of commitment to either faction become the prerequisites for such a position. A generous reading of this trait would be to call it a form of objectivity; a more skeptical response would be to regard it as opportunistic.

■

It's been noted more than once that part of what makes the Manhattan in MANHATTAN so "attractive"—apart from strains of Gershwin and black-and-white CinemaScope views of favorite spots and haunts—is the nearly total absence of blacks and Hispanics. Insofar as this is the Manhattan that a certain class of whites already "see," or want to see, MANHATTAN both validates and romanticizes this highly selective view of the city.

Poverty in Allen's films, apart from the occasional one-liner, is almost invariably Jewish poverty and is rooted somewhere in the past; the contemporary plight of the homeless, for instance, may be apparent to anyone who walks for a couple of blocks in Manhattan, but it is not apparent in the urban exteriors of ANOTHER WOMAN, OEDIPUS WRECKS, or CRIMES AND MISDEMEANORS, and neither is the presence of racism. All of Allen's major characters are protected from such problems by the interiority of their concerns, and by implication the audiences of these films are similarly protected. Serious soulsearching about major world problems and the decline in moral values is the exclusive property of a few upwardly mobile urban whites, whose exclusive vantage points we are invited to share, and any set of assumptions that is located beyond the purview of *The New Yorker* or *The New York Times* is bound to be deemed both esoteric and provincial.

Robert Warshow's critique of *The New Yorker* as a cultural institution (in "E. B. White and *The New Yorker*") seems particularly relevant to the nature of Allen's special appeal:

> *The New Yorker* has always dealt with experience not by trying to understand it but by prescribing the attitude to be adopted toward it. This makes it possible to feel intelligent without thinking, and it is a way of making everything tolerable, for the assumption of a suitable attitude toward experience can give one the illusion of having dealt with it adequately. The gracelessness of capitalism becomes an entirely external phenomenon, a spectacle that one can observe without being touched—above all, without really feeling threatened. Even one's own incompetence becomes pleasant: to be baffled by a machine or by a domestic

worker or an idea is the badge of membership in the civilized and humane minority.

I'm willing to accept on faith Allen's claim in "Random Reflections of a Second-Rate Mind" (*Tikkun,* January/February 1990) that his reputation as a "self-hating Jew" may be somewhat displaced. ("[W]hile it's true I am Jewish and I don't like myself very much, it's not because of my persuasion.") But because of the autobiographical elements in his work, it is still difficult to account for the strong relationship between scoring and winning the love of a beautiful WASP woman (usually Diane Keaton or Mia Farrow) in most of his film comedies—although, to be fair about this, his persona *does* wind up with a Jewish woman just like his (dreaded) mom at the end of OEDIPUS WRECKS. What seems more problematic is the failure of most of Allen's films to face this issue squarely—to the degree that Elaine May's THE HEARTBREAK KID does, for instance, when the Jewish hero (Charles Grodin) ditches his Jewish wife (Jeannie Berlin) during their honeymoon in Miami in order to chase after Cybill Shepherd. The fact that in this case May is directing a Neil Simon script (based on a Bruce Jay Friedman story) which never alludes to the ethnic nature of the conflict in the dialogue makes her success all the more striking: to put it bluntly, May's direction of the actors repeatedly and even uncomfortably exposes the degree to which Grodin's libido is affected by his own anti-Semitism. Allen's hero in OEDIPUS WRECKS may have changed his name from Millstein to Mills, and it's clear that he's dating a shiksa, but these are merely givens in the plot—the conflict is never explored in psychological terms, either in the dialogue or the direction, and eventually it gets resolved sentimentally when the plot offers him a Jewish girlfriend to replace the shiksa.

The usual reluctance of Allen to alienate his constituency—with notable and courageous exceptions, such as STARDUST MEMORIES and his op-ed piece in *The New York Times* criticizing Israeli soldiers—generally mean an avoidance of controversial issues and positions in his movies, in spite of their topical gloss. This is, of course, typical of the commercial American cinema, and it might be added that Allen's popularity with American intellectuals does not automatically mean success at the box office. (Interestingly enough, CRIMES AND MISDEMEANORS has been a commercial disappointment in spite of its rave reviews, and there have been many other such instances in Allen's career.) His unusual freedom to go on making personal films of *his* own choosing clearly has a price tag attached to it—the necessity of turning enough of a profit on some pictures to keep this arrangement going—and it would be naive to assume otherwise. Allen's representation of himself as an artist and an intellectual (as opposed to a "mere" entertainer) obliges us to take him at his own word; and once we do, the issue of what intellectuals and artists both are and should be in our culture immediately comes up. To exempt Allen from that issue is to accept the sort of imposture that the film industry itself is famous for—the notion that art is a form of entertainment that makes money, and that "intellectual" is just a synonym for "pseudo-intellectual."

Noam Chomsky has written, "It is the responsibility of intellectuals to speak the truth and to expose lies. This, at least, may seem enough of a truism to pass without comment. Not so, however. For the modern intellectual, it is not at all obvious." Whether or not we regard Allen as an intellectual depends, in the final analysis, on whether or not we accept Chomsky's view of what should be obvious.

So if we want to see a comedy that tells us something about, say, American idiocy in blundering through the Third World and the Reaganite equation of entertainment and politics, a disreputable piece of goods like Elaine May's ISHTAR will actually come closer to the mark than any movie we can expect to get from Woody Allen. (The notion of a show-biz agent negotiating a peace settlement in the Middle East as part of an entertainment deal might get by as a one-liner in an Allen effort, but only May would have the nerve to use it integrally, as a resolution of her plot.) If we want to learn *some* of the truth about unemployment in the United States in the early eighties—a revelation that might make us shudder as well as laugh—Jerry Lewis's HARDLY WORKING is a better place to go than any film by Allen, just as even a wobbly Mel Brooks effort like SPACEBALLS has more to say about the mercantilism of the film industry than anything we could expect from Woody. Similarly, for a genuinely satirical treatment of blinkered Yuppie sensibilities, one must repair to Albert Brooks's LOST IN AMERICA, not to HANNAH AND HER SISTERS or CRIMES AND MISDEMEANORS. By contrast, what we find in Allen's movies, apart from a lively stream of patter, is flattery to our egos as right-thinking individuals and a kind of soul-searching that excludes any possibility of social change—a provincial narcissism that corresponds precisely to our present situation in relation to the rest of the world.

Reprinted from TIKKUN MAGAZINE,
A BI-MONTHLY JEWISH CRITIQUE OF
POLITICS, CULTURE, AND SOCIETY
Subscriptions are $31.00 per year from
TIKKUN, 251 West 100th Street, 5th floor,
New York, NY 10025

Crass Consciousness

BARTON FINK

★★

BARTON FINK
Directed by Joel Coen
Written by Ethan Coen and Joel Coen
With John Turturro, John Goodman, Judy Davis, Michael
Lerner, John Mahoney, Tony Shalhoub, and Jon Polito

I'm not one of the Coen brothers' biggest fans. I walked out of BLOOD SIM-
PLE, their first feature. The main sentiment I took away from RAISING ARIZONA
and MILLER'S CROSSING—their second and third efforts, both of which I stayed
to the end of—was that at least each new Coen brothers movie was a discernible improvement over the last. RAISING ARIZONA may have had some
of the same crass, gratuitous condescension toward its country characters as
BLOOD SIMPLE, but it also had a sweeter edge and more visual flair. In both
craft and stylishness, MILLER'S CROSSING was another step forward, and even
if I never really believed in either the period ambience or the characters—the
dialogue bristled with anachronisms, and Albert Finney's crime boss seemed
much too blinkered and naive for someone who was supposed to be ruling a
city—the film nevertheless demanded a certain attention.

On its own terms, MILLER'S CROSSING was the work of a pair of movie brats
(both in their midthirties) eager to show their emulation of Dashiell Hammett
but, in spiky postmodernist fashion, almost totally indifferent to Hammett's
own period—except for what they could skim from superficial readings of *Red
Harvest*, *The Glass Key*, and a few secondary sources. Historical and psychological veracity consisted basically of whatever they could get away with,
based on the cynical assumption that their audience was every bit as devoid
of interest in these matters as they were. Unlike their earlier efforts, MILLER'S
CROSSING was a commercial flop—an undeserved one, given its visual distinction and its strong performances. Even if the film was soulless, it showed
an obsession with its Hammett-derived male-bonding theme that suggested
the Coens were aspiring to something more than crass entertainment; for better or worse, it looked like art movies were their ultimate aim.

BARTON FINK confirms this impression with a vengeance. Unfortunately, the movie ultimately founders on the Coens' primary impulses, which drive them to use a festival of fancy effects; whatever their ambitions, midnight movies are still the brothers' métier. The movie's arty surface fairly screams with significance, but the stylistic devices are designed for immediate consumption rather than being part of a coherent strategy. As entertainment, BARTON FINK is in some ways even better than MILLER'S CROSSING, though also just as adolescent and much less engaging when seen a second time. Last May it received the unprecedented honor of being awarded three top prizes at the Cannes film festival—for best picture, best director, and best actor (John Turturro)—which will undoubtedly help it commercially in Europe. Whether these awards will count for much in the more hidebound United States still remains to be seen.

The president of the Cannes jury was Roman Polanski, who took the job only after demanding that he be allowed to handpick his own jury members. Considering the indebtedness of BARTON FINK to Polanski pictures like REPULSION, ROSEMARY'S BABY, and THE TENANT—in its black humor, treatment of confinement and loneliness, perverse evocations of everyday "normality," creepy moods and hallucinatory disorientation, phantasmagoric handling of gore and other kinds of horror as shock effects, and even its careful use of ambiguous off-screen sounds—the group of awards should probably be viewed more as an act of self-congratulation than as an objective aesthetic judgment.

Nevertheless, BARTON FINK is an unusually audacious movie for a major studio to release—not only because of its bizarre form and content, but also because the Coens had complete creative control. Whatever else they might mean, then, the Cannes prizes cannot be regarded as automatic nods to the commercial tried-and-true. In terms of overall meaning, BARTON FINK qualifies as a genuine puzzler. Considering how transparent most commercial movies are, BARTON FINK at least deserves credit for stimulating a healthy amount of discussion.

■

The title hero is a working-class Jewish playwright (Turturro) who has just scored a hit in New York with his first play, *Bare Ruined Choirs*; the year is 1941. Offered a lucrative Hollywood contract by Capitol Pictures that he reluctantly accepts—he doesn't want to compromise his passionate vision of a theater "by and for the common man"—he goes to the west coast, checks into a faded deco hotel called the Earle, and goes to see Capitol's hysterically effusive studio head Jack Lipnick (Michael Lerner), who promptly asks him to write a wrestling picture for Wallace Beery.

Alone in his squalid room at the Earle, Barton finds himself painfully blocked, unable to get beyond a few scene-setting sentences. The sound of sobbing (or is it laughing?) in the next room prompts him to phone the front desk, and a few minutes later his next-door neighbor (John Goodman)—a burly, friendly fellow who identifies himself as an insurance salesman named Charlie Meadows—pays him an apologetic visit. Barton recognizes him as exactly the kind of working stiff he's interested in writing about, and they soon become friends—though Barton is too full of himself to show much interest in learning anything about Charlie (who repeatedly announces that he has stories to tell).

Barton meets with Ben Geisler (Tony Shalhoub), the flinty producer assigned by Lipnick to the wrestling-picture project. He also meets W. P. Mayhew (John Mahoney), an alcoholic southern novelist turned screenwriter clearly modeled after William Faulkner, and Audrey (Judy Davis), Mayhew's abused secretary and mistress, whom Barton clearly takes a shine to.

Stylistically, the movie chiefly consists of three kinds of scenes. There is entertaining if obvious satire about Hollywood vulgarians (Shalhoub—who played the cabdriver in the underrated QUICK CHANGE—and Lerner are both very funny and effective). There are extended mood pieces involving the heat, solitude, and viscousness (peeling wallpaper with running, semenlike glue) of Barton's seedy hotel room, with frequent nods to ERASERHEAD as well as Polanski, and many repeated, obsessive close-ups of both Barton's portable typewriter and a tacky hand-colored photo of a bathing beauty framed over the desk. Finally, there are the scenes between Barton and Charlie, all of which occur in Barton's room (no other room in the hotel is ever seen) and suggest a sort of sweaty homoerotic rapport somewhat reminiscent of Saul Bellow's novel *The Victim* and the tortured male bonding in MILLER'S CROSSING.

There's a certain temptation to follow BARTON FINK simply as a midnight movie, a string of sensations that alternates among styles and moods like a kind of vaudeville. As the plot suddenly veers into outright fantasy and metaphor, incorporating other styles and moods (mainly those of arty horror films), the effect of putting one damn showstopper after another is to almost obliterate any sense of logical narrative. (Moviegoers who don't want their surprises spoiled should check out at the end of this paragraph.) We're essentially invited to take a funhouse ride through these effects rather than ponder too much what they're supposed to mean. But however much it appears to profess otherwise, BARTON FINK is as heavily laden with "messages" as any Stanley Kramer film. Almost all of these messages, I should add, are cynical, reactionary, and/or banal to the point of stupidity.

As I see it, the messages are as follows:

1. *Socially committed artists are frauds.* Admittedly, the only one we see is Barton Fink, but the film has no interest in showing us any others. The principal model for Fink appears to be Clifford Odets (although he's given a George S. Kaufman haircut), and the film is at pains to show us that his ideas are trite, self-centered, and so limited that he ends both *Bare Ruined Choirs* and his wrestling-picture script with virtually the same corny line. We have

no way of knowing whether he's genuinely talented or not, and the movie seems completely uninterested in exploring this question, except for suggesting briefly that the people who praise his play are lunkheads. When the United States suddenly enters World War II toward the end of the movie, it seems not only to catch him completely unawares but to leave him indifferent as well—certainly not the reaction of the socially committed artists the Coens appear to be modeling him after. (As a friend has pointed out, Barton's preoccupations are about a decade off; by 1941, proletarian leftist artists were talking about fascism and the war, not about lower-east-side fishmongers.) He's an infantile sap throughout, and the movie forces us to share his consciousness in every scene.

  2. *Genuine artists like William Faulkner are frauds too—at least partially.* It's true that Mayhew is meant to *suggest* Faulkner rather than duplicate him, but consider how the Coens have loaded their deck. Mayhew looks like Faulkner, and he has both a "disturbed" off-screen wife with the same name as Faulkner's disturbed wife (Estelle) and a secretary (Audrey) modeled in certain respects on Meta Carpenter, the script girl Faulkner was involved with. By contrast, Faulkner was a taciturn drunk whereas Mayhew is a loquacious loudmouth who's successively humming and belting out "Old Black Joe" both times we see him and spouts flowery rhetoric at every opportunity. Although the Coens claim not to have known this until after they wrote their script, Faulkner actually worked on a Wallace Beery wrestling picture when he first came to Hollywood (John Ford's FLESH, 1932), and although it's conceivable that Carpenter or other friends could have helped to write some of his scripts, the suggestion that Carpenter may have helped to write some of the novels is ridiculous and was invented for this movie only to suggest that Mayhew, like Fink, is a poseur who can't really deliver the goods. Certainly the Coens have every right to twist reality as they please, but their alterations ("Old Black Joe"?) are so crass that they tend to rebound. Considering that most audience members won't be closely acquainted with Faulkner, it's disturbing that the only point at which Mayhew and Audrey diverge incontrovertibly from their models is when both of them become victims of a mad serial killer. (Audrey "gets hers," in classic puritanical slasher style, just after she's had sex with Barton.)

  3. *Hollywood producers are frauds.* As indicated above, Lipnick and Geisler are hilarious, but the laughs are easily come by, and they make it difficult to see how such people could have turned out any pictures at all, much less several beautiful ones. (For whatever it's worth, the first "Wallace Beery wrestling picture," THE CHAMP, was arguably one of King Vidor's masterpieces and won Beery, who actually played a prizefighter in the film, an Oscar.) Perhaps the Coens are justified in calling attention to Hollywood bigwigs as illiterate vulgarians, but judging from an early script of BARTON FINK that I happen to have read, they themselves don't even know how to spell such

words as "choir," "playwright," and "tragedy." In short, the rhetorical power of commercial moviemaking, available to anyone with a few million dollars to spend, allows them a free ride over a lot of people's corpses—Louis B. Mayer's as well as Faulkner's and Odets's—a ride that made me slightly nauseous.

4. *The very notion of the "common man" is fraudulent.* Charlie is introduced to us as the embodiment of this cliché, and Goodman's wonderful performance manages to encompass it without ever seeming hackneyed. But the way the movie undermines the common-man cliché is by dragging out a contemporary countercliché that's every bit as hackneyed. When Charlie turns out to be the serial killer, we are offered the revelation that people who chop off other people's heads are nice, ordinary people just like you and me— "common" folks, in fact. (This cliché is promulgated in the news as well as in movies—take those interviews with junior high school teachers about how "nice" the killers seemed to be. Mysteriously, each time the homily is trotted out, whoever's using it—in this case the Coens—seems to think it's brand-new and profound.)

■

So judging from BARTON FINK, what is it the Coens do believe in? Friendship, perhaps. Also, perhaps, an abstraction that the movie designates repeatedly as "the life of the mind" and that it associates with the act of creation— Barton's mind and act of creation in particular—as well as with Charlie himself. (Barton's room is clearly meant to suggest a brain, oozing fluids and all, and Charlie's climactic reappearance when the movie suddenly goes metaphorical—walking down the hotel corridor with a shotgun while the rooms on both sides of him successively burst into flames—is accompanied by his vengeful declaration, "*I'll* show you 'the life of the mind!'")

In order to follow the Coens' shift from one metaphor to another, the wanton abandon of midnight-movie viewing becomes necessary—it might even help if you're half asleep. Ironically, Goodman's Charlie, the most multiple of all the film's metaphors, also proves to be the only real character. (Turturro's Barton seems much too simpleminded to have ever written a successful play, and his so-called struggles with writer's block, as depicted in the film, could easily have been dreamed up in Lipnick's office.)

One way of sorting much of this out is to follow the provocative suggestion of *Variety* reviewer Todd McCarthy and assume that Charlie doesn't exist at all, except as an emanation of Barton's unconscious—the "common man" his blocked imagination is screaming for. This interpretation would make the overheard sobs (or laughs) in the next room, Charlie's murderous impulses, and even the mysterious package Barton receives from Charlie all really emblems of Barton's own tortured mind; significantly, Mayhew indicates that he associates the act of writing with pleasure whereas Barton replies that *he* associates it with pain. According to this scenario, Barton mur-

ders Audrey himself because he can't bear to face the possibility of her creative mind coming to the rescue of his own on the wrestling script.

The only problems with this scenario are that it fails to account for how
Barton finally breaks through his creative block—unless we view Audrey's
murder as the less-than-instantaneous catalyst—and that it fails to mesh co-
herently with some of the other metaphors in the movie. I've been told that
Deutsch and Mastrionotti, the wise-cracking anti-Semitic detectives on the
killer's trail who question Barton and are ultimately killed by Charlie (one of
whom is dispatched with the epithet "Heil Hitler"), are meant by the Coens to
represent the Axis powers. (I suppose that makes Lipnick—whom we last see
dressed as a full-fledged Army officer—the United States.) But if this is the
case, the historical *and* metaphorical imaginations of the Coens must be even
more threadbare and confused than I imagined. In what sense, exactly, were
Hitler and Mussolini trying to track down the common man—or the life of
the mind—and bring him (or it) to justice? And in what sense did this common man or life of the mind that wound up killing Hitler and Mussolini sell
insurance or chop off people's heads?

■

A final point should be made about the broad, comic-book-style Jewish
caricatures in the film—Barton, Lipnick, Geisler, and Lipnick's assistant Lou
Breeze (Jon Polito). Spike Lee was lambasted on the op-ed page of *The New
York Times* and by Nat Hentoff in the *Village Voice* (among other places) for
Jewish caricatures in MO' BETTER BLUES which employed one of the same actors (Turturro), occupied only a fraction as much screen time, and were if
anything *less* malicious than the caricatures in BARTON FINK. So I assume the
reason Lee was singled out for abuse and the Coens won't be to the same extent is that the Coens happen to be Jewish. For whatever it's worth—speaking
now as a Jew myself—I don't consider any of the caricatures in either movie
to be racist in themselves, and it seems to me somewhat absurd that Lee
should be criticized so widely for something that the Coens do at much
greater length with impunity. Being white, having the minds of teenagers, and
believing that social commitment is for jerks are all probably contributing
factors to this privileged treatment.

—*Chicago Reader*, 23 August 1991

Part Five

Inside and Outside the Movie Theater

Introduction

From a journalistic standpoint, what movies are about is always important, but the roles that should be played by content in criticism are not always easy to determine. Ever since I started writing regularly for the *Chicago Reader* in 1987, my principal professional safety net—what helps to guarantee that I'll remain interested in my work on a weekly basis, even if the movies of a given week are not interesting—is my option of writing about the subject matter of certain films. This almost invariably involves a certain amount of short-term research, because even if I already know the subject fairly well, a refresher course in certain specifics is generally necessary. (A good example of this would be the reading and listening I had to do in order to nail down many of my facts and examples for "Bird Watching," in spite—or should I say because?—of my familiarity with bebop and the life of Charlie Parker, which dates back to my teens.)

My greater interest in "content" is a relatively recent development in my criticism, and it parallels the evolution of a critic and theorist who remains one of my biggest influences, Noël Burch (whose work with Thom Andersen on Hollywood films of the blacklist era directly inspired "Guilty by Omission.") An American expatriate filmmaker and writer, Burch started out in his first book, *Praxis du cinéma* (1969)—which I originally read in French, before it was translated as *Theory of Film Practice* (1973)—as a hardcore formalist. After he subsequently became politicized, and duly denounced his earlier work, his research became more and more concerned with questions of content, although in *some* cases this has also meant a reformulation rather than a mere abnegation of some of his earlier formal insights. Burch's work can be criticized both for its lack of historical rigor as well as the inaccuracy of some of his examples, but its imagination and originality have made it for me infinitely more valuable than the relatively accurate but generally tedious theoretical work of his principal American critics; read as a sort of metacritical science fiction, his work continues to be alive with possibilities.

The avoidance of politics in mainstream criticism is broached directly in "Guilty by Omission," and it is also relevant to the various depoliticizing processes at work in the reception of DEEP COVER. The invisible, unstated biases of critics in forming opinions and setting priorities is always a ripe subject for investigation. Consider how many of the hatchet jobs performed on ISHTAR acknowledged, even in passing, the perhaps justifiable hostility felt by many journalists toward the treatment they had previously received from Warren Beatty, the producer and costar. To cite only one instance of what I mean (the many grievances of journalists against Beatty prior to ISHTAR's release are well documented elsewhere), when I recall a Beatty tribute I attended at Toronto's Festival of Festivals well before the release of ISHTAR in which Beatty repeatedly ridiculed and undercut Roger Ebert and Gene Siskel, the two hosts, I can easily understand how ISHTAR eventually offered them an opportunity to exact some revenge—even if the writer-director of the picture unfortunately happened to be someone else.

As an even more covert example that exists outside of film, I can recall a novelist friend writing a rude and scathing letter to the *Village Voice* which was printed. To all appearances, it was a direct, unmediated response to a piece in the magazine, but in fact she admitted to me later that it was mainly motivated by the cruel dismissal of her first novel by someone else in the same magazine. I recall thinking at the time that the pan of her novel might very well have had another agenda as well—such as the reviewer's pique that his or her own first novel *hadn't* been reviewed in the *Voice*.

No doubt the most serious single bias found in criticism today is the eagerness of the press to pander to the U.S. film industry, which means in most cases that even major foreign films will go unnoticed unless a "major" distributor is involved. Writing in the *Reader* in the late 1980s about Souleymane Cissé's breathtakingly beautiful YEELEN (BRIGHTNESS), the greatest African film I've seen (and which has been largely ignored by critics in this country), I ruefully speculated that if Cissé had had the power and the bad taste to cast Tom Cruise or Tom Hanks in blackface as the lead instead of the wonderful Issiaka Kane, he'd have botched his masterpiece beyond belief, but he nevertheless would have gotten some attention from the television reviewers, *Time, Newsweek,* and *The New Yorker*: "The mainstream consensus appears to be that *any* African movie, no matter how great, hasn't a prayer of being treated as seriously as any Cruise or Hanks movie, no matter how atrocious."

■

Apart from "Guilty by Omission"—which grew in part out of a *Reader* column on the rather mediocre Hollywood feature GUILTY BY SUSPICION—all the pieces in this section were written for the *Chicago Reader,* which leads me to a brief consideration of how I wound up in this reviewing job, the longest one by far (as well as the most satisfying) that I've held to date.

When I lost my position at *Soho News* in November 1981, I was literally at loose ends. The only solid writing project of any size I had at that point was *Midnight Movies,* a book I was finishing with Jim Hoberman, a second-string critic at that point for the *Village Voice*; we'd signed our contract with Harper & Row the previous January and had a final deadline in late January 1982. (The fact that Harper & Row had also published *Moving Places* was entirely coincidental. Craig Nelson, an editor there who wanted to commission a book on midnight movies, wrote to several critics—including Raymond Durgnat, who recommended me, and P. Adams Sitney, who recommended Jim. Jim and I were only acquaintances at the time, but we discovered by chance that we both had been summoned to Craig's office about the same project. I had the first appointment, and when I told Craig that I knew he'd be seeing Jim as well, Craig spontaneously suggested a collaboration, which I then proposed to Jim.)

Over the next year, *Midnight Movies* was supplemented by two stints of replacement teaching at the School of Visual Arts, a contract with Arden Press (signed in late June) to write *Film: The Front Line 1983* by the following spring, curating a Straub/Huillet season and editing an accompanying monograph for Fabiano Canosa at the Public Theater in November, and writing for magazines ranging from *AFI Education Newsletter* and *Artforum* to my usual staples, *Sight and Sound* and *Film Comment,* as well as *American Film* (although Hoberman replaced me there that year as contributing editor, just as he later replaced me as adjunct "visiting professor" at NYU—a situation that put some strain on our relationship).

Emotionally speaking, the biggest crisis I had to face that year was not my relative poverty but the unexpected suicide of my older brother David, after a painful divorce and an unsuccessful relationship, in August. Although we'd seldom been very close, and in fact were bitter sibling rivals as children, we'd achieved a certain rapport about half a year earlier, when David had visited me in Hoboken, and the psychosexual implications of his suicide undoubtedly had a major effect in finally putting an end to my own long-term relationship, which had already been coming apart at the seams.

When I luckily got hired to teach for spring quarter in 1983 at Berkeley, I welcomed the chance to escape the east coast with open arms. By early summer, I had moved all my things out of Hoboken into a Manhattan sublet, only to discover as soon as I arrived that I had been hired as an adjunct for another quarter in the fall at the University of California, Santa Barbara. Six years earlier, I had moved all the way from London to San Diego on the strength of a two-quarter job that I'd hoped would become extended. The gamble hadn't paid off, but this time, for want of any better prospects, I was moving all my things to Santa Barbara for a similar gamble based on a single-quarter job.*

This time the gamble paid off, but not right away; for the first year, every request made to a certain dean by the film program chairman that I be rehired for each new quarter was summarily turned down, and it was only after I went to see the dean myself that I got the job. Then, after the first year, I started receiving year-long contracts—the closest thing to job security I ever had in all my years of teaching, and the first time I was able to get health insurance since leaving England. At the same time, I eventually discovered that this security, although better than anything I'd found on the east coast, was wholly finite: the noble efforts of Alexander Sesonske, who briefly served as film chair, to get me and my colleagues onto tenure lines, ended in defeat, and it eventually became clear that no matter how much I published, or, indeed, how much I knew about film, I would never get a permanent teaching job anywhere.

The first time I heard from Bob Roth, the publisher of the *Chicago Reader,* was at some point in 1986, around the time that Dave Kehr was leaving that paper for the *Chicago Tribune*—and, unfortunately, shortly after I had signed a contract for an additional year of teaching at UCSB. Dave, whom I'd met and seen every year since 1981 at the Toronto Festival of Festivals, and who had given me a complimentary subscription to the *Chicago Reader* a couple of years before, had recommended me as a possible replacement, and as potentially appealing as the offer was, the guarantee of a year's employment at UCSB—which Roth couldn't offer as categorically—was difficult to pass up. But I told Bob that if he was still looking for someone in 1987, he should try me again.

This is what Bob wound up doing, and after I learned from the current film chair that the odds of my getting rehired indefinitely at UCSB were very poor, I had no hesitation about showing my interest in the *Reader*. This time, however, Roth and the *Reader* editors had to be convinced first that I was right for the job, and after sending them several sample pieces, I was commissioned to write three separate sample columns for them before they definitively decided to take me. (Only the first of these was printed—a lengthy and mainly negative review of RADIO DAYS, portions of which were later recycled into "Notes Toward the Devaluation of Woody Allen.") Then, after concluding my academic career on a note of relative glory—as director of UCSB's summer school in film studies, for which I was able to hire, among outsiders, David Ehrenstein, Thomas Elsaessar, Paul Jarrico, and, as artist in residence, Samuel Fuller—I moved to Chicago in August and started work the following month.

---

*My father died of cancer of the prostate only weeks after I arrived, and barely a year after David's suicide; I have few doubts that this suicide hastened his own death.

Perhaps the most unusual facet of my job is that, thanks to Dave Kehr and the expectations he was able to establish over a decade at the *Reader,* my knowledge of film actually played some role in my being hired. Strange as it seems, this has rarely functioned as a criterion for the hiring of movie reviewers on American or British papers and nonspecialized magazines, and, I daresay, the degree to which it plays a part in granting tenure to many film professors is debatable as well.

"The media no longer ask those who know something (or love something or, worst of all, know *why* they love something) to share that knowledge with the public," wrote the late Serge Daney, in a review of THE LOVER shortly before his death in 1992—a friend and contemporary who may have been the best French film critic since André Bazin.* "Instead they ask those who know nothing to represent the ignorance of the public and, in so doing, to legitimize it. To 'speak for others' always comes down to claiming *droit de seigneur* over their ignorance."

Moreover, it would be equally naive to assume that these know-nothing critics would necessarily have to educate themselves once they started on the job. During my sojourn in London in the mid-1970s, I often heard the story of novelist Penelope Mortimer, reviewing Hitchcock's TOPAZ for the *Observer* in 1969, remarking that Hitchcock was a "comparative newcomer" who had been directing for only eighteen years. I suspect that any knowledgeable American film critic who has been around a few years could probably cite equivalent howlers from his or her colleagues. Ironically, however, the reasons why most journalistic critics and most academic critics don't have to be knowledgeable about film are very nearly antithetical. In the case of journalists, the lack of a comprehensive film background suggests to many publishers and editors that these critics won't be threatening or intimidating to the general reader. In the case of academic critics, being threatening or intimidating is more likely to be seen by some administrators and professors as a plus, but an arsenal of theoretical terms often serves better in creating this impression than familiarity with film. I realize, of course, that there are many significant exceptions to this rule. But the number of tenured film professors in the United States who know very little about film—and the corresponding number of film professors who know a lot and fail to get tenure—are still large enough to suggest that institutional savvy often counts for more in this world than concrete information about the medium.

What this often boils down to in both realms is a desire for expediency that promotes conformity. Educators tend to look for what's most teachable

---

*We met through Jackie Raynal, a mutual friend, and it was Serge who asked me to become *Cahiers du Cinéma*'s New York correspondent during his last years there as editor (1979–1981). Not long afterward, he began to speak to me about his plan for a more ideal film magazine, *Trafic,* that he finally launched before his death from AIDS in 1992. It's my own favorite today, and I'm proud to be a frequent contributor.

and journalists tend to look for what's most saleable (i.e., available on the marketplace), and this lands both kinds of critic in a climate that prefers the tried-and-true and the status quo to the untested and the potentially problematical. What seems especially unfortunate about this state of affairs is that the potential openness of both students and general audiences to new challenges is often factored out of basic policy decisions at the very outset. Once the passive attitude of most spectators toward what is available to them for viewing becomes essentially shared—and therefore ratified—by teachers and critics, the role of criticism itself becomes degraded, turning the critical process into yet another unacknowledged means for greasing the wheels of commerce.

■

In the previous section, I argued for the advantages of writing for a small but intensely engaged audience over writing for a much larger but generally more indifferent public. In the case of my writing for the *Reader*, it might be said that I've finally reached a position that stands roughly in between these two possibilities. On the basis of a detailed survey about its readership carried out a few years ago, the *Reader*—a free alternative weekly paid for by advertising, and one of the oldest and most successful of its kind in the United States—has a circulation of 137,000 and an estimated readership of about 412,000. Virtually all of this circulation is restricted to Chicago and environs. In the remainder of the country, apart from some comps to friends and colleagues and a small number of paid subscriptions, my *Reader* work gets no exposure at all, so my audience is essentially a third of a million Chicagoans.

The paper, which comes in several sections, is dated Friday and its weekly listings cover Friday through Thursday; the heaps of copies that appear in selected stores and other public buildings on Thursday or Friday are usually gone by the end of the weekend. My contributions to each issue come in two parts—a "column" or longer review in the first section, and detailed listings with capsule reviews or descriptions of theatrical and nontheatrical movie venues in Chicago and its nearest suburbs in the second section. My listings include my own capsule reviews and those of my predecessors (including Dave Kehr) that I choose to retain rather than redo; they appear in all fifty-one issues of the *Reader* that are published annually, and I average about forty-one or forty-two columns (including annual features on the Chicago Film Festival and my ten best list) a year.

On the basis of an extensive *Reader* survey of over 1,200 of its readers, carried out in early 1993, the movie listings and capsule reviews are the most widely read or "looked at" feature in the paper, cited by 58.3 percent of those surveyed. The movie columns—the only samples of my *Reader* work reprinted in this book—come in third (51.4 percent) in the same survey, with front-cover articles in second place and cartoons in fourth. This doesn't, however, make my contributions the most popular. In a separate survey of the two most *enjoyed* features in the paper, my movie columns place sixth and my listings come in ninth. Most of the paper's highly targeted readership is single (77 percent) and white (again 77 percent), with a median age of thirty-one and a median annual household income of $39,500—quite close to my own *Reader* salary.

Each week, one or more capsule reviews are featured with a still and designated "Critic's Choice," and I've often been told that a "Critic's Choice" assigned to an alternative venue will often (though not invariably) guarantee a full house. (The same is true to a slightly lesser degree of films at art houses.) My longer reviews exert the same relative degrees of influence to somewhat lesser extents.

Another indication of the effect of my reviews is the correspondence I receive from readers. It certainly runs the gamut from love letters to hate parcels—I haven't yet received any marriage proposals, but one irate white man objecting to my defense of a Spike Lee movie actually enclosed a piece of his shit in his envelope—though on the whole, the sympathetic responses far outweigh the unsympathetic ones, and some of the former have been enormously gratifying. The fact that I've moved around a lot and lived abroad actually seems to count in my favor—which rarely seemed true in New York, where it was generally assumed that if I hadn't done most of my spadework locally, it couldn't have been very important.

When I combine these responses from correspondents with those I get from Chicagoans whom I personally meet, the net effect of all this steady feedback is that I feel like a respected member of a community—something I've experienced comparably in my career, and to a lesser degree, only when I was in London in the mid-1970s. It's a very nice feeling, and one that I continually try to honor and justify in what I write.

Bird Watching

★★★

BIRD
Directed by Clint Eastwood
Written by Joel Oliansky
With Forest Whitaker, Diane Venora, Michael Zelniker,
Samuel E. Wright, Keith David, and Damon Whitaker

★★

CELEBRATING BIRD
Directed by Gary Giddins and Kendrick Simmons
Written by Gary Giddins

Two telling documents that we have about Charlie Parker, both from the early 50s:

1. During a live radio broadcast from Birdland on 31 March 1951, there's an electrifying moment when Parker leaps into his solo on "A Night in Tunisia," combining cascading machine-gun volleys of notes—wailing sixteenth notes and dovetailing triplets—into what sound like two successive melodic somersaults, each one in a separate direction, that miraculously turn the rhythm around with shifting accents—an awesome tumble in midair over four free bars until he triumphantly splashes into the next chorus.

To understand the genius of that moment—a fusion of passionate acrobatics and spontaneous formal patterning—it might help to detect the evidence of rage that one hears just before the number begins. Symphony Sid Torin, an obnoxiously loquacious disc jockey, has been blathering at length about "Round Midnight," the previous number played by Parker, Dizzy Gillespie, and Bud Powell, which he has repeatedly called "Round About Midnight." He is recounting a long, self-serving anecdote about Billie Holiday when Gillespie plaintively bleats out, "Let me play my number!" Momentarily coming to his senses, Sid turns to Parker and says, "What we gonna do, Bird? We got one number more—"

His voice fairly dripping with disgust, Parker can only say, "Who needs ya?"

" 'A Night in Tunisia'!" Sid grandly announces, deliberately mishearing Bird's jab as the song immediately gets underway. And the remarkable thing about Parker's break one chorus later is that it seems to take over and to take off from his terse, embittered query—as if the quick transfer to music from speech allowed him to unfurl his anger in one dazzling, unbroken string of invective, transforming his three words into four asymmetrical bars of breathtaking invention.

2. On a television show called *Stage Entrance,* aired in 1952, newspaper columnist Earl Wilson and jazz critic Leonard Feather present *Downbeat* awards to Parker and Gillespie, who go on to play a version of the bebop standard "Hot House." This is the only surviving sound-film record of the greatest jazz musician who ever lived, and though Parker's solo is not extended, nor one of his best, it's enough to show his brilliance. The segment can be seen in its entirety (and is, incidentally, the most valuable and instructive thing) in Gary Giddins and Kendrick Simmons's video documentary CELEBRATING BIRD, released last year to coincide with Giddins's book of the same title (and currently available on tape).

In the video, Chan Parker, Bird's last wife, introduces the segment by noting the killing look that Parker gives briefly to Wilson while the awards are being presented, in response to the clear prejudice and condescension in Wilson's spiel. Although Parker smiles winningly and graciously as he accepts his own award, he trains a dark glare on Wilson when the latter calls Gillespie "Diz" and concludes, "You boys got anything more to say?" "Well, Earl," Parker says, with a subtle mixture of molasses and cyanide, "they say music speaks louder than words, so we'd rather voice our opinion *that* way, if you don't mind."

Parker's music *does* speak louder and stronger than words, and if I've lingered over these two fleeting examples of his speech and his anger, it's mainly to indicate a key element that I find missing in Clint Eastwood's remarkable depiction of Parker in BIRD. While it must be said at the outset that BIRD is an extraordinary achievement as a jazz biography, as a portrait of the jazz life, and as a work of screenwriting and directorial craft, it is an achievement bounded by specific limits, most of them ideological and/or musical. The film runs a full 161 minutes, and for a commercial release is an unusually serious and uncompromising treatment of its subject. As a Hollywood fiction feature about jazz, it can't even be said to have competitors, and as confirmation of Eastwood's status as an ambitious auteur, it clearly surpasses everything else he's done—even if no small part of this is due to Joel Oliansky's script, and most likely to Chan Parker's unpublished memoir, *Life in E-Flat,* which served as its principal source.

Without questioning Eastwood's credentials as a jazz buff—it was he, after all, who encouraged Warner Brothers to get behind Bertrand Tavernier's 'ROUND MIDNIGHT—I wonder nevertheless how much definitive wisdom we can get about Parker's life from a staunch conservative Republican, a man who implicitly endorses attitudes and policies that helped to hound Parker to his death. This is not to contest his devotion to the man and his music, only to question the degree of understanding that accompanies it. Although the film leaps about freely in time, covering Parker's life sporadically from his child-hood onward, it is basically structured around the last months in Parker's life—from a suicide attempt after a quarrel with Chan to his final collapse in Bar-oness Nica Koenigswarter's apartment in 1955. The film begins with a quote from F. Scott Fitzgerald, "There are no second acts in American lives," and while it presents Parker with much sympathy, complexity, and accuracy—helped in no small measure by Forest Whitaker's physical resemblance to Parker and his total commitment to the role—it also views him consistently as the sole agent of his own destruction.

Up to a point, this is a defensible interpretation of a man who was a junkie from his teens until his death at thirty-four, and who had gargantuan appetites for alcohol, food, and sex. Beyond that point, however, one has to consider other factors, especially Parker's embattled status as an avant-garde innovator and his extreme sensitivity to racism—two factors the film pays lip service to, but hasn't the room or inclination to explore. Parker's life was an authentic tragedy, and Eastwood regards it as such, but he can't tell us much about what it meant to be a radical artist or a rebellious black man in the 1940s and early 1950s.

To think our way back to what bebop must have sounded like when it was new—in effect, to unlearn the musical culture that surrounds us today—is a difficult if not impossible task. Thus we can forgive (even if we can't fully ex-cuse) one of the film's few musical gaffes: it shows a teenage Parker (played by Whitaker's brother Damon) being humiliated at a Kansas City jam session for his awkward solo, when the drummer hurls a cymbal at his feet. The inci-dent is historically accurate—Jo Jones was the drummer—but the music being played at the session in the film is already bebop, years before it was devel-oped in New York by Parker, Gillespie, Monk, and Powell. Also, as jazz critic Neil Tesser has pointed out to me, the nature of Parker's awkwardness here isn't accurate either. In the session, Parker—a risk taker from the begin-ning—moved out of the original key and got lost. In the film he errs in the opposite direction, playing a solo that the drummer regards as too simple or cornball.

To understand what it meant to be black and American forty years ago is perhaps easier than unlearning bebop, at least in theory, but Eastwood is clearly less interested in this than he is in the music. His previous films are haunted by phallic and/or feisty women, and here Chan, very well played by Diane Venora, is certainly feisty; her first extended meeting with Parker is one of the strongest and most delicately nuanced scenes in the film. But apart from some brief reaction shots when Bird and Chan dance at a ritzy white night-club, Eastwood gives not the slightest hint of what it meant to be an interra-cial couple in this country in the 1950s; it's almost as if the question never occurred to him.

The nocturnal look of BIRD is essentially derived from film noir: lots of rain and thunder, smoky nightclubs, slicked-down city streets, claustrophobic rooms and corridors, a sense of endless night. Part of the function of this oppressive and nearly omnipresent darkness, aside from emphasizing the dark inevitabilities of Parker's life, is to help us concentrate on the music. But the movie's approach to the music is strangely divided, in more ways than one.

During the credits, we get a three-step history of Parker's musical progress—from a Kansas City tot with a tonette riding a pony in his backyard to a teenager traversing his porch while practicing on his alto sax to a full-blown jazzman at the height of his powers in a 52nd Street club, playing "Lester Leaps In." The final transition is almost as dynamic and exciting as the bone-to-spacecraft cut in Kubrick's 2001. Eastwood's panning camera curves slowly around Parker's profile on the bandstand as he pours out torrents of notes and ideas; eventually it frames him head-on, and the effect is galvanizing. The up-tempo tune is by Lester Young, Parker's first major musical love (as well as Eastwood's), and the solo, like many others in the film, is not a familiar one from records, but a rare private recording of Parker's alto that has been remixed with accompaniment by contemporary sidemen—in this case Monty Alexander (piano), Ray Brown (bass), and John Guerin (drums). This strategy functions quite well in the movie: the solo is presented under optimal audio conditions, yet it has the punch of music that's being heard for the first time. But the process of combining Bird with players some forty years later raises a number of aesthetic issues.

Like the colorization of black-and-white movies, this process muddles history even when it is carried out intelligently, as it often is here. For one thing, it leads to many possible misunderstandings. Several months ago, when a prominent film critic reviewed BIRD from Cannes, he surmised that the remixing was done because Parker's original accompanists were poor—an assumption that made my blood run cold as I realized how easily Bud Powell, Miles Davis, and Max Roach (among others) could thus be assigned to the trash can. (This is not unlike the crackpot assumption of some younger viewers that the only reason Orson Welles didn't make CITIZEN KANE in color was that he lacked the proper technology.) The artistic inferiority of the "remakes" of certain Parker numbers by this method, even when Parker's solos remain the same, is patently evident when the two versions are played back to back (as Neil Tesser recently did on his radio show with "Now's the Time"). In the case of a primordial masterpiece like "Koko," the jaggered fury of Parker's solo is sustained by Roach's demonic drum break on the original; the remixed version, which replaces Roach with a string of conventional solos, allows the energy to dissipate into banality.

These complaints apply mainly to the sound-track album. In the film, which has myriad dramatic needs, the technique is much more defensible (indeed, the electric charge and immediacy of "Lester Leaps In" would be partially lost without it). Yet the dramatic needs of BIRD take a different kind of toll on the music. By my own rough estimate, more than ninety minutes of the film have to pass before we hear one full Parker solo from beginning to end without interruption or interference (a buoyant, shrieking version of "Cool Blues"). From this standpoint, BIRD is less satisfying as a listening experience than 'ROUND MIDNIGHT, despite the fact that its music is immeasurably better.

Unless my ears were playing tricks on me, the film *does* manage to improve on three Parker recordings, although in one of these cases improvement is the last thing that's needed. Parker made several mainly unfortunate recordings with strings near the end of his career, a poignant attempt to achieve "class" and legitimacy; the results often sounded like a swan drowning in gallons of bubble bath. Lennie Niehaus, the movie's musical director, created new string arrangements for two such performances, "April in Paris" and "Laura," that minimize the slushy embarrassment and maximize the emotion in Parker's originals. (The most successful Parker foray in this direction, and his own favorite recording, "Just Friends," is not included in the film.) By contrast, the improvement of Parker's disastrous version of "Lover Man" for Ross Russell's Dial label—played on the verge of physical and emotional collapse, and made a good deal more bearable in the film's version through the partial substitution of Charles McPherson's alto sax—limits the tragedy and horror of Parker's performance, one of the most searing evidences of pain on record.

In narrative terms, Eastwood and Oliansky necessarily limit their coverage of Parker's life and career, seeing them mainly from the viewpoints of two white characters, Chan and Red Rodney (Michael Zelniker), and, to a lesser extent, from those of Gillespie (Samuel E. Wright) and an invented black character named Buster Franklin (Keith David). It's amazing how conscientious the film is about honoring certain details, and curious how slack it is about glossing over certain others. BIRD is especially good about drawing attention to Parker's intellectual interests and aspirations, reflected in everything from his flowery speech to his adoration of Stravinsky and the "Rubaiyat of Omar Khayyam." (In Paris, he once befuddled an English jazz critic who was interviewing him by responding to each question with a separate stanza from the "Rubaiyat.") Parker's enjoyment of popular culture was no less intense—he died laughing at a vaudeville routine on television that he remembered from his childhood. Eastwood has gone to the trouble of digging up the kinescope of the original, but then he doesn't bother to make the childhood connection. Similarly, the film records Bird's desperate plea to Chan that he not be buried in Kansas City, but fails to note that he actually *was* buried there—after a funeral service in Harlem, which the film shows—at the insistence of Doris Parker, his previous wife. (To add insult to injury, the date of death inscribed on his gravestone was eleven days off.)

If BIRD lacks the sentimentality of 'ROUND MIDNIGHT, it also lacks the accumulation of feeling that made the climax of Tavernier's film stronger; BIRD's beauty and power come in flashes, and they're rarely allowed to build. There are times when Eastwood seems to be in over his head, but when Pauline Kael calls him "a man who isn't an artist" making an art film, one wants to scream in protest. (Can't he at least be granted the status of an imperfect artist? Or does he have to apply to Kael for permission to make movies at all?) Certainly Eastwood's well-advertised desire to be taken seriously can't be confused with his concrete achievement, but I would defy any two Kael-certified artists working together—say, Brian De Palma and Philip Kaufman—to come up with a jazz film with a tenth as much feeling for the music and the milieu as this one.

What the film mainly lacks, apart from the first meeting of Bird and Chan, is the kind of sustained portrait that we get of Parker in the prologue of Ross Russell's much-maligned but indispensable 1973 biography, *Bird Lives!*—a twenty-four-page rendering of Parker's opening night at Billy Berg's in Los Angeles, his first California date, in the mid-1940s. Although Russell's use of fictional techniques, including imagined conversations, has led many commentators to dismiss his book, the fact that he knew Parker and was present in the club that night gives the scene an epic density that BIRD—which chronicles the same evening rather differently—achieves only in snatches. (Later in the book, there's a heartbreaking letter from Chan to Russell in 1947, when Parker was recuperating in Camarillo, which tells as much in three pages as Eastwood can manage in an hour.)

Although BIRD is stuffed with inside references and in-jokes for musicians and jazz buffs (a bit like the way early French New Wave films are filled with movie references), its basic address is to the unspecialized general public, and from this standpoint its overall treatment of Parker's life is acute but partial. For uninitiated viewers who want to learn more, original Parker recordings and Russell's superb biography would be the best places to start.

The hour-long CELEBRATING BIRD would be a convenient substitute for either or both of the above, as would Giddins's book of the same title, insofar as both do a fair job of filling in major areas that BIRD either neglects or confuses. In the video, we get extended commentaries from Parker's first and last wives (among others), many short clips of musicians who preceded and/or played with him, a coherent chronology of his career (with many still photographs), and a lot of information that confirms, expands, or (in a few cases) contradicts the facts we get in Eastwood's film. (One of the most telling instances of the latter comes from Chan, who says that Parker spoke of wanting to move to Europe—which is directly at loggerheads with a scene in BIRD where Parker, conversing abroad with an expatriate musician, unequivocally rejects this possibility out of patriotism. It's one more indication of how Eastwood's ideological biases seem to play a role that is not exactly neutral.)

Nevertheless, a few caveats about *Celebrating Bird* (book and video) are in order. Giddins may be more up-to-date and reliable than Russell in his research, but he is also much sketchier, and his effort to clear the decks by dismissing *Bird Lives!* in a sentence is not to be trusted. (Calling it "often more roman à clef than biography" is confusing nonsense, particularly because Russell previously published a roman à clef about Parker and Lester Young called *The Sound*—a different matter entirely.)

Turning to the video, the fact that Giddins is basically a writer shouldn't necessarily be held against him, but it does make for certain limitations in his approach. The standard approach of most jazz documentaries—to let us hear a few bars of a solo and then smother the rest under voiceovers—is followed fairly consistently here, even if it's often handled with some discretion. We *are* able to hear what Parker's "Lover Man" solo originally sounded like, but after alerting us to the importance of the famous "Koko" solo, Giddins inexplicably lets us hear only an inferior alternate take, without any acknowledgment of this fact, and then cuts it off before it's over.

Life photographer Gjon Mili shot a documentary film of Parker playing in 1950, the sound of which has been lost, and it is this footage that we see at the beginning of the video and at many subsequent junctures. As J. Hoberman recently wrote in the *Village Voice,* the video "step-prints" this footage of Parker, slowing his motion "so that you can watch him think." Unfortunately the thoughts you're seeing aren't the thoughts you're hearing: another Parker solo is added to the silent footage, so unavoidably the synchronization is off.

Considering the nearly parallel developments of film and jazz as the new art forms of this century, it is disheartening to consider how seldom they've been able to work together interactively without some fatal compromise on either side, which usually means one serving as ballast for the other. Documentaries like CELEBRATING BIRD (and countless others that are much worse) have been hampered by a nervous reluctance to let the music speak for itself, whereas the fiction films have been undone both by ignorance about the music and by an uncertainty about how to integrate it into a dramatic context. For examples of the latter, one could cite otherwise sympathetic fiction films like TOO LATE BLUES and NEW YORK, NEW YORK as well as otherwise unsympathetic ones like PARIS BLUES and THE COTTON CLUB; from this standpoint, Martin Scorsese's effective cameo in 'ROUND MIDNIGHT can be interpreted as a form of penance for his indifference to jazz history in NEW YORK, NEW YORK.

All these problems were admirably faced and solved by a single filmmaker in 1929, the first year of talkies. In two low-budget shorts made respectively with Bessie Smith and Duke Ellington, ST. LOUIS BLUES and BLACK AND TAN, Dudley Murphy set precedents that in some respects no subsequent jazz films have lived up to, 'ROUND MIDNIGHT and BIRD included. Admittedly, both films are fictional, and I am being a bit rhetorical when I state that ST. LOUIS BLUES is valuable chiefly as a documentary record of our greatest blues singer, whereas BLACK AND TAN, with its audacious poetic linkage of death and orgasm with the structure and emotion of Ellington's music, stands as the great example of utilizing jazz within a narrative. The important point is that in these two short and mainly unheralded films, despite some dated racial stereotyping and primitive methods of sound recording, Murphy set down certain fruitful possibilities for jazz and film that have seldom been considered since.

The best that can be said for both BIRD and 'ROUND MIDNIGHT is that they both manage to build on some of these possibilities. Neither is an unqualified success to the degree that BLACK AND TAN is, but each represents an exciting quantum leap after more than half a century of intervening dross about the music. Both significantly build on the poetics of death and dissolution that BLACK AND TAN broached so powerfully, and both help to rectify a form of sociological and artistic neglect that remains one of this country's biggest scandals. Parker was conceivably the greatest musical mind this country has ever produced, and if no movie is ever likely to do him justice, BIRD at least makes an invigorating start on the project.

Jean Vigo's Secret

L'ATALANTE

L'ATALANTE
Directed by Jean Vigo
Written by Vigo, Albert Riéra, and Jean Guinée
With Michel Simon, Dita Parlo, Jean Dasté, Gilles
Margaritis, and Louis Lefèvre

> What was Vigo's secret? Probably he lived more
> intensely than most of us. Filmmaking is awk-
> ward because of the disjointed nature of the
> work. You shoot five to fifteen seconds and then
> stop for an hour. On the film set there is seldom
> the opportunity for the concentrated intensity a
> writer like Henry Miller might have enjoyed at
> his desk. By the time he had written twenty
> pages, a kind of fever possessed him, carried him
> away; it could be tremendous, even sublime. Vigo
> seems to have worked continuously in this state of
> trance, without ever losing his clearheadedness.
>
> —*François Truffaut, 1970*

L'ATALANTE is one of the supreme achievements in the history of cinema, and its recent restoration, playing this week at the Music Box, offers what is surely the best version any of us is ever likely to see. Yet the conditions that made this masterpiece possible were anything but auspicious.

When Jean Vigo started to work on his first and only feature in July 1933, he had no say over either the script or the two lead actors. It wasn't that his producer was unsympathetic; on the contrary, Jacques-Louis Nounez had financed Vigo's 44-minute ZÉRO DE CONDUITE—an anarchic, fanciful, and provocative depiction of a student uprising in a French boarding school—the previous year, and he hadn't interfered with any of Vigo's creative decisions. But ZÉRO DE CONDUITE had been banned in its entirety by France's board of censors (it wouldn't open in France for another twelve years), and in order to recoup some of his losses, Nounez felt that he had to exercise a few commercial restraints on this talented but volatile twenty-eight-year-old filmmaker—the son of an infamous slain anarchist—who had grown up hiding under assumed names.

In fact, Nounez specifically requested that Vigo hold back on his usual impulses to experiment and make social statements and provided him with a highly conventional and unexceptional script called L'ATALANTE, authored by an obscure writer, R. de Guichen, who wrote under the pen name of Jean Guinée. It was a simple love story about a young barge skipper named Jean who marries a provincial woman named Juliette who's never been to the city. Jean brings his bride on board the *Atalante* (the name of his barge), which is also occupied by an old sailor named Père Jules, a cabin boy, and a dog. The only conflict in the plot arises when Juliette meets a young sailor at one of the ports who offers to introduce her to the pleasures of the city. Jean manages to chase him away, but Juliette, still drawn to the city's attractions, escapes anyway, and Jean, upset by her departure, refuses to go after her. Some time later, Père Jules defies Jean's orders and goes out looking for Juliette, finds her, and brings her back. Life on the barge resumes, and Juliette becomes reconciled to her fate.

The popular French stage and movie actor Michel Simon, who had already appeared in four Jean Renoir films, was selected to play Père Jules, and the German film star Dita Parlo, who would subsequently play a lonely war widow in Renoir's LA GRANDE ILLUSION, was cast as Juliette; this package and the script were handed to Vigo, along with a request to include some songs in the film. Vigo—who was delighted with the choice of actors but much less happy with the story—agreed to these terms, requesting only a few minor changes in the script, such as the substitution of a peddler for the young sailor who tempts Juliette, the substitution of several cats for a single dog, and a somewhat more upbeat treatment of the ending.

To help him adapt the script, Vigo hired a friend who had been assistant director on ZÉRO DE CONDUITE, and he filled out the remainder of the cast with other friends, most of whom had acted in ZÉRO as well (Jean Dasté, whom he cast as Jean, had played the only sympathetic schoolteacher in the previous film). He also hired the same cinematographer (Boris Kaufman), composer (Maurice Jaubert), and lyricist (Charles Goldblatt) who had worked on ZÉRO. After several delays, shooting finally started in mid-November.

Vigo had been plagued all his life with weak lungs—a condition he shared with his wife, Lydou, whom he had met in a sanatorium when he was twenty-three—and had been feverish during much of the shooting of ZÉRO, his temperature ranging from 102 to 104 degrees. L'ATALANTE was shot on a barge from November to February (with periodic trips to the Gaumont studios, where sets were built duplicating some of the barge interiors and representing a working-class dance hall), and Vigo was sick roughly half the time. By the time the principal photography and rough cut (which proceeded simultaneously) were finished, he was too ill to work any further. After an abortive attempt at a holiday in the country he took to his bed, and during the seven remaining months of his life he went out only twice—once to view the work in progress with his editor, and once to see the virtually completed film with

Nounez and his associates. (The film's final aerial shot was filmed later according to Vigo's instructions, so it's likely that Vigo himself never saw it.)

Nounez was quite happy with the results, but his associates were not, demanding several cuts. Vigo reluctantly agreed to one major change—an extensive reduction of Père Jules's search for Juliette in Le Havre—and the results were screened on 25 April 1934, for company representatives, exhibitors, and distributors. Most of them disliked the film, and Gaumont then decided to cut it much more drastically, rework the score in order to feature a current popular song ("Le chaland qui passe," or "The Passing Barge"), and retitle the film after the song. At most, only two or three sequences in the film were left intact; this "final" version opened in mid-September at a single Paris theater and closed after a couple of weeks.

A few days after it closed, while Vigo lay dying, a street musician outside his apartment was playing "Le chaland qui passe" on an accordion, and Lydou, who had been cradling her husband in her arms, rushed to the window and tried to leap out. Some friends restrained her, and she was placed in a clinic in a state of delirium. (Vigo had jokingly described the strain of bacteria that caused his illness, streptococcus, as a little fat man in a top hat, and Lydou was asking to speak to the little fat man and demanding that L'ATALANTE be wrapped around the fat producers and set on fire. She died herself less than five years later; the eventual fate of her and Vigo's daughter Luce, born in 1931, is apparently unrecorded.)

■

Attempts to restore Vigo's original version of L'ATALANTE were made in 1940 and 1949, and those efforts produced the only versions of the film that have been visible until recently. (The first of these versions premiered in the United States in 1947 on a double bill with ZÉRO DE CONDUITE.) But in 1989, a few years after repurchasing all the surviving L'ATALANTE material in France, including some outtakes, Gaumont decided to do a more thorough job of restoration and located a nitrate version with the original title (but without the final shot or the excised material of Jules looking for Juliette) at the British Film Institute's National Film Archives. What they aimed for was not a duplication of the version screened on 25 April 1934, but something much trickier—a restoration of Vigo's original intentions based on his notes. Thus a series of short overlapping dissolves punctuating Père Jules's comic demonstration of "Greco-Roman" wrestling, which were indicated in Vigo's script but never executed, was brought about in the lab for the first time, and the placement of certain shots not indicated in the script was carried out by stray clues and guesswork; a few shots from previous restorations were also eliminated.

Some of the decisions made are questionable—I'll be getting to a couple of them later—but shouldn't deter anyone from seeing this version, which runs for eighty-nine minutes (the precise running time Vigo wanted) and contains about ten minutes of new footage. With the possible (and debatable) exception of a new print of CITIZEN KANE, which will be showing here in May, I doubt that a more beautiful film will be showing anywhere in Chicago this year.

Significantly, none of Vigo's four films, including his shorts A PROPOS DE NICE (1929) and TARIS (1931), survives in its original form today. But the fact that Vigo still remains one of the key figures in the history of cinema based on a total oeuvre that runs less than three hours gives some hint of how indestructible his talent remains and how trivial certain losses and alterations are in the broader scheme of things. Even though I've never seen the truncated and mutilated LE CHALAND QUI PASSE that opened in 1934, I've little doubt that Vigo's genius would be evident even there.

■

What does this genius consist of? It's easier to define in ZÉRO DE CONDUITE, an exhilarating celebration of nonstop rebellion against bourgeois propriety and authority informed by free-flowing poetry and fantasy. But having recently seen that film and L'ATALANTE back to back, I've come to the conclusion that the much more "conventional" and commercial L'ATALANTE is an even greater work, for reasons that are less immediately obvious.

Terms like "surrealism"—or "realism," for that matter—prove to be wholly inadequate in dealing with Vigo, despite the fact that he was a strong admirer of both Luis Buñuel's surrealist UN CHIEN ANDALOU ("Beware of the dog—it bites," he declared in a 1930 lecture) and the realist work of Erich von Stroheim. A first-degree reading of ZÉRO might conclude that it's a surrealist film with realist touches, just as L'ATALANTE might initially appear to be a realist film with surrealist touches. But both descriptions fail because they imply a consistent surface speckled with "touches"; Vigo's style and vision in both films are so seamless that the very notion of "touches" is inappropriate.

ZÉRO and L'ATALANTE both begin with shots of steam, vapor, and/or fog—a magical summoning of forces that is grounded in the real, which happens to be a train in ZÉRO, the barge in L'ATALANTE. (Boris Kaufman, who shot both films, later won an Oscar for his work on ON THE WATERFRONT, where he was still working wonders with ethereal textures; a key sequence in a park between Marlon Brando and Eva Marie Saint is virtually orchestrated by fog and the smoke from a burning trash can.) These openings make one think that from this point on anything can happen, but that the world it will happen in is still and always the world we know, however unexpected its form. In ZÉRO, the school principal may be a fastidious, bearded midget and the drawing on a schoolboy's notebook may suddenly turn into an animated cartoon, but the characters and settings still belong to a recognizable and even familiar universe. This is not simply an ordinary place where strange things occasionally happen, but a poetic universe we all instinctively know.

In the supposedly more realistic universe of L'ATALANTE, the barge that travels up and down the river docking at real French towns and cities seemingly holds no cargo at all—save for one fleeting line in the dialogue ("Does unloading take long in a city?"), none is ever seen or mentioned—yet Jean clearly makes his living from some kind of cargo, and at one point even comes close to being fired in a company office in Le Havre, until Jules speaks on his behalf. In an ordinary film, this would be a lapse in credibility, but lapses are as foreign in Vigo's mature filmmaking as touches, and the film's cargoless barge, nevertheless brimming with both possibilities and actualities, is as real—or as unreal, for that matter—as any working boat in movies.

This sense of possibilities and actualities applies to many other aspects of L'ATALANTE as well. When I first saw the new version at the Toronto film festival last fall, I was struck by what seemed to be the film's bisexuality—not a bisexual program of any sort, but a treatment of the character's sexuality that goes beyond the usual heterosexual norms and definitions. We know, for instance, that Jules has some sexual interest in women—we hear him allude a couple of times to someone named Dorothy, see him about to ravish a buxom fortune-teller, and clearly sense his attraction to Juliette as well—but this surely accounts for only part of his sexual nature. I was struck, for starters, by the highly charged ambiguity of his relationship to Juliette—a mysterious kinship that is implied in the similarity of their names—which comes to the fore whenever their responses to certain things suddenly coincide. One scene begins with him demonstrating his skill in using her sewing machine. She then gets him to model her skirt while she adjusts the hem (an experience that fills him with delight), and the sequence ends with them admiring one another's hair and Juliette combing his hair after he has stripped off his shirt to show her his tattoos.

In another scene, in his cabin—where he introduces her to the exotic trinkets he has collected from all over the world on his sea travels—she comes upon a pair of human hands pickled in a jar. Jules indicates that they belonged to a friend who died three years ago (we see his photo) and that they're all he has left of him—a piquant line that suggests that the friend may also have been a lover. (Just before this, to demonstrate the sharpness of his stiletto, Jules deliberately cuts his knuckle and then licks the wound—at which point Juliette instinctively licks her lips.) Jean suddenly enters, obviously upset by the intimacy he recognizes between Jules and his wife, and starts complaining about the cabin's messiness and the smell of the cats; before he starts breaking dishes and a mirror in a rage, he asks Jules to identify a nude black woman in a photograph, and Jules cracks, "That's me when I was young."

In some ways, the behavior of the peddler (Gilles Margaritis) whom Jean and Juliette encounter in a cabaret is equally outrageous. "How nice of you to come," he says to them when they arrive. "We were waiting for you to start the party. Bring on the biscuits, as dry as the duchess's very dry pussy." When he starts to flirt with Juliette in a song, he quickly interjects "You're pretty, too" to Jean, and he wiggles his ass shamelessly when he's dancing with Juliette a little later. (His marvelous sales patter, which mainly takes the form of a musical number, also implies a certain link between Juliette's libido and consumerism that is played out elsewhere in the film.)

There's certainly no question that the sensuality of Vigo's work as a whole—and especially the carnal impact of flesh touching flesh—has a special aura and potency. The key moment that kicks off the schoolboy's full-scale revolt in ZÉRO DE CONDUITE is a fat chemistry teacher stroking the hand of an effeminate, long-haired boy named Tabard—the character in the film who, it is said, most represents Vigo, and who responds by screaming at the teacher, "I say shit on you!" (Vigo's Catalonian father—a controversial anarchist and newspaper editor who was strangled in his prison cell by unknown parties when Vigo was twelve—had composed a headline for his socialist paper which said exactly the same thing, addressed to the government, in large letters. And at the age of seventeen, following his first arrest, Vigo's father changed his name, as an act of defiance, to Miguel Almereyda, the last name a deliberate anagram for a phrase that translates roughly as "There is shit.")

Vigo's biographer, the Brazilian film archivist P. E. Salles Gomes, provides us with one intriguing anecdote that relates to Vigo's attitudes about sexuality. Just after the end of shooting, when Vigo and his actor Jean Dasté were invited to lunch by Margaritis, they arrived arm in arm, both whimsically dressed, according to Margaritis's mother, who was cooking the lunch, "in women's summer frocks, with bare arms and legs, wearing small hats on their heads, one of them apparently in an advanced state of pregnancy."

This carnivalesque gesture seems wholly compatible with Vigo's universe and vision, but whether it pointed to any active bisexuality on Vigo's part is ultimately irrelevant. Just as L'ATALANTE winds up making terms like "realism" and "surrealism" seem inadequate, it also makes terms like "heterosexual," "homosexual," and even "bisexual" seem beside the point. Vigo's grasp of the world is a particular kind of alertness and aliveness that confounds most social and aesthetic categories because it has the freedom to call upon anything and everything that might enhance our appreciation and understanding of what he has to show, ordinary distinctions be damned.

At one point, we're told by P. E. Salles Gomes, when Vigo was scouring Parisian flea markets to fill Jules's cabin with exotic trinkets—he also called on friends to contribute several objects, and even stole some wrought-iron wreaths from the Montparnasse cemetery—he was especially interested in finding one of Alexander Calder's mobiles. The usually astute Salles Gomes concludes that Vigo "must have eventually realized that, although they were not well known in 1933, the presence of a mobile among an old sailor's mementos would have been out of place." On the contrary, I think we have to argue that in a Vigo film—most of all, in *this* Vigo film—a Calder mobile would not have been out of place, not even in an old sailor's junk-strewn cabin. The mystical point at which imagination and observation fuse is present in L'ATALANTE in virtually every shot.

Even without the Calder mobile, many of the shots in the film are simple awestruck discoveries, and the sequences that coagulate around them are often ones that simply arose from these discoveries. Consider the numerous cats of Père Jules's that roam about the barge, affecting the events of the film in numerous ways. We know that they have an autobiographical basis (Almereyda was a fanatical cat lover, and the single-room attic apartment in which Vigo was born was filled with scrawny alley cats), and the poetic mileage the film derives from them goes well beyond their function as suggestive décor. One of them scratches Jean's cheek when he first steps aboard after the wedding, and soon afterward Jean is furious when a litter of kittens is born in his and Juliette's bed—two signals at the outset that Jules and what he represents threaten the sexual health and privacy of the couple, even if it's Jules who ultimately succeeds in reuniting them at the end.

During a pivotal and wonderful sequence in which Jules magically succeeds in repairing an old gramophone, there's a brief shot showing kittens crowded around the machine as if they're listening intently to the record playing, one of them standing inside the shell-like loudspeaker. The gramophone and its repair originally served a minor and quite different role in the scene, but when the kittens unexpectedly became fascinated with the machine between takes, Vigo quickly filmed them that way and then reworked the entire sequence around this improvised shot—turning these kittens into a kind of Greek chorus in the process.

■

During the same sequence, there's a somewhat jarring cut from Jules, the cabin boy, and Jean (brooding over Juliette's absence) on deck to Jean rubbing his cheek against and licking a large block of ice on land. The logical place for this startling and moving shot is a little bit later, after Jean has docked the barge at Le Havre and is looking for Juliette on land; according to *Variety,* the restorers placed it where they did solely on the basis of how certain individual shots were numbered.

My only other major objection to their work (which involved about forty editorial changes in sound and/or image from previous versions) is their artificial prolongation of the final shot, through a technique called step-printing, in order to make Jaubert's score conclude at precisely the same instant that the shot does—a kind of symmetrical neatness that seems counter to Vigo's own looser sense of balance and closure. Letting the music run past the shot, as it did quite pleasurably and naturally in the earlier versions, would surely have done his memory no disservice. (Gracefully sculpted around the action throughout, Jaubert's wonderful score also plays off certain natural sounds—

using the barge's engine as a metronome, much as he used a train engine at
the beginning of ZÉRO.)

■

I can't hope to do more here than hint at a few of the riches in L'ATALANTE,
including the lasting impact it has had on subsequent generations of filmmakers. (There's an extended *hommage* in Bertolucci's LAST TANGO IN PARIS, for
instance; and I think it could be argued that practically all of the good things
in Truffaut's work—most of them realized most fully in his early features—
would have been inconceivable without Vigo's direct influence.) In conclusion, then, let me focus briefly on three aspects of the film that deserve more
detailed consideration than I can give them here:

1. Michel Simon as Père Jules offers what is just about the most wondrous
character acting I know of in movies; but even this performance would be
substantially less than it is if it weren't for Vigo's superb sense of how to integrate him with everything else in the picture. At once the film's only pure
infant and its only pure adult, he embodies a kind of stream-of-consciousness,
polymorphous-perverse behavior that perfectly exemplifies the film's capacity to integrate fantasy and reality. His two extended scenes with Juliette in the
barge's lower cabins are perhaps the richest examples of this—delirious, freeform two-part inventions whose pivots are either props or phrases by Juliette
that send him off into fresh paroxysms of play or demonstration.

The only remote equivalents to Simon's character in the American cinema
are the crotchety comic parts played by Walter Brennan in Howard Hawks's
TO HAVE AND HAVE NOT (a rummy named Eddie) and RIO BRAVO (a cripple
named Stumpy), both of whom play a major role in defining (not to mention
cussing out and irritating) and ultimately uniting the other characters. But
Brennan never quite transcends his function as comic relief, whereas Jules is
much more central. James Agee compared him to Caliban, but in other respects he is even worthy of Falstaff.

2. Conceivably the most erotic sequence in the movie is one that poetically and rhythmically intercuts between Jean and Juliette, each of them in
separate beds many miles apart, suffering from insomnia and longing for each
other. Another powerful two-part invention, as symmetrical as Vigo ever gets,
it rhymes Juliette and Jean fondling their own torsos and musically plays with
their restless movements in and out of the frame; both characters are speckled
mysteriously with polka-dot shadows, implying a common ground to their individual torments and desires—a mutual passion that makes their subsequent
reunion as exciting and fully satisfying as any last-minute Hollywood clincher.

3. Apart from its loose narrative construction, L'ATALANTE is far from
being an art movie in any ordinary sense. If it follows the conventions of any
genre, it comes much closer to being a musical at several critical junctures—
including the climactic moment when Jules finds Juliette in a record parlor,

listening to the sailor's song that serves as one of the score's major themes. Just as the movie confounds our usual understandings of realism and surrealism, documentary and fantasy, and sexuality with its various prefixes, it also collapses what we ordinarily mean by "commercial" and "popular" on the one hand, "arty" and "experimental" on the other. What category can we hope to assign a movie whose beauty and greatness finally rest on the simple gratitude it makes us feel for being alive?

—*Chicago Reader*, 29 March 1991

Guilty by Omission

If one were to undertake a diagnosis of the cultural and historical amnesia that currently afflicts American society in general and the American cinema in particular, the suppression of radical politics as part of our history might be a useful place to start. It is a suppression that comes in many forms, many of them barely conscious.

When a radical youth movie—PUMP UP THE VOLUME—actually gets made and released in the United States today, a repudiation of the 1960s counter-culture becomes an obligatory part of its argument, because otherwise many contemporary teenagers would dismiss it out of hand. And when the same film gets reviewed in the United States, even most sympathetic critics find it convenient to overlook the fact that the film is political, for fear of alienating the public. Or when a recent film about Vietnam such as JACOB'S LADDER has the rare courage to attack the Pentagon (unlike, say, BORN ON THE FOURTH OF JULY and CASUALTIES OF WAR), one can predict that, given the present climate in America, it will be attacked by some critics for being exploitative and un-serious—and praised by others as entertainment—whereas the issues broached by the film won't be addressed at all.

This is nothing new, I hasten to add. When films as antiracist as Cy End-field's ZULU (1964), Herbert Biberman's SLAVES (1969), and Richard Fleischer's MANDINGO (1975) were first released in the States, they were all generally ei-ther ignored in the press—as was Leo Popkin and Russell Rouse's THE WELL back in 1951—or treated as if they were shameless pieces of racist exploita-tion. The diverse methods by which films of social protest become neutral-ized in mainstream discourse, through either misreadings or lack of atten-tion, are too numerous and complex to be explored in detail here, but it is a problem that needs to be acknowledged at the outset. A related problem, to be sure, is the ideological cast of the period we're living in—a period during which, for example, virtual celebrations of the FBI such as MISSISSIPPI BURNING and THE SILENCE OF THE LAMBS have been widely applauded as models of progressive thinking.

If a fear of the social movements of the 1960s has continued to characterize American life since the 1970s, it is equally true that a fear of the social movements of the 1930s was an important ingredient in American life in the 1940s and 1950s. We're still living with the legacy of that fear, which in many cases has seriously warped our grasp of film history. It is difficult, for instance, to understand the full significance of CITIZEN KANE without a comprehensive understanding of Orson Welles's links with leftist politics in his theater and radio work over most of the preceding decade. This is the subject of a forthcoming book by Michael Denning, but most accounts of KANE minimize this background. Few Welles scholars have shown much interest in, say, Welles's original radio play *His Honor the Mayor,* which was broadcast less than a month before KANE's release; it is a remarkable neo-Brechtian effort about racism, union-busting, and the right to free assembly that was widely (and quite implausibly) attacked in the Hearst press as communistic. And when it comes to understanding Welles's subsequent work, the missing political context produces further distortions.

How many people today familiar with the story behind Welles's unfinished IT'S ALL TRUE (1942), which had such disastrous consequences for the remainder of his career, are aware that the reasons why this film was never finished are largely political? Popular accounts usually assume that the project was aborted because Welles got "carried away" by the carnival in Rio, spent too much money, and behaved "irresponsibly." But what scholars such as Robert Stam and Catherine Benamou have recently discovered and demonstrated in copious and persuasive detail* is that Welles's "irresponsibility," "profligacy," "partying," "self-indulgence," and so on were little more than his determination to make a Hollywood movie about Brazil and Mexico that featured poor nonwhites in all the leading roles. So thoroughly has this central fact been papered over by studio propaganda and mythical hyperbole about Welles's personality that even Welles's most sympathetic biographers have failed to see the political dimensions of the project, or fully apprehend that Welles's insistence on spending most of his time in Brazil with working-class blacks was what chiefly constituted his "carrying on" and "partying."

■

How did such a situation come about? To trace a few of its many roots, one has to go back to the 1960s, when Andrew Sarris's writings about auteur-

---

*See "Orson Welles's Essay Films and Documentary Fictions" in part 3.

ism were first appearing and influencing a whole generation of cinéphiles. Auteurism, as formulated by Sarris, was in part a reaction against socially conscious critics who valued films above all for their content and ignored their style. As Sarris wrote in his preface to *The American Cinema,* the bible of auteurism: "The sociologically oriented film historians—Jacobs, Grierson, Kracauer, Rotha, Griffith, Leyda, Sadoul, et al.—looked on the Hollywood canvas less as an art form than as a mass medium. Hollywood directors were regarded as artisans rather than as artists, and individual movies were less often aesthetically evaluated than topically synopsized." There was enough partial truth in this charge to give Sarris's "discoveries"—such directors as Hitchcock, Hawks, Samuel Fuller, and Nicholas Ray, whom he was controversially proposing as artists rather than as "mere" entertainers or studio hacks—the force of a revelation.

But it was a revelation that came at a certain price. "Thesis" cinema at its worst and least artistic was then represented by Stanley Kramer in the United States, André Cayatte in France, and the claims made by Sarris for Ray were strictly formal ones. Insofar as Ray's films were socially conscious, they were inartistic by definition:

> Nicholas Ray has been the cause célèbre of the auteur theory for such a long time that his critics, pro and con, have lost all sense of proportion about his career. Nicholas Ray is not the greatest director who ever lived; nor is he a Hollywood hack. The Truth lies somewhere in between. It must be remembered that THEY LIVE BY NIGHT, THE LUSTY MEN, REBEL WITHOUT A CAUSE, and BIGGER THAN LIFE are socially conscious films by any standards, and that KNOCK ON ANY DOOR is particularly bad social consciousness on the Kramer-Cayatte level. His form is not that impeccable, and his content has generally involved considerable social issues.

It is only when Sarris takes up Ray's visual style, his principal "theme" ("that every relationship establishes its own moral code and that there is no such thing as abstract morality"), and his romanticism—all of which are felt to be divorced from his social meanings—that he can find the director's work artistic.

Over a quarter-century since this was written, Sarris's distinctions of this kind have become critical orthodoxy in the United States, although not in a manner that Sarris himself could have predicted. The immediate consequence of this position in relation to film history is a virtual effacement of certain films and creative individuals whose social orientations are too visible to be ignored or rationalized as something else. It is an unconscious form of censorship that can be found not only in *The American Cinema* and related works of critical reference such as Charles Flynn and Todd McCarthy's *Kings of the Bs,* but even in more recent academic studies whose ostensible interests are social. Thus the names Cyril Endfield and John Berry—two important blacklisted directors I will be discussing later—are missing from Sarris and Flynn-McCarthy, as well as Peter Roffman and Jim Purdy's *The Hollywood Social Problem Film: Madness, Despair and Politics from the Depression to the Fifties* (Indiana University Press, 1981) and, despite the notable contributions of both directors, most studies of film noir.

I don't wish to imply that self-confessed auteurists and academics hold any sort of monopoly on obfuscating our radical past. Turn to "Morality Plays Right and Left," the last essay in Pauline Kael's first collection *I Lost It at the Movies* (1965), for an interesting hatchet job on SALT OF THE EARTH (1953)—the only overtly communist feature ever made in this country, and one of the few American films of the 1950s that qualifies as feminist. Kael links this independent effort—made in the teeth of enormous obstacles by a blacklisted producer (Paul Jarrico), screenwriter (Michael Wilson), and director (Herbert Biberman)—with the wholly forgettable anticommunist NIGHT PEOPLE, a routine Hollywood Cold War thriller of the same period; mutatis mutandis, it's a bit like saying that *Man's Fate* and *Terry and the Pirates* both boil down to the same nonsense. As Jarrico and others later described it, SALT OF THE EARTH was conceived as a "crime to fit the punishment": since he, Biberman, and Wilson were already barred as subversives from work in the industry, they decided to make a subversive film outside the industry that would live up to their reputations.

This is not to suggest that SALT OF THE EARTH is above criticism, or that Kael doesn't make some valid points about certain assumptions of social-realist propaganda (although, for the record, this example of it holds up a lot better than NIGHT PEOPLE, even as entertainment). A closer look at her essay, however, reveals that she's reviewing not the film itself but the published screenplay, which she quotes in copious detail. Perhaps she actually saw the film and is using the script as an *aide de mémoire*; if so, she doesn't bother to mention that some of the material she quotes with such scorn doesn't appear in the movie—a fact first pointed out to me by Jarrico himself. And since there's next to nothing she has to say about the film that couldn't be gleaned from the script and a few stills, it's questionable whether her essay actually deals with the film at all. When we consider that the best-known review of SALT OF THE EARTH in this country is both unreliable as reporting and almost completely negative, it's hardly surprising that few Americans today have much interest in seeing the movie (it's much more widely screened in Europe); but it's a film that cries out for revaluation.

Indeed, when we come to the era of the Hollywood Blacklist, we arrive at another kind of received wisdom: the observation that the writers, directors, and actors most persecuted by the House Un-American Activities Committee were chiefly untalented hacks whose politics were largely irrelevant, both to their martyrdom and to their work in film. But research carried out by Thom Andersen in the past several years suggests another story entirely—a story that needs to be told. Andersen's lengthy, invaluable essay "Red Hollywood," hidden away in a collection entitled *Literature and the Visual Arts in Contemporary Society* (Ohio State University Press, 1985), tells part of it; he and Noël Burch are planning a feature-length documentary on this subject that will undoubtedly tell still more.

Another important piece of radical historiography is Bernard Eisenschitz's massive biography, *Roman américain: les vies de Nicholas Ray,* published last year in France by Christian Bourgeois Éditeur and now being translated into English by Tom Milne.* The information and insights offered by both Andersen's "Red Hollywood" and Eisenschitz's biography formed the basis for "Nick Ray and/in America," a special event at the Rotterdam Film Festival last winter (organized by Eisenschitz) that was an attempt both to recontextualize the films of Ray and to rediscover a tradition in both the American cinema and American history that four decades of amnesia and inadequate understanding have helped obscure. In broad terms, this project suggests the beginning of a revised social history we have only begun to uncover and recognize.

Nicholas Ray

I was born when she kissed me
I died when she left me
I lived a few weeks while she loved me

This brief poem, written and recited by screenwriter Dixon Steele (Humphrey Bogart) to Laurel Gray (Gloria Grahame) in Ray's IN A LONELY PLACE, reflects not only the fleeting and fragile quality of both happiness and tenderness in much of Ray's work, but also the highly limited and circumscribed way that Ray's life and career are generally perceived by the world at large—when in fact they are perceived at all. Known to many chiefly as the man who directed James Dean in REBEL WITHOUT A CAUSE (1955), and to cinéphiles as a maverick director who imposed his romantic, lyrical, and semifatalistic view of the world on a series of disparate features made between the late 1940s and the early 1960s, Nicholas Ray is principally understood and appreciated today without much sense of a context beyond that of Hollywood.

This Hollywood context is complicated only slightly by a general recognition that Ray was *the* exemplary American director during the 1950s for many of the French critics writing for *Cahiers du Cinéma* and preparing to become directors themselves—above all, Jean-Luc Godard and François Truffaut, but also to a certain extent Jacques Rivette and Eric Rohmer. It can even be argued that Ray's work in the 1950s notably anticipates Godard's in the

---

*Subsequently published as *Nicholas Ray: An American Journey* (Faber and Faber, 1993).

1960s in many of its most striking attributes: a strong sense of romantic fatalism, a passionate empathy for adolescents and other solitary existential heroes, a radical discontent with contemporary society, a particular flair for color and CinemaScope, a recurrent (but unfulfilled) desire to film a musical, and a taste for anarchic violence that complicates all of the above—culminating in grandiose fables, parables, and pedagogical "lessons" (THE SAVAGE INNOCENTS and KING OF KINGS, WEEKEND and LE GAI SAVOIR), followed by a complete break with commercial filmmaking and the gradual forging of a new aesthetics based on greater degrees of collaboration and political commitment (WE CAN'T GO HOME AGAIN, Godard's Dziga-Vertov Group films). Many of these parallels come together in Godard's MADE IN U.S.A., a film dedicated jointly to Ray and Samuel Fuller, whose uses of color, Scope, violence, lyricism, and a sense of political betrayal all point toward what Godard learned and applied from his mentors.

Another link between Ray and Godard—the prescient grasp of contemporary social issues before they became part of mainstream culture—suggests a context only incidentally that of Hollywood, pointing toward a wider grasp of cultural currents than are found in most branches of formal film criticism. Consider Ray's handling of youth culture (REBEL), drugs (BIGGER THAN LIFE), ecology (WIND ACROSS THE EVERGLADES), anthropology (THE SAVAGE INNOCENTS), and even pop Christianity (KING OF KINGS suggesting a sort of JESUS CHRIST SUPERSTAR avant la lettre), all of which parallel Godard's early interests in such matters as semiotics (ALPHAVILLE) and Maoism (LA CHINOISE). (By contrast, Godard's own encounter with pop Christianity, JE VOUS SALUE MARIE, was not to take place until over two decades following KING OF KINGS.)

Despite the fact that Ray, born in 1911, was in his late thirties when his first feature was released (THEY LIVE BY NIGHT, 1949), and that he lived for almost another seventeen years after he collapsed during the shooting of his last commercial feature (55 DAYS AT PEKING, 1963), the fifty-odd years of his life not spent as a so-called professional filmmaker have counted for relatively little in most accounts of his work. Broadly speaking, to paraphrase Dix Steele's poem, Ray "was born" when Dore Schary hired him in 1947; he "died" when Samuel Bronston abandoned him in 1963; and he "lived" for the sixteen years in between, during which he directed twenty features and portions of a few others.

■

The inestimable value of Eisenschitz's biography is that it proposes another life (in fact, other *lives,* as the title expresses it)—not one that contradicts the first, but one that furnishes so much additional information that it refines and extends its meanings far beyond the limits of Ray's years in the film industry. Three hundred and twenty-one pages of meticulous and enlightening details are accorded those sixteen years in this mammoth volume, but 230 additional pages devoted to "before" and "after" transform the meaning of that productive period, making it part of a much larger, infinitely richer history. And a substantial portion of what has been uncovered—*excavated,* one is tempted to say—is the buried history of the American radical left during most of this century.

During the 1930s and the early 1940s, for starters, Ray studied with Frank Lloyd Wright, became a member of the radical Theatre of Action, and did work for the Federal Theatre, Birkwood Labor College, the U.S. Government's Resettlement Administration (which involved a great deal of travel across the country, organizing improvisational drama groups with rural workers, and extensive work with Alan Lomax in recording indigenous folk music that led to the discovery of Leadbelly, Woody Guthrie, Josh White, and Aunt Mollie Jackson, among others), and "Voice of America" radio programs.

Much of this activity has some bearing on THEY LIVE BY NIGHT, Ray's first feature, based on a Depression novel by Edward Anderson called *Thieves Like Us* (which also served as the basis for Robert Altman's film in the 1970s). Even before the movie's credits appear, we see the two leading characters (Farley Granger and Cathy O'Donnell) kissing while a subtitle introduces them in consecutive phrases: "This boy . . . and this girl . . . were never properly introduced to the world we live in. . . ." It's as though Ray were parsing the lines of a folk ballad.

If Ray's work as a whole seems founded on a feeling of disequilibrium continually striving for a sense of balance—a feeling especially evident in the poignant, precarious, and momentary symmetries formed by his romantic couples, but also found in the subjectively framed upside-down shots in REBEL WITHOUT A CAUSE, HOT BLOOD, and WIND ACROSS THE EVERGLADES—this instability is already present in the opening (postcredit) images of THEY LIVE BY NIGHT. The first helicopter shots in the history of cinema, they follow the path of a runaway car, and later careen past a bigger-than-life billboard (another important emblem of Ray's cinema). As the plot develops, this disequilibrium is maintained through what might be called an erotic handling of domesticity which turns the continued efforts of "this boy and this girl" to settle down into a scrapbook of fleeting instants.

An image of home and security—represented by either a couple or a troubled, unachieved family—that is shattered into fragments is, of course, a key image of the Depression. It hovers over the remainder of Ray's work like a malediction, without ever canceling out the utopian dreams of shared harmony that are equally a part of that period. Those dreams and their violent betrayals are likewise present in IN A LONELY PLACE, ON DANGEROUS GROUND, and THE LUSTY MEN—films whose very titles evoke the tortured worlds of their protagonists—and in JOHNNY GUITAR they form the core of the famous, embittered dialogue between Johnny (Sterling Hayden) and Vienna (Joan Crawford) about their past love ("Lie to me, tell me that all these years you've been waiting for me").

The precise creative roles played by Ray in each of these films has in the past largely been a matter of conjecture; one of the most valuable accomplishments of Eisenschitz's biography is to clarify as much as possible how much Ray brought to his scripts as well as his direction. In the case of this famous dialogue between Johnny and Vienna, Eisenschitz has discovered that a former relationship between these characters was not even indicated in the various versions of the script—making it highly likely that Ray contributed this crucial element (and this scene) himself.

It has been debated how much of the legacy of Ray's radical background in the 1930s and 1940s can be seen in his films of the 1950s, but there is certainly no question that it is present. Even in a lesser effort, THE TRUE STORY OF JESSE JAMES, one finds an instant lesson in anarchist economics when James pays off the mortgage of a sweet old lady with stolen money, then steals the same money back from her landlord a moment later. Radical considerations of who actually constitute society's outlaws can be found in WIND ACROSS THE EVERGLADES, THE SAVAGE INNOCENTS, and to some degree in the uneven but vibrant HOT BLOOD, Ray's film about gypsy life (which is also the closest he ever came to making a musical). BIGGER THAN LIFE can be read with profit as a disturbing critique of both the arrogance of patriarchy and the sterility of American middle-class life, quite apart from its consideration of the possible ill effects of "wonder drugs" like cortisone. And the contemporary relevance of BITTER VICTORY as a radical statement about war—and about the self-serving deception of what is often regarded as war heroics—was strikingly brought home in Rotterdam, at a symposium about the then-current war in the Persian Gulf, when Eisenschitz had the foresight to screen a devastating clip that ends with Richard Burton mordantly declaring, "I kill the living and I save the dead."

More generally, a philosophical overview of the moral equivalence of male antagonists—in REBEL WITHOUT A CAUSE, BITTER VICTORY, and WIND ACROSS THE EVERGLADES—points to a utopian vision lurking behind the anguished, embattled plots of those films, a dream of symmetry that is closely related to the balances momentarily struck between the romantic couples in THEY LIVE BY NIGHT, IN A LONELY PLACE, ON DANGEROUS GROUND, JOHNNY GUITAR, REBEL WITHOUT A CAUSE, HOT BLOOD, BITTER VICTORY, and PARTY GIRL. In the last, the antagonists, a crippled crooked lawyer (Robert Taylor) and a prostitute-dancer (Cyd Charisse) whose strengths and weaknesses are matched up with a certain compositional balance, wind up as lovers who bring about each other's moral regeneration. (It should be noted in passing that Ray's sensitive direction of both these relatively wooden actors transforms them as fully as the plot does. Robin Wood once noted in these pages that "no one ever gives a bad performance in a Ray film," and Ray's remarkable work with relatively unskilled or inexpressive players is among the steadiest pleasures to be found in his canon.)

After the director's break with commercial filmmaking there are fewer films to speak of, but his projects and interests—the Chicago "Conspiracy Trial," the murder of Fred Hampton, and such completed works as THE JANITOR (1974), two separate versions of WE CAN'T GO HOME AGAIN (1973 and 1976), and even two versions of LIGHTNING OVER WATER (1990 and 1991), Wim Wenders's film about his death—testify more pointedly to the persistence of Ray's radicalism. Chances for examining this still comparatively unexplored period should be improved by the fact that Susan Ray, his widow, hopes to be working in Paris on the restoration of his second version of WE CAN'T GO HOME AGAIN. (Although my only look at this version was ten years ago via a movieola, in my judgment it is substantially different from, and in most respects superior to, the more widely shown 1973 version.)

"Red Hollywood": Cy Endfield/John Berry

It would be absurd to try to summarize the fifty-five-page essay "Red Hollywood"—the best critical history of the Hollywood Blacklist that I've read—in a few lines, but some general remarks about its contents are in order. The first part, "New Inquisitions—Books about the Hollywood Blacklist," identifies and critiques three "waves" or "cycles" of commentary: pamphlets (chiefly ones by John Cogley and Murray Kempton) between 1948 and 1956; books dealing mainly with blacklisters (by Walter Goodman, Robert Vaughn, and Stefan Kaufer), 1968–1973; and books dealing mainly with blacklist victims (by Lillian Hellman, Nancy Lynn Schwartz, Larry Ceplair and Steven Englund, and Victor Navasky), 1976–1982. The second part of Andersen's essay, "Thoughts on Some Unanswered Questions," probes a good many historical issues arising from the first section, including the following:

> There are two questions that need to be borne in mind. Were the films of the blacklist victims *politically* distinctive? Were the films of the blacklist victims *artistically* distinctive? These questions are not independent, and they cannot be entirely disentangled. But we must remember that an answer to one is not necessarily an answer to the other. Surprisingly, none of the histories of the blacklist have addressed either of these questions.

Andersen then offers provisional answers to both questions, formulating in the process a genre associated with six blacklist victims—Berry, Endfield, Jules Dassin, Joseph Losey, Abraham Polonsky, and Robert Rossen—between the first HUAC hearings, in October 1947, and those of May 1951:

> Because this genre grew out of the body of films that have come retrospectively to be called *film noir* and because it may be distinguished from the earlier

film noir by its greater psychological and social realism, I will call the genre *film gris.* The term seems appropriate because we have been taught to associate Communism with drabness and greyness, and these films are often drab and depressing and almost always photographed in black-and-white.

Andersen then cites thirteen films—Rossen's BODY AND SOUL (written by Polonsky), Polonsky's FORCE OF EVIL, Dassin's THIEVES' HIGHWAY and NIGHT AND THE CITY, Ray's THEY LIVE BY NIGHT and KNOCK ON ANY DOOR, Huston's WE WERE STRANGERS and THE ASPHALT JUNGLE, Curtiz's THE BREAKING POINT, Losey's THE LAWLESS and THE PROWLER, Endfield's TRY AND GET ME!, and Berry's HE RAN ALL THE WAY, many of which he discusses—and proposes John Garfield as "the first axiom of *film gris.*"

It's worth noting that, with the exception of Polonsky, all the blacklisted directors in this group were forced into European exile in order to continue working. I can't claim any sort of expertise regarding either Endfield or Berry; but since they're by far the most neglected and I've recently formed some limited acquaintance with both, some preliminary remarks about them might be helpful.

■

Born in Scranton, Pennsylvania, in 1914, Cyril Endfield attended Yale and New York's New Theater School, taught drama and directed for the stage, and worked some time as a professional magician, which brought him into contact with Orson Welles. It was this meeting that led to his first film job in Hollywood, as an apprentice with the Mercury unit at RKO while Welles was away in South America filming IT'S ALL TRUE. He began as a film director in the mid-1940s with several shorts at MGM and a first feature—which he also wrote—at Monogram, GENTLEMAN JOE PALOOKA (1946). That was followed by STORK BITES MAN (1947), THE ARGYLE SECRETS (1948), and JOE PALOOKA IN THE BIG FIGHT (1949).

According to Ephraim Katz's *Film Encyclopedia,* Endfield first attracted attention with THE UNDERWORLD STORY (1950) and THE SOUND OF FURY— also known as TRY AND GET ME!—the next year. These are the two earliest Endfield films I've seen (both have recently turned up on cable and on video). Stylistically as well as politically, they are among the most striking and personal American thrillers of the early 1950s, establishing Endfield as a genuine auteur. Corrosive as social criticism—with a particularly negative view of the American press as a battering ram employed by the ruling class— they are powerfully acted (by Dan Duryea, Gale Storm, and Herbert Marshall in UNDERWORLD STORY, Frank Lovejoy and Lloyd Bridges in TRY AND GET ME!) and directed with considerable sharpness and brio. Both, arguably, are somewhat flawed in their conclusions: UNDERWORLD STORY has a forced happy ending, whereas the superior TRY AND GET ME!, which ends with uncompromising grimness, makes awkward use of a European spokesman to drive home its message. Yet one still comes away from both films shaken. Andersen points out that the lynching that concludes TRY AND GET ME!, headed by cleancut college boys, is not only "a remarkable tour de force of action filmmaking" but also "the most unrelenting and disturbing scene of mob violence I have ever seen in a Hollywood movie." I can only agree with him.

Endfield's last American film was TARZAN'S SAVAGE FURY (1952); most of his remaining films have been English. Because of the blacklist, many of these—LIMPING MAN (1953), THE MASTER PLAN (1954), IMPULSE (1955), CHILD IN THE HOUSE (1956)—are uncredited to him, and many of the others are equally difficult to come by. Of the four I've seen—HELL DRIVERS (1956), MYSTERIOUS ISLAND (1961), ZULU (1964), and SANDS OF THE KALAHARI (1965)—all but the lackluster and formulaic MYSTERIOUS ISLAND are very fine. MYSTERIOUS ISLAND—a Ray Harryhausen "Dynamation" special—is the only Endfield film I've seen apart from TRY AND GET ME! on which he doesn't receive a writer's credit, but I'm told he's done some writing on all his features.

■

Interestingly enough, John Berry also had important links with Orson Welles. Born in New York City in 1917, and starting out as a vaudeville and stage actor during his childhood, he became an integral part of Welles's Mercury Theater in the 1930s and early 1940s—acting in *Caesar, The Shoemaker's Holiday, Danton's Death, Too Much Johnson, Five Kings, The Green Goddess,* and *Native Son,* and serving as stage manager on the last two. He also was assistant director on the film segments of *Too Much Johnson,* and acted in several Mercury radio shows.

After starting out in Hollywood as an assistant to Billy Wilder on DOUBLE INDEMNITY, he directed six features before being blacklisted: MISS SUSIE SLAGLE'S (1945) and FROM THIS DAY FORWARD (1946), CROSS MY HEART (1947), CASBAH (1948), TENSION (1949), and HE RAN ALL THE WAY (plus, according to Robert Aldrich, temporarily replacing the ailing Max Ophüls on CAUGHT, 1949). Most of his subsequent features have been made in France, although he returned to the United States in the 1970s long enough to make CLAUDINE (1974), THIEVES (1977), THE BAD NEWS BEARS GO TO JAPAN (1978), and the television movies ANGEL ON MY SHOULDER (1980) and SISTER, SISTER (1982); his most recent film, A CAPTIVE OF THE LAND, was shot in the Soviet Union. Berry served as the principal inspiration and role model for David Merrill, the fictional blacklisted director played by Robert De Niro in Irwin Winkler's GUILTY BY SUSPICION.

I've so far seen only two of Berry's features, although I'm told that they're two of his very best, FROM THIS DAY FORWARD and CLAUDINE; both were screened at Rotterdam in the presence of Berry himself, who was seeing them for the first time since they were released. It's one sign of the limitations of GUILTY BY SUSPICION as a movie about the blacklist that if I hadn't been told Berry (who played a nightclub owner in the Winkler-produced 'ROUND MID-NIGHT) was the inspiration for the film, I never could have guessed. David Merrill, we quickly learn, is an artist largely *because* he isn't much concerned with politics; as the movie takes great pains to show us, plotting out storyboards is his business, not thinking about the way people live. Yet it was clear from the hours I spent with Berry in Rotterdam that what mattered and still matters to him about FROM THIS DAY FORWARD and CLAUDINE is their knowledge, feeling, and insight about what it means to be poor in a big city.

Both films are concerned specifically with the bureaucratic obstacles that poor people face. FROM THIS DAY FORWARD focuses on the postwar adjustments of a struggling white couple (Joan Fontaine and Mark Stevens) on the job market; CLAUDINE concerns the comic struggles of a black couple (welfare mother Diahann Carroll and garbageman James Earl Jones) with the welfare system. And Berry's mise en scène is wholly a function of his understanding of what his characters are up against, not his capacity to draft pretty pictures à la Hitchcock on a sketch pad.

Coda: Guilty by Omission

GUILTY BY SUSPICION started out as a film to be produced by Winkler, scripted by Abraham Polonsky, and directed by Bertrand Tavernier. Tavernier dropped out when the decision was made to set the story in the United States rather than France; Polonsky, who remained a major source of information about the blacklist, eventually dropped out as well when he saw the approach Winkler was taking, and even refused an executive producer credit that would have paid him a handsome fee. Polonsky's hero, like Berry, was an American communist who refused to recant and ultimately was forced into exile; it was clearly Winkler's perception that the American public would be incapable of sympathizing with such a person, even if he was played by De Niro.

At most the film implies that the Hollywood Blacklist may have stifled social criticism, but it doesn't really show us any social criticism being stifled and it doesn't quite argue that social critics—assuming that any existed—were innocent, either (although, according to the Bill of Rights, they were). In fact, when push comes to shove, the movie doesn't deal with the question of social criticism at all, except to indict the blacklist as an insane, destructive force (which it was). Emotionally speaking, the attention that might have been paid to Merrill's political thinking is supplanted by his relationships with his ten-year-old son (Luke Edwards) and his estranged wife (Annette Bening), and these relationships are shown to be essentially devoid of political associations as well.

The closest the film comes to showing the impingement of rabid Cold War hysteria on Merrill's son is a sequence of his watching a television report on the soon-to-be-executed Julius and Ethel Rosenberg, including their two soon-to-be-orphaned sons; this leads the boy to ask fearfully if Dad is about to be killed too. As it happens, I was ten myself that summer and I recall seeing the headline ROSENBERGS EXECUTED on a family trip to Washington, D.C. Struck by the resemblance of "Rosenberg" to "Rosenbaum," and deeply upset to the point of tears about the two little boys who'd just lost their parents, I plied my own liberal father with troubled questions. Two months later, however, in a Times Square arcade, I was about to have a fake newspaper headline made up bearing my name, and asked my father for a suggestion. He proposed JONNY ROSENBAUM CAPTURES RED SPIES! It seemed like a wonderful idea at the time, and I still have the same headline to prove it.

So the same Jonny Rosenbaum who wept for the Rosenberg boys in June was quite delighted with the fantasy of capturing their parents singlehandedly in August: it was part of the everyday insanity of that period, roughly comparable to the wild standing ovation George Bush got in Congress this year (from adults, I should add) when he declared that this country has the strongest economy in the world. It seems to me, in other words, that GUILTY BY SUSPICION falters by localizing its subject in a few easy targets—restricting the insanity of America in the early 1950s to a few FBI agents, HUAC hearings, and frightened studio executives, without admitting that the fantasies of the period seeped much deeper into the everyday and unexceptional textures of American life.

How effective was the blacklist as a form of ideological warfare? Effective enough, one could argue—given the thousands of individuals who lost friends, livelihood, or both—to demoralize the Old Left so thoroughly that it has never fully recovered. Effective enough to make truly leftist filmmaking in Hollywood highly suspect ever since. And effective enough even to depoliticize most mainstream discussions of the blacklist that have taken place in this country over the past fifteen years.

Readers who find this last claim exaggerated should turn to Andersen's highly persuasive accounts of Lillian Hellman's *Scoundrel Time* and Victor Navasky's *Naming Names,* introduced by Robin Blackburn's statement, "Bourgeois sociology only begins to understand modern revolutions insofar as they fail." Andersen adds, "This dictum may be applied to its dramatic art as well. When it turns to political revolutions for its subject matter, it produces the films VIVA ZAPATA!, THE BATTLE OF ALGIERS, and BURN!, each of which in its own way romanticizes and glorifies revolutionary defeats." Similarly, "what matters about Hellman to the admirers of *Scoundrel Time* is her martyrdom," that seals "her status as a moral exemplar," whereas *Naming Names,* reducing "complex political issues to the ethical issue of informing" and "neglecting concrete historical analysis," uses "abstract models of contemporary American social science" to "occupy the place where we might expect to find political analysis."

From this point of view, it is easy to see GUILTY BY SUSPICION as part of an ongoing tradition of political avoidance and omission whereby blacklist victims become worthy of our attention only to the extent that they become stripped of their political beliefs. I suppose the fact that the film has been made at all shows to what extent we've recovered from the blacklist climate. But the fact that it leaves so much of the story still untold shows to what extent we haven't.

—*Film Comment*, September–October 1991

His Master's Vice

Fuller's WHITE DOG

WHITE DOG
Directed by Samuel Fuller
Written by Fuller and Curtis Hanson
With Kristy McNichol, Paul Winfield, Burl Ives, Jameson
Parker, Lynne Moody, and Marshall Thompson

The best American movie released so far this year, made by the greatest living American filmmaker, was actually made ten years ago, and so far its venues have been restricted to single theaters in New York and Chicago*; but late is a lot better than never, and two cities are certainly better than none. Why it's taken a decade for Samuel Fuller's WHITE DOG to reach us is not an easy question to answer; it was shown widely in Europe in the early 1980s and well received critically. For the past few years it has turned up sporadically on cable, principally the Lifetime channel, but it has never come out here on video.

WHITE DOG started out as an article by Romain Gary published in *Life* magazine and was later expanded into a book. The accounts I've read describe the book as autobiographical, mainly about the author's relationship with Jean Seberg. Gary and Seberg were living in Los Angeles when they found a "white" dog who had been trained to attack blacks; they tried without success to have the dog retrained and eventually had to kill it. Gary's book also deals with Seberg's involvement with the Black Panthers and the FBI's subsequent persecution of her, which eventually led to her suicide; Gary himself committed suicide some time afterward, and Fuller's film is dedicated to him.

The rights to WHITE DOG were purchased by Paramount in the mid-1970s, and Roman Polanski briefly planned to make a film derived from it after CHINATOWN. But eventually Don Simpson, in charge of production at Paramount in the early 1980s, inherited it; he put together a group of film projects

*Since writing this, I've been informed that the film had some brief, unheralded theatrical runs in the United States in 1981, notably in Seattle and Detroit. (1993)

that were designed to be made cheaply (the most commercially successful of which proved to be AN OFFICER AND A GENTLEMAN), and WHITE DOG was among them. The project went through several phases; at one point TOP GUN's Tony Scott was set to direct it, and at another it was planned as a vehicle for Jodie Foster. At least one of the various plans conceived of the film as a sensationalist venture, and when gossip about it leaked out the NAACP lodged a protest, believing—perhaps with some justification—that the film could foster racist violence by inspiring rednecks to train "white dogs." That protest tarnished Fuller's masterpiece when it finally came to be made, despite the fact that it remained unseen by its accusers and is anything but racist or incendiary. When people over the years have alluded to the film as being "controversial," they more than likely have been sharing and perpetrating this misunderstanding.

When Jon Davison, the producer of AIRPLANE!, was first assigned to the project, he reportedly didn't want any part of it. Then he had the brilliant idea of assigning Fuller to the project. Fuller completely rewrote the script with Curtis Hanson, a friend of his who had already worked on one of the earliest drafts; apart from some of the characteristics of the dog Gary described and the white man who ran the animal training compound, all of the Gary book was jettisoned. Instead, the story focused on a white actress who finds the dog and a black animal trainer who tries to recondition him.

After the film was completed, it was briefly test-marketed, tampered with a bit but not significantly altered by the studio, released overseas, and then essentially shelved. Not long afterward Fuller moved to Europe, where he has lived and worked ever since. The move was understandable considering the studio treatment accorded his last two American pictures: four-hour and two-hour cuts of THE BIG RED ONE (1980), his magnum opus about his World War II experiences, were both discarded in favor of a drastically reworked version that wound up pleasing no one (although it is full of extraordinary and beautiful moments even in this form), and WHITE DOG was never released domestically at all. Since Fuller's move to Paris, apart from writing several novels and appearing in several films, he has written and directed three more features and one short film—a Patricia Highsmith adaptation for French television that I haven't seen—none of which has opened in the United States. He is currently seventy-nine, and his chances of working again for an American studio are extremely slim, though he still harbors hopes that his original four-hour cut of THE BIG RED ONE might be restored, even if only for a French miniseries.

In Paris he's still a celebrity; many of his novels have appeared in translation (most recently *The Big Red One*, though it retains its English title) and his movies are regularly revived in theaters. In this country, very few people under thirty seem to know he exists, even though he's as American as apple pie and the uncontested godfather of filmmakers as diverse as Jean-Luc Godard, Steven Spielberg, Martin Scorsese, Wim Wenders, and Peter Bogdano-vich. (A few examples of his influence: Fuller collaborated on the story of Bogdanovich's first film, TARGETS. He appears in Godard's PIERROT LE FOU, Spielberg's 1941, and three Wenders features. There's a clip from his PICKUP ON SOUTH STREET in Scorsese's THE KING OF COMEDY, and extended *hommages* to other Fuller films in Godard's BREATHLESS and Spielberg's INDIANA JONES AND THE TEMPLE OF DOOM.)

Given his eclecticism, it's highly unlikely that he'll ever get an Oscar or an American Film Institute Lifetime Achievement Award; in spite of his major importance, his name has never really registered in the American mainstream. As a novelist and screenwriter, he's unabashedly pulpy, a street prole who writes in short, lurid sentences. He's too full of didactic notions, most of them historical or political, to make it into the current postmodernist pantheon shared by writers like Jim Thompson. Bursting with goofy and exaggerated ideas, his pictures are frontal assaults of explosive conceptual energy that can rarely be rationalized on a naturalistic level. (His brilliant SHOCK CORRIDOR, set in an insane asylum, tells us less than nothing about the mentally ill but practically everything about what's wrong with America in 1963.) A master at depicting violent action, Fuller has a particular flair with both close-ups and long takes, a formal brilliance he exhibited a full decade and a half before any American critic besides Manny Farber recognized the presence of such methods in either Fuller's cheap genre pictures or anyone else's.

The brutish and loutish heroes of most of his pictures tend to be too unromantic to serve as identification figures, but they don't fall into predictable antihero slots, either. (His films are seldom devoid of tenderness, but nearly all of it in his earlier pictures is accorded to children and other victims of adult corruptions.) After critics inaccurately typecast Fuller as a primitive cold warrior and red-baiter—mainly on the basis of the spy thriller PICKUP ON SOUTH STREET (which incidentally won the Bronze Lion at the 1953 Venice Film Festival with the full support of Luchino Visconti, a communist who headed the jury)—they found it increasingly difficult to deal with or even recognize the radical social critiques of American life present in his work. Even in THE STEEL HELMET, the first Korean-war film, made three years before PICKUP, the best ideological points are scored by a Korean communist who lectures a black American G.I. about segregation on buses and a Japanese American G.I. about the American concentration camps during World War II—two matters that no other American filmmaker was dealing with in 1950. The Korean communist may be a "villain," but in contrast to the thuggish and racist American "hero," who eventually goes completely haywire, he's positively charismatic.

Where Fuller differs most strikingly from his acolytes is that he lived the equivalent of two entire lives before he ever got around to making movies—one as a crime reporter and one as a much-decorated war hero. (He directed his first feature, I SHOT JESSE JAMES, in his mid-thirties.) He has a lot to say about both subjects—about war in THE STEEL HELMET, FIXED BAYONETS, HELL AND HIGH WATER, CHINA GATE, VERBOTEN!, MERRILL'S MARAUDERS, SHOCK CORRIDOR, and THE BIG RED ONE, and about crime in PICKUP ON SOUTH STREET, HOUSE OF BAMBOO, UNDERWORLD, U.S.A., and THE NAKED KISS. But this list hardly exhausts the range of his street smarts. FORTY GUNS is one of the wildest westerns ever made, and PARK ROW is the giddiest celebration of American journalism after CITIZEN KANE. Fuller films as diverse as THE STEEL HELMET, RUN OF THE ARROW, CHINA GATE, THE CRIMSON KIMONO, SHOCK CORRIDOR, and WHITE DOG are arguably the most trenchant—and in some cases the most prescient—treatments of racism in the American cinema.

■

Is it possible to remove hatred from the world? If racism is a form of conditioned hatred, is it possible to eradicate it through reconditioning? Does reconditioning itself entail a kind of violence that threatens sanity and emotional equilibrium? These are some of the questions addressed by WHITE DOG, and although the conditioning and reconditioning in this case is done to a German shepherd, Fuller never lets us forget that it's humans, not animals, who are at issue. As in the fables of Aesop and La Fontaine, the hero of Fuller's parable may be a dog, but the subject is the human race.

The nameless title hero of the film is a dog trained to attack blacks, and then retrained during the film to overcome this conditioning by a black man named Keys (Paul Winfield) who's a professional animal trainer. The dog is a tragic scapegoat, neither racist nor antiracist in any human sense. He certainly inspires us to reflect on how conditioning can foster racism, but his own "racism" is purely manmade. We're told how the conditioning of white dogs is usually carried out: a black wino or junkie is paid by the dog's owner to beat the dog mercilessly and repeatedly as a puppy, and a proclivity for attacking blacks grows out of the resulting trauma.

Julie Sawyer (Kristy McNichol), a young actress who lives in the Hollywood Hills surviving on bit parts, accidentally injures the dog one night in her car, takes him to a vet, and then brings him home, hoping she can locate the owner. After no owner materializes and she gradually becomes aware that he's an attack dog, she takes him to a compound called Noah's Ark, where animals are trained for movies and commercials, in the hopes that the dog can be deprogrammed. While the co-owner of the compound (Burl Ives) sadly informs her "Can't nobody unlearn a dog" and advises her to have him killed, Keys agrees to do his utmost to reverse the dog's training, and the remainder of the film is devoted to the intense and heartbreaking drama of this process.

We see the dog's original owner only once in the film—very briefly toward the end—and Fuller takes special care not to depict him as a stereotypical villain. To all appearances he's a kindly grandfather, accompanied by his two young granddaughters, one of whom is played by Fuller's own daughter. The point of making this figure look kindly certainly isn't to excuse or forgive what he's done—it wouldn't occur to Fuller, an Old Testament moralist, to think that way, and the rage expressed by Julie toward this character is clearly Fuller's own—but to give him a human rather than a mythological dimension. There are real people who train dogs to attack blacks, and Fuller wants to impress us with this fact. Unlike the usual clichéd movie iconography, which insists that evil is committed by evil-looking characters—Robert De Niro in CAPE FEAR is the most recent example—Fuller suggests that it can be committed by kindly looking grandfathers as well.

Another example of Fuller's boldness occurs in an earlier sequence, when the dog breaks loose from his cage in the compound and, shortly afterward, chases a black man into the sanctuary of a church and kills him; the camera then cuts to a nearby stained-glass window of Saint Francis of Assisi. (What follows reveals some idiotic studio tampering in the version being shown here, involving redubbed lines as well as cuts in footage. Keys and Julie both turn up at the church; Keys incapacitates the dog with a knockout drug and then enters the sanctuary. In the original, shown on cable, Keys says to Julie when he emerges, "He killed a man—in a church! . . . I'm sure it's not the first black man he's killed." In the release version, this line has been redubbed as "He attacked a black man. He'll live. He'll live." Apparently the notion of a black man dying inside a church was deemed "too controversial" for the American public.)

Part of what makes WHITE DOG so powerful is Fuller's acute and sensitive camera strategy. Close-ups and subjective camera movements repeatedly place us in intimate proximity with the physical world as the dog perceives it, so that he's not merely "a four-legged time bomb" (as Julie's boyfriend puts it, in characteristic Fuller-ese) but also an animal whose perceptions we're invited to share. (Although several dogs were used to portray the German shepherd, what emerges has the miraculous continuity of a single performance and character.) As critic Tom Milne wrote when the film opened in England, "What makes WHITE DOG so moving, finally, is the naked simplicity, worthy of Griffith, with which Fuller deploys emotion: in the repeated close-ups of eyes as man and animal stare at each other in a futile attempt at mutual comprehension, in the sudden rushes of deep and playful affection, in the use of slow-motion to capture the mingled beauty and menace of the canine movements." The plaintiveness of Ennio Morricone's score and the measured musicality of Fuller's tracks and cranes have the same simplicity and directness.

We wind up feeling a lot for this dog because, very much like the donkey in Robert Bresson's AU HASARD BALTHAZAR—a film that Fuller told me he has never seen—he becomes the embodiment of mankind's mark on the world through everything he's submitted to: the love as well as the hate, the tenderness as well as the brutality. He's the litmus test for everything that's best and worst about us, but in his ultimate innocence and helplessness he's far from being the same as us. Like the children in Fuller's war films, he's the ultimate metaphor for the world we engender and nourish and ruin and try to redeem, a cause for some hope as well as despair. In Fuller's marvelously fluid and tragically resonant storytelling, the scope, limits, and consequences of our choices, our efforts, are indelibly clear.

—*Chicago Reader*, 29 November 1991

Government Lies

THE PANAMA DECEPTION and DEEP COVER

———————————————————————————

THE PANAMA DECEPTION
Directed by Barbara Trent
Written by David Kasper
Narrated by Elizabeth Montgomery

———————————————————————————

DEEP COVER
Directed by Bill Duke
Written by Henry Bean and Michael Tolkin
With Larry Fishburne, Jeff Goldblum, Victoria
Dillard, Charles Martin Smith, Sydney Lassick,
Clarence Williams III, Gregory Sierra, and
Roger Guenveur Smith

I wonder how many people under thirty-five know that one of the most frequent taunts hurled at President Lyndon Baines Johnson during antiwar demonstrations at the height of the Vietnam war was, "Hey, hey, LBJ, how many kids did you kill today?" Johnson did considerably more than any other U.S. president of this century to turn the civil rights movement into law—even going so far as to appropriate the movement's theme song, "We Shall Overcome," for a speech to Congress. But because of his behavior regarding nonwhites overseas, especially in Southeast Asia, a considerable part of the youth of the late 1960s regarded him as a mass murderer and told him so on every possible occasion. It seems plausible that Johnson's decision not to seek reelection in 1968, announced only four days before Martin Luther King was assassinated, had more than a little to do with the repeated sting of that relentless chant.

If any of the young people of today consider George Bush—who has done precious little for civil rights—a mass murderer because of Panama and the Persian Gulf, I have yet to hear about it. Some of this may be the fault of the media, which, as part of their totalitarian coverage of military interventions in those countries, have tended to minimize and undercut most public opposition to them, and some of it probably has to do with the fact that our economy—which was unusually strong during the 1960s—now makes many of us less prone to care about the fates of innocent nonwhites in foreign countries. (Whether it makes us totally indifferent, as some claim, is another matter. If we were, the tightly controlled state censorship in the cases of Panama and the Persian Gulf—which wasn't in effect during the war in Vietnam—surely wouldn't be necessary.)

■

As luck would have it, I happened to see most of Barbara Trent's highly informative THE PANAMA DECEPTION immediately before George Bush's upbeat speech at the Republican National Convention last week. As a result, I had the surreal experience of going directly from the somber parade of horrors caused by the U.S. invasion of Panama in 1989—20,000 Panamanians homeless, more than 18,000 forced into detention centers, 7,000 arrested without charges, thousands of civilian deaths, mass graves evoking Nazi exterminations, an estimated doubling of local cocaine traffic since Noriega's capture, a brutal U.S. military occupation now projected into the indefinite future—to Bush in Houston euphorically boasting "I feel great!" and "The Cold War is over and freedom finished first."

Like Trent's COVERUP: BEHIND THE IRAN CONTRA AFFAIR (1988), THE PANAMA DECEPTION is clearly timed to influence the presidential election, and it will be interesting to see if the carefully documented Bush bashing will reach a more receptive audience this time around. (Either way, perhaps we can look forward to a documentary from Trent about the Persian Gulf in time for the 1996 election—though I hasten to add that Bill Clinton appears to support the mass murder of innocents in that venture almost as fully as Bush does. As one commentator in the film points out, Panama was in many ways a "testing ground for the Persian Gulf war one year later," and the progression from Iran-contra to Panama seems equally logical.) Back in October 1988—fourteen months before the Christmas-season invasion of Panama was launched—COVERUP started an extended run at Chicago Filmmakers, which is now granting the same treatment to THE PANAMA DECEPTION. PBS, however, reportedly agreed to show COVERUP only if every reference to Bush in the film were deleted—a highly comical suggestion almost tantamount to removing every reference to Panama from the new film. (PBS also recently refused to show DEADLY DECEPTION, the documentary short criticizing General Electric that won this year's Academy Award. Naturally the GE-owned NBC and CNBC won't be showing it either, but I'm told that Evanston and Lincolnwood cable subscribers can see it on Monday, 31 August at 6 P.M. on public access channel 29. Ain't freedom grand?)

Both of Trent's documentaries—the first scripted by Eve Goldberg, the second scripted and edited by David Kasper—are careful and lucid after-the-fact clarifications of government lies. So, in a way, is DEEP COVER, a powerful and beautifully directed Hollywood thriller about Bush's so-called war on drugs that opened on April 15 and has been running almost continuously in Chicago ever since. The three movies give compatible, even complementary views of Bush's support of the drug industry—dating back at least as far as his using Noriega as his principal Panamanian contact when he became director of the CIA in 1976, upping Noriega's annual salary to over $100,000, and agreeing to stop monitoring his drug dealing. In fact, one could go directly from THE PANAMA DECEPTION to DEEP COVER, as I recently did, and discover a coherent account of how our freedom-loving government has directly collaborated in the proliferation of crack babies and related fruits of free enterprise.

As far as I can tell, hardly any of DEEP COVER's reviews, press coverage, or advertising (assuming that one can distinguish between the three) has even so much as hinted that the movie is a frontal assault on the hypocrisy of Bush's war on drugs. It's an essential part of that much-celebrated freedom of ours—the freedom that "finished first," and that now theoretically allows the former communist bloc to compete with the United States in the crack market, starvation, and firearms—that we rigorously enforce what we already believe to be true so that we don't run the risk of proving ourselves even slightly wrong. Critics constantly maintain that no one ever goes to movies for political reasons or responds to movies politically, and they write their reviews accordingly. So when a movie like DEEP COVER comes along and clearly strikes a chord in audiences, critics don't notice. It's also part of our received wisdom that no one cares at all whether or not Bush is a mass murderer—that people vote for candidates exclusively on the basis of their own pocketbooks. This means that DEEP COVER must be drawing people in for reasons other than its story or its theme, and that Bush's failing popularity has nothing to do with his foreign policy.

The problem is, given the limits of our allegedly free mass media when it comes to certain matters—the *Washington Post, New York Times, Los Angeles Times,* and *Wall Street Journal* all uncritically supported the absurd government pretexts for invading Panama, and as Trent's movie shows, the United Nations' condemnation of the invasion got ten seconds from Dan Rather on CBS and no mention at all on NBC—how can we evaluate what's going on in the world in the first place? We're landlocked about a good many matters, and often as not we don't even know it. Postmortems like THE PANAMA DECEPTION are certainly helpful in pointing out how we were misled, but because most media events depend on our short attention spans—so that, for instance, Woody Allen was a flawless visionary genius in the spring, has become a pathetic degenerate numbskull this summer, and surely will embody some equally hyperbolic fabrication in the fall—they don't necessarily prepare us for seeing through future media bamboozlements.

Although THE PANAMA DECEPTION does a fair job of showing how the invasion of Panama was systematically misrepresented in the U.S. press, it leaves out one prime instance of obfuscation, based on a mistranslation from Spanish to English, that surely would have enhanced its overall analysis. An official statement in Spanish saying in effect "It's as if we were at war with the United States" was translated without the subjunctive in early media reports and became an alleged (albeit farfetched) declaration of war on the part of Panama, thereby serving to justify the indiscriminate slaughter of civilians more effectively that the bogus claim of "protecting American lives" ever could.

THE PANAMA DECEPTION also makes us acutely aware of the wider problem of evaluating any information we get in the news. Defending the basic integrity of the U.S. press, a friend recently argued that the only possible reason no one except Lynda Edwards in the March 1992 *Spy* ever reported on the two additional sworn testimonies from women about sexual harassment by Clarence Thomas—testimonies that never came up either during the Hill-Thomas hearings or in the press immediately afterward, though they were presumably available at the time—is that the story didn't check out; if it had, my friend said, the *New York Times, Washington Post,* et al. would surely have run it. Why, then, I wondered, couldn't they have run a story showing that the *Spy* story didn't check out? On a recent trip to Europe I discovered that the London *Guardian* had run essentially the same story as *Spy,* and for all I know countless other foreign papers ran it as well. But unless we have access to these overseas reports (and most people don't), we have to depend on what our own press chooses (or chooses not) to shove our way.

Part of what keeps THE PANAMA DECEPTION so watchable is the various styles of lying it offers. Bush, a Pentagon spokesman, an Army general, and a Panamanian government flunky each have a different manner of contradicting the evidence of our eyes and ears (including blocks of ravaged neighborhoods and the eloquent and angry testimonies of many Panamanian civilian victims), though it shouldn't be assumed that none of the military officials we see is candid or forthcoming. (It's Rear Admiral Eugene Carroll who freely admits about the invasion, "The fact that it could cause tremendous peripheral damage, damage to innocent civilians on a wide scale, was not of concern in the planning.") A capsule history of relations between the United States and Panama since the 1800s helps to show that the grim logic behind our present military occupation is nothing new, and a commentator toward the end explains how "the invasion sets the stage for the wars of the twenty-first century." All that seems relatively new about Panama and the Persian Gulf, really, is the degree to which the public's initial understanding of such events can be orchestrated, and Trent's movie is invaluable precisely for showing us the strings of the puppeteers.

■

DEEP COVER is a fable about a black undercover drug agent who calls himself John Hull (Larry Fishburne). The son of a junkie who was killed holding up a liquor store one Christmas, Hull joins the police force determined to put an end to the drug trade, not realizing that it's the police and the government who contrive to keep the drug trade flowing and the kingpins protected. The kingpin in this case proves to be a Latin American politician named Guzman who could easily be mistaken for Bush's pal Noriega before he got uppity; we learn that Guzman "goes fishing with George fucking Bush" and "is a friend of our president" (for the record, Noriega is mentioned directly in the dialogue as well). Hull is appalled to discover that he has to disobey his white boss (Charles Martin Smith) and get fired in order to go after this creep.

I've been told that when Michael Tolkin (THE RAPTURE, THE PLAYER) wrote or cowrote the original version of the script, the hero was white, but the studio that financed the deal got either him or someone else—perhaps cowriter and coproducer Henry Bean—to make the character black, then dropped the project altogether when NEW JACK CITY came out and became associated with ghetto violence. The new script got picked up by New Line Cinema. The movie is a telling case of how sometimes the best results can grow out of the most incoherent or arbitrary deliberations.

I'm not sure when Bill Duke—the talented black actor who previously directed A RAGE IN HARLEM and the television film THE KILLING FLOOR—got assigned to direct this, but there's no question that his remarkable feeling for editing and acting rhythms does as much for this movie as the punchy vernacular dialogue and the moral force of the plot. A good example of Duke's editing rhythm is his use of staccato jump cuts, including what appear to be forward zooms broken up by skip framing, or eliminating every other frame—a rhythm that suggests a needle skipping across a record and that perfectly captures the panicky Los Angeles drug milieu the hero penetrates. In direct contrast to this druggy, hyperactive editing is Fishburne's manner of registering dramatic points by calmly raising or lowering his eyes, motions that come across as cool fluctuations in the center of a hurricane.

Other riffs in the movie include the hero's narration, which approximates at times a kind of rap poetry; the structure of the plot, which pointedly uses blood-soaked paper money as a motif and has the hero oscillating between his boss and his drug partners; and the implications of the hero's impersonation of a drug dealer, which recalls a memorable line from Kurt Vonnegut's *Mother Night*: "We are what we pretend to be, so we must be careful about what we pretend to be." (His undercover identity has a kind of dialectical irony worthy of Bush himself, and one that the script milks at every opportunity. "Undercover, all your faults will become virtues," the hero's boss tells him at the onset of his adventures; much later, the hero mordantly remarks off-screen that although he used to be a cop pretending to be a drug dealer, now he's a drug dealer pretending to be a cop.)

I can't claim that DEEP COVER is a masterpiece. There's an uncertainly conceived subplot involving an implausibly synthesized "designer drug," and the religious beliefs of another black cop, evoking some of Tolkin's preoccupations in THE RAPTURE, are shoehorned awkwardly into the proceedings. The denouement is neatly brought off, but it mixes in so many fanciful Hollywood wish fulfillments that it ultimately mars—or at least needlessly complicates—the singular bitterness and lucidity of the closing scene.

Duke's corrosive direction of the violence, however, and the sheer stench given off by Jeff Goldblum's uncharacteristically slimy performance as a jumpy Jewish lawyer-gangster are as striking as anything I've seen in an American movie this year. And the moral and political force of DEEP COVER's statement is so clear that I suspect only a film critic could fail to recognize it; to all appearances, sizable portions of the public have already found their way to this movie's truth without benefit of media "experts"—mainly, it would seem, through word of mouth. In other words, a significant part of the public has already voted against Bush's euphoria; whether they'll carry this insight all the way to the polls is of course another matter.

—Chicago Reader, 28 August 1992

A Cinema of Uncertainty

Films by Michelangelo Antonioni

> Jean-Luc Godard: The drama is no longer
> psychological, but plastic . . .
> Michelangelo Antonioni: It's the same thing.
>
> *—from a 1964 interview*

Just for my own edification, I've put together a list of the twelve greatest living narrative filmmakers—not so much personal favorites as individuals who, in my estimation, have done the most to change the way we perceive the world and are likeliest to be remembered and valued half a century from now. The names I've come up with are Michelangelo Antonioni, Ingmar Bergman, Robert Bresson, Federico Fellini, Samuel Fuller, Jean-Luc Godard, Hou Hsiao-hsien, Stanley Kubrick, Akira Kurosawa, Nagisa Oshima, Alain Resnais, and Ousmane Sembene.

Only five have had their most recent feature distributed in the United States—Bergman, Bresson, Kubrick, Kurosawa, and Sembene. Fellini may have recently earned a special Oscar, but that doesn't mean we can expect to see his latest film anytime soon, and though Godard's next-to-last feature, NOUVELLE VAGUE, has finally come out on video, that doesn't mean we can expect to see it properly, on a big screen.

We can, however, see nearly all of Antonioni's work—fourteen of his fifteen feature films and most of the dozen or so shorts—in brand-new prints at the Film Center this month and next. (The missing feature is THE PASSENGER, of 1975, which Jack Nicholson, the film's star, owns the American rights to and is withholding from this retrospective for mysterious reasons of his own. It's available on video only with the image cropped and in incomplete form.)

All things considered, this is the most important retrospective to have come to Chicago during the five and a half years I've lived here, and for those unfamiliar with most of Antonioni's work—probably most people—it provides the opportunity for some major, mind-bending discoveries. Although it's regrettable that the films are being shown out of strict chronological

307

sequence because of print availability—L'AVVENTURA won't turn up until next month, many weeks after its immediate successors, LA NOTTE and ECLIPSE, have shown—this is not as serious an impediment to the understanding of the work as it would be with a filmmaker like Godard.

Whatever one thinks of Fellini, it seems to me inarguable that Antonioni is far and away the greatest living Italian filmmaker; indeed, with the exception of Roberto Rossellini, he is probably the greatest of all Italian filmmakers. Although he is hardly known at all to younger viewers, that's not because his films—made between the late 1940s and the early 1980s—have dated in any significant way; it points, rather, to the fact that the critical community and most of the rest of world cinema have regressed to the point where they can no longer even remember why such a fuss was made over Antonioni in the 1960s—or even that there *was* a fuss. Because of the basic challenges his work has posed from the beginning—challenges to our notions about storytelling, realism (including Italian neorealism), drama, society, the modern world, and reality itself—he has been more consistently misunderstood and attacked than any other modern filmmaker of comparable importance. (The only time audiences truly kept abreast of him was during his period of popularity in the 1960s.)

Moreover, the supplementary tools at our disposal for clearing the air are far from ideal. There are only two book-length critical studies of Antonioni in English in circulation; one of these is highly problematic and the other is first-rate, but it's the problematic one—Seymour Chatman's *Antonioni, or the Surface of the World* (1985)—that is most readily available. (The other one is Sam Rohdie's *Antonioni,* published in 1990 by the British Film Institute, and it's well worth hunting down.)

The period when Antonioni was fashionable—though he certainly remained controversial even then—stretches from the 1960 premiere of L'AVVENTURA at Cannes to the catastrophic release of ZABRISKIE POINT in 1969. Undoubtedly his commercial success peaked with BLOWUP in 1966, but perhaps the most significant indication of his reputation during this period was *Sight and Sound*'s top-ten survey—a poll of international critics conducted every ten years since 1952. The Winter 1961/1962 survey placed L'AVVENTURA in the number-two slot, right below CITIZEN KANE. L'AVVENTURA slipped down to fifth place in 1972, then seventh place in 1982, and finally went off the list entirely last year. (Perhaps significantly, the only other time the critics had given a recent film comparable standing in this poll was 1952, when THE BICYCLE THIEF, made in 1949, scored first place; curiously, CITIZEN KANE, first in all four polls since 1962, didn't place at all in 1952.)

The degree to which Antonioni remained in intellectual vogue in the United States during this period fluctuated wildly. The original defenders of L'AVVENTURA were mainly literary types like Dwight Macdonald and John Simon, both of whom turned against ECLIPSE only a year or so later, as did a rising star named Pauline Kael (who had also championed L'AVVENTURA). Andrew Sarris, who later came back in force to defend BLOWUP, was already cracking jokes about "Antoniennui" in the early 1960s. Many American critics tended to be scornful of Antonioni's continuing use of Monica Vitti (in four features in a row) because of her limited technical range as an actress, much as Godard was criticized concurrently for repeatedly using Anna Karina. And the fact that Antonioni's concentration on the idle rich in L'AVVENTURA and LA NOTTE coincided with the milieus of such contemporaneous movies as LA DOLCE VITA and LAST YEAR AT MARIENBAD was enough to make Kael ignore the radical formal differences between Fellini, Resnais, and Antonioni and link them all together in an otherwise amusing broadside called "The Come-Dressed-as-the-Sick-Soul-of-Europe Parties."

The problem was, many of these people were already starting to adopt a critical attitude that assumed it was possible to know immediately and without a doubt what was good and bad in a movie the precise moment it appeared—an attitude that Kael's disciples have subsequently adopted with even more shrillness and impatience. Intricate, melancholic mood pieces like Antonioni's, which invite and reward—and occasionally even require—weeks of mulling over, could find no place at all within this approach, so fewer and fewer critics wound up dealing with them, seriously or otherwise. Better to come up with a clever quip about them right away than continue to think about them for a week or two, or even revise an opinion about them when the review got reprinted (which Kael has never done about a single movie in any of her eleven books—confidence with a vengeance, and one that necessarily rules out a whole cinema of uncertainty). In a marketplace virtually predicated on planned obsolescence, movies that stick in one's craw rather than speed through the digestive system are bound to cause trouble.

■

Born to a middle-class family in 1913 in Ferrara, a small provincial capital in northeast Italy near the Po River, Antonioni didn't shoot his first feature until his midthirties. He studied business and economics at the University of Bologna, worked in a bank, flirted with playing professional tennis, and became interested in cinema during the last decade of Italian fascism. Starting out as a film critic and short-story writer for his hometown newspaper, and displaying a taste for atmosphere rather than plot or character, he made a few abortive stabs at filmmaking before moving in 1940 to Rome, where he contributed articles to several film journals.

Although the prevailing aesthetics of his colleagues at the time were realist, populist, and socially committed, Antonioni was more interested in formal experimentation. As Rohdie and other critics have pointed out, it wasn't that he didn't share the preoccupations that would eventually blossom into Italian neorealism; it's just that he came at them from a different angle.

This difference can already be felt in his early short documentaries, mostly made during the late 1940s, but it becomes decisive in his first feature, CRONACA DI UN AMORE (STORY OF A LOVE AFFAIR, 1950), which broke with the popular perception of neorealism not only in its attention to form but in its choice of an upper-class milieu—a milieu that he stuck to for most of the remainder of his career. Only IL GRIDO (THE CRY), made in 1957, is situated squarely in a working-class environment, and Antonioni himself has said, "I prefer to set my heroes in a rich environment because then their feelings are not (as in the poorer classes) determined by material and practical contingencies."

One good example of Antonioni's distinctive version of neorealism is his sketch TENTATO SUICIDIO (SUICIDE ATTEMPT), his remarkable contribution to the 1953 neorealist feature L'AMORE IN CITTÀ (LOVE IN THE CITY), made the same year he turned forty and after he already had three features under his belt. A number of men and women who have attempted to commit suicide (as we learn from the male off-screen narrator) are seen filing into the bare white confines of a film studio and are framed in various clusters. Then the stories of a few women among them are recounted, both by the narrator and by the women themselves, most often in the original settings where these attempts took place, with the narrator often asking questions and the women, in the process of answering, restaging certain portions of what originally happened.

In the second story, the camera itself partially "restages" a woman's trying to drown herself in the Tiber by moving toward the center of the river and then lingering on the choppy surface of the water around the base of a bridge while she narrates off-screen—not exactly point-of-view shots, yet images that clearly imply *someone's* subjectivity. In the final story, a young aspiring actress lying on her bed describes slitting her wrist and rather unconvincingly re-creates the gesture with a razor before suddenly showing the camera the actual scar on her wrist; then she continues to describe what happened, in the past tense.

For critics like Chatman, who echoes the objections of many of Antonioni's contemporaries, such procedures qualify only as failed neorealism: the aspiring actress, for instance, is "suspiciously photogenic" and "one could perversely imagine her attempting suicide just to get into Antonioni's movie. . . . No real effort is made to find out what lies under the surface." But it might be argued that for Antonioni, the mysteries he is investigating exist precisely *in* surfaces—the recitations and actions of these women, the settings, even the ugly scar revealed on a woman's wrist. We quickly perceive that the original suicide attempts themselves may have been partially feigned—staged gestures designed to produce certain effects—and that their restaging can only compound our uncertainties rather than dissipate them. The fact that the narrator remains unseen further foments our doubts and suspicions without confirming any of them. Chatman's self-admittedly perverse imagination is not shared by Antonioni. The filmmaker is not interested in "penetrating" artificiality to "get at" the truth—as Chatman, with his comic-book version of the neorealist aesthetic, would have him do. In the context of this sketch, it would constitute a violation of the women involved.

Antonioni is interested, rather, in the truth of not knowing, the truth of surfaces, the truth of reality and falsity alike. Agnostic toward what is commonly labeled "reality," he is ultimately more interested in posing the right questions than in coming up with easy answers, and in this respect he becomes the blood brother of a true neorealist like Rossellini. The Italian title of THE PASSENGER, one should note, is PROFESSIONE: REPORTER. If we consider Antonioni an investigative journalist in all of his features, he is one with a painter's eye, a choreographer's sense of movement and rhythm, and a metaphysical imagination—a journalist whose questions never stop.

■

Indeed, many of Antonioni's features—CRONACA DI UN AMORE, LE AMICHE (THE GIRLFRIENDS), L'AVVENTURA, BLOWUP, THE PASSENGER, IDENTIFICATION OF A WOMAN—resemble detective stories for long stretches. But especially in the case of the last four, their mysteries are not solved but eventually displaced by other mysteries. The pivotal narrative event in L'AVVENTURA is the sudden disappearance of Anna (Lea Massari) from a volcanic Sicilian island during a pleasure cruise she is taking with her lover Sandro (Gabriele Ferzetti), her best friend Claudia (Monica Vitti), and a few others. Her affair with Sandro, a once-idealistic architect who has become more concerned with money than creativity, has not been going well, and her earlier behavior leads us to suspect that she has either committed suicide or escaped from the island on a passing fishing boat as a malicious prank. (Interestingly, until Anna disappears, the island itself is simply a picturesque setting for a yachting party. But once Sandro and Claudia begin to search for Anna, covering and recovering the same areas, it comes alive with clues and potential meanings, as if a character in its own right.)

Following a trail of leads back on the mainland, Sandro and Claudia travel together from town to town in search of Anna, and embark on an affair of their own in the course of their investigation. Much of what they encounter on their journey expands the thematic scope of the film—with reference to eroticism, love, and lost ideals—but none of it solves the mystery of Anna's disappearance. Our growing suspicion that the movie isn't "going anywhere," that it's constantly in danger of collapsing into random incidents, corresponds precisely to the characters' doubts—emotional, ethical, and existential—about their own experiences. The slow pacing central to Antonioni's masterful establishment of mood and atmosphere grants us ample space in which to wander and worry, just like Claudia and Sandro. At the same time, the sheer and constant beauty of Antonioni's framing, his choreography of camera and actors, his musical sense of duration and editing, and his sculptural sense of space all leave powerful and lingering after-effects. In contrast, aesthetically empty movies usually satisfy our narrative needs and leave us with nothing after they're over—except room for more of the same.

Still, given the unsettling displacement of our narrative expectations, which occurs in different forms in the other films, it's not difficult to understand why Antonioni's films can provoke anger. It's rather as if CITIZEN KANE concluded without telling us what Rosebud meant—and significantly, perhaps no other filmmaker ever expressed more irritation with Antonioni's methods than Orson Welles, whose similarities with Antonioni in terms of deep-focus and mobile mise en scène and black-and-white chiaroscuro are offset by radical differences in his approaches to actors and various theatrical elements. (For all his profound links with architecture, sculpture, painting, music, dance, and the novel, Antonioni has virtually no relation at all to theater, and he isn't even remotely a director of actors in the sense that Welles was. For him, actors are Jamesian "figures in the carpet," not fellow weavers.)

But Antonioni's thwarting of narrative conventions fails to account for the fury of the American responses to ZABRISKIE POINT, the Chinese responses to his documentary CHINA (which inspired Umberto Eco's essay "The Difficulty of Being Marco Polo"), or Vincent Canby's review of IDENTIFICATION OF A WOMAN in *The New York Times,* which virtually terminated Antonioni's career a little over a decade ago. (A subsequent stroke has rendered Antonioni paralyzed, so the odds of his working again are practically nil, though I'm told that he remains alert: he was present at symposia on his work accompanying this touring retrospective held in New York and Los Angeles.) The reasons his work as a whole poses profound threats to any number of ideologies is too vast a subject to be broached here, but brief considerations of the first and last of these "disasters" may offer a few helpful clues.

ZABRISKIE POINT, Antonioni's only American feature, came on the heels of his biggest success, BLOWUP, a movie that put sexy, "swinging London" on the map even more decisively than either DARLING or A HARD DAY'S NIGHT did. Evidently expecting Antonioni to similarly glamorize radical youth in the United States, MGM was disappointed with the spectacular and fanciful poetic fable that resulted, as was almost everyone else. Intellectuals and ordinary spectators, radicals and conservatives, and everyone else in between—including the romantic leads—denounced the movie in no uncertain terms. But today it's clear that the film has aged a lot better than its detractors. Perhaps because Antonioni regarded "America" as a natural site for iconographic fantasies, he worked more expressionistically and less realistically than he had in any of his Italian movies, including even the color experiments in RED DESERT, and he did at least as much with billboards as any of the best pop art. And in the final, apocalyptic sequence—a dream of destruction in which a striking desert ranch house repeatedly explodes, raining down a profusion of consumer products that add up to an astonishing catalog of the modern world—

Antonioni created what is surely one of the most powerful and beautiful images of his career. (It's the precise antithesis of the lovely fantasy sequence near the end of RED DESERT—a peaceful, utopian story recounted by the neurotic heroine to her little boy about a girl and the sea.)

For all its beauty, IDENTIFICATION OF A WOMAN (1982) is probably not one of Antonioni's best films, though it's still one of the great Italian films of the past decade. It represents such a departure in terms of its studio filmmaking style and its theme (the personal life of a filmmaker) that when I saw it at the New York Film Festival over ten years ago I found it difficult to come to terms with (even while I found myself passionately defending it for its highly erotic handling of female sexuality and its distinctive view of life in contemporary Italy). It's certainly every bit as mysterious and enigmatic as his previous work, but by 1982 the lack of instant certainty that is the staple of today's reviewing, especially on television, was becoming harder and harder to defend.

Prior to its festival premiere, the film had found a small U.S. distributor and tickets to its screenings were sold out. Then came Canby's review, which suggested that "Mr. Antonioni" make a careful study of the films of Woody Allen so that he could learn to be less pretentious, and immediately afterward hundreds of tickets were returned to the festival box office and the distributor promptly dropped the film. The movie was never released in the United States, and thanks in part to this loss of potential revenue, Antonioni was never able to finance another feature, though he had many projects. The biggest irony of all came when Woody Allen—who'd paid extended homage to Antonioni in an episode of EVERYTHING YOU ALWAYS WANTED TO KNOW ABOUT SEX . . . BUT WERE AFRAID TO ASK ten years earlier—hired Carlo Di Palma, who shot IDENTIFICATION OF A WOMAN (as well as previous Antonioni pictures in color), for many of his own pictures.

I don't mean to imply that Canby's imbecilic review—written four years after unpretentious Woody's INTERIORS—was responsible for ending Antonioni's career. I'd place most of that blame on the shoulders of Canby's hip New York audience (including distributors), who were so fearful of having to make up their own minds that they forfeited that privilege for audiences everywhere else. (With our tacit consent and approval, they're still doing it to other pictures, too.)

■

In all fairness, one can't accuse Antonioni's pictures of fostering uncertainty about *everything*. The stories and even the characters and their identities may eventually start to dissolve, forcing us to reconsider various elements in the pictures that we have taken for granted, but the sheer persistence of certain locations is so strong that it calls to mind a famous line from a poem by Stéphane Mallarmé: "Nothing will have taken place but the place." These locations haunt our memories like sites with highly personal associations from our own pasts. A few examples among many would include the English parks where corpses are discovered in both I VINTI (1952) and BLOWUP, an abandoned set of newly constructed buildings in the middle of nowhere in L'AVVENTURA that suggest Giorgio De Chirico's surrealist paintings, and a marshy industrial wasteland bordering a factory—presented as surprisingly beautiful in certain shots—in RED DESERT (1964).

The aforementioned apocalypse at the end of ZABRISKIE POINT is only one of three extraordinary codas in Antonioni's work, each involving a startling rupture in style and narrative, while at the same time centering on the spell cast by a specific location as dusk approaches. At the end of THE PASSEN-GER—a film that, like BLOWUP, is much better in handling physical environments than in grappling with literary conceits—the hero's mysterious death on a motel bed in rural Spain occurs off-screen; the camera has momentarily turned away from him and drifted out the window to contemplate the seemingly everyday comings and goings of people in a village square. As in the sequence at the end of ZABRISKIE POINT—and in the majority of other great moments in Antonioni's cinema, for that matter—the absence of dialogue helps a lot. Antonioni's selective use of sound and choreographed images tend to be a lot more potent and intuitive than his words. Unfortunately, it's only the latter that can get quoted in reviews; the charges of pretentiousness lodged against Antonioni nearly always derive from this disproportionate emphasis.

In the final scene of ECLIPSE (1962)—my favorite Antonioni feature, and the one that concludes the loose trilogy started by L'AVVENTURA and LA NOTTE—a lingering over an urban street corner while night begins to fall, effected through montage rather than an extended take, becomes one of the most terrifying poems in modern cinema simply through its complex poetry of absence. The lead couple in this film, played by Alain Delon and Monica Vitti, have previously planned to meet at this corner, in front of a building site. (Another building site figures in the opening sequence of L'AVVENTURA.) The unexplained fact that neither character shows up is perturbing, but because their affair has been more frivolous that serious, it hardly accounts for the overall feeling of desolation and even terror in this sequence.

It's almost as if Antonioni has extracted the essence of the everyday street life that serves as background throughout the picture, and once we're presented with this essence in its undiluted form, it suddenly threatens and oppresses us. The implication here (and in every Antonioni narrative) is that behind every story there's a place and an absence, a mystery and a profound uncertainty, waiting like a vampire at every moment to emerge and take over, to stop the story dead in its tracks. And if we combine this place and absence, this mystery and uncertainty into a single, irreducible entity, what we have is the modern world itself—the place where all of us live, and which most stories are designed to protect us from.

—Chicago Reader, 9 April 1993

Bibliography

The following list of articles and reviews, given in chronological order of publication, is far from exhaustive. It merely consists of a selective (and subjective) choice of my best critical pieces up through July 1993 not included in this collection; in a few cases I have indicated only portions of some pieces, but capsule reviews and letters are omitted, as are pieces printed, reprinted, or excerpted in my books *Moving Places* or *Film: The Front Line 1983*. Entries that have been reprinted in other books are preceded by an asterisk.

The following abbreviations are used: *CR* = *Chicago Reader, FC* = *Film Comment, MFB* = *Monthly Film Bulletin, S&S* = *Sight and Sound, SN* = *Soho News, VV* = *Village Voice*.

1. Review of Andrew Sarris's *The American Cinema: Directors and Directions 1929–1968, Film Society Review* 4, no. 5 (January 1969): 41–44.
2. "Moviegoing at Cannes: Classics without Labels" (on CITY LIGHTS, FOUR NIGHTS OF A DREAMER, BROTHER CARL, PUNISHMENT PARK, HOW TASTY WAS MY LITTLE FRENCHMAN, and Portabella's VAMPYR), *VV* (17 June 1971).
3. "Show Business in the End" (on GLEN AND RANDA), *VV* (21 October 1971).
4. "Paris Journal" (on *Cahiers du Cinéma* and *Positif, publicité* films, PEAU D'ANE, Jean-Daniel Pollet, LA FAUTE DE L'ABBÉ MOURET, TRAFIC, and L'AMOUR FOU), *FC* (Fall 1971): 2, 4, 6, 68. See also letter and reply in *FC* (Spring 1972): 74–75.
5. "Paris Journal" (on PLAYTIME), *FC* (Winter 1971–1972): 2, 4, 6.
*6. Review of Pauline Kael's "Raising Kane," *FC* (Spring 1972): 70–73. See also corrections in *FC* (Summer 1972): 80. To be reprinted in *Critical Essays on "Citizen Kane,"* ed. Harry M. Geduld and Ronald Gottesman (New York: G. K. Hall & Co., forthcoming).
*7. "Paris Journal" (on L'AMOUR FOU, PARK ROW, and Yasujiro Ozu), *FC* (Summer 1972): 2, 4, 6. Ozu section reprinted in *Yasujiro Ozu: A Critical Anthology,* ed. John Gillett and David Wilson (London: British Film Institute, 1976), 32–34.

8. "Surprises at Cannes: Huston Redeemed, Tashlin Reincarnated" (on FAT CITY; KING, QUEEN, KNAVE; SUMMER SOLDIERS; UMBRACLE; and WINTER SOLDIER), *VV* (29 June 1972).

9. "Portabella at the NFT—A New Vision from Spain," *Time Out* (22–28 September 1972): 45.

10. Review of REMINISCENCES OF A JOURNEY TO LITHUANIA, *VV* (2 November 1972).

11. "The Voice and the Eye: A Commentary on [Orson Welles's] HEART OF DARKNESS Script," published with the script's introductory sequence, *FC* (November–December 1972): 24–32. See also p. 72 for additional material from Welles interview and correction in *FC* (January–February 1973): 71.

*12. "Interruption as Style: LE CHARME DISCRET DE LA BOURGEOISIE," *S&S* (Winter 1972/ 1973): 2–4. Reprinted in *Foreign Affairs,* ed. Kathy Huffhines (San Francisco: Mercury House, 1991), 102–107.

13. Review of *Gravity's Rainbow, VV* (29 March 1973).

14. Notes on LA NUIT DU CARREFOUR in "Paris Journal," *FC* (May–June 1973): 4.

15. "Tati's Democracy" (interview), *FC* (May–June 1973): 36–41.

16. "Raymond Durgnat," published with responses from Durgnat, *FC* (May–June 1973): 65–69.

17. "Cannes Journal" (on LA MAMAN ET LA PUTAIN, DEAD PIGEON ON BEETHOVEN STREET, SOME CALL IT LOVING, WHO IS BETA?, A PAGE OF MADNESS, etc.), *FC* (September–October 1973): 2, 4, 62, 64.

*18. "Circle of Pain: The Cinema of Nicholas Ray," *S&S* (Autumn 1973): 218–221. Reprinted in modified form in *Cinema: A Critical Dictionary,* ed. Richard Roud (New York: Viking Press, 1980), vol. 2, 807–812.

19. Notes on Leo McCarey in "Paris Journal," *FC* (November–December 1973): 4, 6.

20. Review of F FOR FAKE in "Paris Journal," *FC* (January–February 1974): 58, 61.

21. "Paris Journal" (interview with Alain Resnais on the set of STAVISKY), *FC* (March–April 1974): 2, 4, 6.

22. "Rencontre avec Jim McBride" & "Introduction à Jim McBride," *Positif,* no. 158 (April 1974): 37–43.

23. Review of LACOMBE, LUCIEN in "Paris Journal," *FC* (May–June 1974): 63.

*24. "Second Thoughts on Stroheim," *FC* (May–June 1974): 6–13. Reprinted in *Passport to Hollywood: Film Immigrants Anthology,* ed. Don Whittemore and Philip Alan Cecchettini (New York: McGraw-Hill, 1976), 130–145; reprinted in modified form in *Cinema: A Critical Dictionary,* vol. 2, 973–987.

25. On LANCELOT DU LAC, *S&S* (Summer 1974): 128–130.

26. "Phantom Interviewers over Rivette" (with Lauren Sedofsky and Gilbert Adair), *FC* (September–October 1974): 18–24.

27. Reviews of JUGGERNAUT, BLACKMAIL, and TONI, *MFB,* no. 489 (October 1974): 224–225, 234, 236–237.

28. Review of Dwight Macdonald's *Discriminations, VV* (10 October 1974).

29. Reviews of BADLANDS and THE NIGHT PORTER, *MFB,* no. 490 (November 1974): 245–246, 255–256.

30. Review of Gore Vidal's *Myron, VV* (14 November 1974).

31. Review of CALIFORNIA SPLIT, *MFB,* no. 491 (December 1974): 269–270.

32. Review of LA MAMAN ET LA PUTAIN, *S&S* (Winter 1974/1975): 55.

33. Review of Noël Burch's *Theory of Film Practice, S&S* (Winter 1974/1975): 60–61.

34. "Dream Masters I: Walt Disney" & "Dream Masters II: Tex Avery," *FC* (January–February 1975): 64–71. Unsatisfactory, much-condensed versions of both articles appear in *Cinema: A Critical Dictionary,* vol. 1.

*35. Review of THE LIFE OF OHARU, *MFB,* no. 494 (March 1975): 66. Reprinted in *Foreign Affairs,* pp. 84–87.

36. Review of I WAS BORN, BUT . . . , *MFB*, no. 494 (March 1975): 68.
37. "Improvisations and Interactions in Altmanville," *S&S* (Spring 1975): 90–95.
38. Reviews of LOVIN' MOLLY and LA SIGNORA SENZA CAMELIE, *MFB*, no. 496 (May 1975): 110–111, 120–121.
39. Review of THE PASSENGER, *MFB*, no. 497 (June 1975): 143–144.
40. Review of LETTER TO JANE, *MFB*, no. 498 (July 1975): 157.
41. "Richie's Ozu: Our Prehistoric Present," *S&S* (Summer 1975): 175–179.
42. Reviews of JACQUELINE SUSANN'S ONCE IS NOT ENOUGH and NUMBER SEVENTEEN, *MFB*, no. 499 (August 1975): 176–177, 186–187.
43. "London Journal" (on NASHVILLE and F FOR FAKE; interview with Geraldine Chaplin), *FC* (September–October 1975): 4, 70.
44. "LES FILLES DU FEU: Rivette X 4" (on the shooting of DUELLE and NOROÎT, with Gilbert Adair and Michael Graham), *S&S* (Autumn 1975): 234–239.
*45. Review of NASHVILLE, *S&S* (Autumn 1975): 254–255. Reprinted in *Sight and Sound: A Fiftieth Anniversary Selection,* ed. David Wilson (London: Faber and Faber, 1982), 261–265.
46. Review of SOME CALL IT LOVING, *S&S* (Autumn 1975): 256–257.
47. Review of FOX AND HIS FRIENDS, *MFB*, no. 504 (January 1976): 6.
48. Review of THE HOMECOMING, *MFB*, no. 505 (February 1976): 29–30.
49. Reviews of THE MAIDS, NOT RECONCILED, and WHAT'S UP, TIGER LILY?, *MFB*, no. 506 (March 1976): 57, 60, 65–66.
50. Review of NUMÉRO DEUX, *S&S* (Spring 1976): 124–125.
51. Reviews of HOT TIMES, THE MAN WHO FELL TO EARTH, and RENDEZVOUS AT BRAY, *MFB*, no. 507 (April 1976): 83, 86–88.
52. Review of SPIONE, *MFB*, no. 508 (May 1976): 112.
53. Review of four books on Jean Renoir, *FC* (May–June 1976): 60–61.
54. Review of FAMILY PLOT, *S&S* (Summer 1976): 188–189.
55. Reviews of jazz films and THE RING, *MFB*, no. 510 (July 1976): 148, 156–159.
56. "DUELLE: Notes on a First Viewing," *FC* (September–October 1976): 27–29.
57. "Afterword" (reply to Lucy Fischer's "'Beyond Freedom and Dignity': An Analysis of Jacques Tati's PLAYTIME") & review of THE TENANT, *S&S* (Autumn 1976): 239, 253.
58. "Regrouping: Reflections on the Edinburgh Festival 1976," *S&S* (Winter 1976/1977): 2–8.
59. Review of NOROÎT, *S&S* (Winter 1976/1977): 59–60.
60. Editor's Introduction, *Rivette: Texts and Interviews* (London: British Film Institute, 1977), 1–8.
*61. "The Solitary Pleasures of STAR WARS," *S&S* (Autumn 1977): 208–209. Reprinted in *The Broadview Reader,* ed. Herbert Rosengarten and Jane Flick (Peterborough, Canada: Broadview Press, 1987), 192–196.
62. "Film Writing Degree Zero: The Marketplace and the University" (on two anthologies, Richard Koszarski's *Hollywood Directors 1914–1940* and Bill Nichols's *Movies and Methods*), *S&S* (Autumn 1977): 248–251.
63. "A la recherche de Luc Moullet," *FC* (November–December 1977): 50–55.
64. "Obscure Objects of Desire: A Jam Session on Nonnarrative" (with Raymond Durgnat and David Ehrenstein), *FC* (July–August 1978).
65. "Sound Thinking," *FC* (September–October 1978): 38–41.
*66. Review of THE DEER HUNTER, *Take One* 7, no. 4 (March 1979): 9–10. Reprinted in slightly abridged form in *Love and Hisses,* ed. Peter Rainer (San Francisco: Mercury House, 1992): 484–487.
67. Review of REMEMBER MY NAME, *Film Quarterly* (Spring 1979): 55–58.
68. "Getting Personal in Milwaukee," *American Film* (September 1979): 16, 66–67.

69. "Cinema Via Videotape," *American Film* (November 1979): 23–24.
70. "Venetian Panels," *American Film* (December 1979): 14–15, 76.
71. Entries on John Boorman, Paul Fejos, Elia Kazan, Norman McLaren, Otto Preminger, and Yulia Solntseva, in *Cinema: A Critical Dictionary*, vol. 1, 135, 339–340, 536–542; vol. 2, 654–655, 794–799, 941.
72. Review of Graham Greene's *Doctor Fischer of Geneva, or the Bomb Party, SN* (14 May 1980).
73. On shopping malls, *Omni* (July 1980): 28.
74. "Sam Fuller Reshoots the War" (interview), *SN* (9 July 1980).
75. "A Fond Madness" (on *Mad*), *SN* (16 July 1980).
76. Review of John Kennedy Toole's *A Confederacy of Dunces, SN* (27 August 1980).
77. Review of Sirk's early German films, *SN* (27 August 1980).
78. "Bringing Godard Back Home" (interview), *SN* (30 September 1980).
79. "Hollywood or Bust," *SN* (8 October 1980).
80. Review of Susan Sontag's *Under the Sign of Saturn, SN* (12 November 1980).
81. Review of Vladimir Nabokov's *Lectures on Literature, SN* (26 November 1980).
82. On Louis Hock, *Omni* (December 1980): 34, 146.
83. "Speaking with Alain Resnais," *SN* (23 December 1980).
84. "Vietnam Dispatches," *The Movie* [London], no. 82 (1981): 1621–1624.
85. "Cinema at a Distance" (interview with Peter Gidal), *SN* (14 January 1981).
86. Review of Mary McCarthy's *Ideas and the Novel, SN* (4 February 1981).
87. Review of ICI ET AILLEURS, *SN* (18 February 1981).
88. "The PRESENTS of Michael Snow" (interview), *FC* (May–June 1981): 35–38.
89. Review of Roland Barthes's *Camera Lucida* and Italo Calvino's *If on a Winter's Night a Traveler, SN* (18 August 1981).
90. Review of COMIN'AT YA!, *SN* (8 September 1981).
91. "Playing Oneself" (on LIGHTNING OVER WATER and MY DINNER WITH ANDRÉ), *SN* (27 October 1981).
92. "Old Wave Saved from Drowning" (with Sandy Flitterman), *American Film* (November 1981): 67, 70–74.
93. Review of David Bordwell's *The Films of Carl Theodor Dreyer, FC* (November–December 1981): 77–79.
94. "Nick's Kicks" (on Nicholas Ray retrospective), *SN* (24 November 1981).
95. "Looking for Nicholas Ray," *American Film* (December 1981): 55–56, 72–76.
96. Review of LONESOME, *The Movie* [London], no. 117 (1982): 2328–2329.
•97. "Course File: Experimental Film: From UN CHIEN ANDALOU to Chantal Akerman," *AFI Education Newsletter* (January–February 1982): 4–7. Reprinted in *College Course Files,* University Film and Video Association Monograph no. 5 (1986): 78–82.
98. "Jack Reed's Christmas Puppy: Reflections on REDS," *S&S* (Spring 1982): 110–113.
99. Review of books on the Hollywood musical, *Film Quarterly* (Summer 1982): 34–36.
100. Review of William S. Pechter's *Movies Plus One, FC* (July–August 1982): 78–79.
101. "Tournage de THE THING: Méfiez-vous des imitations," *Cahiers du Cinéma*, no. 339 (September 1982): 24–26.
102. "Introduction: Once It Was Fire . . ." & "Transcendental Cuisine," in *The Cinema of Jean-Marie Straub and Danièle Huillet*, ed. Jonathan Rosenbaum (New York: Film at the Public, 2–14 November 1982), 2–4, 17–18. Latter piece reprinted in truncated form in *Film: The Front Line 1983.*
103. On the Toronto Festival of Festivals, *Artforum* (December 1982): 85–86.
104. Program notes on THE TIGER OF ESCHNAPUR and THE INDIAN TOMB, *Film Forum* 1 (14–27 September 1983).
105. On Manuel De Landa, *Omni* (December 1983): 36, 164.

106. "Rotterdam," *S&S* (Spring 1984): 83.
107. "Avant-Garde in the 1980s," *S&S* (Spring 1984): 130–133.
108. "Split Images" (on Rotterdam Film Festival), *FC* (June 1984): 65–67.
109. Review of REAR WINDOW, *Video Movies* (June 1984): 9–10.
110. On Cornell Woolrich adaptations, *FC* (October 1984).
111. Review of Rudolph Wurlitzer's *Slow Fade, Los Angeles Reader* (14 December 1984).
112. "Rotterdam," *S&S* (Spring 1985): 80–81.
113. Review of 1984, *Video Times* (June 1985): 37.
114. "How to Live in Air Conditioning," *S&S* (Summer 1985): 162–168.
115. "Thinking about (Personal) History Lessons: The Movie Paintings of Manny Farber," *New Observations*, no. 36 (1985): 2–7.
116. Review of GREMLINS, *Video Times* (December 1985): 93.
117. "The Invisible Orson Welles: A First Inventory," *S&S* (Summer 1986): 164–171.
118. Review of books on Orson Welles, *Film Quarterly* (Fall 1986): 26–30.
119. "Pour quitter quelque chose" (interview with Jim Jarmusch), *Cahiers du Cinéma*, no. 389 (November 1986): 50–52.
120. Response to Robin Bates (on CITIZEN KANE), *Cinema Journal* 26, no. 4 (Summer 1987): 60–64.
*121. Review of THE HORSE THIEF, *CR* (18 September 1987). Reprinted in *Foreign Affairs*, pp. 369–373.
*122. Review of FATAL ATTRACTION, *CR* (2 October 1987). Reprinted (slightly abridged) in *They Went Thataway*, ed. Richard T. Jameson (San Francisco: Mercury House, 1994), 284–289.
123. Review of LES VAMPIRES, *CR* (9 October 1987).
124. Afterword to Orson Welles's THE BIG BRASS RING: *An Original Screenplay* (Santa Barbara: Santa Teresa Press, 1987), 137–148.
125. Review of Ruiz's MAMMAME, *CR* (6 November 1987).
126. Review of WALKER, *CR* (4 December 1987).
127. Review of EMPIRE OF THE SUN and THE LAST EMPEROR, *CR* (18 December 1987).
128. Review of BROADCAST NEWS and WALL STREET, *CR* (25 December 1987).
129. On the ten best movies of 1987, *CR* (8 January 1988).
*130. Review of HOUSEKEEPING, *CR* (22 January 1988). Reprinted in *Produced and Abandoned*, ed. Michael Sragow (San Francisco: Mercury House, 1990), 192–198.
131. Review of ANATOMIE D'UN RAPPORT and MIX-UP, *CR* (26 February 1988).
132. On Sergei Paradjanov, *CR* (25 March 1988).
133. Review of AN ACTOR'S REVENGE and ALONE ON THE PACIFIC, *CR* (3 June 1988).
134. Four reviews of MIDNIGHT RUN, *CR* (22 July 1988).
135. "Entertainment as Oppression," *CR* (23 September 1988).
136. "Myths of the New Narrative (and a Few Counter-Suggestions)," in *Independent America: New Film 1978–1988* (catalog) (New York: American Museum of the Moving Image, 7 October–11 November 1988), 3–8.
137. Review of TALKING TO STRANGERS, *CR* (4 November 1988).
138. Review of THEY LIVE, *CR* (18 November 1988).
139. Review of THE DEATH OF EMPEDOCLES, *CR* (2 December 1988).
*140. Review of MISSISSIPPI BURNING, *CR* (16 December 1988). Reprinted (slightly abridged) in *Love and Hisses*, pp. 388–395.
141. Review of GOLUB, *CR* (17 February 1989).
*142. Review of PARENTS, *CR* (7 April 1989). Reprinted in *Produced and Abandoned*, pp. 277–282.
143. Review of HENRY: PORTRAIT OF A SERIAL KILLER, *CR* (14 April 1989).
144. Review of MACAO, OR BEYOND THE SEA, *CR* (14 July 1989).

*145. "Say the Right Thing," *CR* (4 August 1989). Reprinted in *Love and Hisses,* pp. 395–404.
*146. Review of DISTANT VOICES, STILL LIVES, *CR* (18 August 1989). Abridged version reprinted in *Foreign Affairs,* pp. 400–403.
147. Review of CASUALTIES OF WAR, *CR* (1 September 1989).
148. Review of REMBRANDT LAUGHING, *CR* (29 September 1989).
*149. Review of PARADE, *CR* (1 December 1989). Abridged version reprinted in *Foreign Affairs,* pp. 231–237.
150. On William Klein retrospective, *CR* (8 December 1989).
151. Review of books on Orson Welles, *Film Quarterly* (Winter 1989/1990): 44–46.
152. On the ten best movies of 1989, *CR* (5 January 1990).
153. On music videos, *CR* (23 February 1990).
154. Review of THE PLOT AGAINST HARRY, *CR* (9 March 1990).
155. Review of Thomas Pynchon's *Vineland, CR* (9 March 1990).
156. Review of SWEETIE, *CR* (30 March 1990).
157. Review of THE TEN COMMANDMENTS (6 April 1990).
*158. On *Twin Peaks, CR* (20 April 1990). Revised version printed in *Full of Secrets: Critical Approaches to "Twin Peaks,"* ed. David Lavery (Detroit: Wayne State University Press, 1994).
159. Review of MR. HOOVER AND I, *CR* (18 May 1990).
*160. "Inner Space" (on SOLARIS), *FC* (July–August 1990): 57–62. (Revision of a *CR* review.) Reprinted in *Contemporary Literary Criticism,* vol. 75 (Detroit: Gale Research, 1993), 408–411.
161. Review of THE FRESHMAN, *CR* (27 July 1990).
162. Review of WILD AT HEART, *CR* (24 August 1990).
163. Review of WHITE HUNTER, BLACK HEART, *CR* (28 September 1990).
164. On Jean Rouch, *CR* (20 November 1990).
165. "Movies: The Big Shill" (on trailers), *CR* (21 December 1990).
166. "Criticism on Film," *S&S* (Winter 1990/1991): 51–54.
167. On the ten best movies of 1990, *CR* (4 January 1991).
168. Review of PRINCES IN EXILE and THE SILENCE OF THE LAMBS, *CR* (22 February 1991).
169. Review of PRIVILEGE, *CR* (8 March 1991).
170. Review of JU DOU, *CR* (19 April 1991).
171. Review of MORTAL THOUGHTS, *CR* (26 April 1991).
172. Review of Eric Lax's *Woody Allen, New York Newsday* (28 April 1991).
173. Review of Richard Schickel's *Brando, New York Newsday* (7 July 1991).
174. "The Seven ARKADINs," *FC* (January–February 1992): 50–53, 57–59.
175. On the ten best movies of 1991, *CR* (3 January 1992).
176. On Mike Leigh retrospective, *CR* (10 January 1992).
177. Review of NAKED LUNCH, *CR* (17 January 1992).
178. Review of HEARTS OF DARKNESS: A FILMMAKER'S APOCALYPSE, *CR* (24 January 1992).
179. Review of RHAPSODY IN AUGUST, *CR* (21 February 1992).
180. Review of DUELLE and NOROÎT, *CR* (28 February 1992).
181. Review of THE PLAYER, *CR* (1 May 1992).
182. Review of THE 4TH ANIMATION CELEBRATION: THE MOVIE, *CR* (22 May 1992).
183. Review of A TALE OF THE WIND, *CR* (29 May 1992).
184. On Cy Endfield retrospective, *CR* (10 July 1992).
185. Review of . . . AND LIFE GOES ON, *CR* (23 October 1992).
186. On Toronto Festival of Festivals (ACTRESS, FAMILY PORTRAIT, THE DAY OF DESPAIR, etc.), *FC* (November–December 1993): 57–59.
187. On Sadie Benning videos, *CR* (15 November 1991).
188. Review of ROCK HUDSON'S HOME MOVIES, *CR* (20 November 1992).

189. Review of MALCOLM X, *CR* (11 December 1992).
190. "Eight Obstacles to the Appreciation of Godard in the United States," in *Jean-Luc Godard: Son-Image 1974–1991,* ed. Raymond Bellour and Mary Lea Bandy (New York: The Museum of Modern Art, 1992), 197–203.
191. "The Undistributed," *CR* (25 December 1992).
192. Review of Endfield's INFLATION and THE ARGYLE SECRETS, *CR* (15 January 1993).
193. Review of THE MATCH FACTORY GIRL, *CR* (19 February 1993).
194. Review of NIGHT AND DAY, *CR* (26 March 1993).
195. Review of EL MARIACHI, *CR* (16 April 1993).
196. Review of THE STORY OF QIU JU, *CR* (28 May 1993).
197. Review of CLIFFHANGER, *CR* (11 June 1993).
198. "Missing the Target," *CR* (18 June 1993).
199. Review of HISTOIRE(S) DU CINÉMA, *CR* (16 July 1993).
200. Review of THE LONG DAY CLOSES, *CR* (30 July 1993).

Index

Designer:	U.C. Press Staff and Janet Wood
Compositor:	Prestige Typography
Text:	10/12 Times Roman
Display:	Runic and Times Roman
Printer:	Maple-Vail Book Manufacturing Group
Binder:	Maple-Vail Book Manufacturing Group